ADAM SMITH AND THE CLASSICS

Adam Smith and the Classics

The Classical Heritage in Adam Smith's Thought

GLORIA VIVENZA

OXFORD

UNIVERSITY PRESS

OXFORD
UNIVERSITY PRESS

Great Clarendon Street, Oxford OX2 6DP

Oxford University Press is a department of the University of Oxford.
It furthers the University's objective of excellence in research, scholarship,
and education by publishing worldwide in

Oxford New York

Athens Auckland Bangkok Bogotá Buenos Aires Cape Town
Chennai Dar es Salaam Delhi Florence Hong Kong Istanbul Karachi
Kolkata Kuala Lumpur Madrid Melbourne Mexico City Mumbai Nairobi
Paris São Paulo Shanghai Singapore Taipei Tokyo Toronto Warsaw
with associated companies in Berlin Ibadan

Oxford is a registered trade mark of Oxford University Press
in the UK and in certain other countries

Published in the United States
by Oxford University Press Inc., New York

British Library Cataloguing in Publication Data
Data available

Library of Congress Cataloging in Publication Data
Vivenza, Gloria.
[Adam Smith e la cultura classica. English]
Adam Smith and the classics : the classical heritage in Adams Smith's thought/Gloria Vivenza.
p.cm.
Translation of: Adam Smith e la cultura classica.
Includes bibliographical references and index.
1. Smith, Adam, 1723–1790—Knowledge and learning. 2. Classical education.
3. Economists—Great Britain. 4. Classicism—Great Britain—History—18th century.
I. Title.
HB103.S6 V57813 2001 330.15'3—dc21 2001033853

ISBN 0–19–829666–5

1 3 5 7 9 10 8 6 4 2

Typeset by Newgen Imaging Systems (P) Ltd., Chennai, India
Printed in Great Britain
on acid-free paper by
T.J. International Ltd., Padstow, Cornwall

Preface

It was after some hesitation that I agreed to translate a book on Adam Smith published in 1984 into English without any significant changes other than the addition of a postscript. On the other hand this volume represents the foundation of my studies in this field, and I still consider my conclusions to be valid. I am aware that the book may leave a slightly strange impression on today's reader. When I wrote it, no general works on Adam Smith's classical culture were available, with the exception of *The Social Physics of Adam Smith*, by Vernard Foley, which I have reviewed in a separate article. Two good annotated editions of Smith's work existed, and these were extremely useful: the German edition of *The Theory of Moral Sentiments* by W. Eckstein (1926), and *The Glasgow Edition of the Works and Correspondence of Adam Smith*, which was being published as I was working on my book.

Other than these, and as it has frequently been observed, there were only scattered observations in articles by a number of authors which highlighted this or that analogy with the classical texts. I made great use of these, not only for completeness of information, but also because I found it helpful to discuss the few points which had already emerged on the subject.

If I were to rewrite this book today, I would probably adopt a different strategy. Much has been written on Smith and the classical authors in recent years, and it would no longer make sense to conduct a survey of the various opinions in this type of book. In the meantime, my knowledge of Smith's debt to the classics has also increased and I would write with greater certainty and within a wider context, as indeed I have done in a number of subsequent articles. (For example, here I analysed the relationship between Smith and Plato in terms of the division of labour, but I highlighted Smith's debt to Xenophon in a later article published in 1990; while in a brief essay of 1989 I developed the reference to musical metaphors in Smith's work contained in note 22 to Chapter 2 of the book.)

It should also be remembered that the book was written for a non-specialist, Italian readership: this explains the numerous references to Italian authors, and also the copious summaries of Smith's texts, unnecessary for those who are already acquainted with his work, as well as certain details (for example, on classical studies in England or the Scottish legal system) which are superfluous for the British reader.

The book is thus presented here in its original form, with some cuts which do not, however, alter the substance. In fact, they are, in part, the outcome of a somewhat modified approach to the subject: a subject which includes both an author attracting a great deal of attention, and a cultural heritage which enjoyed renewed interest throughout the centuries. Consequently,

I have to do with endless bibliographies. In the scholarship of the past, the good methodological approach was that of defining the *status quaestionis* each time that a debated subject was treated. I do not know to what extent this is possible today, unless we wish to write a monograph on each individual topic. When I wrote this book, I adopted the traditional approach, because although Adam Smith himself had already been treated widely, his relationship with the classical authors had not. Today this situation also has changed, and I felt it was appropriate to restrict myself to the main theme, including wherever possible references to issues which I have examined more thoroughly in separate articles.

I have used the same criteria for the List of References, as it would have been pointless to provide a 'comprehensive' bibliography on an author like Smith. I have replaced the original bibliography, which was subdivided by topic, with simple references to the quoted texts, including those used to write my original book (and naturally I have taken advantage of this opportunity to rectify some minor inaccuracies), as well as those used to write the additional chapter, which I have entitled 'Postscript'.

This translation would never have seen the light of day without the help and precious advice of Prof. David D. Raphael, whom I will never be able to thank enough. Words cannot repay my debt to his competence, his readiness to help, and his kindness. I would like also to thank Emma Rothschild for helpful advice and encouragement.

This book has been translated by Clive Cheesman (Chapters 1–4) and by Nicola Gelder. Quotations from texts in languages other than English, including the classical authors, are by Clive Cheesman unless otherwise specified.

G.V.
Verona, December 2000

Contents

Abbreviations

Adam Smith's Works:

'AN'   'Anderson Notes', *History of Political Economy*, 8/4 (1976), 466–77
          (Appendix to Meek, 1976*a*)

Corr.   *The Correspondence of Adam Smith*, ed. E. C. Mossner and I. S. Ross,
          Oxford, Clarendon Press, 1977

EPS   *Essays on Philosophical Subjects*, ed. W. P. D. Wightman and J. C. Bryce,
          Oxford, Clarendon Press, 1980 ('HA' = 'The History of Astronomy';
          'HAP' = 'The History of Ancient Physics'; 'HALM' = 'The History of
          Ancient Logics and Metaphysics')

TMS   *The Theory of Moral Sentiments*, ed. D. D. Raphael and A. L. Macfie,
          Oxford, Clarendon Press, 1976

WN   *An Inquiry into the Nature and Causes of the Wealth of Nations*, ed. R. H.
          Campbell and A. S. Skinner, Oxford, Clarendon Press, 1976

LJ   *Lectures on Jurisprudence*, ed. R. L. Meek, D. D. Raphael, and P. G. Stein,
          Oxford, Clarendon Press, 1978 (*LJ* (A) = Report of 1762–3; *LJ* (B) = Report
          dated 1766)

LRBL   *Lectures on Rhetoric and Belles Lettres,* ed. J. C. Bryce, Oxford, Clarendon
          Press, 1983

Exceptional mentions have been made of Cannan's edition of *LJ* (New York, August McKelley, 1964 reprint), of Lothian's edition of *LRBL* (London, Thomas Nelson and Sons, 1963), and of Eckstein's German translation of *TMS* (Leipzig, 1926).

The works of classical authors have been quoted, as usually, with the reference to book, chapter, section. The titles in the notes, and sometimes also in the text, have been abbreviated as usual: e.g. Aristotle's *NE* for *Nicomachean Ethics*.

Classical authors of a single surviving work have been quoted without giving any title, only with the reference to book, chapter, etc.

Some well-known dictionaries or repertories have also been abbreviated:

RE   Pauly-Wissowa, *Real-Encyclopaedie der classischen
                            Altertumswissenschaft*, Stuttgart, J. B. Metzlerscher, 1894–

TGL   C. B. Hase, G. R. L. de Sinner, and T. Fix (eds.), *Thesaurus
                            Graecae Linguae*, 3rd edn. Paris, Firmin Didot, 1831–

Liddell, Scott, and Jones   H. G. Liddell, R. Scott, and H. S. Jones, *Greek-English Lexi-
                            con*, Oxford, Clarendon Press, 1961

Other abbreviations used:

Raphael and Macfie, 'Introduction'	D. D. Raphael and A. L. Macfie, introduction to *TMS*
Raphael and Skinner, 'General Introduction' to *EPS*	D. D. Raphael and A. S. Skinner, general introduction to *EPS*
Wightman, 'Introduction'	W. P. D. Wightman, introduction to Adam Smith, 'HA', 'HAP', 'HALM', in *EPS*

Introduction

Adam Smith's cultural heritage was one of great breadth, enriched by lively interests. The aim of this book is to shed light on an aspect of it that cannot in any way be regarded as marginal or limited: his formidable grounding in the classics, which—though not at all exceptional for the period and environment in which he moved—was one of its lynchpins.[1] It is perhaps of some interest that in this area he owed no great debt to his teachers at Oxford, given the poor quality of teaching at that university. We must go back to Smith's years at the Glasgow College (where he arrived at the age of fifteen and remained three years) in order to see the earliest germ of a predilection that lasted his whole life—as shown by the 'blank half hours' in the custom-house at Edinburgh, his last work place, spent reciting passages from the classics by heart, in competition with his colleague James Edgar.[2]

The man responsible for sowing that seed was almost certainly Francis Hutcheson, who introduced and revitalized the study of the classics at Glasgow;[3] but the college could muster other strong classicists. Smith, one might say, caught the bug. In all his writings, without exception, one can recognize the lasting impression made by this early classical education, even if filtered through the stimulating cultural experiences which abounded in the age and the milieu in which he lived.

---

[1] The reason for the general lack of awareness of this is, I believe, the fact that Smith achieved his renown in the 'modern' area of economic studies. I would like, however, to mention the article by Pappé (1979), 295–307. The astonishing course of instruction undergone by John Stuart Mill which it recounts (at the age of seven he knew Aesop, Xenophon, Diogenes Laertius, Isocrates, part of Lucian, and six of Plato's dialogues; at twelve, he had got as far as Thucydides, Polybius, Demosthenes, Aeschines, Pindar, Anacreon, Homer, Theocritus, a fair number of tragedies and a few comedies, the *Rhetorica*, and the first four books of Aristotle's '*Organon*'; and at thirteen he undertook Plato's *Gorgias*, *Protagoras*, and the *Republic*) derived above all from the fact that his father James Mill, was—it can be said without much doubt—a fanatical Greek scholar, comparable with Montaigne's, who, as is well known, surrounded his son with people speaking nothing but classical Latin. But, while noting these individual cases (and remembering that the two illustrious 'victims' evinced the most heartfelt gratitude for the education they had received), one should not forget that situations of this sort arise, even in the case of sons of 'normal' parents, when a genuine love for the classics is expressed in the form of solid, intense, youthful study. It is the present writer's opinion that training of the sort cannot have failed to leave its trace in these adolescents' minds when they became men.

[2] Scott (1937), 40.

[3] Cf. Taylor (1965), 12 f. I have touched on the instruction Smith received in his youth in Vivenza *et al.* (1980), 10 f.

Certain circumstances need to be borne in mind in examining the classical heritage that underlies the corpus of Smith's work. In essence, the reader discerns two types of classical influence, which one might term direct and indirect. Within the former group one can further class two types of reminiscence: the one explicit and, so to speak, conscious, including all the express references, quotations, recounted episodes, parallels, and so forth; the other unconscious but of great significance, observed when Smith, not always aware of doing so, echoes classical phrases or passages that he has clearly read over and studied so much that they stick in his memory and re-emerge as his own expressions. A few examples follow (though I would emphasize that these are merely individual instances and that I do not pretend to have traced every classical allusion of this sort that is there to be found in Smith's work).

In *TMS* i. 3. 2. 12 Smith states: 'Human virtue is superior to pain, to poverty, to danger and to death'; and in the same work (iii. 3. 6) we read that:

there is no commonly honest man . . . who does not inwardly feel the truth of that great stoical maxim, that for one man to deprive another of any thing, or unjustly to promote his own advantage by the loss or disadvantage of another, is more contrary to nature, than death, than poverty, than pain, than all the misfortunes which can affect him, either in his body or in his external circumstances.

This sort of phrase has an unmistakably Ciceronian tone; compare it with *De Off.* iii. 21:

detrahere igitur alteri aliquid, et hominem hominis incommodo suum commodum augere, magis est contra naturam quam mors, quam paupertas, quam dolor, quam cetera quae possunt aut corpori accidere aut rebus externis
for a man to take something from his neighbour and to profit by his neighbour's loss is more contrary to Nature than his death or poverty or pain or anything else that can affect either our person or our property.   (W. Miller's translation)

Placing this passage side by side with the second one by Adam Smith given above, one can see that the quotation is word-perfect, astonishingly so in a writer as imprecise as Smith often was, not only when quoting from memory but even when referring to the author.[4] The allusion to the 'stoical maxim', furthermore, implies that when he made it he was to some extent thinking of the classical passage—a highly appropriate one in view of the title of the chapter in which it appears ('Of the Sense of Duty'), which made a reference to Cicero's *De Officiis* almost obligatory.[5]

---

[4] On this point it will suffice to take a look at the editorial notes in the new University of Glasgow edition of Smith's works—the edition referred to in this book. In fact the Cannan edition of the *WN* and Eckstein's German edition of the *TMS* had already engaged in some 'fine tuning' in this area.

[5] The harsh judgement we might form today of this mode of quotation, done without making even an allusion to the original author, is entirely inappropriate. At a time when classical culture was the common heritage of all cultivated individuals, conventions were not so strict. As Hutcheson stated, the educated reader would have been able to tell at once how much of his

The phrase quoted first, however, has a different context. Smith is expounding his own philosophy, and echoes Cicero's dictum in a fashion that can perhaps be regarded as unintentional, when one considers the frequency of expressions of this sort in the *De Officiis*:

detrahere autem de altero sui commodi causa magis est contra naturam quam mors, quam dolor, quam cetera generis eiusdem
for anyone to rob his neighbour for his own profit is more contrary to Nature than death, pain and the like   (iii. 24);

qui alterum violat . . . aut nihil existimat se facere contra naturam aut magis fugiendam censet mortem, paupertatem, dolorem, amissionem etiam liberorum, propinquorum, amicorum quam facere cuiquam iniuriam
if a man wrongs his neighbour . . . he must either imagine that he is not acting in defiance of Nature or he must believe that death, poverty, pain or even the loss of children, kinsmen, or friends, is more to be shunned than an act of injustice against another   (iii. 26);

sine fugiendum id quidem censet, sed et multo illa peiora, mortem, paupertatem, dolorem while such a course should be avoided, the other alternatives are much worse—namely, death, poverty, pain   (ibid.);

nemo enim iustus esse potest, qui mortem, qui dolorem, qui exsilium, qui egestatem timet   (ii. 38)
no one can be just who fears death or pain or exile or poverty   (W. Miller's translation).

Nothing could be easier to explain than the dogged persistence of these turns of phrase in Adam Smith's memory, in view of the importance ascribed to Cicero's philosophical works in the moral-philosophy teaching at Glasgow and the fact that, following this example, Smith set aside part of his lecture course each year to a commentary on the *De Finibus*.[6]

Smith's great familiarity with the Latin orator also accounts for certain unmistakably classical rhythms in his prose. Consider, for instance, the cadence of *TMS* iv. 1. 8: 'and sometimes more exposed than before to anxiety, to fear, and to sorrow; to diseases, to danger, and to death', or the anaphora of 'HA' ii. 7: 'there is no break, no stop, no gap, no interval'.[7]

Furthermore, Smith took certain images from the classics. Compare, for example, *TMS* ii. 2. 2. 1: 'In the race for wealth, and honours, and preferments, he may run as hard as he can, and strain every nerve and every muscle, in order to outstrip all his competitors. But if he should justle, or

work was garnered from other sources, from Cicero and from Aristotle (Hutcheson, *Introduction to Moral Philosophy*, cited in Taylor (1965), 25).

[6] See, respectively, W. Richardson, *Discourses on Theological and Literary Subjects by the Late Rev. Archibald Arthur* (cited in *LJ*, introd. p. 12 n. 37) and Stewart (1828), ii. 351. It can be safely assumed that the *De Officiis*, as well as the *De Finibus*, played an important part in Smith's education: see below, Ch. 2 n. 8, and relevant passage in the text.

[7] Smith was not, indeed, the only writer in Britain to employ a Ciceronian style: it was the distinguishing feature of an important group of prose writers including Joseph Addison, Edmund Burke, Edward Gibbon, Samuel Johnson, and Jonathan Swift. See on this Highet (1949), 327 f.

throw down any of them, the indulgence of the spectators is entirely at an end' with the remark of Chrysippus cited by Cicero in *De Off.* iii. 42:

qui stadium . . . currit, eniti et contendere debet, quam maxime possit, ut vincat; supplantare eum, quicum certet, aut manu depellere, nullo modo debet.
When a man enters the foot-race . . . it is his duty to put forth all his strength and strive with all his might to win; but he ought never with his foot to trip, or with his hand to foul a competitor.

The latter continues:

sic in vita sibi quemque petere, quod pertineat ad usum, non iniquum est; alteri deripere, ius non est
Thus in the stadium of life, it is not unfair for anyone to seek to obtain what is needful for his own advantage, but he has no right to wrest it from his neighbour   (W. Miller's translation).

As may be seen, here we have another very close parallel, deployed by Smith in his own context.

Other significant examples can be produced. In *TMS* i. 3. 2. 2 Smith remarked that tragedy only concerns itself with the misfortunes of kings, not with those of ordinary mortals. Epictetus had said as much: the rich, tyrants, sovereigns—these are tragedy's subject matter, not poor folk (Epict. *Diss.* i. 24. 15). Consider too the elegant example of the infant hitting the stone which it has bumped into (*TMS* ii. 3. 1. 1), taken, without a hint of quotation, from Epictetus, *Diss.* iii. 19. 4–5 (where, however, the job of 'punishing' the stone, should the child burst into tears, is delegated to the nurse). From the examples given, Smith's painstaking study of Stoic philosophy will already be apparent: the Ciceronian passages are on Stoic subjects, while Epictetus was studied by Smith when he was a boy.[8]

On occasions, one can discern echoes of a literary character, such as the *elogium* Smith composed for his friend David Hume (which has reminded Raphael of the concluding passages of Plato's *Phaedo*), or apparently banal turns of phrase that in reality have a history dating back to the jurisconsults or—needless to say—to Cicero, by way of scholasticism: phrases used by Smith and other seventeenth-century economists, such as 'necessaries and conveniences of life' and 'necessaries, conveniences and amusements of human life'.[9]

Some pieces of classical imagery came down to Smith by way of modern authors. For instance, the Virgilian description of the boat which, drawing away from the shore, gives its passengers the impression of being stationary while the coast retreats was employed by Copernicus (and re-employed by Smith in 'HA' iv. 37) to explain how the earth, though moving, might seem

---

[8] Scott (1937), 33. The turn of phrase used at *TMS* vii. 2. 13, which according to the editor derives from Xen. *Mem.* i. 7, may also go back to Epict. *Diss.* ii. 18. 2.
[9] With regard to these passages I have summarized the comments of Caruso (1973), pp. xlii–xliii. On the parallel with Plato cf. *TMS*, app. II., p. 401.

stationary to its inhabitants. Admittedly, in this case one cannot state with certainty that Smith had no knowledge of the original, but the usage he makes of it recalls the modern author rather than the ancient one. Here, however, the Scots philosopher explicitly refers to neither one of the two sources, much as at 'HA' iv. 62, where he makes use of an example from Lucretius (though deploying it in a contrary manner to that of the Latin poet) to illustrate the Cartesian concept of the inexistence of the vacuum, with reference to motion in a 'full' space.

As for those influences we have defined for convenience as indirect, they are distinguished from those just described in that they do not arise from Smith's more or less conscious recall of his youthful studies, firmly fixed in the memory—or, at least, not from this alone. They are more a matter of ideas, concepts, kernels, or trains of thought of classical origin which, passing through a lengthy process of transformation, adaptation, and 'rediscovery' from century to century, had finally arrived, somewhat modified, in the Age of Enlightenment. There they were received into a world that was radically different not only from the ancient one that spawned them, but even from that of the humanist Renaissance which had in many cases made them flower again.

It goes without saying that this second type of classical influence holds a greater interest for the present study. Smith shared it with the majority of his civilized contemporaries, but the fact that these ideas were common currency in learned circles should not prompt the conclusion that he did not bring his own mind to bear on the subject, restricting himself to absorbing in pedestrian fashion whatever was presented to him. All the evidence suggests, rather, that he allowed himself to be influenced by it only to the extent that it could broaden his mind and stimulate its capacity for independent thought. These were the motives that prompted him to analyse and discuss specific problems: while the technical capacity for doing so he also derived from classical civilization, with its rational and logically appropriate division of distinct and interrelated subjects, suitable for separate and ordered treatment.

The subjects he dealt with, however, almost always display essential links with the contemporary world.[10] As a result, even when their classical mould may be clearly discerned, their manifold connections with present-day events are simultaneously evident, giving the classical author or thought a character quite different from the original one. Alternatively, one specific classical reference may be chosen in preference to another on the grounds that it is felt to be more sensitive to the problem in hand—to say nothing of cases in which Smith, without referring to any particular authority, nonetheless makes use of a procedure deriving from a classical origin and since then traditionally in use in the relevant discipline.

---

[10] This applies, I believe, even to the questions of natural philosophy, given the significance of Newton's physical theories for the whole culture of the time, and to those of moral philosophy, since Smith's ideas, even those relating to economic activity, must be viewed as part of a general representation of human behaviour.

To anticipate briefly in outline the more detailed exposition we will undertake in the course of this study, one may observe that the chief areas of classical influence in Smith's work are the origin of scientific thought, with Platonic motifs on the structure of astronomical theories, Aristotelian ones on the psychological origins of research, and others deriving (at least partly) from Stoicism on the requirements that must be met by scientific knowledge; the elaboration of a model of social and, indeed, economic behaviour, characterized by two classical virtues, namely Epicurean prudence and Stoic self-control; and the recognition of Roman law as a source of the first importance for historical and legal understanding, and, indeed, one with an exemplary systematic approach.

Even these brief notes make it clear that we are dealing with a far from unimportant phenomenon. One must add, furthermore, that on occasions Smith also offers an explanatory essay on what he knows of classical civilization, writing a history of astronomy, of ancient physics, of ancient logic and metaphysics, or giving the broad outline of certain systems of moral philosophy, ancient education, and the political evolution of the classical world.[11] His occasional critical judgements on individual classical authors or on this or that school of thought, indeed, have a specific character: they are instances of Smith exercising his critical awareness and putting himself at one remove from things; in other words, examining the question from the outside—or so he believes (given that some of the criteria for his judgements themselves derive from the classical world).

Returning for a moment to our rudimentary classification, we can say that the first type of reminiscence (direct), whether conscious or not, is an index of Smith's tastes: the turns of phrase and thought that he found striking, that he most easily recalled and loved to repeat. The second type, on the other hand, points to his conceptual tendencies, discernible in the coincidence (not always complete or precise) between the classical text and whatever his own mind had worked out or was working out for itself: harmony with one particular manner of thought in preference to others. The note-form histories of the various disciplines, however, with the criticisms and judgements expressed in them, constitute a different sort of relationship, and offer an example of Smith thinking about the classics. As far as any possible 'parentage' for Smith's tastes goes, for his conceptual tendencies and critical evaluations, mention has already been made of the importance of the instruction he received. Adolescence is a highly receptive phase, and Smith was most likely influenced in part by his teachers' inclinations. We have seen that he was taught a great deal of Cicero and Stoic philosophy; and, since

---

[11] Apart from three essays on ancient astronomy, physics, and logic and metaphysics, we have part VII of the *TMS*, dedicated to an account of the various systems of ancient moral philosophy; a brief excursus on the three parts of Greek philosophy in *WN* v. 1. f. 23–31; the history of education in *WN* v. 1. f. 39–44; and a history of the political evolution of the classical world in *LJ* (A) iv. 56–113 and *LJ* (B) 31–49, as also in *LRBL* ii. 142 f.

education is not merely a matter of receptivity, it is appropriate to record here the responsibility of whoever designed the courses that Smith followed, since it is certain that he did so on definite principles.[12] The tenacious (albeit not exclusive) persistence of Stoic philosophy in Smith's thought could perhaps be ascribed precisely to his systematic, first-hand reading of Cicero (and, as has been mentioned, Epictetus); Plato and Aristotle by contrast not being studied directly in the original. Furthermore, it is perhaps well to take account of a greater modernity on the part of Stoic thought: certain requirements—for instance, that of calming anxiety and restoring the imagination's 'tranquillity'—could indeed still be valid right up to the present day, while the satisfying picture of a perfect universe, waiting to be contemplated, was likely to gain the approbation (and high approbation at that) of an eighteenth-century man—for all that Smith rejects it, at least on the ethical score. At Oxford, as is known, Adam Smith studied the classics almost by himself, and later his personality was sufficiently sharp and independent for him not to be overawed intellectually either by the exceptional men whose company he shared in the extremely lively cultural world in which he had occasion to move, or by the ancient authors whom he loved, read, and without the slightest difficulty brought to terms with the thought of the eighteenth century.

We shall therefore be examining, for the most part, the second type of classical influence in Smith's work, since it is without doubt the more important. But we shall not overlook, wherever it appears to be of significance, the type of influence we termed 'direct', it being generally more easily identifiable (and to some extent already identified). The best method of approach seemed that of subdividing the material according to subject matter, thereby creating different chapters under the heads of the various central disciplines, such as philosophy, jurisprudence, and literature, and examining in each case the evidence that serves to illustrate it. Chronological order has also been followed, though not with any rigidity, and it has where appropriate been ignored. One such case is the placing of the chapter on Smith's literary interests at the end of the volume, although his surviving *Lectures on Rhetoric and Belles Lettres* belong to an early phase of his career.

The parts with greatest interest with regard to Smith's thought—including his economic thought—will form the nucleus of this book, but it has been considered appropriate to place them after an examination of what is termed his natural philosophy. This is perhaps a less enthralling subject for students of Smith's ideas, and a somewhat limited one in that only three

---

[12] Smith himself, when the time came, joined the ranks of the teachers and did not break away from the preferences he had been imbued with—as shown not only by the details of his teaching and his lecture notes, but also by the lists of books he ordered for Glasgow University library between 1758 and 1760, which include two editions of classical texts (Scott (1937), 178–82), and the long list of classical authors he ordered from the publisher Foulis for the Duke of Buccleuch in summer 1759 (*Corr.* 57–8 (no. 41)).

essays on it survive, two in much reduced form. But these contain conceptual and methodological elements that are to reappear later in Smith's more mature thinking, clearly indicating how he had already, at the time of these youthful efforts, taken up a definite position. Those elements that are common to more than one group—evidently, the subject matter cannot be divided into watertight compartments, and subdivision is made merely for the sake of practicality and clarity—will be referred to from time to time as opportunity arises. Since the bicentennial edition of Smith's works, produced by the University of Glasgow, contains exhaustive notes with precise references to the sources—including the ancient ones—it has been considered unnecessary to repeat them, and it is there that the reader is accordingly directed.[13] In cases where the editors did not identify the source, or where it has been thought appropriate to add some detail, direct reference is made to the classical author.

[13] For the purposes of checking classical authors I have mostly made use of modern critical editions, while ensuring that the text was substantially unaltered from that in use in the eighteenth century.

1

The Natural Philosophy in Smith's Essays

1.1. 'THE HISTORY OF ASTRONOMY'

Philosophy covers a vast area, subdivided into many compartments, and these have not maintained their composition unaltered over the centuries. One need only think of the great uncertainty which obscured the boundaries separating 'philosophy', 'natural philosophy', and 'science' in the period that interests us, and the almost interchangeable uses that were made of these terms. The simple fact that Newton entitled his great work *Philosophiae naturalis principia mathematica* emphasizes, as Wightman has pointed out,[1] that what we think of as a scientific subject today, in the aftermath of Kant's distinction between the two disciplines, was then regarded as a component of philosophy. Relevant to this question is a group of three essays composed by Smith with the chief aim, explicit in their titles, of using the history of certain areas of study (astronomy, physics, logic and metaphysics) to reveal the principles that direct philosophical enquiry—taking 'philosophical' in the sense already indicated. To be precise, it is only in the first of these essays, 'The History of Astronomy',[2] in an introductory section,[3] that Smith sets out the guiding principles of philosophical/scientific enquiry. Various scholars have accordingly looked at this work precisely in order to extract from it the basic outlines of Smith's philosophy.[4] Nor is this only of methodological interest: the essay on astronomy is distinguished from the other two in that it offers the fullest treatment of its subject,[5] and is, furthermore, not limited in chronological terms.[6]

---

[1] Wightman (1975), 46; id., 'Introduction' to 'HA' 12. On Smith's usage of 'philosophy', 'science', and other related terms see Campbell (1971), 27–9.

[2] The full title, the first part of which is common to all three essays, is 'The Principles which Lead and Direct Philosophical Enquiries Illustrated by the History of Astronomy'.

[3] To be seen as a sort of general introduction to all three essays: cf. Raphael and Skinner, 'General Introduction' to *EPS*, 17.

[4] Chiefly Thomson (1965); Lindgren (1969); Skinner (1972); id. (1974a); Wightman (1975), *passim*; id., 'Introduction' to the three essays, *EPS*, 5–27.

[5] The others are 'little more than fragments': Wightman (1975), 44; cf. id., 'Introduction', 27.

[6] Unlike the other two essays, the titles of which expressly qualify their subject matter as 'ancient'; interpreted by Wightman ('Introduction', 22–3) as meaning that it was not Smith's intention to deal in any depth with these topics in a post-classical context.

As has often been pointed out, Smith made mention of this essay in a letter to his friend David Hume, who would have been his literary executor, with the duty to dispose of his manuscripts, had he survived. Smith describes the essay as 'a fragment of a great work', one of his youthful projects, and leaves the question of whether to publish it or not up to his friend— though for his own part he strikes a note of caution, saying: 'I begin to suspect myself that there is more refinement than solidity in some parts of it'.[7] Despite this observation, however, this was the only one of the essays saved from destruction just before Smith's death that he names, not without a certain sense of appreciation.

The work had been drawn up at least in its basic features while Smith was still at Oxford, and properly composed soon after he went down from that university, but internal evidence shows that additions were made later.[8] Black and Hutton, in a note at the end of their edition of the text, also point out that certain notes found by them demonstrate the author's dissatisfaction with the last part of the essay, which deals with Newton's astronomy, and which Smith felt required revision and amplification. Nonetheless, the work is of great importance, being in itself 'one of the best examples of theoretical history', apart from its interest, referred to above, as an exposition of Adam Smith's view of the principles that should direct scholarly enquiry.[9]

For one aspect of these principles, Smith was indebted to the classics. To put it another way, his approach reflects the specific formulation of a problem whose roots lay in classical literature.

1.2. THE 'CONNECTING PRINCIPLES' OF NATURAL PHENOMENA

According to Smith, the most desirable element in a philosophical system is the ability to provide an explanation that reduces to a small number of simple 'principles' the various discordant aspects of reality.[10] The success of any system in doing so is proportionate to the progress attained by philosophical/scientific thought at the point when the system is produced: for, men's capacity for observation and analysis has varied, along with their experiences,

---

[7] *Corr.* 168 (no. 137).

[8] Wightman, 'Introduction', 7. Thomson (1965), 212–13, dates the essay to Smith's years at Oxford. Moscovici (1956), 3–4, connects it with a series of lectures given between 1749 and 1752/3 at the Philosophical Society of Edinburgh.

[9] Raphael and Skinner, 'General Introduction' to *EPS*, p. 2, recalling a view expressed by Stewart (1980), ii. 49, in *EPS* p. 294. A similar opinion is stated by Thomson (1965), 213.

[10] Expressed in its best-known instance at 'HA' ii. 12, though cf. also 'HALM' i., p. 119. The editorial comment on the 'HA' passage (p. 45) draws an analogy with the statement regarding moral philosophy at *WN* v. 1. f. 25. Relevant to this is the link between scientific methodology and moral philosophy in the age of Newton—on which see Mittelstrass (1979), 54—reflecting as it does the classical notion of a relationship between the physical universe and moral behaviour: Maguire (1947), 162; Fassò (1966), 25–6, 79.

throughout history. Each system is therefore destined to be superseded by another that more closely accords with the cultural phase from which it emerges. Since the faculty responsible for working out any system is the imagination, the goal that such a system represents is not objective truth, but rather one possessing enough likelihood to satisfy the imagination at that particular point in the development of science. Not even Newton's system is exempt from this critique, added rapidly though it is at the end of the essay, and qualified by the explicit admission that in this case the system's degree of perfection guaranteed it brief acceptance as 'the truth'.[11]

With regard to astronomical theories, this method of interpretation was ultimately derived from a distinction which arose in the classical era between the respective tasks of astronomy and physics; a distinction that was elaborated by such philosophers as Posidonius, Proclus, Ptolemy, and Simplicius, whose commentary on Aristotle's *Physics* transmitted it to modern science.[12] This indirectly explains why it was precisely in his 'History of Astronomy' that Smith chose to enunciate the fundamental principles of science. According to the distinction in question, one task belonging exclusively to astronomy was that of using mathematical hypotheses to reduce the apparently irregular movements of the planets to a simple motion of uniform, circular character. This idea dated back to the Greek astronomer Eudemus; from him (by way of Sosigenes) it too came to Simplicius, who speaks of it in his commentary on Aristotle's *De Caelo*.[13] Its aim was to achieve that essential goal of *sozein tà phainomena*—'safeguarding' or 'explaining' 'the phenomena'.[14] One of the most striking aspects of this method of approach, which the science of the middle and early modern ages received from its Greek origins by way of the Arabic and Latin literary tradition,[15] is its hypothetical nature. It is found in express form as early as Simplicius, who states that it goes back to Plato,[16] and was accepted by almost all the great

[11] 'HA' iv. 76. 'Newton also looked upon his fundamental doctrine, the general theory of gravitation, only as such a provisional point of rest': Cassirer (1951), 52. Interestingly, Smith's view has been interpreted both as a deep-seated resistance to gravitational theory (Foley (1976), 33–4) and as the recognition of an intellectual advance (Moscovici (1956), 9–10). In the face of such widely differing interpretations, it is prudent to stay close to what Smith actually wrote: thus Lindgren (1969), 902 n. 9, commenting that Smith saw Newton's theory as a satisfactory alternative to ancient superstition. [12] Mittelstrass (1979), 49.

[13] Mittelstrass (1979), 48; Duhem (1913), i. 103 f.; Cassirer (1967a), 207.

[14] The Latin translation being *salvare apparentias*, reflected in Galileo's *salvar l'apparenze*: Mittelstrass (1979), 53 n. 1. Dijksterhuis (1961), 15, explained the verb *sozein* ('to save') as implying saving the phenomena 'from the verdict of unreality that seems to be invited by their irregularity'.

[15] Wightman, 'Introduction', 17; Mittelstrass (1979), 50 f. Especially noteworthy is the lively strain of Anglo-Saxon medieval thought and its distinction between physical and mathematical theories, first drawn by Michael Scotus in his translation of Alpetragio's *Liber Astronomiae*, and continued in the work of Robert Grosseteste and Roger Bacon: Mittelstrass, loc. cit.

[16] Cassirer (1967a), 206–7. Simplicius reports Plato as asking: 'What are the circular, uniform and perfectly regular motions which, *supposing them to be true*, explain all the phenomena of planetary movements?' (ibid. 207; my italics).

astronomers up to the beginning of the modern age, who 'constructed a
highly ingenious and complicated system of celestial spheres, by which
means they sought to explain all the known data, to "safeguard the phenomena". But that does not mean that these objects of hypothesis were "real"
things.'[17]

According to the ancient distinction between astronomy and physics, the
latter was meant to 'explain' the nature of the physical world (on the basis of
the theory of the four elements), while the job of the former, which was
equipped with mathematical concepts such as the eccentrics, epicycles,
equants, and deferents of Ptolemaic astronomy, was to 'explain the phenomena'. In this way a schism that was to last for centuries grew up between
Aristotelian physics, which dealt with 'real' elements, and Ptolemaic
astronomy, which was connected to ideas such as that of the eccentric and
epicyclic system—a system which classical astronomers were able to show
was geometrically consistent, but which nothing could prove to have real
existence.[18]

Physics, furthermore, was supposed to identify the causes of the phenomena that came within its purview. Astronomy, on the other hand, was not
interested in causes: it limited itself to formulating hypotheses between
which, as long as they were of equal explanatory value, the choice was
entirely arbitrary.[19] 'Physics—which they regarded as a branch of philosophy—was entrusted with the task of explaining the final causes of phenomena, while that of astronomy was limited to conceiving such "geometric
hypotheses" as were capable of accounting for the external aspects of the
phenomena themselves.'[20]

A later period would see both a conclusion to this contrast and the development of a new, Newtonian method of 'safeguarding the phenomena' by a
mechanistic mode of explanation.[21] Here, however, it is, rather, our purpose
to note that Smith's essay preserves in recognizable form traces of an
analytical principle of Greek origin—for which the young essayist (perhaps
under the influence of his recent studies of the subject) seems to display
some sympathy.

Classical origins also lie behind the axiom that the more satisfactory theory
is that which manages to rationalize a mass of varied phenomena on the basis
of a simpler set of principles—though it was only in modern times that it was
viewed in the context of scientific methodology. Formulated by Kepler,

---

[17] Cassirer (1967*a*), 209.   [18] Mittelstrass (1979), 49–51.
[19] Dijksterhuis (1961), 62.
[20] Schiaparelli (1873), 415; cf. also 411 n. 88. Still of fundamental importance on the
difference between the methods of astronomy and physics is Duhem (1908), 115–23: though see
Mittelstrass (1979), 48 n. 2, for a suggestion that the paternity of the argument should be
re-attributed from Plato to Eudoxus.
[21] Mittelstrass (1979), 53 f.; Neugebauer (1957), 3. Wightman ('Introduction', 23) remarks
that 'Smith never made explicit the cardinal distinction between "physics" and "astronomy" ';
but his approach certainly presupposed it and was clearly influenced by it.

taking his lead from Plato,[22] this approach is also seen in Smith's two principal works. Indeed, it underlay his philosophy in such a way as to lead to a conclusion of fundamental importance: for Smith, though at no point does he seem aware of the origin of his method, the *whole* of reality (moral and economic reality, not just scientific) was to be interpreted in this fashion.

1.3. 'WONDER'

There is quite a different aspect of Smith's theory of science, one relevant to the question of what prompts research. Every human attempt to explain the world as it is seen and experienced has at its base a sense of 'wonder', a feeling that impels man to try and account for what he observes. According to Smith, it is from this feeling that philosophy (in the usual sense of scientific research) arises, engendered by the need to link up in a sufficiently intelligible fashion phenomena whose interrelationship is not, at least on the face of things, comprehensible. This task, as stated above, is that of the imagination, which must work out 'explanations' that are convincing enough to bring the enquiry to a close, and to do so with a double satisfaction: that of assuaging the sense of wonder, and that of contemplating the beautiful vision of a universe that is so wisely 'ordered'.[23] Man is by nature inclined to seek this sort of satisfaction: he must satisfy his instinct for enquiry, an instinct based upon three fundamental sensations: wonder, surprise, and admiration.[24] Faced with something that catches the attention because it is out of the ordinary, man feels an amazement that is in itself a sense of unease arising precisely out of the phenomenon's anomalous nature, for which some explanation is necessary. According to the definition with which Smith begins the essay, 'wonder' arises in the presence of the exceptional and little known; 'surprise', when something unexpected occurs; and 'admiration' in the face of magnificence or greatness, even in something already known.

This notion of 'wonder', then, calls for investigation. There are two sorts: the first when one encounters something new that does not fit into any known category, and the second resulting from an unaccustomed succession

[22] Cassirer (1967*b*), 136. Cf. also Dijksterhuis (1961), 490: 'the tendency to seek for a small number of explanatory principles was not foreign to Aristotle', which supports the idea that this principle of theory was widely espoused in ancient philosophy. Smith applied it not only to scientific theory but—as stated in the text—to ethical and economic ones too: cf. Campbell (1971), 54; Skinner (1972), 313–14. I do not agree with Lindgren's comment that Smith objected to philosophers such as Epicurus who 'indulged a propensity . . . to account for all appearances from as few principles as possible': Lindgren (1973), 4 n. 4, on *TMS* vii. 2. 2. 14. Smith does make objections to Epicurean philosophy, but not on the basis of this tendency, which he presents as common to mankind in general and philosophers especially.

[23] Satisfaction termed by Smith 'repose and tranquillity of the imagination' ('HA' iv. 13): cf. Cropsey (1977), 44. This 'tranquillity' may owe its origins in part, if not exclusively, to Locke: Campbell (1971), 33 n. 2. On the importance of the aesthetic factor see Lindgren (1969), 904–5; Thomson (1965), 217, 219–21; Skinner (1972), 313 n. 7.

[24] 'HA', intro. 1—sect. ii. 12.

of things which inspires an initial reaction of surprise, followed by a sense of wonder;[25] and the latter gives rise in turn to the spirit of scientific research, dealing as it does with an unanswered question: the mind is aware of a discontinuity, a sort of logical gap between the two things, and cannot be quiet until it has filled it by means of as complete and exhaustive an explanation as possible, and thereby can pass from one to the other. In the first case there is no point of reference: in a significant phrase used by Smith twice, the object 'stands alone in the imagination' ('HA' ii. 3, 4). In the second, a sequence has been interrupted. In both cases a connection is missing, and though they are, so to speak, of opposite value, the sense of unease they create is analogous. The specific nature of this unease is what impels man—as stated above—to seek an explanation.

After this long preamble, Smith states: 'Philosophy is the science of the connecting principles of nature' ('HA' ii. 12), and proceeds to illustrate the way in which philosophy can bring to light the 'invisible chains' that link the various, more or less discordant, aspects of reality as seen by human eyes.

As described by Smith, this sense of wonder under whose aegis philosophy is born finds a correspondence in an analogous Aristotelian concept. Referring precisely to the origin of philosophy, Aristotle states: 'Men were moved to philosophize, then as now, by wonder; being astonished at first by the more obvious problems, and then progressing gradually to set themselves questions of a much greater loftiness'.[26] In the third section of Smith's essay (the section entitled 'Of the Origin of Philosophy') a very similar reconstruction appears, albeit in a form that is much lengthier and fuller of colour and fantasy, describing the savage's first amazement in the face of natural phenomena.[27] Aristotle's concise reference to the progression from simpler to more complex problems has a fitting conceptual parallel in Smith's observation that the savage is unaware of many incoherences of a minor sort, which are destined to perplex the philosophers of a later age, but is startled by comets, eclipses, thunder, lightning, and so forth.[28]

The first result of the enquiries made by our forebears in their savage state was mythology.[29] Shaken by the more imposing natural phenomena, and liable through fear to exacerbate the state of uncertainty and danger in which they lived, they found it natural to ascribe the object of their terror to an

---

[25] 'HA' ii. 5. The concept is, however, explained at length throughout sect. ii.

[26] Arist. *Met.* 982^{b}11–15. The motif is also found in Plato, *Theaet.* 155d.

[27] 'HA' iii. 1–2, the argument being briefly recapitulated in *WN* v. i. f. 24. Smith's savage is naturally of eighteenth-century stamp, capable of subtle analogies and reflections on the ways of nature and his own reactions.

[28] 'HA' iii. 1. Aristotle too, repeating the notion that 'we all begin, as was stated, by wondering that the thing really is thus' (*Met.* 983^{a}12–13), makes passing reference to events in the heavens. For the Stoics it was the horror aroused by thunder, lightning, and all the other remarkable natural phenomena, in addition to the movements of the stars and planets, that gave rise to the idea of divine beings: Pohlenz (1970), i. 94.

[29] Smith draws a distinction between myth and philosophy that was unknown to the pre-Socratics: Zeller (1881), 4–5.

angry deity.[30] Bit by bit they developed an interest in less 'terrifying' occurrences: the unceasing cycle of the seasons and irregularity in rural events. The explanation for these irregularities was found in polytheism, and, characteristically, Smith illustrates this by drawing on examples from the classical repertory; enter, therefore, the serried ranks of dryads and naiads, with Bacchus, Ceres, and Neptune.

With a slightly disdainful phrase—'Hence the origin of Polytheism, and of that vulgar superstition which ascribes all the irregular events of nature to the favour or displeasure of intelligent, though invisible beings, to gods, daemons, witches, genii, fairies'[31]—Smith turns to the consideration that primitive man's mind was not yet sufficiently mature to wonder about the physical laws behind 'regular' events. Having posited the existence of the aforesaid divine beings, one tends to imagine that, like man, they exercise their will only in halting or changing the 'natural' course of events.

Of possible relevance in this connection is a view dating back to Aristotle, though Smith holds it, so to speak, in reverse. For Aristotle, the purpose of scientific research is to determine what is normal or natural, in contradistinction to the fortuitous or accidental. Smith's savage, on the other hand, seeks to explain those facts that deviate from the norm.

For this reason, 'regular' phenomena are of no account: they do not require the intervention of any god, and still less that of the 'invisible hand of Jupiter', that characteristic component whose mention has drawn the attention of a distinguished scholar[32] intrigued by this early appearance of the well-known motive force of Smith's later theory, but in pagan dress, and in a role quite opposite to the one it is ascribed in his two main works.

1.4. THE PREMISES OF RESEARCH

Primitive and superstitious beliefs begin to be gradually left behind, and the first rudimentary steps to be made in research, ultimately leading to a sound and correct brand of philosophy, only when an element of central importance arises in society: law, bringing with it order and security, and making the business of sustenance a less precarious one. The result is more leisure and freedom to use time as one chooses. Man acquires security, and with it an ever-increasing sense of scientific curiosity, which—in the absence of

---

[30] The motif of early man's fear and terror, which can be traced back to De Pauw, is frequent in seventeenth- and eighteenth-century literature: Landucci (1972), 232–46. The ultimate inspiration is a line of Statius (ibid. 237). Contrast, however, the Stoic and Epicurean notion that an understanding of natural phenomena drives out fear of death and religion: Cic. *Fin.* iv. 11.

[31] 'HA' iii. 2. Smith's position can be explained in terms of the European belief, deriving from the initial contacts with the New World, that all pagans, ancient and modern, attributed natural phenomena to 'idols'. This ethnographic analogy facilitated a 'secular explanation—destined to emerge victorious in the Eighteenth Century—of the fact that historically distinct peoples could show cultural convergences as the result of their shared human nature': Landucci (1972), 198; cf. also 191–2. [32] Macfie (1971), 595–9.

economic difficulties—he can happily dedicate himself to satisfying. This link between economics, politics, and culture is typical of Smith, and demonstrates that at least one characteristic aspect of his philosophy is already present in his youthful work.

Once again, however, there is a parallel with Aristotle:

Since, then, men undertook philosophy in order to flee ignorance, it is clear that they sought knowledge for the pure love of it, not to make use of it for some practical end. This is proven by the very fact that this sort of knowledge began to be sought when the necessities of life and the things that make it comfortable and healthy were, so to speak, entirely provided.[33]

There are thus two elements in common between Smith's view of the origin of philosophy and that of Aristotle: cause (wonder) and time (in the sense of an actual set of circumstances—in the case in point, the moment at which economic worries are shrugged off). But there are differences, and they explain how a different interpretation of the subject leads to a different concept of the motives involved. First of all, man's reaction to wonder needs analysis. 'Whoever feels wonder in the face of a difficulty', Aristotle states in true Greek fashion, 'feels himself to be ignorant': and so men began to engage in philosophy precisely to avoid this sense of unease that results from their own ignorance. This reaction is one of an intellectual and typically Greek sort. In Smith's version, however, the sense of unease that wonder provokes makes itself felt first and foremost as terror and consternation in the face of frightening phenomena, with reciprocal relief and delight in the face of pleasant ones; and, later, as an inquisitiveness, nourished by the availability of time and wealth, and favoured by the fact that the anxiety that marked the previous phase is now over. As a result, some individuals undertake, for pleasure, to seek the explanation that will bestow perfect coherence on the picture of the universe, and in this way satisfy not only their thirst for knowledge but also their aesthetic sense, while restoring the sense of tranquillity that was riven by doubt, perplexity, and fear.

It will be seen that this reaction is one that bears upon the feelings more closely than, or at any rate before, it touches the intellect—even if the latter is naturally of great relevance. One upshot of this is that legal and economic security (two closely connected states), by removing the fears and anxieties of the 'savage' state, constitute a *sine qua non* for the dedicated, undisturbed, and untrammelled use of the imagination.

In Aristotle, then, man's attitude bears resemblance to Socratic knowledge, the knowledge that one knows nothing.[34] It is on account of this

---

[33] Arist. *Met.* 982^{b}19–24. The motif was also used by Hobbes, in connection with the relationship between science and technology stressed by Francis Bacon: Landucci (1972), 129; cf. also 179.

[34] For the 'methodical doubt' characterizing the sort of wonder posited by Aristotle see Mondolfo, in Zeller and Mondolfo (1932), i. 347. It was noted as early as the seventeenth century: Malusa (1981a), i. 285–6.

knowledge that men engage in philosophy, their only aim being to flee ignorance. Economic well-being seems to earn a mention specifically in order to put the question of profit out of court: philosophical enquiry, it is averred, began only when fundamental economic problems had been resolved. Man, according to Aristotle, desires only knowledge and ignores questions of how he might benefit economically thereby. It is in the nature of things that it is necessary already to have whatever is essential for life in order to lose interest in such matters—and it is perhaps only in order to clarify this point that Aristotle mentions it at all.

Smith, however, puts economic well-being in a different light. In one passage only—one which (I think deliberately) echoes Aristotle[35]—does he refer to the benefits or advantages that man might extract from the pursuit of philosophy, and agree with Aristotle that these things are not what prompts man to conduct research. But previously Smith has taken care to explain that man can only undertake enquiries of a scientific nature when he has attained a certain level of psychological and economic tranquillity: it is not so much that he ignores such matters, but rather that he takes them for granted. For Aristotle and the ancients in general, the economic sphere was the sphere of necessity, in the sense of man's dependance on the material world: an inescapable relationship and therefore synonymous with slavery or, at any rate, with the lack of freedom; a bond, in other words, of which the philosopher needed to be free.[36] By the time that Smith wrote, however, the notion that man must have resolved all the problems relating to his vital needs before he can turn his mind to anything else had acquired enough conceptual authority to be recognized as a scientific matter. Smith therefore states that freedom from economic concerns is a priority, an indispensable requirement for the philosopher, who *must not need* to earn if he wishes to philosophize. For Smith, the philosopher is free because he has money; for Aristotle, because money does not interest him (as illustrated by the well-known anecdote about Thales).[37]

---

[35] 'HA' iii. 3 to the end. See also the editorial note ad loc., and Raphael and Skinner, 'General Introduction' to *EPS*, 17. I hold this to be a conscious echo of Aristotle because of its singularity and lack of resemblance to Smith's general approach to the topic as shown by the rest of the cited paragraph. This approach achieves a kind of reversal of the argument, starting from Aristotle's conclusion, or rather his counter-example, namely the necessity of economic security to the philosopher. Only in the passage of 'HA' just cited does Smith refer to any gain that might be earned from philosophy: and he does so in a few lines and in such a way that it seems not a fundamental part of his thought but rather an addition, only superficially linked with what goes before. It is not that Smith asks what profit a philosopher might be able to derive from his calling, then to conclude that he does not wish for profit as he already has all he needs. Rather, the opening statement that the philosopher must be comfortably off prompts in Smith the unplanned thought, without any logical connection to his preceding line of argument, that profit could in fact be got from philosophy.

[36] Cf. Musti (1984), 10–11. Greek philosophy's fiercely maintained concept of independence can also be seen in the fact that the manufacturing trades or manual labour were not seen as 'inferior' by their nature, as generally believed, but rather because they obliged those who pursued them to depend on other men: see below, Ch. 4 n. 85.

[37] Arist. *Pol.* 1259^{a}5–18. Cf. Barbieri (1958), 22.

The Aristotelian concept of science, according to which its value is intrinsic to itself rather than the result of any useful product it gives rise to, is perhaps worth brief consideration. It is a view expressed both in the fragments of the *Protrepticus* and in the introductory chapters of the *Metaphysics* by way of arguments directed particularly against those such as Isocrates who proclaimed the utility of science. One account advanced by Aristotle is mythological in character (though it has a historical reference at *Met.* 981^{b}23–4): it maintains that the arts relating to the provision of the necessities and even the pleasures of life were developed before philosophy, which is therefore untainted by the pressures of utility. Another explanation offered takes up the already mentioned Platonic concept of 'wonder', with the aim of showing that nothing arising from it can have any practical function.

Smith clearly makes use of these two arguments, but no one acquainted with his work would maintain that he subscribes to the concepts on which they were based. It is unnecessary to compare him with Isocrates: it will suffice, I believe, to think back to what Bacon said. This is a fine example of the way in which Smith assimilated classical teachings and turned them to his own ends, preserving the topics but understanding and interpreting them differently. Of the two Aristotelian arguments, one becomes in Smith's hands a demonstration of the primary role played by 'material' questions in the development of human activity, rather than the essentially anti-utilitarian value of scientific research. The other, instead of relating to the admission of ignorance, concerns man's inborn need for reassurance in the face of what he finds disconcerting or frightening—an interpretation with clear Stoic resonances.[38]

The disinterested attitude of the Aristotelian philosopher, then, driven as he is by his unalloyed love of understanding, does to a certain extent find its counterpart in the way that Smith's exemplary thinker, though he is partly impelled by his sensations and to that extent more involved emotionally, nonetheless remains untouched by material concerns. He does not engage in philosophy for private gain, it is true, but his philosophizing is not its own end, unlike that described by Aristotle (*Met.* 982^{b}20–1); its function is rather that of assuaging his sense of turmoil in the presence of the unknown. In short, Aristotle represents the ultimate end as 'the truth'; Smith sees it as no more than a temporarily satisfactory solution to the problems thrown up by the real world in its various manifestations.[39]

---

[38] For this aspect see above, n. 30. Aristotle's influence on Smith is, furthermore, seen in the fact that the former, in both the *Protrepticus* and the *Metaphysics*, deals with knowledge in relation to the heavens and the stars, or rather the gods that govern them. This has certain consequences in the religious sphere: Einarson (1936), 281. On the origins of philosophy see also id. 277.

[39] This shows that Smith's approach continued to be one appropriate to astronomy, while Aristotle—a philosopher in the complete sense (see below, n. 60)—took his cue from physics: cf. above, Sect. 1.2. Smith speaks of 'philosophical enquiries' in general, making no distinction in this sense between the systems of astronomy and physics: cf. Wightman, cit. n. 21 above.

It should also be recalled that by Smith's day there was already a long history of studies into man's primitive condition and the role played by his need for sustenance: this was a subject in which Smith felt a particularly close interest. For him, economic security is not proof that the wise man has no interests beyond pure research, but it is still of vital importance, inasmuch as it brings about the conditions in which he can work. Such matters may be of no interest to the wise man himself, but Smith cannot overlook them. He knows that they are central to everything, and that to ignore them in favour of some other pursuit is a luxury no one can permit himself, even from an intellectual standpoint. This is doubtless something of which the primitive philosopher in Smith's account is himself unaware, and indeed he is ascribed an attitude that is, in short, Aristotelian; but the account itself is clearly couched in these terms.

Nor should the political element in Smith's reconstruction be overlooked. In relating how the great eastern monarchies of Asia and Egypt had established the conditions of public order and the rule of law necessary for the birth of philosophy, Smith bemoans the fact that, despite passing references to Chaldean or Egyptian culture, there are no documents that might show 'whether there ever was in those nations any thing which deserved the name of science, or whether that despotism which is more destructive of security and leisure than anarchy itself, and which prevailed over all the East, prevented the growth of Philosophy'.[40] According to Smith, in other words, scientific research can begin in a well-ordered and -governed society, as long as it is not stifled by tyranny.

1.5. THE ORIGINS OF PHILOSOPHY

The first stirrings of philosophical enquiry, then, took place in the Mediterranean world; but it was in the Greek colonies, rather than the mother country, that the first consistent philosophical notions were produced, for the fundamental reason that economic well-being was achieved there first.[41] After stating that the production of poetry also depends on economic prosperity, for the first great poets in Greek were, like the philosophers, from the islands and the colonies, Smith gives a brief résumé of pre-Socratic philosophy. Here too one can observe traces of an Aristotelian form of categorization. The first two philosophers whom Smith examines are Thales and Pythagoras: as a point of departure, this is a traditional choice, since it was to Thales that Aristotle ascribed the beginning of philosophy in the true sense of the word, following on after the supremacy of mythical beliefs; and

---

[40] 'HA' iii. 4, with editorial note 9 ad loc. Only later was the significance of these peoples to Greek science appreciated: cf. Zeller and Mondolfo (1932), i. 82–5.
[41] 'HA' iii. 4–5. Smith makes a distinction between colonies, which achieved wealth and in the process surpassed the country that spawned them, and the islands, for which the aim was peace and security.

from the same two progenitors classical scholars had deduced two intellectual lines of descent, the Ionic and the Italic.[42]

After the absurd fables of mythology, the first steps taken by science were
not very encouraging, Smith felt; he laments the 'inextricable confusion' of
the Ionic school headed by Thales and carried on by way of Anaximander
and Anaximenes down to Anaxagoras and his pupil Archelaus.[43] He does,
however, recognize the insufficiency of the available documentary evidence
that survives on the matter, which prevents one from establishing, for both
Ionians and Pythagoreans, not only the essential outlines of each system but
even whether their respective doctrines were well enough ordered to merit
the name of a system at all. The Pythagoreans earn slightly more approval
for having been better at making progress 'in the study of the connecting
principles of nature', as Smith somewhat vaguely puts it without offering
further details. Later on, though, this hurried judgement seems to be
implicitly contradicted by the statement that both Plato and Aristotle
derived the fundamental elements of practically their whole philosophy from
the Pythagoreans. It should be said here that Smith is almost certainly
referring to the Pythagoreans of the Christian period.[44] Once again following
Aristotle (though not by name), Smith emphasizes that the Pythagoreans
explained everything on the basis of the properties of numbers,[45] and that it
was from their theories of the earth's movements (involving its rotation and
revolution, not about the sun but about a central fire) that Copernicus drew
his inspiration for a similar hypothesis.[46]

[42] Arist. *Met.* 983^{b}7–984^{a}3. Aristotle has been followed in this not only by Smith but by
many moderns: Zeller (1881), i. 166, 216; Malusa (1981*b*), 11 and *passim*.

[43] 'HA', iii. 6. According to Zeller (1881), i. 243–4, those writing later than Anaximander
give contradictory information about him, which must be regarded as conjectural and derived
not from his own writings but from Aristotle's: this is perhaps what gave rise to the 'inextricable
confusion'. In fact Anaximander devised the theory of the spheres, on which account 'he claims
an important place in the history of astronomy': Zeller (1881), i. 254. Anaximenes was
responsible for the concept of the crystalline heavens; cf. Mondolfo, in Zeller and Mondolfo
(1932), ii. 238. From Anaximander the theory of the spheres was transmitted to the Pythagorean
astronomers, perhaps by Pythagoras himself: Zeller, ibid. 517–18.

[44] 'HA' iii. 6: 'From the Pythagorean school, both Plato and Aristotle seem to have derived
the fundamental principles of almost all their doctrines'. Cf. Zeller (1881), i. 309: 'the
Pythagorean of the Christian period could even maintain that the Philosophers of the Academy
and the Lyceum had taken their so-called discoveries, one and all, from Pythagoras'. In reality
the opposite was true: ibid. n. 2; pp. 505–6.

[45] 'HA' ii. 12. Aristotle, *Met.* 985^{b}23–6, states that the Pythagoreans, the first to advance the
study of mathematics, believed that the principles of the latter underlay everything: cf.
Abbagnano (1961), i. 23–4; Zeller (1881), i. 369, 372. Smith's methodology of 'familiarity' or
'analogy', which he also applied to economics and moral philosophy (Skinner (1972), 315–16,
318–19; cf. Thomson (1965), 223–4, *contra* Lindgren (1969), 906 n. 10), thus has its own
classical roots. Apart from the Pythagoreans, Smith also refers to the example (taken from
Cicero) of the musician Aristoxenus, who identified the soul with harmony.

[46] 'HA' iv. 28; cf. Dreyer (1953), 41–2, 314–16. In truth Pythagorean theory was not
heliocentric: Schiaparelli (1873), 382 f. Nor did Copernicus commit the error which Smith
ascribes to him of mistaking the Pythagoreans' central fire for the sun.

To reach something that resembles a philosophical system according to Smith's criterion, one has to come down as far as the teachings of Empedocles, Architas, Timaeus, and Ocellus of Lucania, the most renowned philosophers of Magna Graecia.[47] The last two inspired Plato and Aristotle respectively; the first can be called the founder of ancient physics; and the second, the inventor of the categories, merits the same designation in the field of dialectic.

When he comes to speak of the two 'greats' of Greek philosophy, Smith attempts to outline the debt they owed to their predecessors. With regard to Timaeus and Ocellus, he suffers from certain widespread errors of his age,[48] while to all the philosophers of the Heraclitan tradition and the school of Elea he is inclined to apply that famous epithet of Heraclitus, 'the obscure'. Indeed, he avers, it was because of the extraordinary obscurity of their teachings that the thinkers of these schools—Cratylus and Heraclitus in the former, Xenophanes, Parmenides (whose influence on Plato he greatly undervalues, as is stated in the editorial note on the passage), Melissus, and Zeno in the latter—failed to achieve renown on their own account.

After Smith's recognition of the pre-Socratic influences on Plato and Aristotle, it comes as something of a surprise to find him stating that not one of these ancient sages is worth saving from the oblivion that shrouds them. The two greatest Greek philosophers have preserved in their own systems as much of their predecessors' philosophy as deserved preservation—and that is enough. This attitude was quite widespread in eighteenth-century Britain, where not much attention was paid to classical philosophy: while Socrates was venerated (as depicted in Xenophon's *Memorabilia* rather than in Plato's dialogues), both Plato and Aristotle were held at arm's length, and the pre-Socratics were not appreciated at all. Even Lord Monboddo, that fervent admirer of ancient philosophy as opposed to the mean speculations which the moderns engaged in, states in his *Antient Metaphysics* that the Ionic and Eleatic schools were unable to offer anything that might deservedly be called philosophy. It should be added that Monboddo made up for this severe judgement with his extraordinary admiration for Pythagoras.[49]

Smith makes a final, passing, reference to the atomistic theories of Leucippus, Democritus, and Protagoras, which he considers to have been elbowed out of

---

[47] 'The Italian School', as Smith terms them: a phrase also used (as the editor notes on 'HA' iii. 6, p. 52 n. 12) in 'HAP' 3 f., referring to the Pythagoreans of Croton. The Pythagoreans were already denominated 'Italic philosophers' in classical times: Zeller (1881), i. 337–8.

[48] Only at the start of the 20th century was it concluded that the works ascribed to Ocellus and Timaeus (who despite long-lasting beliefs to the contrary probably lacks any existence outside the Platonic dialogue named after him) really belong to Neo-Pythagorean literature. The effect of the false ascription was to attribute works of the Neo-Pythagorean school to the earliest Pythagoreans, from whom Plato and Aristotle supposedly derived the basic elements of philosophy. In fact the precise opposite was the case. The Neo-Pythagoreans, being of a later date, plundered Plato and Aristotle: cf. the brief remarks above, n. 44. See *RE*, xxxiv (1937), 2364–5 (s.v. 'Okellos'), and xi (1936), 1204–5 (s.v. 'Timaios'). Smith was not of course in a position to foresee later critical developments.

[49] Clarke (1945), 112–17.

view by Plato's hostility before being brought to the fore again by Epicurus.[50] He then embarks on the history of astronomy properly so called.

It is true that Smith's historical sense, which was acute but nonetheless not isolated from contemporary cultural views, still prevented him from describing the earliest Greek thinkers as scientists, a title which modern commentators would ascribe to them without any hesitation.[51] But it is also true that much work on the pre-Socratics has been carried out since his day. In Smith's time, these philosophers were known by way of other classical authors' citations of them—we have already referred to the important role played by Aristotle in their transmission—rather than being the object of study themselves. Indeed Smith is inclined to take them into brief consideration only to the extent that he feels the greater philosophers might have made use of them, and tends not to go into the details of what particular elements they may have used, limiting himself instead to general and unspecific statements. His intention, it should be remembered, was to give a broad view of studies undertaken with the aim of accounting for celestial movements by means of certain fundamental principles; the aim, in other words, of safeguarding or explaining the phenomena. His judgement therefore is based on the extent to which these philosophers have managed to achieve this task. He was not in a position to evaluate their purely astronomical contributions, such as the theory of the heavens' rotation, introduced into cosmology by Anaximander and, later, by way of the Pythagoreans, Plato, and Aristotle, a cardinal element in the world system down to Copernicus, or the concept of the earth as a sphere, introduced by Parmenides.[52] It is probable that Smith only named the pre-Socratics at all for the sake of completeness, his intention being to give a brief but full account of the origins of philosophy.

1.6. ANCIENT ASTRONOMY

In the true sense of the term, ancient astronomy began with the system of homocentric spheres devised by Eudoxus and Callippus. Smith, who still talks of 'concentric' spheres, calls this system 'rude and inartificial', while accepting that it fulfilled every obligation imposed by the requirements of the age— among them the necessity of preserving an element of secrecy, out of respect for the widely held view that to know the instruments of divine wrath was to be guilty of impiety.[53] This remark would perhaps be better directed at

---

[50] It is wrong to classify Protagoras with the Atomists, but it does explain the reference to Plato's criticism: cf. editorial notes 16 and 17 at 'HA' iii. 7, p. 53.

[51] Zeller and Mondolfo (1932), ii. 37–8.   [52] Ibid 45.

[53] 'HA' iv. 4, where the editorial note states that the epithets 'rude and inartificial' are unmerited. The unfavourable evaluation perhaps goes back to Bailly, who called Eudoxus' system 'absurd', and derives from the prejudice that, although there was enough source material to reconstruct the system, Eudoxus was not a member of the Alexandrian School and was not accorded the status of a true astronomer: Schiaparelli (1875), 2–3.

Pythagorean philosophy,[54] but the fact is that one cannot say with precision whom Smith intends it to refer to: for all that he includes it in the context of a description of Eudoxus' system, it sounds like a more general comment upon the tendency of 'these early philosophers' to maintain the secrecy surrounding their doctrines, which would reveal the causes (simple in themselves) of natural phenomena and endow those who knew them with power. Astronomical theories, as has been stated elsewhere, could not in fact explain 'causes': this too suggests that the remark was incidental, indeed rather tangential, to the context in which it appears, intended only to explain in 'conjectural' manner a mode of behaviour known from antiquity onwards. Smith does recognize some value in the system propounded by Eudoxus and Callippus, not only from the scientific point of view but also from the aesthetic one, on account of the harmonious beauty of its depiction of the universe. His opinion on this point accords perfectly with that of a modern scholar: 'in this way the world's fabric continued to be endowed with a degree of elegance, from which the reconstructions of Hipparchus, Ptolemy and all the others, including Copernicus, were far removed, and which did not find its match until the time of Kepler'.[55]

To give a better explanation of the system of homocentric spheres, Smith steps back and refers again to the cruder theories of earlier philosophers: a flat earth surrounded by ocean; the sky as a solid hemisphere arching over it and joining up with ocean at the edge of the horizon; the sun, the moon, and the other heavenly bodies moving from east to west where they set and, by way of some subterranean passage, come up again in the east. These were the opinions of Xenophanes, founder of the Eleatic School, and probably also of Thales, who according to Aristotle considered that the earth floated on ocean; as Smith notes, the astronomical discoveries attributed to Thales by Plutarch and Apuleius were probably of a later date.

This is the only mention Smith makes of pre-Socratic astronomy, and he does so chiefly in order to show up its *naïveté*, though he mitigates that by referring, as normal, to the primitive mentality which would have found it both valid and, in its way, enchanting. He adds that it was probably this that gave Plato his notion of harmonic proportion in the movements of and distances between the heavenly bodies, and the Pythagoreans their 'wild and romantic idea' of the music of the spheres.[56]

---

[54] Schiaparelli (1873), 382. It is also possible that here we have a distant and elaborate echo of Plato's idea that if the gods are heavenly bodies, one must know astronomy in order to do them honour: Einarson (1936), 280–1. According to this notion initiates possess a degree of power—perhaps the same power mentioned by Smith.

[55] Schiaparelli (1875), 8. Compare id., 42, where the system is described as 'the simplest and most symmetrical until Kepler's day', with Smith, 'HA' iv. 4: 'And if there had been no other bodies discoverable in the heavens besides the Sun, the Moon, and the Fixed Stars, this old hypothesis might have stood the examination of all ages, and have gone down triumphant to the remotest posterity.'

[56] Presumably not a displeasing theory in Smith's eyes, possessing as it did the beauty that he required of every theoretical system, though he makes no reference here to its general 'consonance', of which he was aware in other contexts; cf. Bonar (1926), 336; below, Ch. 2 n. 22.

The discovery of the 'irregularity' of celestial motion (in other words, the stations and retrogradations of the planets), which obviously took place when human capacity for observation was somewhat refined, was a troubling revelation for minds that were by nature disposed to appreciate regular and ordered movement. What resulted was an attempt to reduce this aberrant behaviour to clarity by way of a new explanation. According to Smith, this attempt was also prompted by the sense of a missing connection between one event and the next, which made it necessary to formulate a hypothesis[57] to link them: it was Eudoxus of Cnidus who came up with it.

Among the pupils of Plato, Eudoxus was the one who 'took up the challenge'[58] and worked out a system of homocentric spheres (for the description of which Smith by and large was to rely on Aristotle's *Metaphysics*).[59] In order to account for the phenomena and explain the 'irregularities' and positional changes of the planets, Eudoxus increased the number of the spheres. It was now necessary to provide not just one but several for each planet. Callippus and then Aristotle followed Eudoxus' approach in turn,[60] but the progress made in observation continually brought to light new and varied movements in the heavens, and the method was shown up as excessively complicated and, above all, an ineffective solution to the problem. The spheres had to be multiplied incessantly, not only by the ancient authors, but by their Renaissance heir, Fracastoro: in his desire to make ancient astronomy live again this scholar found himself constrained to increase the number to seventy-two—and even that did not suffice.

For these reasons the system of homocentric spheres was superseded even in antiquity: its complexity was not capable of resolving the sense of difficulty and dismay inspired in the imagination by so many apparent discordant elements. Much better, as Smith states, was the system of eccentric spheres and epicycles devised by Apollonius,[61] perfected by Hipparchus,

[57] The term 'hypothesis' in this context fits perfectly with the spirit of ancient astronomy, but it also accords to some extent with later astronomical work. Thus Cassirer (1967a), 209: 'The ancient astronomers Eudoxus and Callippus used their crystal spheres as working hypotheses, but did not feel obliged to demonstrate their physical existence. This point of view was considered "orthodox" even at the outset of the modern era.'

[58] The expression used by Schiaparelli (1875), 7. Cf. id. (1873), 402–3, for Eudoxus' debt to Plato, who in book X of the *Republic* provided the starting-point for the theory of the spheres, to be taken up anew by the Peripatetics, the schoolmen, and by Fracastoro.

[59] Arist. *Met.* 1073^{b}17–1074^{a}16. Cf. the editorial comment on 'HA' iv. 7, p. 58.

[60] Though the point went unnoticed by Smith, it should be emphasized—to translate Schiaparelli (1873), 415—that 'the astronomers Eudoxus and Callippus introduced for each planet only that number of spheres that was necessary to explain the phenomena; while Aristotle believed himself obliged as a physicist to complete their system so as to explain additionally how the motions of the various heavenly bodies' spheres could be mechanically produced without mutual disturbance'. Likewise Dijksterhuis (1961), 33, ascribes the fact that Aristotle's geocentric theory lasted for centuries to 'the totality of his doctrine'. Aristotle was not a mathematical astronomer, but rather a synthetic thinker, unable to study cosmology without connecting it with physical reality.

[61] Cf. Schiaparelli (1873), 416: the theory of epicycles, in reality 'invented by certain anonymous Pythagoreans and submitted to geometric study by Apollonius, furnished a convenient basis for the application of geometry and trigonometric calculus'.

and transmitted to later centuries by Ptolemy. By means of successive refinements Ptolemy was able to lend some coherence to the speed and direction of celestial motions, and thus meet the more and more exacting demands imposed by the imagination.

In judging this second important system, Smith applies the same test as before: How satisfactorily does it bring together in one account the apparent movements of the various celestial bodies? Better than the homocentric-sphere system does, he concludes, though he recognizes some virtue in the latter.[62] The system propounded by the Stoic Cleanthes, on the other hand, which differs from both the systems just mentioned, failed to achieve any coherence or present a connective principle underlying celestial movement: for that reason it won little support even among the ancients.[63] It might be felt that Smith included it in his account largely by way of an act of regard towards Stoic philosophy, which in other areas he treated with such respect; or merely, perhaps, out of a desire not to miss out any system of note.

And so, at last, to Ptolemy, in whose system the data from lengthy observations carried out in the reign of Antoninus Pius were used to refine what had already been concluded on the basis of the theories of eccentrics and epicycles. Such was the general degree of acceptance this account attained that it did not undergo further attempts at refinement but merely formed the subject of commentaries, principally those of Proclus and Theon.[64] Smith precedes his remarks on this topic, however, with some sharply worded comments about the fact that Ptolemy's predecessor Hipparchus is passed over in silence by authors such as Cicero, Seneca, Plutarch, and Pliny the Elder.[65] This, he says, results from the marked tendency of ancient philosophers to disregard natural science in favour of ethics, rhetoric, and dialectic: an arrogant and ignorant prejudice, in his view. In fact, as stated above, and as Smith himself was aware, astronomy was in antiquity one of the mathematical sciences, while physics was, if anything, a component part of philosophy. Smith uses vague terms of reference in speaking of 'natural

---

[62] 'HA' iv. 9–14. This opinion too has been echoed by more recent writers: thus Schiaparelli (1873), 403: 'this theory [i.e. the theory of homocentric spheres] held the field in astronomy until, chiefly as a result of the work of Hipparchus, wide diffusion was achieved by the theory of eccentrics and epicycles, which was much less elegant even if better able to represent the phenomena faithfully'.

[63] 'HA' iv. 14–15. In truth the Stoics had a reply that was consistent with their philosophy, namely that since the planets were divine beings they were capable of finding their own orbits, on account of their understanding of the cosmic order of things: Dijksterhuis (1961), 45, 62. This is a system without any place for mathematics, which is perhaps why it did not satisfy Smith. [64] 'HA' iv. 20.

[65] To be precise, the scant regard shown by 'those professed instructors of mankind' ('HA' iv. 18) for Hipparchus, on whose fortune in antiquity Smith apparently conducted a survey. In Pliny's case, he is perhaps too harsh: there is a glowing reference to Hipparchus at *Hist. Nat.* ii. 53–4.

science', but the authors he names were in this case philosophers and men of letters, not mathematicians.[66]

The long path that astronomy was to travel thereafter, though still characterized by the need to make the continuing discoveries from experience meet the requirements of simplicity and coherence that are implicit in every theory, was no longer concerned with classical doctrine. Smith pursues his account of the subject, briefly lingering over the researches of Arabic scholars and the medieval schoolmen (whose work on the basis of classical astronomy obviously required a recap of the latter's salient points) before at last reaching Copernicus, Kepler, and Newton—to mention only the most important. This section is thus outside our ambit, despite the occasional, unpredictable return to a classical theme, usually made in order to emphasize the extent to which modern theories have advanced and their closer conformity with the required nature of a scientific system. Examples of this are seen in Smith's discussion of the speed of movement of heavenly bodies, where he sets out the laws of motion as expressed by Aristotle, and Copernicus' objections to those laws;[67] in his explanation of the difference between circular orbits (the characteristic element of all ancient astronomy) and elliptical ones, Kepler's fundamental discovery;[68] in his account of equinoctial precession as calculated by Hipparchus and as understood at a later date;[69] and in his relating that, unlike modern astronomers, the ancients had located comets in the sublunar sphere.[70]

To read this essay is to become conscious of the high degree of awareness that Smith had of ancient astronomy,[71] particularly when one considers the fact

---

[66] Wightman, 'Introduction', 12, states correctly that the term 'philosophers' is used here in its ancient and medieval sense, without distinguishing them from 'scientists'. There was, however, some awareness of a link between Greek philosophy and mathematics, being invoked for instance by Newton's teacher Isaac Barrow: Sandys (1908), ii. 350. Smith's comment on the oblivion into which Hipparchus fell can be justified with regard to astronomy: according to Neugebauer (1957), 145, 'Ptolemy's astronomy is probably built to a large extent on results obtained 300 years earlier by Hipparchus'. Less sustainable is the accusation of intellectual 'isolationism'—as Thomson (1965), 221, put it—against authors who had some idea of astronomy but not enough to form a critical judgement of the merits of an astronomer whose ideas were later to turn out to be fundamental.

[67] 'HA' iv. 38. Smith here uses a 'modern' standard, namely the great distinguishing feature of Newtonian astronomy in comparison with its classical predecessor, the application of the laws of dynamics to astronomical phenomena: Neugebauer (1957), 3.

[68] 'HA' iv. 51. The authority of the axiom relating to circular and uniform motion 'was only fully destroyed when as a result of the efforts of Galileo, Newton and their successors the metaphysical element was completely banished from natural science': thus Schiaparelli (1875), 8.

[69] 'HA' iv. 73. In Hipparchus' day it had merely been observed that the longitude of the fixed stars gradually increased. Later this was interpreted and denominated 'precession of the equinoxes': Dijksterhuis (1961), 60.   [70] 'HA' iv. 74.

[71] It should be emphasized that classical methods in mathematical astronomy remained valid until Newton's day. 'One can perfectly well understand the *Principia* without much knowledge of earlier astronomy but one cannot read a single chapter in Copernicus or Kepler without a thorough knowledge of Ptolemy's *Almagest*. Up to Newton all astronomy consists in modifications, however ingenious, of Hellenistic astronomy': Neugebauer (1957), 3–4.

that he took his first steps in the study of the subject when still a student. It should also be borne in mind that, until recently, the study of non-Alexandrian, Greek astronomy was impeded by a lack of information—a deficiency which, like other such deficiencies, has ultimately led by way of ignorance or imperfect understanding to an unmerited prejudice against the subject.[72]

Unfavourable comment has admittedly been made on the fact that Smith was silent on two figures of great importance, namely Heraclides Ponticus and Aristarchus of Samos.[73] Leaving aside this and the few other such gaps,[74] however, his essay is interesting as proof of his vast understanding of classical culture, as also of his tendency to analyse its fundamental elements by contemporary intellectual standards, in a way that would now be considered 'unhistorical'. But this approach is not only, in all probability, inevitable: it is also, perhaps, typical of every era that truly manages to make the classics live again.

Others have already written with authority on the value of the essay from a methodological point of view. My aim here has been merely to display Smith's grasp of a subject which at first sight might appear foreign to his main area of study, and the classical origin of certain basic principles which, notwithstanding some modification, were to remain important in his later philosophy.

On the first of these points I have refrained from rehearsing in detail any of the descriptive passages of purely scientific character which Smith includes in the essay, such as the accounts he gives of the various systems: to do so would be beyond my capabilities and is, in any case, unnecessary since they have already been examined critically—by Wightman, for one, who has indicated some of their shortcomings. Furthermore, this is not for our purposes the most interesting aspect of the essay. Of greater relevance for us is the presence in Smith's account of two lines of approach that can be traced back to antiquity: the hypothetical nature of astronomy, together with the need for 'connecting principles' to bring together the whole of reality in a coherent system; and the identification of a psychological origin for scientific research, namely man's natural sense of wonder.

The first of these elements—the hypothetical character of astronomical theories—is a principle which modern astronomers still have recourse to. With regard to its conceptual content, it is at least analogous to Smith's general

---

[72] Schiaparelli (1875), 2; Neugebauer (1957), 145–6.

[73] For their importance as supporters of heliocentricity (certainly in Aristarchus' case, and probably in Heraclides') see Schiaparelli (1873), 403 f.; Duhem (1913), 404–23; Dijksterhuis (1961), 63; Mondolfo, in Zeller and Mondolfo (1932), ii. 628–9. On Aristarchus see Geymonat (1970), i. 292, and—for a clear statement of his lack of success—Dreyer (1953), 138–41.

[74] Such as the lack of any emphasis on the long scientific work that necessarily preceded the system devised by Eudoxus, which in Smith's account springs forth fully formed, like Athene from Zeus' brow. Other gaps are noted by Wightman in his erudite 'Introduction' (especially 15–17), though he concludes that despite its omissions and errors the essay is 'acceptable to a modern historian in its main lines' (ibid. 11), and that Smith manoeuvres himself through his account of ancient astronomical systems 'not indeed with complete mastery, but with a remarkable degree of precision and understanding' (ibid. 15).

scientific theory,[75] for all that the latter can certainly not be said to limit itself to an account of what is apparent, independent of objective reality. Smith's own view of the 'philosophy of science' has already undergone authoritative study. We shall merely say that his work in general presents a distinction between natural and moral philosophy, namely that the latter does not have this hypothetical character, being based instead on directly discernible and analysable human behaviour.[76] Another very important aspect of Smith's theory is also of astronomical origin: the view that it is on the few, simple connecting principles of nature that every system turns. This, of course, is modern astronomy's fundamental bequest to Smith: as has been pointed out with suitable emphasis (in a study describing 'HA' 's 'Newtonian' methodological foundations),[77] it informs the methodology of all his works.

The other element, wonder, is founded on a basis of recognizably Aristotelian origin, but one which has been too highly embellished by eighteenth-century notions regarding primitive man's mental state to have preserved its previous classical appearance. In Smith's scientific writings, the sense of wonder is closely bound up with psychological theories of association, but it does not have an exclusive role.[78] At any rate, it displays the remarkable coherence of his philosophical outlook, for it shows that even scientific research has its origin in sentiment: man had resort to research as the result of an impulse of pleasingly psychological, rather than rational, character. It is only later that reason intervenes, just as we shall observe to be the case in moral philosophy. Wonder is perhaps, of the two classical elements here discussed, the more circumscribed; but it is not isolated from the recurrent references in Smith's writings to the as yet 'uncivilized' state of early man.[79]

1.7. 'THE HISTORY OF ANCIENT PHYSICS'

Descending to earth with his next essay,[80] Smith begins by putting the theories of ancient physics to the usual test: How and to what extent did

---

[75] See above, Sect. 1.2; cf. Wightman (1975), 58. It is perhaps in order to emphasize that in the early modern age of astronomy, and for Newton in particular, gravitation was not hypothetical: it is just that its ultimate cause was unknown, and the important point was held to be that it explained the phenomena better than any other hypothesis; cf. Dijksterhuis (1961), 482; Wightman (1975), 60; id., 'Introduction', 22.　　　[76] Raphael (1979), 90–2.

[77] On the basis of Smith's own distinction (*LRBL* ii. 132–4) between Aristotelian and Newtonian method: Skinner (1972), 314.　　　　　　　　[78] Skinner (1974a), 178.

[79] See Vivenza *et al.* (1980), 18. Scientific 'wonder' of this sort should not be confused with what might be called emotional or aesthetic wonder, which has its own Aristotelian principle; ibid. 53–4. But note that in Smith's account even intellectual or scientific wonder assumes, in the end a psychological nature: see above, Sects. 1.3 and 1.4. The distinction referred to, then, is more Aristotle's than Smith's.

[80] Wightman questions this 'descent' ('Introduction', 23), on the grounds that there is no support for Smith's account of philosophers turning to sublunary matters only after they had investigated the heavenly spheres. Smith is in fact repeating a phrase of Cicero: *Tusc.* v. 10. 69.

philosophers manage to reduce the various elements and phenomena of nature to a few familiar principles. His two shorter essays on the subject, though incomplete, cannot be overlooked here, for they may well contain important evidence on his grasp of ancient scientific theory. There are many possible reasons for the preliminary, unfinished form in which they survive, and it would be futile to try to pinpoint one; but it is perhaps appropriate to emphasize that, while ancient astronomy would not be completely foreign territory to an early modern astronomer, ancient physics remained in such a rudimentary state that it has been called 'a futile wandering'.[81] The historian's task, in an age when interest in this sort of enquiry had only recently arisen, was thus rendered somewhat difficult by the virtual impossibility of placing oneself in the context of those early researches, which to modern eyes were so bereft of certain fundamental requirements for the early progress of that science.

Smith begins his account by recapitulating in his own words the basic points of the Empedoclean doctrine of the four elements, and submitting it to the familiarity test. The criterion for the test, he explains, is the extent to which, 'upon such an inattentive view of nature as must be expected in the beginning of philosophy',[82] the doctrine made it sufficiently easy to bring together in a few fundamental principles all the phenomena of the sublunary world.

In the context of this discussion, Smith lays down a form of methodological guideline which is of some interest: one should not imagine that the work of ancient philosophers can contain, even by chance discovery or by the application of reason, understandings that derive from modern science but were beyond the reach of early thinkers. This statement is correct in so far as it is intended to save early science from judgement by hindsight, but it also shows a basic incomprehension of the real deficiencies that impeded the development of ancient physics.[83] Smith's words appear in the course of his explanation of the upward and downward motions that Empedoclean theory ascribed to the four elements on the basis, respectively, of their positive levity or gravity. The former of these concepts fits with appearances and for that reason led ancient philosophers astray.[84] But the reasoning, which Smith felt might well have been a partial substitute for experimentation, was

[81] Dijksterhuis (1961), 68.

[82] 'HAP' 5. It is evident that here, as in 'HA', Smith uses a conjectural approach in assessing the history of ideas just as much as that of events. The whole essay is based on this approach: cf. Wightman, 'Introduction', 23; id. (1975), 54: 'in his elegant "account" of Ionian natural philosophy . . . [Smith] gives the reader no guidance as to how much this is merely his own conjecture'.

[83] Deficiencies linked by Dijksterhuis (1961), 70–2, with the lack of a critical approach to empirical data, the lack of interest in verifying hypotheses experimentally, the lack of interaction of science with technology, and the exaggerated value placed on uncontrolled speculation.

[84] 'HAP' 5. Cf. *EPS*, p. 109, editorial nn. 4 and 5, pointing out that modern understandings— at least those relating to the weight of air—were not in fact achieved by chance, and that Anaxagoras, while not knowing its weight, demonstrated that air has mass: as recorded by Aristotle in book IV of the *Physics*.

not up to the task, and its resolution had to await Archimedes' principle of
the upward motion of bodies in fluids. Empedoclean doctrine was till then
characterized by its attribution of a true upward motion to fire and air.[85]

Using Aristotle as a source (though he never names him), Smith dedicates
about half of the essay to the exposition of the theory of the four elements,
which he approves for being a sufficiently trustworthy means of enabling
early men to reason scientifically, notwithstanding its lack of connections,
and, furthermore, for being endowed with the harmonious beauty that every
system should have. The remainder of 'The History of Ancient Physics' is
chiefly taken up by a discussion that starts with Aristotle's theory of the
Fifth Element and passes by way of the processes of generation and corruption deriving from the movement of the spheres to culminate in a treatment
of the problems of immortality and the existence of God. Here, to emphasize
how completely foreign to our ancestors was the concept of a divine mind
responsible for creation, Smith returns to the theme of early man's habitual
fear and ignorance, which prompted him to attribute every unforeseen event
to the will of divine beings, acting impulsively for their own particular
purposes and without a preordained plan. This is his version of the Hesiodic
myth of the earth as offspring of chaos and progenitor of the gods through
union with the heavens that arose out of it. For Smith the most troubling
aspect of this myth is the fact that ancient philosophers were capable of
supposing the birth of the gods to be later than that of the world: earth and
heaven, in which according to the tale they had their abode, predated them.
Smith seems amazed that this curious aberration of a theory found adherents
even among educated men, and it is almost as if to preserve the level of the
eighteenth-century reader's sense of astonishment that he mentions the
exceptional case of Anaxagoras, whose concept of *nous* was posited as
predating the world. Smith cites with evident approval Aristotle's remark
that Anaxagoras spoke like a sober man amongst drunkards. He then returns
to his previous subject of primitive theogonies, this time citing (again by way
of Aristotle) the Pythagorean theory that the last work of nature must be the
most perfect production; he also emphasized that the notion of the world's
spontaneous origin was not even considered as disrespectful to religion,
which the Pythagoreans were careful to observe.

Leaving religious considerations to one side, Smith's view and opinion of
ancient theories on this topic at least was coloured by a notion that was
particularly widely held in the eighteenth century, and which lies at the heart
of all his thinking. This is the notion of the world as a coherent system,
governed by laws and serving as an end its own preservation and well-being;
and of course directed by a divine mind, by providence, or by whatever other

---

[85] Cf. *On External Senses*, 15, where Smith cites the difficulty with which ancient philosophers learnt that air was a substance with mass, capable of pressure and resistance—clearly
being aware of the topic referred to in the previous note—and states that for modern philosophers the same difficulty has arisen with regard to light.

name might be bestowed upon its guiding spirit. Smith finds a view analogous to his own in some ancient philosophers, at least as regards the origin of the concept of creation, or rather of a mind responsible for creation. The principle of creation understood as the work of a higher intellect than those responsible for man-made machines, Smith states,[86] derived from the analogy drawn between 'mechanisms' thought up by the human mind and the immense and perfect mechanism that is the universe, for which a much loftier mind was of course necessary. In his view, then, the ancients arrived at their idea of a single creative force by way of a mechanistic analogy.[87]

A similar argument is found in Stoic philosophy, being deployed to prove the existence of God:[88] here it proceeds from an analogy with a mind that can plan a fine building or a work of art; the capabilities, in other words, of the human mind. Smith does the same, but adds to the picture an element which gives the whole a typically eighteenth-century flavour: the machine. From the united character of creation, of the system created, early philosophers made the short step to imagining a single creative principle: 'The unity of the system, which, according to this ancient philosophy, is most perfect, suggested the idea of the unity of that principle, by whose art it was formed; and thus, as ignorance begot superstition, science gave birth to the first theism that arose among those nations, who were not enlightened by divine Revelation' ('HAP' 9).

Smith next undertakes a brief discussion of the way this question was handled in the teachings of Plato, Aristotle,[89] and the Stoics. Plato marked a step forward in relation to previous enquiries inasmuch as he posited a higher divinity, responsible for a temporally located act of creation. In his essay on metaphysics Smith notes that this being (which he variously terms the 'intelligent Being', 'the great Author of all things', and 'the Deity') is said to have created the world in the image of the supercelestial,[90] and that the theory thus presupposes the latter. This is not, therefore, a creation from nothing: indeed, the matter of creation is posited to have existed from eternity. But, rather than the idea of a creator that is 'anterior' to everything, Smith seems interested in showing the different manner in which ancient authors approached the basic concept of a world that was created and is directed towards ends laid down by a providential plan. Even in this brief passage, then, it is possible to detect two approaches that were to characterize Smith's later thought: the mechanistic argument, and the proposal of a providential design.

The concise treatment that follows of the Aristotelian theory of the first cause, or prime mover, is expressly drawn from the last book of the *Physics*

---

[86] At 'HAP' 9 Smith speaks of Anaxagoras, Timaeus, and Plato.

[87] Used by Smith in other areas as well: see Skinner (1972), 315; cf. n. 45 above.

[88] Cic. *Nat. Deor.* ii. 15. 87.

[89] 'HAP' 9–10, still treating Timaeus and Ocellus as the sources used by Plato and Aristotle respectively. On this see above, n. 48. [90] 'HALM' 2.

and the last chapters of the *Metaphysics*.[91] Towards the end of it, Smith allows himself a pointed remark: if, despite causing the changes of the physical world by means of the movement of the spheres, heavenly intelligences 'neither knew nor intended the effects which they produced' ('HAP' 10), there would be no point in any human form of worship; and yet (in a great irony) Aristotelian metaphysics was in large part the basis of scholastic theology.

Smith ends with a short description of the Stoic system, drawing an unspecified connection between it and Platonic theory which, he maintains, it corrected and refined.[92] He retraces the Stoic form of monist pantheism to the ancient belief (which he doubtless regarded as superstitious) that behind the various natural phenomena of the world lay a variety of divinities. He does note in this context, however, some progress on the part of the Stoics towards the sense of unity that he appreciates in any philosophical system: namely their conclusion that since all nature is a worthy object of admiration,[93] the whole must be inspired by a single deity.

The essential outline of the essay, then, is determined by its purpose of enquiring into the way in which ancient philosophy resolved the question of the prime cause. Smith's view of ancient physics in this connection seems to be in line with the classical notion of a subject that seeks to explain sublunary phenomena in terms of their fundamental causes. Indeed, after briefly expounding the theory of the four elements, and dismissing out of hand those early philosophers who posited a multiplicity of gods, or deities that predated the creation of the world, he dedicates the entire second portion of the essay to the question of whether they fulfilled that classically defined role. His summary account of Plato, Aristotle, and the Stoics proceeds along similar lines.

Though he makes no explicit reference to it, there are sporadic indications in the essay that the question of the design or providential plan behind the world's operation was in some degree in Smith's mind throughout. But the essay is not only fragmentary and unfinished; it also deals exclusively with ancient physics, and Smith may have thereby lost sight of the fact that—on a more general level—the Stoics took a 'providential' approach, and that to mention this would not have been at all out of place in a discussion of physics, since that subject for them coincided with metaphysics.

---

[91] 'HAP' 10. Smith deplores the obscurity of these chapters of the *Metaphysics* (not in fact part of the last book, as noted by the editor ad loc.), stating that they have caused commentators more difficulty than any other part of Aristotle's writings. His account of them, if somewhat abbreviated, is nonetheless comprehensible: Bonar (1966), 10.

[92] 'HAP' 11. As the editor has noted (p. 116 n. 25), Smith repeats this reductive judgement of the value of Stoic philosophy elsewhere; it is only in the 20th century that the originality of formal logic and other Stoic doctrines has been appreciated.

[93] 'HAP' 11. Of the three reactions of wonder, surprise, and admiration, Smith here twice names the third—perhaps not by chance, since it is the one resulting from scientific explanation: Campbell (1971), 60.

In conclusion, it is clear that Smith's intention in writing this essay was not to examine the various physical theories in their entirety—this is, indeed, hardly touched on—but rather to enquire more specifically how man as 'not [yet] enlightened by Divine Revelation' sought to explain the fundamental problem of the 'cause' that lies at the root of earthly, physical phenomena.

1.8. 'THE HISTORY OF ANCIENT LOGICS AND METAPHYSICS'

Before examining the third essay, which bears this title, it would be useful to bring together a few references, some from later works, which make Smith's opinion of metaphysics quite clear. One passage that demonstrates his reservations on the subject[94] is *WN* v. i. f. 28–9. Smith looks back to the traditional subdivision of ancient philosophy into physics, ethics, and logic,[95] which, he says, accords perfectly with 'the nature of things', and emphasizes that matters concerning the deity (a part of the system of the universe, whatever might be its essence) came within the purview of physics. But European universities, mostly ecclesiastic institutions dedicated to the training of the clergy, taught philosophy as the handmaiden of theology, and it was not long before spiritual problems began to gain at the expense of physical ones, 'till at last the doctrine of spirits, of which so little can be known, came to take up as much room in the system of philosophy as the doctrine of bodies, of which so much can be known'.[96] In this way a clear opposition between physics and metaphysics was born. Needless to say, the resulting neglect of the former in favour of the supposed superiority of the latter is something that Smith, imbued as he was with the triumphant scientific spirit of his age, thoroughly deplored. He held that metaphysics, or pneumatics, produced nothing but sophisms and subtleties and, as such, was not only useless in itself but gave rise to an even more useless subject, namely ontology, that 'cobweb science' of the schoolmen, which in great measure coincides with metaphysics itself.[97] His objection to metaphysics as a subject was not so much the fact that it sought an explanation for reality beyond sensible experience, as its degeneration into a confused mass of philosophical wrangles, typically medieval in form and quite foreign to the

---

[94] Noted by, among others, Morrow (1966), 158; Bittermann (1940), 722–3; Campbell (1971), 28; Raphael (1972), 336.

[95] *WN* v. i. f.23. The subdivision had its origins in the Academy, but was firmly established by the Stoics: cf. Pohlenz (1970), i. 33.

[96] *WN* v. i. f.28. Further on, Smith remarks in similar vein that physics latterly lost so much ground as to be 'almost entirely neglected'.

[97] *WN* v. i. f.29. Ontology is treated as superfluous, if in a somewhat different manner, at 'HALM' 1, p. 120, where it is stated to have been for the schoolmen a subject distinct from logic, inasmuch as the latter, from the time of Porphyry onwards, included the principal doctrines of Aristotelian metaphysics, leaving precious little over for ontology. Smith was thus quite aware of the difference between Aristotelian doctrine and the scholastic interpretation of it. Cf. Dijksterhuis (1961), 278; Malusa (1981*a*), 234.

spirit and mentality of the eighteenth century. Part and parcel of the same impatient attitude is the pointed critique of casuistry as a debased form of the 'legalistic' and conservative moral science of the Middle Ages, which Smith makes at *WN* v. i. f. 30–2 and at various points in *TMS*, particularly towards the end.

It is impossible to know whether this view was one that Smith already held in its full form when he sketched out the third essay in the series, the 'History of Ancient Logics and Metaphysics'. He may not, perhaps, have yet developed all the lines of attack that he later used, as just summarized, but a clear distaste for the subject, or at least for its degenerate medieval descendants, was certainly already in place, even though his topic was ancient (rather than medieval) metaphysics and ought therefore to have been exempt. Smith's essay begins with a few propaedeutic remarks, as it were, on the concepts of substance and accidence, matter, essence, and species, as well as on the relationship between logic and metaphysics on the one hand and physics on the other;[98] but what follows amounts to little more than the Platonic doctrine of Forms, with brief additional references to Aristotelian, Stoic, and other ancient theories (with the sole, somewhat inexplicable, exception of the Atomists).[99]

In a lengthy note of considerable interest, Smith uses several arguments to refute the view that Plato's theory did not accord the Forms real existence other than in the mind of God. In evidence he summons Aristotle, Cicero, and Seneca, the meaning of the Greek word *idea* ('idea' or 'form') and its evolution, and the fact that Seusippus and Xenocrates remain silent on the subject of any arbitrary attempt to interpret it in that way: the only ancient author, in short, to give it that interpretation was Plutarch, and Smith argues in a critical spirit that he is not to be relied on (though it has to be said that he uses him as a source fairly frequently).[100]

The section dealing with Platonic Forms is sound throughout, and has led Wightman to say that it 'is almost the only part that carries conviction that the author had adequately prepared himself for the ambitious task he had

---

[98] The father of logic was Aristotle; before him, logic and metaphysics made up the ancient subject of dialectics 'of which we hear so much, and of which we understand so little' ('HALM' 1, p. 120). Logic and metaphysics, being indispensable tools for communicating knowledge of the physical world, should be learnt before natural philosophy, for all that historically they developed from and thus postdate it: ibid., p.119. Cf. *WN* v. i. f. 26: logic, though the newest arrival, provides the tools by which right reason can be achieved. Note that at 'HALM' 1, p. 120, Smith states that logic is founded on metaphysics, which in turn derives from natural philosophy, while at *WN* v. 1. f.26–28 metaphysics is said (with reference to teaching in the medieval university rather than the classical period) to derive from theology, and logic from philosophers' need to demonstrate the truth of their own reasoning and the falsehood of that of others. Smith does not draw attention to the difference between this Aristotelian position, according to which logic is a tool of philosophy, and the Stoic one, according to which it is one of philosophy's three component parts: see above, n. 95; Geymonat (1970), i. 314.

[99] 'HALM' 9 (*ad fin.*), p. 128 n. 28.

[100] 'HALM' 3, n. Cf. the editorial notes in the recent Oxford editions of *TMS* and *WN*, as well as Scott (1940), 87–8.

undertaken'.[101] Here too, however, Smith gives rein, if briefly, to his taste for conjectural reconstruction of the past, and explains as obvious the fact that a philosopher who lived in the days when the subject was just beginning should have considered matter and form to predate the world and to have been separate from it *ab aeterno*. His briefer references to the various views adopted at different times by Aristotle emphasize the care with which the latter examined Plato's formulations, before he concluded that they were incapable of meeting the requirements imposed by the imagination. Though rapid, this résumé makes it clear that Smith's intention is to apply to metaphysics the mode of explanation he adopted for astronomy.

What Smith wishes to deny is the possibility of a priori knowledge and innate ideas.[102] This also emerges from his exposition of the theory of anamnesis, which allows him to make reference to the 'fallacious experiment' ('HALM' 3) of the Socratic method. In a particularly interesting passage regarding the pre-existence of matter and form in regard to the sensible objects that are made from them, Smith echoes Aristotle's criticism that Platonic doctrine has a purely verbal coherence, more to do with language than with concept.[103] This judgement is scarcely mitigated by the remark which follows, that an 'attentive consideration' ('HALM' 7) of Plato's teaching (such as Aristotle had carried out) is necessary to reveal its errors.

Smith then deals at length with certain basic concepts of Aristotle's doctrine, such as his notions of potentiality and actuality, before concluding (as already stated) with a brief discussion of Stoic, Peripatetic, and Neo-Platonic teachings, and the Arabic and scholastic commentaries on Aristotle.

1.9. A 'CONJECTURAL' HISTORY OF THE SPIRIT OF SCIENTIFIC ENQUIRY

The foregoing summary of the structure of Smith's essays—if perhaps a little dull to read—has been necessary, partly in order to give an idea of their

---

[101] Wightman, 'Introduction', 25.

[102] Cf. Bittermann (1940), 498. This theoretic denial does not prevent Smith himself, according to some critics, from holding to a fundamental a-priori proposition, namely his faith in a natural order according to which the opposing forces of self-interest would bring about a state of equilibrium: Lindgren (1969), 897. This view is slightly softened in Morrow (1966), 169: Smith's position is 'partly empirical, but mainly . . . a priori'.

[103] 'HALM' 5–7. Cf. Arist. *Met.* 991ᵃ20–2: 'so to say that they [ideas] are models and that other things share in them, is to voice empty phrases and poetic metaphors'. In addition to this, Smith's phrase 'to substitute words in the room of ideas' recalls Cicero's strictures on Stoicism (*De fin.* iv. 21 and esp. v. 22, precisely repeated at 'HALM' 9 in relation to the dependence of the Stoics from Plato and Aristotle). This is an old and polemical line of argument, dating back to antiquity and the distinction between *verba* and *res*, whose aim is to discern a purely verbal distinction between two doctrines, which amounts to imputing lack of originality to one of them. In the case of Cudworth—whose thought was far removed from that of Plato, but whose terminology was largely derived from the latter—Smith deployed the same tactic in order to level the opposite charge, namely that a real difference had been covered up by similar language: 'HALM' 6.

contents, which are not as well known as those of his two major works, but also to enable certain conclusions to be drawn.

Smith had a strong tendency, as we have already noted, to judge ancient philosophy, which he evidently knew well, according to the standards of the Enlightenment, and thereby sometimes alter its characteristics or even, on occasions, its basic significance. One of the most frequent examples of this is the way he refers to the 'primitive' quality of certain theories, by which he means that they are naïve, making crude observations and drawing crude conclusions from them; furthermore, particularly in the case of the more ancient schools of thought, they are guilty of superstitious fear in the face of apparent manifestations of divine anger and the uncertainty of social conditions in an age in which the rule of law could not yet guarantee peace and freedom of possession.

The extent to which Smith applied this mode of analysis in concrete fashion to specific philosophical doctrines, or their mythological and religious antecedents, is far from clear; his conviction was deep-rooted, but the period in question was too remote for there to be supportive evidence in the historical record. This does not, however, undermine his approach. In all three essays, indeed, Smith goes out of his way to excuse those aspects of ancient philosophy that might bring a smile to the lips of his enlightened contemporaries but which 'in the beginning of philosophy' were plausible or appropriate for their task. This stance, an early instance of a view he adopts in his maturer work, reflects the belief that for every stage in the development of human civilization there is a corresponding step forward in the arts and sciences. Smith retraces these steps, so to speak, wishing to show that at that given stage of cultural development (interpreted as including all the elements that make up a civilization), the system in question was precisely what was needed in order to meet the requirements then in place.

A regularly recurring feature of Smith's analysis is the question of a theory's aesthetic value, its 'beauty' in the sense of harmonious internal coherence, a requisite for any scientific system. He finds it to be a common characteristic of astronomic theories, from the most rudimentary to the most sophisticated, itself standing, naturally enough, in proportion to the degree of civilization reached at the time of the theory in question; it is also found in the physical theory of the four elements. Only the third essay is an exception: Smith makes no reference to any 'beauty of the system', nor—apart from a tentative remark relating to the Platonic theory of Forms[104]—to the appropriateness of any given theory to the stage reached by Greek civilization at

---

[104] 'HALM' 5; cf. above, Sect. 1.8. Smith lingers over the difficulty of abstract reasoning, making reference to the authority of Locke and Malebranche and adding that even now the problem remains a fundamental one; the Platonic solution, meanwhile, is worthy of appreciation, no better solution having been found despite centuries of trying. Plato lived at the dawn of philosophy; while the great Malebranche, two thousand years later, was unable to come up with anything much better.

the time of its propagation. The subject matter of this essay is probably too closely linked to principles that Smith did not share, and the debate regarding them was still, in certain aspects, alive in his day. The third essay, in other words, seems to display a slight tendency towards polemics, or at least towards the disavowal of certain positions (even if not explicit), while the first two show a more detached attitude, together with a 'historical' attempt at reconstructing a past that has been altogether superseded. For the supremacy of modern science was by now triumphantly confirmed, and both Aristotelian physics, with its teleological approach, and Ptolemaic astronomy, with its mathematical hypotheses, belonged to the past: to study them was, in a sense, to do archaeology, and Smith allows himself to adopt a re-evaluative and somewhat paternalistic attitude to them. In the case of metaphysics, however, the battle was still undecided; and, bearing in mind that metaphysical questions to a large extent are matters of religion and theology, on which Smith's position was not always strictly traditional,[105] one will appreciate that the approach he adopts in the third essay is slightly different from the one he uses in the first two, for all that the tone is mainly that of impartial exposition, devoid of the barbed criticisms he directs at metaphysics in the *WN*. At any rate, Smith makes no use, or only the very rarest use, of the criteria he applies in the first two essays.

From all this one can conclude that Smith's attitude to philosophical and scientific theories (leaving aside for the moment moral philosophy) is characterized by being at once hypothetical and relativistic. The theories described cannot, for him, lay any claim to absolute validity: they are hypotheses framed so as to satisfy the imagination. This point of view—with the exception of the psychological interpretation of the imagination—is partly classical in origin, deriving from astronomy, but Smith combines it with a typically eighteenth-century element: the importance of the relationship between every intellectual phenomenon and the age and the people that produce it.[106] In a sense, Smith to a certain extent 'historicized' the various manifestations of Greek thought, attempting to put each one back into the historical moment that gave it birth, the moment in which it made most sense: an analytical process which one might characterize as a modern 'treatment' of a classical principle.

A similar process can be detected in relation to the aesthetic worth which Smith ascribes to every valid scientific system, and which also has classical origins;[107] this too is understood in a relativistic fashion—not as the absolute

---

[105] At least in the sense that he favoured a 'natural' moral system, whose rules derived not from dogmas or commandments dictated by an external authority but from a 'natural theology', the aim of which was to provide 'a foundation for morality independent of positive religion': thus Morrow (1966), 170.

[106] One thinks at once of Montesquieu, who was the first to identify the influence of time and place on laws and institutions, and his Scottish disciples Dalrymple and Kames, who were in contact with Smith: Meek (1976*b*), 106–7.

[107] The argument relating to the grandeur and beauty of creation, presupposing a providential plan and compelling man to contemplate it, is a Stoic one: Pohlenz (1970), i. 94. Cf. also Cic.

characteristic of a definitive world-view, but rather as an essential attribute of each single member of the chain of successive hypotheses. Even the few connecting principles, simple and familiar though they are, change and evolve along with the theories themselves; from Plato's circular, uniform motion to Newton's theory of gravitation, they are the various instruments devised by the human mind to enable answers to be fashioned to the questions of the day.

Smith viewed scientific thought, therefore, as a process. It is not a view that has much in common with his better-known 'stadial' theory of history, for all that one can discern a link, at least in principle. Indeed, he began by declaring that speculative thought depended on economic well-being; but he did not develop the idea, other than in the form of the general principle, underlying all his work, that the growth of commerce and economic activity is favourable to the arts and sciences.

We have already spoken of the Aristotelian origins of the concept of wonder; all that remains is to emphasize, once again, Smith's ability to use his classical heritage to the advantage of his conceptual thinking. If man's initial impulse to philosophy came from the observation of the external world and its phenomena, it was his immediate, fundamental psychological reaction that set in motion the whole series of questions ultimately leading (along determinate paths) to the consequent formulation of scientific hypotheses. Far from simply taking over certain hallowed principles, Smith was capable of making use of the part which was best suited to his conception of the origins of scientific research; thus it was that he took from the classics—with the difference already referred to—a principle of fundamental importance for his work.

In addition to what has already been remarked, Smith obviously derives from the classics specific pieces of information on each philosophical school and its theories. There is not much that needs to be said about his judgement of the classics. His principal sources in these essays are Plato and Aristotle, and though he regularly cites the Stoics, whose importance for moral philosophy is great, his analysis of their system is somewhat irrelevant and fails to exercise any obvious influence on the overall form of his treatment; one feels it was added to complete his history of ancient doctrines. His references to the two 'greats' of Greek philosophy come chiefly from Plato's *Timaeus* and Aristotle's *Physics*, *De Caelo*, and *Metaphysics*, though he may not in every case have been consulting them directly, given the vast amount of secondary work that had been done on these writings from late antiquity onwards.

Fin. iv. 12 for the pleasure that comes from understanding: this too is a frequently recurring motif in Smith's work. At *TMS* vi. 2. 3. 5 Smith shows that he is fully aware of the 'contemplative' implications of this concept, and distances himself from it on account of its tendency to encourage an inactive approach to moral behaviour. The situation is different in the essays, which do not concern the whole of human activity but only the speculative: they represent the aesthetic value of a theory as merely one of its attributes, albeit an indispensable one.

In his note on the Forms, Smith declares Aristotle to be superior to Plato in every way, save in eloquence. But traces of each survive in equal quantities in his essays, for all that Aristotle more or less explicitly underlies a good part of the argument. Nor is the latter spared the occasional criticism,[108] in the midst of the praise, despite the fact that Smith uses him to confirm his own view of Plato.[109]

The concluding section of Smith's essay on metaphysics contains some rather hasty judgements. He discerns a similarity of concept as well as of expression between Aristotle's theory of potential existence and Plato's separate universal essence; he ascribes a Pythagorean origin to Aristotle's concepts of matter and form; he holds the Stoic view of cause to be close kin to the idea of specific essence in Plato and Aristotle, from whom a large part of Stoic doctrine is said to have derived—this being the reason for its hybrid nature, resembling the theories of the Peripatetics, the Neoplatonists, and even, perhaps, the Arab and scholastic commentators on Aristotle.[110]

On these grounds, one could broadly conclude that the predominant influences in Smith's essays derive from the two greatest Greek philosophers: Plato being the origin for the notions of the hypothetical character of astronomy and the structural role of the connecting principles in scientific theory; while Aristotle is the source for the themes relating to the birth of scientific research, namely the ideas of wonder and economic independence, as also for the succinct historical data on the earliest philosophers.

And yet one cannot entirely grasp the nature of Smith's thought on the 'principles which lead and direct philosophical enquiries' without bearing in mind the underlying motives of the Stoic *explicatio naturae*: to chase away human terror of the gods and of death (an attitude shared by the Epicureans); to instil a sense of moderation, of order, and magnanimity, and assist in instilling a sense of justice; and to communicate the pleasure obtained from contemplating the works of nature or God.[111]

The analysis of Smith's essays that follows will not, I hope, seem too 'conjectural'. In his attempt to reconstruct the origins of scientific thought, Smith first took certain psychological phenomena, such as the fear of the gods and of exceptional events, from the classics, and located them in the eighteenth-century category called superstition—thereby displaying a need, thoroughly typical of the Enlightenment, to drive out fear and doubts by means of understanding. The process works by association: the imagination ceases to torment itself when it uncovers a relationship between two or three

---

[108] For example, 'HAP' 10; 'HALM' 8.

[109] On the doctrine of Forms, 'HALM' 3 n. (pp. 121–3).

[110] Respectively 'HALM' 7 (*ad fin.*); 8; 9. I do not mean to pass strict and precise judgement on what is perhaps a rather loose use of terminology on Smith's part, but I would again advert to the fact that the essay was not finally revised: indeed Wightman ('Introduction', 27) felt that Black and Hutton might have been more cautious in arranging its publication and that of 'HAP'. [111] Cic. *Fin.* iv. 11–12, referred to above, nn. 30, 107.

phenomena, a link that transforms their enigmatic apparition into a familiar sequence of events. Smith uses the Aristotelian sense of wonder to represent the initial phase of this process: that point at which the connection between the phenomena, and with it their explanation, has not yet been discerned. Since the questions that occur to mankind can be resolved (in true Enlightenment fashion, once again) by the gradual progress of human understanding, and the refinement of human methods of observation, it is enough for each explanation to satisfy the intellectual requirements of the time, without regard to the extent to which it corresponds to 'objective reality'.

But it is Stoic philosophy, so notably neglected in Smith's exposition, that contains the most characteristic general motivations behind his conjectural history of scientific research: at the outset, fear of gods and death; then, a sense of order and measure; a vision of the universe as predisposed in accordance with wisdom, prompting the idea of a system which man can contemplate with serenity and pleasure. Stoicism, one might argue, gave Smith the general framework for his picture, using as it does quite precise elements to characterize man's original psychological impulse towards the study of nature: fear on the one hand and tranquillity on the other. Overcoming the former is achieved by acquiring the knowledge to open up the way to the opposite mental state, one of serene consciousness. Aristotle and Plato, for their part, furnished Smith with elements of great importance. He used these elements singly, however, as and when they were relevant to particular perspectives or particular moments in the history of research; and he put them in eighteenth-century contexts and thereby transformed them considerably.

Adam Smith's 'history' of the evolution of scientific thought, then, is both complex and intriguing. His youthful forays into the subject closely intertwine Enlightenment and classical philosophy, acquiring in the process a very particular flavour of their own, personal to Smith and with the occasional hint of the great things to come. An example of this is his ultimately Aristotelian reference to the philosopher's need for *otium* or leisure, the only way in which he can be free of unwanted interferences and dedicate himself to his brainwork: the older Smith, investigating the nature and sources of the wealth of nations, was to ascribe to the same phenomenon of leisure the invention of machines.[112] With typical decisiveness, Smith takes up for his own use the classical motif of science as a disinterested subject, and philosophy as an aristocratic calling, and reapplies it so as to give the man of ideas a vital and specific role in the machine-based culture of the industrial age.

---

[112] For the connection with classical thought on the division of labour into manual and intellectual sectors see below, Ch. 4.

2

The Classical Heritage in
Adam Smith's Ethics

2.1. ADAM SMITH'S MORAL PHILOSOPHY

The twelve years that Smith spent as Professor of Moral Philosophy at
Glasgow were the ones he recalled as his best.[1] A true evaluation of the
extent to which classical influences operated on this important phase of his
life and work can only be formed by examining his most systematic work on
philosophy, the *Theory of Moral Sentiments*, side by side with the elements it
contains of classical origin: very easily discerned, these mostly derive from
the Stoics, but also from Plato, Aristotle, and others. But, rather than a set of
authorities requiring homage, the ancient sources relied on will be seen to
form a kind of cultural seed-bed, in which a quite new species of ethics could
take root and grow.[2]

A not entirely unjustified charge levelled at the *TMS*—long overtaken in
terms of academic attention and esteem by its much better-known successor—is that it is somewhat pedantically and rhetorically, not to say boringly,
written. In mitigation it can be pointed out that the work is nothing more
than a printed version of Smith's Glasgow lectures,[3] and its style is a
reflection of its pedagogical origins. The Glasgow moral-philosophy course
was structured so that 'natural' theology was taught in the first year, ethics in
the second, jurisprudence in the third, and what we would today call
political economy in the fourth.[4] The very way in which moral philosophy
was placed between theology and jurisprudence, and the fact that a large
proportion of the students were destined for a career in the Church,[5] may be
used to support the assumption that only a truly capable teacher could make
the subject agreeable. There is sound evidence that Smith was such a

---

[1] *Corr.* 309 (no. 274).

[2] The classical antecedents of which have been listed in full by Macfie (1967*b*), 44: 'It is just the
accepted classical ethical background of the eighteenth century—Platonic—Aristotelian—Stoic'.

[3] Macfie (1967*b*), 42–5; Raphael (1969), 244.

[4] This sequence was accepted by all the central names of eighteenth-century Scottish
learning—Carmichael, Hutcheson, Hume, Smith himself, Ferguson, and Dugald Stewart—
endowing their writings with an unmistakable flavour and making the Scotland of their day one
of the centres of European culture: Macfie (1967*a*), 21.

[5] Macfie (1967*e*), 106; Bonar (1926), 335.

teacher[6]—but giving a lecture is a different matter from writing. Furthermore, it should not be forgotten that the book had considerable success.[7] We should perhaps be asking ourselves whether we find it less interesting today simply because it deals with questions of less proximity to us than economic ones.

The main source Smith used for his lectures was Cicero, whose *De Officiis* and *De Finibus* had the additional advantage of being well known to the students.[8] From the sixteenth century onwards the teaching of moral philosophy had been based on Cicero,[9] and by Smith's day the great orator's modified Stoicism was 'almost conventional',[10] though changes were under way that were to prompt some to re-evaluate Stoicism as a whole and the position of Seneca in particular.[11] But Smith, as we shall see, remained faithful to Cicero on the one hand and on the other to Epictetus and Marcus Aurelius—for all that certain hints of Seneca are to be found.

Despite the fact that Smith's fame as an economist has for a long time overshadowed his reputation as a moral philosopher, his moral writing has nonetheless been studied and related in different ways to his other, better-known work. To summarize briefly what scholarship has highlighted in this respect: Smith belonged to that group of British philosophers known as 'sentimentalists' because of their conviction that man's defining element is not reason but sentiment, or passion. It was not on reason, therefore, but rather on specific sentiments that they based their moral theories. In Smith's case the sentiment was 'sympathy': a sense of sharing in one's neighbour's sentiments, universally felt to a greater or lesser degree, and therefore to be considered an essential characteristic of human psychology. An immediate point to make is that despite the similarity of terminology Smith's 'sympathy' has little in common with classical *sumpatheia* apart from the basic sense of taking the part of, or 'suffering together with', another person.[12]

On sympathy Smith bases the principle of approbation, the lynchpin of his moral philosophy: action, and the passion that gives rise to action, is held morally praiseworthy or reprehensible according to the extent that it seems proper or fitting in the circumstances. This is measured in terms of sympathetic emotion, not of utility. The 'propriety' is accordingly based on an

---

[6] Rae (1965), 53–7; Stewart (1980), I. 21–3 (pp. 275–6).

[7] See Hume's friendly and oft-cited letter, reporting that copies of the book were selling like hot cakes (in *Corr.* 33 f. (no. 31)). Within the author's own lifetime there were six editions.

[8] Macfie (1967*b*), 44; cf. above, Introduction. n. 6.   [9] Baldwin (1944), ii. 581.

[10] Macfie (1967*c*), 60, defines Smith's position as 'eclectic, with a distinct bias towards the modified stoicism typical of Cicero, and almost conventional in the Enlightenment'.

[11] Highet (1949), 324 f.

[12] A distinction is necessary between the 'cosmic' significance of the word in the Stoic context (cf. Raphael and Macfie, 'Introduction' to *TMS*, p. 7) and the purely literal sense it is used in by Smith at *TMS* I. i. I. 5, as relating to its radical meaning of 'pity and compassion'. Neither of the two fits with Smith's explanation of 'sympathy' as 'our fellow-feeling with any passion whatever' (ibid.).

affective principle and the experience of relationships between individuals. It follows that Smith's moral theory is founded on an empirical psychology, and is an attempt to furnish 'a satisfactory alternative to *a priori* accounts of conscience and morality generally'.[13] The rules of behaviour are therefore based on experience and observation—as appropriate to Smith's lack of patience with aprioristic solutions and metaphysical dogma, not to mention his detestation of casuistry.

This doctrine might well have been excessively individualist, had Smith not entrusted the task of forming moral judgements to a figure that might be considered a case of split personality, the impartial spectator. It is the judgement of the impartial spectator which lends approval to actions, and such approval is the essence of the individual's conscience; thus conscience is viewed as a social product.

Thus Smith's ethical theory, being based upon reciprocity of sentiment, is social in character. Society, in turn, is viewed as a machine; an organism, in other words, whose operations are ordered and synchronized to produce a final result. One may thus see a parallel, in the moral sphere, with what Newton had imposed on scientific thought.[14] It must be pointed out, of course, that society is not a machine built by human reason. It is therefore legitimate to ask whether reason is wholly absent from Smith's moral theory. Evidently this cannot be the case. The ethical theories of the time were seeking a rational foundation for morals, independent of theology and ecclesiastical authority. In Smith's case, the rational foundation is provided by the impartial spectator, who is ever-present in moral judgements. Furthermore, reason is held to be indispensable for discerning the future consequences of our actions, for judging right and wrong, and for inductively working out the rules of morality. This, however, does not alter the fact that the initial perception of what is morally good or bad belongs in the sphere of sentiment; reason only enters the formula afterwards. Further, an important role in the constitution of moral judgement is left to imagination, by means of which one may partake in someone else's feelings.

The essentially practical nature of Smith's moral theory—its general formulation as a 'practical philosophy', embracing both ethics and economics—has been pointed out.[15] But it is also right to emphasize another aspect of the topic, related to his rejection of the traditional ascetic medieval doctrine of self-denial, namely the fact that for him 'the true moral philosophy is concerned with human happiness and welfare in this world'.[16] This

[13] Raphael (1972), 352; cf. ibid. 337.
[14] Garin (1941), 224; Willey (1940), 137; Raphael (1979), 88; Mittelstrass (1979), 54–5.
[15] Garin (1941), 225; cf. also Raphael (1972), 337. It has been repeatedly emphasized in all important studies of Smith and his work that the subject matter of the *WN* flowed from the organization of the moral philosophy course at Glasgow.
[16] Morrow (1966), 160. Morrow stresses that to adopt this position was to avoid the contrast between an ethics of complete renunciation and the comforts of the modern world; cf. also Garin (1941), 241.

was a point held in common with classical writers, at least as far as happiness is concerned: their ethics had happiness as a final aim, without perceiving any contradiction between the two.

Another important characteristic of Smith's moral philosophy, with considerable significance for his economic thought, is his conviction that private and public good are one and the same thing, leading to the coincidence of the interests of the individual and of society as a whole.[17] Connected to this is a principle which brings reason—a suprahuman reason—squarely back into the heart of reality. This principle too has classical origins.

This is merely a brief sketch of the layout of the essential points in Smith's moral philosophy.[18] The aim of the chapter is to examine each point in turn, bearing in mind that the purpose is not to attempt a further explanation of Smith's moral philosophy, but merely to discern its connections with classical ethics. For that reason only those topics will be examined that might admit of some relationship with similar areas in ancient thought.

2.2. POLYBIUS AND 'SYMPATHY'

It was long ago suggested that Smith took one of his main philosophical concepts, that of 'sympathy', from Polybius.[19] In the course of his brief account of early human societies in vi. 4–7, Polybius declares the necessity of establishing mutual solidarity between parents and their children: if adults fail to give back to their parents the affection and care they received as children, this contemptuous behaviour is disapproved of by society because each individual—thinking rationally—can foresee the possibility that the same might happen to him. This consideration is then extended by means of generalization to interpersonal relationships outside the family: if someone receives assistance in a time of difficulty and does not return it, or perhaps repays good with evil, his conduct offends the observer, who shares the other party's indignation and imagines himself in his shoes. Polybius concludes from this that this sort of situation endows men with a certain sense of duty, which is the root of justice.

One certainly cannot deny that Smith and Polybius have many elements in common, in particular the figure of the observer who shares in the injured party's resentment and the fact that this is the origin of the sense of justice. Writers who have dealt with the hypothesis in the past were rather

[17] Morrow (1966), 168; Myrdal (1953), 46. The principle is also found in English writing on economics from the 16th century onwards: see Chalk (1951), 335, 340.

[18] Many scholars have subjected the concept of sympathy and other ideas in Smith's moral philosophy to a closer and fuller analysis than is possible here: in addition to the already cited works of Garin, Limentani, and Campbell, cf. Bagolini (1976), *passim*; Viner (1972), 78–9; the cited articles by Bonar, Morrow, Raphael, and Macfie; Anspach (1972); Morrow (1923); Campbell (1975), 70–4.

[19] The first to make this suggestion, in 1797, was John Gillies, the well-known English translator of Aristotle.

vague: Smith knew his Polybius, of course, and it is possible that he was recollecting it when he wrote on the same subject, but this does not in any way detract from the originality of his own moral theories.[20]

An examination of the passages in question is perhaps in order. In Gillies's translation, the section of Polybius that most closely resembles Smith's thought reads as follows:

Thus again, when anyone who has been succoured by another in the time of danger, instead of shewing the like kindness to his benefactor, endeavours at any time to destroy or hurt him; it is certain, that all men must be shocked by such ingratitude, *through sympathy with the resentment of their neighbour*; and from an apprehension also, that the case may be their own.

A literal translation of the same passage would run as follows:

When someone has received aid or succour from another in moments of danger and does not show favour to his rescuer, but even tries to harm him, it is evident that he is likely to displease and offend by such conduct those who observe, since they share their neighbour's indignation and imagine themselves in his position. (Polyb. VI. 6. 6)

Gillies's translation is faithful, but it uses Smith's own terminology, and the phrase I have italicized invokes two concepts that are fundamental to his philosophy: 'sympathy' and 'resentment'. The Greek, however, uses only a single verb: impossible to translate with one word, it means 'to be vexed along with'. To translate it in terms of sympathizing with the injured party's resentment, then, overemphasizes the sympathetic aspect. While he has not wholly misrepresented the meaning of the original, I am convinced that Gillies, persuaded by the similarity between the two authors, has translated Polybius so as to bring out as clearly as possible the link with Smith.

According to Gillies, then, Adam Smith's moral theory was in substance a development of the passage of Polybius cited above. The difference between the two authors would lie in the fact that the former located a sentiment at the basis of ethical judgement, while Polybius followed Aristotle in founding ethics on the action of reason on the appetites. He thus identified a dual origin.[21] But in reality the Polybian passage itself ascribes a notable role to sentiment, while for his part Smith scarcely overlooks the rational element. A better formulation would perhaps be that the two authors start from

---

[20] Discussed initially by Dugald Stewart (1980), 334–6, defending Smith from the charge of plagiarism in a long note where he acknowledges the coincidence but states that Smith's originality lies not so much in the general principle as in the use he puts it to in setting out his own moral theory. As far as I know the only scholar to examine the original and point out the debatable nature of Gillies's translation hitherto has been Scott (1940), 84–5. Bonar (1926), 340, mentions the problem in passing. Foley (1976), 100 f., states that Smith drew directly on Polybius, but does so on the basis of his own physico-anthropological interpretation of Smith's thought—for which see Vivenza (1982a), 65–72—thus moving rather far away from the real problem. [21] Quoted in *EPS*, 334–5.

opposite points. The view of Polybius is that man, whose ability to reason distinguishes him from the animals, observes ungrateful behaviour, recalls the events that led to it, and can foresee that it might happen again—perhaps to his own disadvantage. As a result, he takes the side of the injured party and feels anger at the one who gave the injury. In Smith's version, the first reaction derives not from reason but from the immediate sense of sharing the injured party's feelings. Then, when all the circumstances relating to the action have been worked out (this being where reason plays its part), and the propriety of the reaction adjudged by means of the impartial spectator, approval is reached. In this case too, moral judgement is made up of an emotional element and a rational calculation, but the valuation process is set up differently: it is, indeed, the other way around. Another point to note is that Polybius' exposition of the reactions involved, unlike that of Smith, relates to human beings in the very earliest stages of society.

My view is, in short, that though there is certainly an analogy between the two authors, it does not suffice to allow the conclusion that Smith's work derived from that of Polybius. A more compelling similarity than that of the concept of sympathy lies in the notion that the injured party's resentment (when approved, in Smith's version) is the foundation of the principle of justice.

2.3. THE 'GOLDEN MEAN' AND THE IMPARTIAL SPECTATOR

Returning briefly to Smith's concept of sympathy, we may recall that it is a form of identification with the feelings of other people but without experiencing them with the same intensity: the spectator has the feeling to a weaker degree. Moreover, a necessary condition for the sympathetic relation is that the person sympathized with should exercise self-command: too great a display of joy or grief would inhibit the sympathetic reaction of the spectator. It is therefore essential to curb the excess of one's own feelings and to reduce them to a lower degree than would occur naturally. When a harmony[22] has been reached between the passion of the person affected and the sympathetic emotion of the spectator, the former's behaviour is approved and considered 'just and proper' (*TMS* i. i. 3. 1); that is to say, proportionate

---

[22] Smith's use of musical metaphors in this context was perspicaciously spotted earlier by Bonar (1926), 336, 340. Hume too spoke of the meeting point between the subject and others and the necessity of touching 'a string to which all mankind have an *accord* and *symphony*': quoted in Morrow (1969), 25 (my italics). The use of terms implying being in the same key or 'in tune' to express ideas of accord is a figure of speech with a distinguished lineage—still operative in modern language, as my own phraseology indicates—stretching back to Cicero's *concordia ordinum* and beyond to the Pythagoreans' 'celebrated fancy' ('HA' iv. 5) of the music of the spheres, putting the idea of *concentus* in the context of cosmic order. In humanist writing on the history of philosophy the motif was used to emphasize agreement between different thinkers: Malusa (1981a), 31f.

to the causes which gave rise to it. The propriety is therefore the suitability of a passion (and of the action it provokes) to the relevant circumstances; the action must not be disproportionate to the situation from which it springs if it is to obtain moral approbation. In other words, human passions, according to Adam Smith, must be kept down to an intermediate degree. This reminded many scholars[23] of Aristotle's 'golden mean', which consists in considering each virtue to be situated at a point equidistant from two opposite vices.

Smith himself points out a connection between Aristotle's theory and his own, stating that it closely agrees with his own treatment of the 'propriety and impropriety of conduct' (*TMS* VII. ii. 1. 12).[24] In fact the Scottish philosopher affirmed in *TMS* I. ii. intro. 1 that propriety consists 'in a certain mediocrity'. One must emphasize, however, that here this concept refers to the passions 'excited by objects peculiarly related to ourselves', with the avowed purpose of allowing the spectator to participate.

In this instance Smith consciously uses a classical concept, emphasizing its similarity to his own but placing it within the framework of his theory and thereby modifying it to some extent. The Aristotelian concept did not in fact depend on the requirement that passions should be reduced to a degree that would allow others to share it; it was, rather, an ideal of equilibrium arising from the typically Greek dislike of whatever is excessive.[25]

Nevertheless, one must allow a certain similarity between the two doctrines. Aristotle says:

virtue must have the quality of aiming at the intermediate. I mean moral virtue; for it is this that is concerned with passions and actions, and in these there is excess, defect, and the intermediate. For instance, both fear and confidence and appetite and anger and pity and in general pleasure and pain may be felt both too much and too little, and in both cases not well; but to feel them at the right times, with reference to the right objects, towards the right people, with the right motive, and in the right way, is what is both intermediate and best, and this is characteristic of virtue. Similarly with regard to actions also there is excess, defect, and the intermediate. (*NE* 1106^{b}15–24, W. D. Ross's translation)

Moreover, Aristotle's concept of virtue is defined not only by the subjective attitude but also by its being appropriate to a given situation,[26] just like Smith's propriety, whose mediate character must suit causes and circumstances. There is also another aspect of Smith's concept which has a parallel in Aristotle's *Ethics*: the 'point of propriety' differs for different passions, so

---

[23] Limentani (1914), 75–6; Macfie (1967e), 119; Bonar (1922), 163, 166; Bittermann (1940), 511; West (1969), 104, 108; Campbell (1967), 572.

[24] Cf. Limentani (1914), 75. Morrow (1966), 174, notes that after having listed components of virtue such as benevolence, justice, and prudence, Smith 'borrows from ancient ethics a fourth constituent, propriety'. Scott (1940), 84, puts the concept of propriety in relation to Greek *tò prépon*, which roughly corresponds with Latin *decorum*.

[25] Bonar (1926), 340; Aubenque (1963), 165.

[26] Arist. *NE* 1106^{a}26–32; cf. Aubenque (1963), 64.

that an excess in some (e.g. the 'social' passions such as affection, friendship, esteem) is less blameworthy than an excess in others.[27] Finally, for both authors the ideal 'measure' expressed by propriety constitutes the perfection of moral action.[28]

One element closely connected with these aspects of Smith's thought is represented by the key figure of moral judgement, the impartial spectator. He makes an evaluation which is objective because it is disinterested and thereby guards against the risk of being subjective. Once again we find in *Nicomachean Ethics* a character who may be considered somewhat analogous to Smith's personage: 'Virtue, then, is a state of character concerned with choice, lying in a mean, i.e. the mean relative to us, this being determined by a rational principle, and by that principle by which the man of practical wisdom would determine it' ($1106^b36-1107^a2$, Ross's translation).[29] Some scholars have seen a connection between Aristotle's *phronimos* (man of practical wisdom) and the impartial spectator;[30] rightly enough, to my mind, though Smith's concept is much more complex and elaborate, and therefore, in the end, different. In Aristotle the prevailing idea is that, since the mean is a relative standard, only practical wisdom can succeed in establishing it, while in Smith (leaving aside the various characterizations of his spectator) the prevailing concept seems to be the inadequacy of sympathy, and of reason too, to determine the golden mean. All the same, both thinkers find it necessary to establish a fundamental element of control beside the subjective judgement, whether it arises from reason or feeling, and they entrust this task to the wisdom of the upright man.

One specific situation in which the evaluation of propriety can cause problems is the application of justice in the strict sense. Bonar discerned an analogy between the well-known passage in which Aristotle states that since in certain cases unwavering observance of the law can be thoroughly unjust, recourse must be had to the virtue of equity, and a section of the *TMS* where Smith states that the 'rules' of duty are a good, but imperfect, guide to moral behaviour: the best results are obtained by the few who have the

---

[27] Arist. *NE* 1109^a34: 'For of the extremes, one is more erroneous, one less so . . .' (Ross's translation); cf. *TMS* I. ii. intro. 2, illustrated with examples in the treatment of self-command in VI. iii. 14 f. On this point see Limentani (1914), 76.

[28] 'Hence in respect of its substance and the definition which states its essence, virtue is a mean, but with regard to what is best and right an extreme': Arist. *NE* 1107^a5-7; cf. *TMS* I. i. 5. 8–9, VI. iii. 23. See Limentani (1914), 90.

[29] Arist. *NE* $1106^b36-1107^a2$. The analogy between this figure and the impartial spectator lies in their capacity to discern the golden mean; apart from this, the frequent translation of *phronimos* as 'prudent' can, if done in connection with Smith, create confusion with the latter's 'prudent man'; cf. next note.

[30] Bonar (1926), 340, and (1922), 166; Limentani (1914), 75. Scott (1940), 89 n. 4, makes the objection that Smith distinguishes carefully between the spectator and the 'prudent man', which he connects with Aristotle's figure. Morrow (1969), 54, seems to link the latter not with the spectator but with the man 'of the happiest mould', who—by consulting the spectator—is capable of discerning the 'degree of propriety' with accuracy and subtlety.

ability of regulating their behaviour according to the best propriety of the instant situation.[31] This is an example of the frequently remarked conflict between an abstract and insufficient normative principle and the attempt to apply it in specific situations.

The two figures that are compared in this case are Aristotle's judge and Smith's man 'of the happiest mould', the only one who may establish with exactness the point of propriety, but who differs from the impartial spectator in that he is a real man, however rarely to be found. Both he and the judge are able to grasp what is the most suitable behaviour for any given factual situation. It is important to note that Aristotle's *epieikes* judge, in applying equity, performs the same operation in terms of justice as the *phronimos* performs for *all* virtues, i.e. is able to recognize the mean or, as Smith would have it, propriety. The man of the happiest mould is perhaps to be considered the (somewhat infrequent) embodiment of the impartial spectator. He certainly shares the latter's evaluative ability with regard to propriety, but— not being exempt from action himself—he also applies it to his own behaviour. What these two individuals imagined by Smith and Aristotle have in common is their ability to determine the precise degree of virtue, the measure of ethical behaviour, without reference to laws or established systems. It is on the basis of this similarity that comparisons are drawn between, on the one hand, Aristotle's *phronimos* and Smith's impartial spectator, and, on the other, as has been done by Morrow as well as by Bonar himself, between the former and Smith's man of the happiest mould.

If, however, we examine the notion of 'following the rules precisely' we see that Smith viewed this as leading to acceptable and even praiseworthy conduct, for all its imperfections; for Aristotle, however, it resulted in true and undiluted injustice. It should indeed be emphasized that the two authors are dealing with separate questions: Smith's topic is 'the general Rules of Morality', while Aristotle's is justice, a very specific virtue whose 'rules' translate into practice as civil and criminal laws. Aristotle's judge is the individual who goes for the intermediate, and to that end knows the golden mean: if he did not, he would tend towards one of the two extremes, distancing himself from virtue.[32] Smith observes no contrast between the man who can locate and arrive at propriety, on the one hand, and the man who, on the other hand, merely follows rules that he has learned, rules that amount to normative principles worked out on the basis of experience with the aim of bringing human behaviour as close as possible to perfection—to propriety, in other words. For both authors, then, perfection lies in the mean: but for Aristotle this always signifies equidistance from the two extremes, so that any movement away from it is viewed negatively, and in the field of justice it will amount to a distancing from what is just; while for Smith, dealing as he does

[31] Bonar (1926), 346; cf. *TMS* III. 4. 8–5. 1, and Arist. *NE* 1137^{b}8–27.
[32] Arist. *NE* 1132^{a}21–4, 1133^{b}30–4.

with empirical moral principles, their application in practice is precisely an attempt to move closer to that perfection that not everyone can discern. Although therefore there is some similarity between Aristotle's judge and Smith's man of the happiest mould,[33] inasmuch as in each case the rigour of the established rule is overcome by a superior individual's sensitivity and intuition, one cannot entirely agree with Bonar. The two writers present quite different judgements of behaviour that veers away from what is proper. Aristotle's argument essentially expresses the contrast between natural and positive justice, for which one may simply refer to the well-known *summum ius, summa iniuria*. Smith, on the other hand, refers to precepts of moral behaviour whose function is to govern human conduct, and states that to act solely in accordance with them (in other words, in accordance with a conventional sense of duty), though far removed from perfection, is morally acceptable. The precepts in question are clearly ones designed to regulate social behaviour, and do not necessarily have any connection with justice. As we shall see, Smith did not regard justice as the same as the other virtues: treating it as if it were, indeed, was something he blamed Aristotle and Cicero for. Its 'rules' are constructed differently from moral ones, being defined with a degree of accuracy that is unknown in the case of other virtues, since they are the most important for social life, which has in justice 'the main pillar that upholds the whole edifice'.[34] In the case of justice, therefore, propriety (or the mean) is not merely a matter of sensitive judgement: it must admit of objective, mathematical (or, in Smith's eyes, grammatical) proof.

2.4. RESENTMENT

In Smith's sympathetic theory appreciation of resentment has a special place. When a man is injured, it is natural to feel sympathy with his resentment, as long as the latter, like his other emotional reactions, is kept at a moderate level of intensity. Smith distinguishes the sort of resentment that belongs to the negative movements, so to speak, of human behaviour[35] from the natural reaction to an offence, a reaction given us by nature for our own defence: 'It is the safeguard of justice and the security of innocence'.[36]

For that reason this impulse has a social function within the area of justice, inasmuch as it allows the formation of a rule system that prevents overbearing individuals from prevailing. The advantage of this legitimate resentment is

---

[33] Namely his ability to recognize propriety and take part in specific situations: cf. Bagolini (1976), 84.   [34] *TMS* II. ii. 3. 4; cf. also VII. iv. 37; III. 6. 11.

[35] That is, the 'unsocial passions' (*TMS* I. ii. 3). These, incidentally, are distinct not only from the 'social passions' but also from the 'selfish' ones, indicating once again that Smith did not regard the latter as unsocial. The 'unsocial passions' (hate and resentment) need to be controlled much more than the others to meet with approval, and yet they too 'are regarded as necessary parts of the character of human nature' (ibid. 3. 3).

[36] *TMS* II. ii. 1. 4. On resentment, cf. also I. ii. 3. 8.

that it makes it dangerous *for others* to use violence, and their punishment will meet with general approval, because it will be considered just.

Classical precedents for this feature of Smith's ethical thought have been discerned by Limentani: Plato's doctrine of 'spirits' (the irascible part of the soul), and certain passages in Aristotle where the inclination to forgiveness beyond certain limits is condemned as a moral defect.[37] Even Theophrastus, who early on wrote critically of anger, later considered it a natural and necessary reaction on the part of a victim of unjust or criminal actions.[38] The classical tradition, therefore, contained a strain of support for justified resentment: no one, of course, was in favour of blind, unfettered rage. But it was on resentment that Smith founded his conception of justice, which amounted to the application (in the form of civil and criminal laws) of the principles of 'natural jurisprudence' that reflect the universal sense of disapproval towards an offence and the desire to see it punished.[39] 'Resentment', then, it has been rightly said, presupposes justice's essential nature as the '*sine qua non* of any manifestation of practical life'.[40]

2.5. JUSTICE

For Smith the essential characteristic of justice, which he deals with at several places in his works, is that it is—in his words—a 'mere negative virtue'. Its negative quality arises from the fact that its fundamental function is to prevent men from harming other people; it is, as he famously says, possible to fulfil its requirements 'by sitting still and doing nothing' (*TMS* ii. ii. 1. 9).

To view justice principally in terms of the individual's behaviour towards others is a conception that goes back by way of Aquinas to the basic definition it receives in Aristotle, as a virtue that relates to others and therefore governs interpersonal relationships; a definition in complete contrast to the exclusively ethical one given by Socrates and Plato. Many scholars have underlined this feature of Smith's justice, together with the connected claim (itself too of ultimately Aristotelian origin) that it is an essential virtue for the constitution of society: other virtues (such as beneficence) might be lacking, he states, but not justice.[41] A typical example of this necessity is given at *TMS* ii. ii. 3. 3: even robbers and murderers, if there is any society among them, must refrain from robbing and murdering one another. This phrase probably derives from Cicero (*Off.* ii. 40), who in a comparable passage on the necessity of justice states that even among evildoers there must be rules.[42] From this follows

---

[37] Limentani (1914), 147–8 and p. 238 n. 5.

[38] See Pohlenz (1970), i. 173.

[39] *TMS* vi. ii. intro. 2; cf. also the manuscript fragment printed ibid. app. ii, p. 389, on which see Raphael (1972), 340–1. Stewart ((1828), i. 130–1) states that Smith and Kames applied their theory of resentment to jurisprudence: cf. also Raphael and Macfie, introd. p. 13.

[40] Bagolini (1966), 99.

[41] Bonar (1926), 338; Raphael (1973), 94–5; Cropsey (1975), 137; Haakonssen (1981), 93f.

[42] For a similar point made in Plato's *Republic* see Bonar (1922), 127 (cf. also 168).

another feature that distinguishes justice from the other virtues: observance of its rules can be imposed by force (*TMS* II. ii. I. 5), thanks to the fact that if a man does not wish to do good he cannot be compelled to do so, but if he wishes to do ill, he must be prevented.

Some of Smith's remarks on justice are traditional. Its coerciveness, like its social quality and abstract nature, was specified by Aristotle. But in other respects his interpretation is quite personal. In his scheme the sense of justice develops out of the 'natural' sense of indignation people have on seeing it violated and their sense of solidarity with the victim. In other words justice too has sympathy at its root, inasmuch as it is, in the final analysis, founded on a 'sympathetic understanding of human motivations'.[43] It nevertheless can be subjected to a more accurate form of evaluation than other virtues and, unlike them, it has rules that are absolute in their precision: they can be compared with the rules of grammar, while the rules of the other virtues, less clearly defined and less able to produce a fixed and unwavering directive, are more like the guidelines of stylistic elegance.[44]

Smith's view of justice has been compared with Aristotle's 'commutative' justice,[45] called by Aristotle 'corrective', inasmuch as its function is precisely that of maintaining equality and correcting any disparities that may arise in the sphere of personal relations. Justice of this sort regulates social relationships, whether in the civil area (contracts and so forth) or the criminal one (theft, murder, insult),[46] and it is clearly to the latter group that Smith refers when he says that his treatment of justice is not far removed from the one according to which 'we are said to do justice to our neighbour when we abstain from doing him any positive harm, and do not directly hurt him either in his person, or in his estate, or in his reputation' (*TMS* VII. ii. I. 10). Not long previously he has stated that this interpretation is that which Aristotle and the schoolmen had of commutative justice.

Chief among the injuries that an individual can do to another, and which justice must prevent or punish, are those inflicted on the other's property. Aristotle, it will be recalled, remarked that 'Justice is the virtue through which everybody enjoys his own possessions in accordance with the law' (*Rhet.* 1366^{b}9–10). This comment did not go unheeded in antiquity, and was the basis for, among other things, the Stoic belief that the main motive force

---

[43] Bittermann (1940), 731; cf. also Raphael (1973), 93f., and Bagolini (1976), 94–5.

[44] *TMS* III. 6. 11; cf. Bagolini (1966), 65–6, and Campbell (1967), 574, where the interesting point is made that the comparison with grammar suggests that the rules in question were arrived at by way of a slow process of social consensus, and fixed for long periods without alteration; in other words that they are variable but only slowly and by degrees.

[45] Smith's comments on commutative justice are at *TMS* VII. ii. I. 10; cf. also ibid., app. II, p. 390.

[46] Arist. *NE* 1131^{a}1–9. For Aristotle at least, the practical nature of justice is evidenced by the fact of its 'mediate' character: one searches a mean between gain and loss, or between damage suffered and damage inflicted. Indeed, a word for the judge in such a situation is 'mediator'; ibid. 1132^{a}14–24.

for the creation of a State is the desire to guarantee the security of private property.[47] Not only Locke, then, but Aristotle too, stood behind Smith's statement that the job of justice is to maintain property.

Since to safeguard property is the State's chief task, the fundamental characteristics of this sort of justice should be sought rather in the *WN* than in the *TMS*. Broadly speaking, it has been remarked that the perspective in the former is wider but not essentially different: in the *TMS* justice is the virtue that prevents the individual from harming others; in the *WN* it guarantees a degree of impartiality in the social order, barring privileges and unfair restraints. Scholars have found the concept to be broadened in the later work, and treated as the basis of social policy; doubt arises, however, as to whether the impartial spectator is appropriate in the latter context, being a figure that fits better with individual moral development. According to this interpretation, then, justice functions on the level of interpersonal relations in the earlier work and on that of relations between groups in the later one.[48]

The fact that for Smith the essence of justice is avoiding causing injury to others connects with a further classical component of his thought, namely resentment. His view of justice has at its root, in my opinion, the double conceptual foundation whereby the individual sympathizes with the resentment of the injured party, and thus objects to injury not only against himself but against others too. Therefore to classical resentment (which always refers to the injured party, and amounts to no more than a natural sense of indignation at the offence suffered) is added Smith's concept of sympathy, which takes the former away from its original egocentric formulation and endows it with objectivity. In this way even justice is founded in the sphere of sentiment, to which is also linked the feeling of remorse that arises from the individual conscience at having broken the laws of justice. Anspach correctly pointed out that the individual who persists in wrongdoing not only loses the sympathy of the spectator but draws his own resentment on himself: this, in short, is remorse.[49] To illustrate this dramatic sentiment, which brings the double torment of the fear of punishment and the need to atone for one's guilt, Smith uses an argument with its origins—though he does not cite them—in classical literature: the guilty man, even if safe in the knowledge that his crime will remain undiscovered by all, is so fiercely persecuted by his bad conscience that in some cases he will end up confessing his crime voluntarily, thereby to remove himself from the terror and remorse, and give himself up to justice.[50]

---

[47] Thus Panaetius, who regarded private property as 'ein notwendiger Bestandteil der staatlichen Rechtsordnung': Pohlenz (1970), i. 205.

[48] Campbell (1967), 576; Bittermann (1940), 728; *pace* Grampp (1948), 327–8, for whom the view of justice presented in the two works is different.

[49] Anspach (1972), 184; cf. *TMS* ii. ii. 2. 3 and 3. 4.

[50] *TMS* iii. 2. 9, very probably taken from Cic. *Fin.* i. 50–1, ii. 53. Other similar passages in Lucretius and Plato are noted by Mondolfo (1903–4), i. 63.

2.6. PRUDENCE

Prudence plays an important role in economic activity. Smith defines it as the virtue predisposed to the care of health and fortune, rank and reputation: the things, in other words, on which depend the comfort and ease of life. The prudent man is presented in a detailed description as simple and modest in conversation; sincere; cautious but faithful in friendship; not endowed with great brilliance; tending to respect the established usages and customs of society. His specific qualities, additional to these characteristics, are industriousness, frugality, and the ability to renounce a present benefit for the sake of a greater one to come. Behaving in this manner, he gains the impartial spectator's wholehearted approval. Financially, he lives off his own income, aiming bit by bit to improve his situation in a very gradual fashion; he pays attention to no one's affairs but his own, and he is not given to ambition of any sort. He is wedded to his tranquil existence and has no desire to be deprived of it even in order to take on responsibilities that might carry him to success and authority. In conclusion, Smith states, virtue of this sort is respectable and perhaps even agreeable; but it earns only a 'cold esteem', rather than 'ardent love or admiration'.[51]

The section of the *TMS* in which this description of the prudent man is given was added to the sixth edition, which was the product of revision by Smith shortly before his death in 1790. As has been justly stressed, this shows the renewed attention that Smith gave to such behaviour after he had written his major work.[52] But a section of the *TMS* forming part of the first draft—and therefore written in the 1750s—contains a similar if more synthetic definition, and a phrase that is worth quoting. Having demonstrated how the impartial spectator approves of the carefully thought out behaviour of the person who denies himself a present pleasure for a future one, and how rare those who exercise this form of self-control actually are, Smith states: 'Hence arises that eminent esteem with which all men naturally regard a steady perseverance in the practice of frugality, industry and application, though directed to no other purpose than the acquisition of fortune'.[53]

The clear relationship between prudence and economic activity which this passage makes explicit has often been emphasized.[54] Prudence is obviously a virtue that implies a cautious ability to renounce something in favour of a carefully calculated future benefit. Smith's prudent man, level-headed, thrifty, and industrious as he is, does not bother about getting sensationally

---

[51] For the full description see *TMS* VI. i. 5–14.
[52] Raphael and Macfie, 'Introduction', p. 18; cf. also the editorial note 22 at *WN* II. iii. 19.
[53] *TMS* IV. 2. 8. For the link with the virtue of self-control see Raphael and Macfie, 'Introduction', p. 9: 'The moral quality of prudence depends on its association with the Stoic virtue of self-command'.
[54] Anspach (1972), 196; Campbell (1971), 178–80; Gee (1968), 287–90; Salvucci (1966), 84–91; Macfie (1967c), 71–5; Campbell (1967), 573.

rich, nor does he undertake great enterprises. His field of operations is limited and not particularly bold; his aim is to increase his substance bit by bit, without risks and without excess. This behaviour is considered virtuous, its essential premise being the related approach by which present interests are subordinated to future ones.

This last point has obvious connections with Epicureanism, but Smith does not make the relationship explicit in the two passages outlined above, leading one to conclude that he does not merely concur with the Epicurean motif that they express, but has rather assimilated it as his own. In *TMS* VII, however, when placing Epicureanism among the philosophical systems for which virtue consists in prudence, he returns to the topic and specifically links it with the doctrine of 'pleasure', according to which all beings naturally tend towards pleasure. Indeed part of this doctrine is the idea of an accurate form of comparative assessment on the basis of wisdom: pleasures are not to be sought for their immediate quality, since some—liable to produce painful results in the long run—must be avoided, while on the other hand certain painful events are to be tolerated because advantage may derive from them in the future. This type of selection of pleasures and pains results in a mode of behaviour which can be well defined as prudent, in the etymological sense of foresight. Its fundamental characteristics are in the main described, once again, by Cicero.[55]

Though he does not expressly draw attention to this link between his philosophy and that of the Epicureans, it is clear that Smith is aware that prudence has certain characteristics that are necessary elements in the behaviour of his virtuous man. It is perhaps relevant that in the passage added to the sixth edition of the *TMS* he writes of sacrificing present 'ease and enjoyment' (VI. i. 11), while in the other two passages he uses a more strictly Epicurean terminology: thus, at IV. 2. 8, he refers to 'present appetites' and 'pleasures'; while at VII. ii. 2. 2ff. not only does he write again of 'pleasures', but he draws a distinction between prudence and temperance, stating that 'Temperance . . . was nothing but prudence with regard to pleasure' (2. 9). In the course of his examination of prudent behaviour, Smith discerned qualities that were essential components of profitable, creditworthy conduct in the general—and indeed the economic—sense. He then tried to diminish the emphasis on pleasure pure and simple, and make it clear that favourable future results can derive also from the renunciation of an immediate good or advantage.

As described by Smith, then, prudence implies a degree of self-mastery which brings it into proximity with Stoic self-control. It might be said on this basis that it represents a mixture of Stoic and Epicurean elements.

---

[55] Cic. *Fin.* i. 32–3, 48. Describing the philosophy of Epicurus in *TMS* VII. ii. 2. 2f., Smith refers back to *Fin.* i as a whole, as well as to Diog. Laert. x: the essential point can be found at x. 129; cf. Mondolfo (1903–4), i. 12.

Of self-control something will be said in the next section, but Smith's own contribution, the reference to economic behaviour, is closely connected with the positive moral quality ascribed to prudence, as indicated by the impartial spectator's approval.

The difference between Smith and Epicurus, in this instance, is that the latter did not consider the virtues desirable in themselves, but only for their capacity to help the individual attain pleasure and avoid pain—the only end at which man's natural desires aim. Therefore prudence, being a circumspect state of mind focused on the furthest consequences of every action, is not a 'pleasant and agreeable' thing in itself, but only for its ability to make provision for future results. Smith, on the other hand, though considering prudence respectable but not worthy of love, approves of it in itself. It is not, after all, for its tendency to achieve the good and avoid the bad that the spectator appreciates prudent behaviour, but rather because the man who practises it exercises a form of self-control. The spectator, detached from both present and future circumstances, can judge with objectivity. The agent, however, is emotionally caught up in the moment, and accordingly under greater pressure from his own desires than from far-off, scarcely conceivable advantages, with little influence over his immediate decisions. Indeed, Smith notes, very few men behave in this way. But it is precisely this capacity for self-control—the ability to say no now in order to have later on—that arouses the impartial spectator's approval. He appreciates the prudent conduct in itself, for the discipline it imposes, not only for the positive results that derive from it.[56] This might seem partly to contradict Smith's view that in forming a judgement one should look not only at the intention behind an act but also at its results: this view, to which we shall return, is different from the Stoic one, and formulated with a greater sense of realism. In general, however, Smith does not restrict morality within the bounds set by the mere consideration of consequences, and thus—as has been observed—distinguishes himself from the utilitarian views of his contemporaries, resorting instead, like Shaftesbury, to the ethical tradition of antiquity.[57]

In the current case, however, there is no sharp contrast, because intentions and future results ought to be precisely coterminous; the spectator's approval of temporary sacrifice in reality arises from the awareness that it is the best choice in terms of future outcome. A permissible conclusion, perhaps, is that approval of this virtue is prompted both by the intention behind it and by the consequences of acting in accord with it. Smith's point

---

[56] *TMS* VII. ii. 2. 8–13; cf. IV. 2. 8 for 'self-command'. Bagolini (1975), 108, shows that Smith favours the ethic of 'propriety' over that of 'utility'. He was certainly no utilitarian: Macfie (1967*b*), 45–8, and (1967*c*), 59–60.

[57] Morrow (1969), 30–1. To ignore consequences entirely would reduce moral judgement to a test of intentions; to take them into account reflects nature's aim of safeguarding 'the happiness and perfection of the species': *TMS* II. iii. 3. 2. We may add that, viewed in this way, Smith did not altogether reject a utilitarian criterion.

of view, then, is partly Stoic and partly Epicurean. Besides, prudence presides over that inclination to 'take care of oneself' which even Stoic philosophers regarded as one of man's natural instincts[58]—a point on which they were not so far removed from the Epicureans.

There is also a 'superior' form of prudence, which looks not to the good of the individuals but to that of the community.[59] Rather than Epicureanism, it is the philosophy of the Academy and the Peripatetics which Smith presents as the source for this quality, which must go together with a wide range of other moral and intellectual virtues, and for that reason is associated with a lofty degree of excellence. All in all, Smith's view of prudence is highly classical, and quite consistent with the etymology from *provideo* which was known to Cicero.[60]

2.7. SELF-CONTROL

It has been remarked that in the sixth edition of the *TMS* Smith considerably amplified his description of this virtue, an indication of the fact that Stoic philosophy maintained its hold over him throughout his life.[61] It is indeed a virtue with undeniably Stoic characteristics; but it should be pointed out that these are more in evidence in section III. iii ('Of the Influence and Authority of Conscience') than in VI. iii ('Of Self-command').

There is something Stoic about the very way the subject is initially set out, with the statement that egocentric instincts must not be allowed to prevail in man, whose duty is to consider himself as a part of the whole, and who for that reason has no justification for putting his own interests before those of the many—or indeed before those of any other single individual.[62] There are two ways of fulfilling this demanding requirement: by elevating our sensitivity to other people's needs;[63] or diminishing our awareness of our own needs. Smith's clear preference is for the latter, which is indeed the Stoic approach, and he illustrates it by way of a phrase from Epictetus. A better idea of the relationship between this aspect of Stoicism and Smith's thought can be gained from certain comments in the second and following editions, but removed in the sixth, where the whole section was recast. Although it is difficult to attain this high level of magnanimity and steadiness, he argues, we must strive to reach it:

Though few men have the stoical idea of what this perfect propriety requires, yet all men endeavour in some measure to command themselves, and to bring down their

---

[58] Limentani (1914), 175; Paolucci (1955), 496.

[59] The prudence of the statesman, general, or lawmaker: *TMS* VI. i. 15; cf., in brief, Anspach (1972), 187–8, and Cropsey (1977), 41, who adduces precedents for it in Aristotle and Aquinas.

[60] *De Leg.* i. 60.   [61] Raphael and Macfie, 'Introduction', 5–6, 18.

[62] *TMS* III. 3. 5–6, where Smith repeats the Ciceronian remark (quoted above in the Introduction) that to deprive anyone of anything unjustly is contrary to nature.

[63] *TMS* III. 3. 8–14; cf. Limentani (1914), 81.

selfish passions to something which their neighbour can go along with. But this can never be done so effectually as by viewing whatever befals themselves in the light in which their neighbours are apt to view it. The stoical philosophy, in this respect, does little more than unfold our natural ideas of perfection.[64]

This passage is Smith's comment on the Epictetan example preserved in the sixth edition: when your neighbour loses his wife or son, you consider it a misfortune which is nonetheless part of the natural order of things; if it happens to you, you regard it as an unbearable calamity, for all that it is no less part of the natural order of things. Smith states that some degree of self-control is natural to man, and that in this respect Stoicism does little more than display to us our own, natural, ideas of perfection. But the remark about each man trying to lower his selfish passions to a level at which his neighbour can share in them is typical of Smith. The idea of the 'neighbour' is a refinement of the one which he took from Epictetus (who uses the general term ἄλλος), and seems to lie at the root of his notion of how self-control might be attained: by viewing what happens to you in the same light as your neighbour would—with, in other words, a degree of detachment.

However, Smith does not completely share Stoic views on this topic. Immediately afterwards he defines two categories of misadventures that an individual can be affected by, according to whether they afflict someone he holds dear, or himself. In the former Smith displays a less unbending approach than the Stoics, who are well known for not drawing a distinction between one's nearest and the rest of the world, though they did admit a natural affection on the part of parents for their offspring.[65]

The paragraphs that Smith allots to this topic (*TMS* III. 3. 13; cf. also VI. ii. 1. 3–6) almost certainly go back to Aristotle (*NE* 1161^{b}26–1162^{a}4), though a similar motif can be found in Cicero, *Off.* i. 54. They repeat, with some slight variations, Aristotle's comments on the dependence between children and their parents, and the progressively less close relationships binding siblings, cousins, friends, and so on. Here too, then, Smith starts from a principle of Stoicism (namely that the individual must care for himself), but departs from it when it no longer meets his requirements: he finds it natural that one should feel stronger sentiments for those who are closer to oneself; whence it follows that not only self-preserving actions are virtuous,[66] but that those calculated to safeguard the interests of one's nearest neighbours—family, friends, fellow-countrymen—are too.[67]

---

[64] *TMS*, editorial note on III. 3. 11 (p. 141); cf. the similar note at III. 3. 4 (p. 136).

[65] Cic. *Fin.* iii. 62; *Off.* i. 11–12. Other sources in Mancini (1940), 111–12; cf. Bryson (1945), 149.

[66] Raphael and Macfie, 'Introduction', 8; West (1969), 103–5; cf. Bonar (1922), 162: 'his [man's] chief business is to govern the affairs of his own daily life'.

[67] At *TMS* VII. ii. 1. 43–4 and III. 3. 14 Smith expresses his disagreement with Stoicism on this point; cf. Raphael and Macfie, 'Introduction', 9–10; Anspach (1972), 195.

On this subject too Smith ends up criticizing Stoic 'apathy', on the grounds that the coldness it imposes on the warmest affections is in reality unnatural and offensive to propriety.[68] The situation where Smith feels that apathy *can* act as a valid rule is in putting up with misfortunes that strike one directly, in regard to which a reduced or at any rate not excessive sensitivity is approved of. Epictetus' notion (treat your own misfortune as your neighbour would) may well have been of considerable importance to Smith,[69] in that he elaborates the relationship between agent and spectator throughout the current section.

Self-control, then, has a fundamental importance in Smith's philosophy:[70] approval is not earned if the passions are not kept under control and below a certain level. It is therefore the virtue which endows all the others with value, and must always be deployed to moderate and regulate the emotions;[71] to bring them down, that is to say, to the level of propriety which Smith himself likens to Aristotle's golden mean. Once again we see the coexistence in his philosophy of elements with quite distinct origins.

To this brief account of a Stoic virtue (more properly a virtue peculiar to a mitigated Stoicism, because its extremes are criticized) I shall add only that it plays a part of some importance in Smith's economic theory. The link between it and prudence enables the man who seeks to moderate his present appetites and thereby attain a future goal—a praiseworthy end in Smith's evaluation—to engage in the required frugal and far-sighted behaviour. Furthermore, control of one's own passions leads to beneficial results for society, and is thus necessary in interpersonal economic relationships too: 'according to Smith, the free market *demands* not only contractual justice and prudence, but the possession of self-command in terms of discipline for all producers and purchasers; a personal self-control within each individual'.[72]

In *TMS* vi Smith examines self-command from the specific point of view of the classical subdivision of the passions into the 'irascible' and the 'concupiscible'.[73] Many of his illustrative examples are drawn from the classics: the death of Socrates, to exemplify suffering overcome for the sake of a great idea; Cicero's *Catalinarians* and Demosthenes' *Philippics*, expressive of justifiable indignation reined in with difficulty; Odysseus, Lysander, Themistocles, and Crassus, demonstrating the usefulness of the ability to

---

[68] *TMS* III. 3. 14; cf. Limentani (1914), 81.

[69] As noted by Raphael (1972), 342, 346, Smith first used the epithet 'impartial' with reference to the spectator when reconciling Stoic self-control with Christian love.

[70] Resembling Stoicism in this respect: cf. Limentani (1914), 82, where the point is made that self-control is insufficiently valued by the other 'sentimentalists', and Campbell (1971), 168.

[71] Macfie (1967), 118; cf. also Raphael and Macfie, 'Introduction', 6: 'For Adam Smith, self-command has come to permeate the whole of virtue, an indication of the way in which Stoicism permeated his reflection over the whole range of ethics and social science'.

[72] Lamb (1974), 681, author's italics.

[73] *TMS* vi. iii. 2–3. Smith does not use the classical terminology, but rather divides the passions according to the difficulty in overcoming them for short or long periods: the former group includes the violent passions, the latter the pleasant ones. See Cropsey (1977), 48.

dissemble and control one's emotions in political life;[74] and so on. The section amounts to a gallery of 'characters', after the manner of Aristotle or Theophrastus, and in accordance with a seventeenth-century literary fashion in Britain, often followed in writings on ethics.[75]

Certain classical characters, of course, had inherent weaknesses, and Smith, despite reflecting the ancient tradition, does not fail to subject these to his eighteenth-century judgement. Thus great men such as Alexander the Great and Caesar suffered from the fault of regarding themselves as of divine birth; and even Socrates, though not claiming to be the offspring of his *daimonion*, nonetheless imagined he was privately addressed by it—a fantasy that would, in Smith's eyes, naturally be the least serious were it not entertained by such a beacon of wisdom as Socrates. Exaggerated self-esteem is, for the most part, a defect, often nourished by good fortune, on the basis of which these individuals come in for more than their fair share of admiration.[76] The man who is spoiled by success and prosperity loses his sense of proportion and becomes capable of the most hateful forms of violence: the classic example is Alexander, to whom Smith had previously opposed the wise Parmenides, who knew the true value of approbation, and for whom Plato alone was a sufficient public (*TMS* VI. iii. 31–2).

Smith ends with a lengthy comparison between the 'proud' man and the 'vain' one. Both characters are to be criticized, but in certain circumstances some aspects of the former may be positive or even noble. Smith draws a parallel between pride and the 'magnanimity' of Aristotle's *Nicomachean Ethics*, and then—true to his habit of connecting ancient and modern—likens the Aristotelian magnanimous man to the Spaniard of the two last centuries. The former has, it should be said, been taken both as a caricature or idealization by Aristotle of his contemporary fellow-countrymen, and as a more or less realistic self-portrait.[77] Smith's Spaniard is somewhat different from these models but nonetheless constitutes further proof of the perennial fascination exerted by the Aristotelian character. And, like Aristotle, Smith holds it better as a rule to exceed slightly in pride than in humility.[78]

The classical sources identified by the editors in this third section on 'self-command' in *TMS* VI are Cicero, Plutarch, Quintus Curtius, Plato, Suetonius, and Demosthenes. But, apart from displaying Smith's huge

---

[74] *TMS* VI. iii. 12. The examples come from Cic. *Off.* (cf. editorial note ad loc.) and *Tusc.* i. 98, v. 7 (cf. Eckstein's edn., ii. 580).

[75] Ussher (1966), 72 f.; cf. Raphael and Macfie, 'Introduction', 18.

[76] At *TMS* VI. iii. 30 Smith argues that if Caesar had lost at Pharsalus, the accepted judgement of him would have been different, and his attack against his own country heavily criticized. Apart from good fortune, the chief merits that Smith seems willing to ascribe to him are taste and elegance in his writings, eloquence, military prowess, courage when in difficulty and coolness in danger, loyalty to his friends, and generosity to his enemies. But had he lost, his 'character' would have been set at little better than that of Catiline, whose 'real merit', Smith adds, 'is acknowledged at this day'. See below, Ch. 5.

[77] Aubenque (1963), 37.

[78] *TMS* VI. iii. 52; cf. Arist. *NE* 1125ᵃ17–35.

knowledge of the classics, the section evinces a closer connection with Aristotle than with the Stoics. This is apparent not only in the depiction of characters, but in the use of the point of propriety as a criterion for self-control in all the passions; different in each case, but not to be overstepped, either in excess or in default.

2.8. EPICTETUS AND 'SELF-INTEREST'

Towards the end of the *TMS*, while demonstrating his disagreement with Stoicism, or rather with a part of it, Smith twice lays weight on man's 'private, partial and selfish affections' (VII. ii. 1. 46–7). Stoic apathy would eliminate these, but Smith regards them as indispensable to man's fulfilment of his obligations on earth; indeed, that is why nature gave them to him. Seemingly self-centred feelings of this sort are necessary to give direction to human actions. The unexpected aspect is that a Stoic origin can be found even for Smith's well-known theory that certain self-centred instincts encourage activities which, taken together, act to society's advantage.

That nature has endowed man with an instinct for preserving and looking after himself is a Stoic principle (though not exclusively so), and is frequently repeated by Smith.[79] Likewise of Stoic origin is the statement that society is not harmed in any way by this tendency of each individual to pursue his own interest. It was propounded by Epictetus, an author close to Smith's heart, as the two following passages show:[80]

In general he [sc. Zeus] has so constituted the nature of the rational animal man, that he can attain nothing of his own proper good unless he contributes something to the common interest. Hence it follows that it can no longer be regarded as unsocial for a man to do everything for his own sake   (*Diss.* i. 19. 13–14, Oldfather's translation)

This [sc. taking care of oneself] is not mere self-love; such is the nature of the animal man; everything that he does is for himself.   (ibid. i. 19. 11)

Self-love, then, the universal and only principle of action, fits perfectly well with the common good.[81] Elsewhere[82] I have briefly touched on the similarity between this position and the one apparent in the two famous sentences considered fundamental to the understanding of the theoretical foundation of Smith's economic thinking: 'It is not from the benevolence of the butcher, the brewer, or the baker, that we expect our dinner, but from their regard to their own interest' (*WN* I. ii. 2), and the passage employing the well-known

---

[79] *TMS* VII. ii. 1. 15; VI. ii. 1. 1; II. ii. 2. 1; cf. esp. Cic. *Off.* i. 11; *Fin.* iii. 16, iv. 19, 25, v. 24; Raphael and Macfie, 'Introduction', 8.

[80] The translation is slightly adapted from that of Oldfather.

[81] Le Hir (1954), 88.

[82] Vivenza (1982*b*), i. 165 f. Viner (1960), 48, connected the idea of harmony between the interests of the individual and of society with Aristotle's theory of man as a social animal, but I find the Stoic derivation more probable.

image of the 'invisible hand' that furthers the common interest while the individual, unaware of its action, pursues his own interest (*WN* IV. ii. 9; cf. *TMS* IV. i. 10).

I am not convinced that Smith had Epictetus in mind at the precise time of writing these remarks. But I feel there can be no doubt that they are based on the admission that man possesses a natural, inborn tendency to pursue his own interest, and the belief that this must produce a positive final result for society. The notion is not to be found only in classical philosophy. Its journey can be traced from John Chrysostom to Campanella, Milton, Pierre Nicole, Boisguilbert, and on to Mandeville.[83] I do not, in any case, consider it right to ask whether Smith 'took' it from this or that author, as if he had not made it in reality entirely his own.

So Smith states that the good of society can be served with everyone furthering their own interests. This has nothing to do with pure, unrestrained egoism, of course, but rather the legitimate self-love with which each man is endowed by nature.[84] Here one should perhaps note the much-discussed question of whether or not Adam Smith could have propounded a morality of egoism, or rather one of self-interest, in the *Wealth of Nations* when he had put forward one founded on altruism and benevolence in *TMS*.[85] On this point I agree with those who see no real difference between the two works, bearing in mind that, far from being criticized, behaviour inspired by a reasonable degree of self-love is in fact commended in *TMS*; while egoism in the true sense is not encouraged in *WN*.

Furthermore, even though it is important to remember that economic questions were, in Smith's view, within the ambit of moral philosophy,[86] the fact is that even in his day there was a distinction between ethics in the strict sense and political economy. Therefore there is no requirement for coherence, of the sort exemplified by a theorist who believes that man should be free and unencumbered in the economic sphere to follow his interests, and

[83] Spiegel (1976), 488–91, where the 'invisible hand' is given a theological/providential interpretation. Rosenberg (1979), 24, makes it correspond with the competitive market.

[84] Note the important distinction between self-love or self-interest and selfishness made by Raphael and Macfie, 'Introduction', 22.

[85] Raphael and Macfie, 'Introduction', 20 f; cf. also Garin (1941), 225–6. The main interpretations of the topic are briefly recalled here. Morrow (1966, 161–7) stressed the role of the minor virtues (prudence, frugality, industry, self-reliance) which, ruled by justice, lead to private as well as to public welfare also in *TMS*. Viner's classical thesis of the irreconcilability of *TMS* and *WN* (1966) is on the opposite side to Macfie's essays (1959, 1961) which represent the 'economic' man of *WN* as the projection, in the field of economics, of the 'prudent' man of *TMS*. Anspach's (1972) and Lamb's (1974) ingenious interpretations are centred on the 'sympathy' felt for 'the rich and the great', and, excluding discrepancy between the two works, end by placing sympathy as a foundation of *WN*, too. According to Colletti (1979), 211–12, a difference between the two works is irremediable because it symbolizes the essence of the bourgeois civilization. See also Wilson (1976), and Heilbroner (1982).

[86] Similarly in Scottish universities of the day: cf. the point made by Raphael and Macfie, 'Introduction', 24, and never sufficiently repeated: 'lectures on economic matters were a recognized part of Moral Philosophy as taught in the Scottish Universities at that time'.

likewise in the moral one to follow his instincts, whatever they are. Nor is it to be expected that Smith should have founded economics on altruism and sympathy just as he had founded ethics on them. To return to the famous quote beginning 'It is not from the benevolence of the butcher'—I am not the first to doubt whether the impartial spectator would in fact sympathize with a butcher who gave away his meat,[87] or even sold it at a lower price than he should. My feeling is that the answer must be no. Smith evidently meant that if both parties in a transaction pursue their own interests, the end result will be the satisfaction of both, rather than satisfaction for one only and damage to the other.[88] Pursuit of one's own interests; bartering or exchanging one product for another; the desire to better one's situation; the fundamental instincts that govern economic activity are not considered morally bad by Smith, inasmuch as they do not cause harm. On the contrary, they bring about well-being for all, lead to the division of labour that allows economic progress, improve manners, and accustom people to meet and get to know each other.[89] Naturally there is no sanction in any of this for behaviour that damages the interests of others; each man's actions are limited by the equal rights of others.[90]

In the context of exchange between two parties, each one can discern what is in the other's interest as well as in his own. In a wider context it is difficult to predict the results of one's actions: but the outcome is nonetheless a good one. The quasi-theological invisible-hand argument refers to the relationship between individual and society, and to the general matter of the distribution of goods. As is well known, this states that even though all members of society will pay attention only to their own interests they will in the end unwittingly, and perhaps even unwillingly, further those of society as a whole.

There is accordingly quite a close connection between the Stoic view encapsulated in the dicta of Epictetus quoted above and the celebrated principle of the invisible hand. Even the lack of intention on the part of the individual in bringing about the final result is in origin a Stoic element. But Smith approaches the problem in a different way, starting from the individual and his natural instincts towards self-preservation and the search for happiness. These, he argues, must be followed, for they can bring advantages to all, notwithstanding that each individual is thinking only of himself.

---

[87] Cf. Lamb (1974), 678: 'Although the benevolence of the butcher would be more strongly approved by an impartial spectator than his prudent self-interest, in most ordinary cases we do not disapprove of him for selling rather than giving meat away'.

[88] Wilson (1976), 77. See *LJ* (A) vi. 160 for a very interesting reference to this sort of transaction, invoking prudence: 'and if the bargain be managed with ordinary prudence it must be profitable for both'.

[89] Cf. in particular *LJ*, ed. Cannan, 234, 253 *LJ* (B) 303, 326–7. The originally Stoic notion of universal brotherhood is associated with the principle that commercial activity favours human contacts and, in some way, civilizes them; see Viner (1972), 36 f. The personal qualities necessary to the acquisition of fortune (prudence, frugality, etc.) are no less approved of by the impartial spectator than the end to which they are directed: Skinner (1974*b*), 95 n. 87.

[90] Macfie (1967), 110; Bittermann (1940), 728; Napoleoni (1970), 56.

Stoic theory, on the other hand, starts from the contemplation of the whole, the cosmic viewpoint.[91] Everything in the universal economy, so to speak, has a precise function: human instincts are preordained towards a providential end, which is necessarily good; and therefore what men do in accordance with these instincts will necessarily be good for the universe as a whole.

I earlier noted the oddness of the fact that in turning from Smith's remarks on apathy, directed against all forms of selfish affections, to those passages offering considerable support for the proposition that each individual must pursue his own interests, one immediately finds them to have a precedent in Stoic thought. On the basis of what has been noted since then, it is clear that the relevant Stoic principles (the idea of universal harmony and the reciprocal notion of the accord between the selfish interests of the individual and the common good) make up a theoretical explanation the purpose of which is to demonstrate that providence has ordered things this way for its own inscrutable—but certainly good—ends. In other words Stoicism values the individual only as a part of the whole, while in the ethical sphere it reduces his active role to the entire acceptance of the divine plan, since reason tells him that the latter must be perfect. Smith, on the other hand, starting from an ethical position, and moving on the basis of experience, formulates a model of behaviour for the individual. The fact that the theoretical account he ends up with might coincide with the Stoic one does not suffice to outweigh the distinction that in Smith's theory the individual is fully responsible and acts autonomously. When the Stoics elaborated an ethical theory, they produced a doctrine which tended to counter the passions, viewed as the main obstacle to wisdom. Smith was aware that this did not meet his needs. As a result, by applying a Stoic theoretical principle to an ethical framework that was at least in part unStoic, he was unable to pursue his 'model' to its logical conclusions. Accordingly he could not accept apathy, suicide, the paradoxes,[92] and the lack of 'gradations' so characteristic of Stoic ethics. Smith's own ethical theory, though firmly based upon the aforesaid Stoic theological principle, has certain fundamental elements that are Aristotelian rather than Stoic.

2.9. BENEVOLENCE

While justice is the indispensable basis for all forms of society, Smith considers other virtues—in particular prudence and benevolence[93]—necessary for the quality of social existence. These virtues frequently interact, and on occasions conflict, with each other. Thus benevolence and justice, in

---

[91] Cf. Limentani (1914), 82: 'Stoic teaching relies on a system of metaphysics; that of Smith on empirical psychology'.

[92] *TMS* VII. ii. 1. 39–44. Smith evinces disbelief that Zeno and Cleanthes could have dishonoured their sublime eloquence sufficiently to be the authors of these 'mere impertinent quibbles' (ibid. 41), preferring to ascribe them to Chrysippus, who is portrayed in the tradition as 'a mere dialectical pedant, without taste or elegance of any kind'.

[93] Campbell (1971), 178–85.

particular, have reference to two different types of moral action, and two different theoretical points of view.[94] But benevolence always conflicts with egotistical behaviour, and to that extent accords with justice, whose role is to regulate and moderate those other virtues, such as prudence and frugality, that operate according to the agent's own interests and therefore easily merge with egoism.

So when Smith states that 'the man who acts according to the rules of perfect prudence, of strict justice, and of proper benevolence, may be said to be perfectly virtuous' (*TMS* VI. iii. 1), the three virtues cited each have a different end: the first is directed towards taking care of oneself, the second towards not harming other people, while the third consists of wishing others well, and acting accordingly—which makes it similar to the related virtue of beneficence. Benevolence thus surpasses all forms of self-centred motive, and indeed for this reason is considered the only motive behind divine actions, unlike those of mankind, which are driven by the manifold impulses imposed on nature by man's imperfection and the resulting necessity of external factors for survival.[95] In the chapter 'Of Universal Benevolence' (VI. ii. 3) the concept of a benevolent providence, directing natural and human affairs so as to bring about the maximum amount of happiness for all, has as its background the observation that man must accept his share of difficulties, inasmuch as they are part of an already established plan that will lead to the common good. There is a distinctly Stoic flavour to all this, of course[96]—notwithstanding the concluding statement that man is made for action, not for contemplation.[97]

So Smith's treatment of benevolence alludes to a providential plan responsible for the functioning of human society,[98] a topic which might not in this case be of economic concern, but which nonetheless has relevance to economics on account of the benevolent design that is inherent in the idea of the invisible hand. Apart from this, however, benevolence is not a particularly significant theme in Smith's economic thought, and its importance is largely restricted to the moral sphere. Human economic activity is determined in the first instance by each individual's instincts for protecting his own interests.[99] The virtue of benevolence does not play a major part among

[94] Morrow (1969), 54: 'an abstract individualism, proper enough in the discussion of legal relations, is inadequate to express the higher realities of the individual moral experience'; cf. also Garin (1941), 222.

[95] *TMS* VII. ii. 3. 18. God's self-sufficiency is an Aristotelian motif.

[96] Raphael and Macfie, 'Introduction', 6: 'He [Smith] departs from Stoicism in his views on beneficence, but even there, when he comes to discuss universal benevolence in VI. ii. 3, he introduces Stoic ideas and Stoic language to a remarkable degree.'

[97] A principle to which Stoicism opposes that of contemplation. Smith does not make this statement here, but later on, at *TMS* VII. ii. 1. 21 and 46.

[98] For the omnipresence of this idea in all branches of eighteenth-century social and political thought, in the form of an abstract 'natural order' existing by divine providence or by virtue of its own intrinsic rationality, cf. Morrow (1969), 16.

[99] Lamb (1974), 682: 'In *Moral Sentiments* as in *Wealth of Nations* Smith makes exactly the same assertion, that he expects men to act first in accordance with their self-interest before

these,[100] unless one considers agreements that meet the interests of all to be its works.[101]

Evidence of a link with the related classical concept of *beneficentia* is provided in *TMS* vi. ii. chs. 1–2, where Cicero's treatment of that virtue is recalled quite precisely. Smith makes no express mention of the Latin author, but makes use of his subdivision of beneficence into that directed towards individuals, and towards society as a whole,[102] as well as other lines of argument too closely similar not to derive from the same source. Thus the love of one's own country is characterized by a double aim: to help further the interests of the whole community, and those of the citizens considered individually. If possible, one tries to achieve both together. The distinction is identical to the one made by Cicero,[103] who went on to add that government is established to safeguard private property, and therefore must not draw on private individuals' possessions for its own advantage, then to distribute what it has expropriated among others. This is a point on which Smith was later to express his full agreement, though not in the present context.[104]

Smith follows up his treatment of the subject with his well-known comment that one should not use violence to change the established order, but rather seek peaceful means, for all that this is a difficult thing to do in troubled times when people are invariably tempted by the 'man of system', imposing from above his political framework: perhaps a good one, but necessarily a constrictive one. Here Smith is edging towards a form of general political theory, one may almost say a philosophical position. Cicero, more modestly, restricts himself to the topic of agrarian laws and war levies, but in some ways his approach is similar: if, regrettably, a tax should become necessary, he states:

danda erit opera ut omnes intellegant, si salvi esse velint, necessitati esse parendum
every effort must be made to let all the people realize that they must bow to the inevitable, if they wish to be saved   (W. Miller's translation)[105]

In the matter of beneficence towards single individuals, however, a partial difference between the two authors becomes apparent. Both ask the obvious

thoughts of benevolence'; though cf. ibid.: 'In neither book does self-interest eliminate sympathy'.

[100] Viner (1966), 130.
[101] Anspach (1972), 189–90f.
[102] In point of fact Smith uses the term 'beneficence' only in the second of these cases, the two chapters being entitled respectively 'Of the Order in which Individuals are Recommended by Nature to our Care and Attention' and 'Of the Order in which Societies are by Nature Recommended to our Beneficence'; cf. Cic. *Off.* ii. 69–71 and 72–4.
[103] *TMS* vi. ii. 2. 11–12; Cic. *Off.* ii. 72.
[104] Cic. *Off.* ii. 73; cf. *LJ* (A) vi. 19 and (B) 210. See below, Ch. 3 nn. 65 and 99 and the related passage in the text.
[105] *Off.* ii. 74: cf. Smith, *TMS* vi. ii. 2. 16: 'When he cannot conquer the rooted prejudices of the people *by reason and persuasion* he will not attempt to subdue them by force' (my italics). I have referred to this problem elsewhere: Vivenza (1980), 32–3.

question as to whether one should benefit a rich person or a poor one. Cicero concedes that when it comes to it the gratitude of a rich and powerful man is more useful than that of a poor man, no matter how honourable. But he maintains the praiseworthy view that the correct thing is to show favour to respectable people, without regard to their wealth. Unfortunately, he concludes, decadence and fashion have led to the admiration of wealth. This theme was taken up by other ancient authors,[106] hence Smith had to fight against a principle which was well established and, in a certain way, more agreeable than his own. Smith's declaration that man has a natural penchant towards the rich and powerful, and that this is a good thing, is well known. Accordingly, after he has dutifully stated that our benevolence is owed to those we are connected with, to those who are endowed with fine qualities, or those who have on earlier occasions shown benevolence to us, Smith finally turns his attention to those who have been smiled on by fortune or alternatively dogged by misfortune. The powerful rich and the wretched poor are objects of the most important human sentiments. Smith claims that the respect and admiration naturally felt towards the former are the basis of society's class divisions or distinctions of rank, and therefore of social peace and order; while the sense of pity felt for the latter is the foundation of every relief and comfort to human misery. Of these two tasks, maintaining order and relieving misery, the former is by far the more important. So, despite the concerted appeals of moralists to charity and compassion, and their warnings against the glamour of riches, the glamour is irresistible. Nature knew what she was about when she established that peace and order should be founded on clearly visible differences of birth and fortune, rather than the vague and debatable ones of wisdom and virtue. Then, to reinforce his argument, Smith adds a psychological point of some subtlety: if wealth and power are conjoined with wisdom and virtue, the 'sympathy' for people of high rank rises still further, and if they should by chance suffer adverse luck, people will share more deeply in their misfortune than in that of a common man, be he ever so virtuous. The argument concludes with the observation that the misadventures of kings and princes are precisely the stuff of tragedies and romances—another classical echo.[107]

Throughout the section on benevolence, then, there are clear signs of its close relationship with Cicero; but this relationship was for Smith a point of departure, not a blueprint to follow closely. The 'conservative' thinking that underlies many of his statements on the matter, as detailed here, has already

---

[106] Cic. *Off.* ii. 71. The theme reappears in Livy and Sallust especially.

[107] *TMS* vi. ii. 1. 20–1. Here too the classical source goes unnamed, but, as noted above, in the Introduction, the comment can be traced back to Epictetus. 'Great men' are also specified as tragic protagonists in Aristotle's *Poetics*. A distinguished writer on the classical tradition, however, has seen the prevalence of kings, princes, and emperors among the principal characters of baroque tragedy more as a reflection of the social hierarchy of the day than as a mark of obedience to a classical precept: Highet (1949), 298. See also Heilbroner (1982), 437–8: Smith depicts the descent from riches to poverty, not chronic poverty itself, as arousing sympathy.

been pointed out, and perhaps bears certain similarities to Cicero's. Smith seems to be detaching himself from it by the frank admission that public order is served by the human tendency to admire the powerful; but Cicero was not, in the end, far from concluding that too much benevolence towards the poor will ultimately throw the social order into chaos.

This sort of virtue—as is the case with justice[108]—is related to economic matters only in certain respects: in the main, its character is political.

2.10. THE PROBLEM OF GOOD AND EVIL

According to the most recent studies,[109] Stoicism's influence on Adam Smith's thought was not limited to the field of moral philosophy: 'a Stoic idea of nature and the natural forms a major part of the philosophical foundations of *TMS* and *WN* alike'.[110] The context here is the view of reality as a harmoniously functioning 'system', presided over by an 'all-wise architect and conductor',[111] and forming part of a pre-set plan in which human virtues and vices alike play a necessary role, leading ultimately to the establishment of good (i.e., in economics, prosperity) for all. The importance of this concept has been too often emphasized for it to need repeating here. Apart from Stoicism, its relationship with the well-known 'fable' of Bernard Mandeville has been recognized. Here we shall restrict ourselves to emphasizing its connections with classical thought.

Smith seems to be quite aware of the relationship between his own ideas and those of Stoicism, even when he distances himself from the latter. Thus, at *TMS* I. ii. 3. 4 he writes:

The ancient Stoics were of opinion, that as the world was governed by the all-ruling providence of a wise, powerful and good God, every single event ought to be regarded, as making a necessary part of the plan of the universe, and as tending to promote the general order and happiness of the whole: that the vices and follies of mankind, therefore, made as necessary a part of this plan as their wisdom or their virtue; and by that eternal art which educes good from ill, were made to tend equally to the prosperity of the great system of nature.

Smith rejected the conclusion of this argument: no philosophical theory of this sort would ever be able to relieve man of his 'natural abhorrence' for vice, arising from the immediate deleterious effects of vicious behaviour, which are visible at once and in that way unlike its remoter consequences, too hard to imagine as they are and therefore not present in the mind. Here Smith seems

---

[108]   On the relationship between these two virtues cf. Morrow (1969), 45 f.

[109]   Most recent, that is, at the time of first publication of this book, in Italian, in 1984.

[110]   Raphael and Macfie, 'Introduction', 7. Lindgren does not consider Smith's moral philosophy to be connected to Stoicism but rather, ultimately, to sophistics: Lindgren (1973), 35 n. 11.

[111]   A figure which—like many other writers from Descartes onwards—he took from the Stoics: Pohlenz (1970), i. 470–1.

to be not so much rejecting the notion that this principle of Stoicism can be maintained, but rather averring that human nature finds it impossible to accept because of the strain it imposes on the imagination.[112] Macfie regarded the passage quoted above as one evincing 'obvious approval' for the Stoic theory in question: presumably the theory as a whole, that is, rather than just its conclusion; but against this one needs to note Bittermann's observation that though the similarity between the Stoic theology and that of Smith is undeniable, one cannot ignore the important difference that the latter does *not* consider evil to be a necessary part of the divine plan.[113]

A fuller picture of Smith's thinking on the subject can be gained from another passage in the same work (*TMS* VI. ii. 3. 3):

If he [the wise and virtuous man] is deeply impressed with the habitual and thorough conviction that this benevolent and all-wise Being can admit into the system of his government, no partial evil which is not necessary for the universal good, he must consider all the misfortunes which may befal himself, his friends, his society, or his country, as necessary for the prosperity of the universe.

The context of this passage is the wise man's complete adherence to the will of the supreme being, who is capable of sacrificing individuals for the good of the whole. Despite the undoubted Stoic flavour of the phraseology, further intensified by the statement that if the wise man were aware of the divine plan he would himself wish things to be arranged according to its provisions,[114] Smith is here in fact speaking of 'universal Benevolence', and expressing an idea of his own, as demonstrated, among other things, by the classification of relationships into degrees (friends, society, country)—not of Stoic origin.

The terminology used in the two passages shows a discernible and quite significant softening: in the first, Smith speaks of the 'vices and follies of mankind'; in the second, of 'partial evil' and 'misfortunes'. The former come under the heading 'unsocial passions', discussion of which opens with the observation that in certain conditions one has a reaction of sympathy for the resentment felt by the injured party, which is to say that complete resignation is not approved of.[115] In the latter case, however, one is dealing with the individual's understandable reluctance to confront misadventure, a reluctance which can arouse a sense of solidarity. Evil wilfully perpetrated, however,

---

[112] It is not only in the sciences, but also in morals, that imagination is a key element in Smith's thought. The remote 'distance' of some of the results of human activity is a problem for the imagination, just as it is in the laws of physics. On occasions Smith believes it possible for humans to determine their behaviour on the basis of calculations extended over long periods, as in the case of prudential self-control; but here, where it is a matter of approving an immediate evil on the grounds of a too-distant good, the imagination is not capable of the process.

[113] Macfie (1967c), 78 n. 50; Bittermann (1940), 724.

[114] A principle given further emphasis at *TMS* VII. ii. 1. 20. Effectively present in Stoic ethics (cf. Epict. *Diss*. ii. 6. 10; 10. 5), it had by Smith's time been given greater weight in one strand of 18th-century thought on the origin of evil: see Lovejoy (1970), ch. 7: 'The Principle of Plenitude and Eighteenth-Century Optimism'.

[115] *TMS* I. ii. 3. 1–3.

excites resentment, even in the party not directly involved. There are moreover two aspects to consider when judging a wicked act, inasmuch as there is a
party performing it and another party suffering it. Smith's whole concept of
social relations is directed towards a free development of human activity,
provided that it is not harmful to others: in those instances where it is, there
must be intervention, of a repressive sort, enacted by justice. He is therefore
reluctant to accept the idea of evil as a universal necessity, inevitable in both its
aspects, and against which all human efforts are futile.[116] Unlike the Stoics,
Smith is disposed to accept as part of the providential plan only that form of
evil that can be seen as misadventure, or a difficulty to overcome. The Stoics
had 'derived from Heraclitus' theory of contrasts the logical necessity of evil as
a companion for good; a logical necessity from which followed, of course, a
metaphysical necessity'.[117] It was from this line of thought that Christianity,
despite its different formulation of the designs of providence, derived both its
logico-metaphysical understanding of evil as the necessary counterpart of
good, and its principle of not treating physical suffering as an evil.

   This is not, of course, the place to attempt an answer to the intractable
question of the role of providence in human destiny; but in seeking to grasp
Adam Smith's view of the matter, one can recall his invocation, quoted at the
outset, of 'that eternal art which educes good from ill', as well as his immediately subsequent statement that, in spite of this, man has a natural aversion
to evil; a way, perhaps, of implying that he is not content to leave everything
up to providence. Smith was not ready to adopt lock, stock, and barrel Stoic
theories of the unity of physical and logical necessity, according to which evil
itself was part of a universe that was rationally disposed, and thus without
contrasts, wrongs, or evils in need of setting right. The Stoic position was
that the reality of the cosmos was in itself already endowed with rationality,
wisdom, and happiness.[118] That of Smith was, implicitly at least, dualistic.
He certainly only accepted Stoic theories on this question up to a point. And
in the course of dealing with a subject that spotlights a huge contradiction in
Stoic moral theory, from the Christian point of view at any rate, he makes a
decisive move away from the principles of the Stoa.[119]

   According to the Stoic rule whereby one should act in accordance with
nature, the individual, despite being imbued with an instinct for

---

[116] In this way Smith is also at odds with 17th-century optimism, the chief defect of which,
as noted by Voltaire, was that it amounted to a doctrine of the conservation of evil. Thus
Lovejoy (1970), 245: 'If all partial evils are required by the universal good, and if the universe is
and always has been perfectly good, we cannot expect that any of the partial evils will
disappear.'

[117] Pohlenz (1970), i. 100.   [118] Aubenque (1963), 87–8.

[119] *TMS* VII. ii. 1. 25–34. The section was completed in the 6th edition, which Smith revised
shortly before his death, probably influenced by the posthumous publication of an essay by
Hume in which approval was given, in certain cases, to suicide: Raphael and Macfie, 'Introduction', p. 6. The addition did not represent a substantial change in Smith's view of Stoic
philosophy: Mizuta (1975), 123 n. 27.

self-preservation, feels himself a part of the universal whole, and must thus be ready at any moment to sacrifice himself for the salvation and prosperity of the many; for, it is no less a commandment of nature that each person must place the universal good above that of his own.[120] He must therefore 'choose'[121] whatever is laid down for him, abiding as closely as possible to divine will. This requires of him total and enthusiastic agreement and co-operation, wearisome in the achieving, and excellently portrayed by Smith in *TMS* VII. ii. 1. 18–22, with frequent reference (both expressed and otherwise) to Epictetus. Communicating these basic motifs of Stoic ethics to his students was clearly something Smith was able to do with warmth and conviction, as can also be seen in the lively and detailed account he gives at *TMS* VII. ii. 1. 15–47.[122] In this latter passage one can even perhaps glimpse an awareness on his part that there was an educational value to a doctrine that impelled one to fulfil all one's duties, and not give up when one's efforts met with no success, or indeed outright failure.

Notwithstanding Smith's deep appreciation of this doctrine, there remained a practically ineradicable point of difference. Given the limits on man's range of choice,[123] the results of his actions were not something over which he had any power. Stoic philosophers grasped that in order to avoid advocating a form of untrusting inertia the consequences of man's activity must not be set up as the element of greatest importance, and that emphasis must instead be placed on the moral perfection of the activity itself. The aim of human life, according to this schema, is to carry out one's duties as well as possible, whatever they are.

In this connection Smith restates, with evident approval, another well-known Stoic principle: life is like a game, in which the important thing is playing well, not winning.[124] Underlying this analogy is a simple consideration. In a game, as in life, there can be interventions on the part of chance (perhaps actually unrecognized divine will, or divine will only recognized as

---

[120] *TMS* VII. ii. 1. 18. In operation here is a fundamental Stoic principle according to which the universal laws of nature can be taken as a whole rather than one by one. Cf. Pohlenz (1970), i. 393–4.

[121] The Stoics drew a careful distinction, which need not be rehearsed here, between what is held out by nature as 'eligible' and what is not: cf. *TMS* VII. ii. 1. 16–17, with a note (removed in the 6th edition) apologizing for the awkwardness of the relevant terminology in English.

[122] The section on Stoicism is known to have been reworked for the 6th edition, passages being cut, added, or reordered. I do not believe that this undermines my observation about the doctrine's pedagogical value, for all that the 6th edition does not faithfully reflect the order in which the lectures were given. As the editors point out, they probably began with the excursus on preceding theories found at the start of part VII: cf editorial note on *TMS* VII. i. 2 (p. 265).

[123] Man's only option is to refuse to play the part destined for him; he cannot change it. At the most, he can 'act it out' unwillingly. In reality, for the Stoics, 'wisdom is to know the world's order and consent to it': Mancini (1940), 12.

[124] For the importance of this concept in Smith's thought in general see Macfie (1967), 118. See also the remarks of Giuliani (1954), 534–6, discerning here an interest in the method of play, and a relationship with the adversarial nature, of legal institutions.

such after the event).[125] Therefore even a good player can be defeated; but he cannot be deprived of the merit of having played well. Difficulties and adverse destiny are personified in the character of a strong athlete, to fight against whom is a glorious thing.[126] In short, if a man makes it the purpose of his life to behave in the right way, he can be its master. As Smith correctly points out, this doctrine implies that for the Stoics life itself was a thing of no importance,[127] not worth getting too anxious about. Partly for this reason, when the need arose, the Stoics were relatively happy to relieve themselves of it. But here Smith was unable to agree.

The Stoics, as is well known, did not consider suicide in certain cases a contemptible act, or even an irrational one. For them life, like everything else, could be 'the proper object either of our choice or of our rejection' (*TMS* VII. ii. 1. 25), independently of the personal situation of the individual deciding whether to preserve it or not; a conscious evaluation of his duty, indeed, might impose the choice on him.[128] In his attempt at understanding an act that is without exception regarded as impermissible for Christians, who are therefore bound to pass an intrinsically negative judgement on it, Smith notes that it was allowed by all the ancient schools of philosophy, including 'the peaceable and indolent Epicureans'. He goes on to examine this curious tendency in the light of the historical circumstances in which each of the 'sects'—a strongly classical word he makes frequent use of— arose.

At *TMS* VII. ii. 1. 30–3 Smith groups together an interesting selection of ancient cases of suicide, which starts with the observation that, all in all, the Greeks killed themselves quite rarely. Drawing a distinction between philosophers and men of action,[129] he notes that, while there are hardly any cases at all of 'patriots and heroes' committing suicide, the practice was, alas, quite widespread amongst philosophers. He even throws some doubt on the trustworthiness of the ancient biographies of the philosophers, holding them to have been drawn up at a later date with liberal use of fantasy, as a result of the fact that their subjects made no real mark during their lives; a situation quite unlike that of the men of action, whose exploits were renowned and related in their own day. Indeed the degree of attention Smith paid the

---

[125] Smith speaks of 'chance, or of what is vulgarly understood to be chance': *TMS* VII. ii. 1. 24. This is another point on which, perhaps unconsciously, he was at odds with the Stoics, for whom chance did not of course exist: Pohlenz (1970), i. 102.

[126] *TMS* VII. ii. 1. 23. The image is probably derived from Epict. *Diss.* iii. 22, 51–2; 25, 2–4; iv. 4, 30–1, and from Seneca, *Ep.* 78, 16; 80, 3. At *TMS* VI. ii. 3. 4 Smith makes use of a similar image, that of the good soldier, certainly taken from Cic. *Tusc.* i. 101. Epictetus was also given to comparing life with a military campaign—*Diss.* i. 9, 16; iii. 13, 14; 24, 31; 99–102; 26, 29—as indeed was Seneca; *Ep.* 96, 5. The image ultimately derives from Plato; cf. *Apol.* 28d.

[127] 'Human life . . . ought, according to the Stoics, to be regarded but as a mere two-penny stake': *TMS* VII. ii. 1. 24.

[128] *TMS* VII. ii. 1. 25–7, with sustained reference to Epictetus and to Cic. *Fin.* iii. 60, which Smith repeats and amplifies.

[129] *TMS* VII. ii. 1. 31, repeating a distinction already drawn at 1. 28.

question of ancient suicide is demonstrated by the documentation adduced throughout the digression.[130] There is even an attempt at source criticism: not sharing the attitude of ancient writers to the subject,[131] he calls the authenticity of Zeno's suicide into doubt,[132] as if it were an act of homage by the biographers to the coherence of the philosopher who had declared suicide to be a moral duty.

Turning from the Greeks to the Romans, Smith was faced with a formidable figure whose exemplary status would have cowed many into submission: but not even the shadow cast by Cato Uticensis could dim Smith's convictions, for all the difficulty of questioning a view enshrined for centuries. Smith ascribed Cato's prominence to the literature on the theme, noting that in managing to present him as the martyr of the republican cause, Cicero's eloquent oratory outdid the criticism of Caesar. With a certain malice he adds in support of this a comment of Seneca demonstrating that in that writer's day Cato already enjoyed a surprising degree of renown as a man of virtue.[133] He displays no sign of awareness that Cato killed himself in a true Stoic attitude 'because to continue to live in those circumstances would have been contrary to his nature'.[134]

With another brief mention of the unconscionable frequency of suicide under the empire—drawing this time on Pliny the Younger—Smith concludes with the expected statement that suicide is against nature. His words betray, however, a note of humane pity, rather than censure, towards these overweak victims of an irresistible desire for self-destruction. He is not appalled by the act; but he takes objection rather to the approval of it, the attempt to justify it in moral terms—something he regards as 'altogether a refinement of philosophy' (*TMS* VII. ii 1. 34), foreign both to the savage (in his eighteenth-century guise as man in his natural state) and, usually, also to those civilized men who qualify as men of action. Smith treats as similar the savage's fighting behaviour and that of the earliest Greek and Roman heroes,

---

[130] The examples given of Greek 'heroes' who gave themselves up to their enemies rather than kill themselves are for the most part taken from Plutarch: cf. Eckstein's commentary on the German edition of *TMS* (1926), ii. 587–8. Smith goes on to cite, somewhat imperfectly, the three versions of Zeno's death and their treatment in authors such as Diogenes Laertius, Lucan, and Lactantius.

[131] 'The notion that man is master of his own life and can therefore, when certain factors impel him, put an end to it, was a fact beyond debate for Seneca and the Stoics, as for Greeks in general': Pohlenz (1970), i. 323.

[132] *TMS* VII. ii. 1. 31. Smith relies on Persaeus, the only source contemporary with Zeno, but is wrong in stating that he speaks of 'natural death'; he simply does not speak of suicide (cf. the editorial note ad loc.). In reality Smith's scepticism over the suicide of Zeno and others is almost certainly due to his difficulty in reconciling his deep respect for these ancient thinkers with an act he considered unworthy of them.

[133] *TMS* VII. ii. 1. 32. Cato was partial to drink, Seneca admits: but whoever accuses him of being a drunkard will more easily show drunkenness to be a virtue than Cato to have been guilty of any vice (*Tranq. An.* 17. 9). Note, in passing, that Smith makes no mention of Seneca's own suicide; perhaps, as it was ordered by the emperor, he regarded it as equivalent to a death sentence.

[134] Pohlenz (1970), i. 266.

inclined as they were to let themselves be captured rather than kill themselves; this attitude accords with 'nature', who 'in her sound and healthful state' never drives us to suicide. The philosopher too can support the comparison, but only as long as he accepts life: 'In so far as they are *struggling to live* through tyranny, factions and war, both the Stoic and the savage provide a good example of self-control for men in civil society'.[135] The conclusion, it seems, is that both the Stoic and the savage, each in his own way a master of himself, regulate their behaviour according to an ethical standard clearly connected with the stage reached by culture and civilization in their respective societies, and—one might add—with the station within those societies that they occupy (if one bears in mind that some of the 'heroes', i.e. statesmen or soldiers, whom Smith admires were not so much earlier than the suicide of Zeno to allow one to argue that they represent some primitive stage of the Greek world which the latter postdated).[136]

Smith thus adopts those parts of Stoicism that sit happily with a bold, fighting spirit (emphasized by historians of philosophy as early as the seventeenth century),[137] but discards those that seem to him leading to self-denial—an example of this is suicide, a self-destructive instinct, approved only by means of a 'refinement of philosophy'—without considering that for the Stoic, suicide itself is as much a way of following nature as an aggressive, unyielding attitude is for the savage. This shows, it can be added, just how far Smith truly was from the Stoic attitude, at least on this issue.

2.11. AGAINST APATHY

In the context of a comparison between the moral philosophies of the Peripatetics (that is, the followers of Aristotle) and the Stoics, interesting among other things for the way he formulates ancient philosophy according to his own categories (e.g. 'sympathy', the 'impartial spectator'), Smith states:

The Peripatetics seem to have thought that no passion exceeded the bounds of propriety as long as the spectator, by the utmost effort of humanity, could sympathize with it. The Stoics, on the contrary, appear to have regarded every passion as improper, which made any demand upon the sympathy of the spectator, or required him to alter in any respect the natural and ordinary state of his mind, in order to keep time with the vehemence of its . . . emotions. A man of virtue, they seem to have thought, *ought not to depend* upon the generosity of those he lives with for pardon or approbation. (*TMS*, edns. 1–5, VII. ii. 1. 17, p. 273; my italics)

The Stoics had taken from the Socratic tradition the idea of the self-sufficiency of the wise man,[138] dependent not on outside circumstances but

---

[135] Mizuta (1975), 125; my italics.
[136] Phocion and Eumenes died in Zeno's lifetime; Philopoemen almost a century later.
[137] By Heinsius in particular: cf. Tolomio (1981), i. 130.
[138] Differing from self-sufficiency in Aristotle, whose wise man must be brought to terms with the circumstances: Aubenque (1963), 78–81.

only on his own virtue. This independence is arrived at by avoiding the desire of things that are not within our reach, freeing oneself of fear that is no more than empty opinion, and wishing only for what supreme reason or *logos* wishes for. Smith appreciates this point of view, but he also sees that this independence led in the end to detaching the Stoic from society. Platonists and Aristotelians, by his account, admitted the passions up to a certain point, as reason alone does not suffice to govern man's behaviour. (Smith does not hesitate to attribute to them a method that is typically his, namely that of admitting the passions to the extent to which the impartial spectator would sympathize with them.) For the Stoic, however, any and every option was of necessity indifferent in itself, and his decision as to choice or rejection depended solely on which of the two was prescribed by 'the rule which the gods had given him for the direction of his conduct' (ibid. 274): that is, by reason.

So for Smith the distinction between Stoicism and the teachings of the Peripatetics was the different levels of self-control they required: complete in the former case, applied so as to keep the passions below a certain level in the other. For both schools, virtue consisted in living in accordance with nature—but this was understood differently, and precisely in relation to the amount of rein given to the emotions: 'The peripatetics . . . allowed of some degree of perturbation as suitable to the weakness of human nature, and as useful to so imperfect a creature as man' (ibid. 273).

Smith's commentary on ancient philosophers allows us to understand his own position better, and makes it clear that his understanding of self-control, the Stoic virtue he so admired, possesses certain Aristotelian aspects. This probably derives from the fact that self-discipline and mastery over the passions were tenets of Stoicism, and therefore when he propounded keeping the emotions under control Smith naturally recalled the Stoics; while the measure of this control, the precise degree to which the emotions had to be contained, was a question dealt with by Aristotelianism, one which fulfilled, so to speak, Smith's conception.

Confirmation that Smith did not fully accept Stoic moral theory comes from his trenchant critique of apathy[139]—that absolute insensitivity to the most basic of human emotions (compassion, anger, pain), as proposed by early Stoics, and criticized even in the ancient world.[140] Smith was unable to accept this; if for no other reason, then on account of that fundamental concept in his thinking, sympathy, which might have nothing in common with the classical concept but nonetheless refers to one person's reaction to another's emotions, and must therefore treat all emotions as legitimate. But

---

[139] *TMS* VII. ii. 1. 46; cf. also III. 3. 14.
[140] The claim that sentiments such as compassion and sensitivity over the death of a loved one could be eradicated aroused opposition from Peripatetics and Academics, who propounded a moderate line accepted even by the sceptics. The Stoics themselves were later to water down their views: Pohlenz (1970), i. 173–4.

his criticism of Stoic apathy (*TMS* VII. ii. 1. 46) is particularly indicative, and merits quotation at length:

By the perfect apathy which it [Stoicism] prescribes to us, by endeavouring not merely to moderate, but to eradicate all our private, partial and selfish affections, by suffering us to feel for whatever can befall ourselves, our friends, our country, not even the sympathetic and reduced passions of the impartial spectator, it endeavours to render us altogether indifferent and unconcerned in the success or miscarriage of every thing which Nature has prescribed to us as the proper business and occupation of our lives.

Smith, it is clear from this passage, considered that according to Stoicism the result was, and had to be, of no importance. The view of life as a game was something, as we have seen, that he accepted only as a form of boldness, not as true indifference to the outcome of any act. The risk of a contemplative scheme of life is ever present in that part of Stoic teaching that culminates in apathy, indifference, and cosmopolitanism, leading inevitably as it does to passivity and inertia. For all that in its initial formulation this theory scarcely prevented an active life or consigned the Stoic to a strictly fatalist outlook, it nonetheless inherently possessed the detachment from the things of this world that recommended itself, albeit in modified form, to the Christians, by whom it was at length to be equated with asceticism.[141] This inclination towards 'divorce from the world' appeared in different forms and different degrees, ranging from that exemplified by Posidonius, who combined the pursuit of theory with an active attitude, to that of the Neoplatonist Plotinus, whose only inclinations were to a life of contemplation.[142] The only point to make here is that Smith was well aware of the inevitable result of apathy, namely an indifference to worldly activities; this much is clear from a warning which he cites against the contemplative life,[143] occasioned by the consideration that Marcus Aurelius is perhaps better remembered for his *Meditations* than for what was achieved during his reign, and that Avidius Cassius was able to reproach him for ignoring the empire in favour of philosophy. That posterity should hold the Emperor's philosophical activity in higher esteem than his political life is regarded by Smith as an injustice, a case of the contemplative life being privileged over the active one: here he is clearly making a philosophical point. But he also finds unjust Avidius'

---

[141] Grilli (1953), 89. Although Stoicism encouraged involvement in public life, the abstract nature of its ideals and the political circumstances of the time conspired to bring about a contradiction between theory and practice. In fact Stoic thinkers refrained from any activity of the sort, apart from the great Roman exceptions, Seneca and Marcus Aurelius: ibid. 90–3.

[142] Pohlenz (1970), i. 396. Posidonius was a close acquaintance of Cicero, and in that way had a certain influence over western philosophy. Plotinus, though a Neoplatonist, had strong links with Stoicism, from which in particular he drew his concept of the 'wise man', the model of behaviour.

[143] *TMS* VI. ii. 3. 5–6, in a chapter entitled 'Of Universal Benevolence' and dedicated to celebrating the idea of providence, immediately after a description of the temptation for the thoughtful man to pass through life in contemplation of its harmonious perfection.

charge as directed against Marcus Aurelius: this is rather a historical point, reflecting his view that to recall his writings rather than his actions is to do the Emperor wrong.

I have no intention here of reopening the well-known question, Aristotelian in origin, of the superiority of the contemplative life over the active one—an idea which has been discussed for its elements of possible equivocation.[144] There is no doubt that Smith comes across as opposed to contemplation, like a great number of British thinkers from Bacon onwards; though admitting that it can have a sublime aspect, he sets against it even 'the smallest' practical duty.

Stoic ethical theory, then, judged actions by disregarding their results and looking solely at the intentions behind them. Smith for his part considers it an 'Irregularity of Sentiments' that it is impossible to have regard only to intentions, since the results of any action—whether good or bad in itself—will always have some effect on the way it is judged. He recognizes that in the abstract case it would be juster to restrict oneself to the intention. But in reality, and even if one places appropriate emphasis on whatever the action was motivated by, what it led to—whether the desired end was achieved or not—is bound to have a notable effect on one's judgement. For instance, the gratitude or resentment aroused by a specific action will vary in intensity according to whether benefit or harm have been effectively brought about or left in the realm of intentions.[145] The agent too can judge his own actions differently according to their results. Unintentional fault, inducing an innocent party to feel responsible for the grave consequences of his actions, instils what has been called a 'fallacious sense of guilt', the substance of several ancient and modern tragedies: Oedipus and Jocasta are instances cited by Smith. His view of this point matches that expressed by Aristotle in the *Poetics*,[146] but actually derives from his own close interest in the relationship between results and intentions and, more especially, his refusal to give weight only to the latter when forming moral judgements. When it comes to judging specific actions, Smith—an anti-utilitarian in respect of the motives of human activity, even in so specialized an area as justice—considers consequences of some importance at least.

---

[144] Schalk (1971), 232–7. For a clarification of the Aristotelian concept and its modern interpretation, particularly that of Bacon and Bodin, cf. Mondolfo (1982), 121. Smith may have drawn elements of the concept from Bacon and Bodin that he did not get from Aristotle: Bodin's idea of the philosopher 'doing nothing' but nonetheless making observations on the practical life; and Bacon's view that the contemplative life cannot be a foundation of moral philosophy. See Cassirer (1953), 45–6 f., and Garin (1941), 21.

[145] *TMS* II. iii. intro. 1–6; cf. ibid. iii. 1.7 and the two chapters following, 'Of the Extent of this Influence of Fortune' and 'Of the Final Cause of this Irregularity of Sentiments'. See above, n. 57 and the related passage in the text.

[146] *TMS* II. iii. 3. 5; cf. Eckstein (1926), pt. i. 294 n. 49, and id. (1927), 387, where certain juridical principles of Smith are derived from his moral theory: see below, Ch. 3 n. 71. Aristotle's view is that tragic heroes are motivated not by cruelty or wickedness but by 'guilt' (or 'error') which cannot be ascribed directly to them: *Poet.* 1453^{a}9, 16; 1453^{b}29–30.

The aspects of Stoicism so far examined, then, appealed to Smith, but only up to a certain point: only until they did not result in contemplation, indifference, or self-negation. One strand of Stoic philosophy was brilliantly adept at avoiding these perils,[147] and there was no shortage of Stoic thinkers able to reconcile apathy and public life, contemplation and action. Smith was quite capable of extracting from his close understanding of Stoic thought those elements that were of most use to his own ethical theory. Therefore it would not be right to say that he did not appreciate the value of a positive attitude in the face of difficulty or hardship, seeking to overcome but paying closer attention to the rectitude of one's actions than to the end result. He was, however, conscious that if one ignores the latter totally, one arrives willy-nilly at a species of indifference that cannot fail to have an effect on the quality of one's actions.

2.12. ADAM SMITH'S HISTORY OF CLASSICAL ETHICS

Smith was not only interested in the history of ancient astronomy, physics, and logic and metaphysics; he dedicated a complete section of the *TMS* (part VII) to an exposition of the various systems of moral philosophy.[148] Within this section the first subsection is entitled 'Of those Systems which make Virtue consist in Propriety' and deals with the theories of Plato, Aristotle, and the Stoics. The second, 'Of those Systems which make Virtue consist in Prudence', deals with the Epicureans. The third, 'Of those Systems which make Virtue consist in Benevolence', opens with a merely passing reference to the eclectics and Neoplatonists.[149] Various aspects of the way these schools of thought relate to Smith's own philosophy have already been touched on: here we will restrict ourselves to elements that have been overlooked.

The Platonic concept of the tripartite soul, divided into the elements of reason, 'spirit', and appetite, as described in book IV of the *Republic*, is treated with a brief commentary on each of the elements. In dealing with the spirited (or 'irascible') emotions—resentment among them—it is interesting to note that Smith discerns their origin in the necessity 'to defend us against injuries'; a point on which the two authors coincide.[150]

---

[147] Particularly Roman Stoicism, of which Smith was well aware: cf. Raphael and Macfie, 'Introduction', 7.

[148] See Raphael (1972), 335, and Morrow (1969), 28. Here obviously we will deal only with classical systems. A brief excursus on the three main branches of Greek philosophy is also found at *WN* v. i. f. 23–8.

[149] The editorial note at *TMS* p. 300 points out that the attention paid to benevolence was more characteristic of late Stoicism (Seneca, Epictetus, Marcus Aurelius) than of Neoplatonism, and suggests that Smith's study of the latter may have been influenced by the teachings of Christian thinkers, who were indebted to Neoplatonism in other respects.

[150] *TMS* VII. ii. 1. 5; cf. Plato *Rep.* iv. 440e.

Moving on to the concept of justice, Smith distinguishes different sorts, drawing on the *Nicomachean Ethics* among other sources, and again has recourse to his regular standby, the impartial spectator. He concludes that Plato's view of the nature of virtue fits with his own 'propriety of conduct'. Shortly afterwards, however, he says the same thing of Aristotle's golden mean (*TMS* vii. ii. 1. 11–12). It is probable that in the former case he is speaking of propriety in the sense of each passion having an appropriate area of operation, while in the latter the word refers to the specific degree of intensity that each passion or sentiment can be allowed to reach.

Book II of the *Ethics* is then used as a source for certain motifs regarding the quality of actions and persons, and the criteria for judging the heart's motives and dispositions, whether momentary or habitual, in relation to the actions accomplished. Smith finishes by distinguishing between Aristotle's ethical theory, based on habit, and Plato's, based on the intellect, according to which men act immorally only through ignorance (*TMS* vii. ii. 1. 14).

The account of Stoicism that follows is more diffuse than the two just given, but this school of philosophy has received quite substantial treatment in the preceding pages, and only one further point is made here: the two underlying principles of Stoic moral theory, Smith states, are absolute submission to the providential order of things, combined with total indifference to life and death, and a sense of complete satisfaction with whatever event life might throw up (*TMS* vii. ii. 1. 35). Epictetus well exemplifies the former principle in practice; Marcus Aurelius the latter. A slightly unusual interpretation, this, but one that displays Smith's tendency to pay close attention not only to the substance of a work but also to its author's personal circumstances, which he evidently regarded as capable of influencing both thought and character.

Turning to Epicurus, Smith recounts how that philosopher derived all forms of happiness, including the spiritual, from physical pleasure, and argued that pain can always be put up with because when it is intense it is of short duration, and when it is long-drawn-out it is moderate: a well-known proposition, treated with a degree of ridicule by Cicero.[151] The Epicurean treatment of prudence is quite similar to Smith's, but is, as already noted, distinguished by its largely utilitarian nature, according to which the only reason for acting prudently is the positive consequences that doing so gives rise to. Analogously, Epicurus argued that justice can be reduced to prudent and discreet conduct towards others so as not to endanger one's own tranquil state. This analysis, Smith declares, is wholly incompatible with his own. As for why it had proved such an attractive theory, though, he argues that this was because it treated virtue as advantageous, and vice as the contrary. Virtues are accordingly practised not only for their intrinsic value, but also

---

[151] *TMS* vii. ii. 2. 5; Cic. *Fin.* i. 40, ii. 22, 93–4; *Tusc.* ii. 44–5. The phrase often reappears in Seneca.

for the benefits they bring.[152] In introducing this principle, Epicurus 'indulged a propensity which is natural to all men, but which philosophers in particular are apt to cultivate with a peculiar fondness, as the great means of displaying their ingenuity, the propensity to account for all appearances from as few principles as possible' (*TMS* vii. ii. 2. 14). The significance of this point in Smith's philosophy has been indicated elsewhere.[153] Here he illustrates the Epicurean tendency to take this reductionist approach both in the context of moral theory—by reducing every desire or aversion to a matter of physical pleasure and pain—and in that of natural philosophy—by atomistically accounting for all the powers and qualities of physical entities in terms of the 'obvious and familiar, the figure, motion, and arrangement of the small parts of matter' (*TMS* vii. ii. 2. 14).

At *TMS* vii. ii. 4. 5 Smith states that there is something important to learn from each of the three groups of philosophical systems under examination: fortitude and magnanimity; humanity; and—from Epicureanism—the use of virtue as a certain guide for our own benefit. But one cannot fail to note that he accords the moral doctrines of Plato and Aristotle considerably less treatment than Stoicism or even Epicureanism. This is not without reason: the latter two philosophies played important roles in Smith's thought in general, and specifically in his economic theories.

The last section within *TMS* vii deals with the problem of practical rules, moral norms, and how these have been treated by different thinkers. These are classed in two groups, according to their approach. The first are the descriptive moralists, as they might be termed, numbering among them all the ancient philosophers: they do no more than illustrate vices and virtues. The others are those moralists who set down precise rules of behaviour: the medieval and post-medieval casuists. The only classical thinker to appear in both groups is Cicero.[154] The 'juridical' character of these rules is closely examined, with special attention paid to the difference between jurisprudence and casuistry.

Smith's conclusion is the well-known remark that ethics and jurisprudence are the only useful parts of moral philosophy (*TMS* vii. iv. 34). But to this he appends a clear rejection of casuistry and a positive evaluation of the methods of ancient philosophy, relying as it does not on setting out an

---

[152] *TMS* vii. ii. 2. 13; cf. also 4. 5, where Smith suggests that it was on account of his theory of the good effects of virtue that Epicurus was studied so closely even by his philosophical opponents Cicero and Seneca.

[153] See above, Ch. 1.2. Note also Campbell (1971), 89: 'Smith's broad interpretation of the term [sc. sympathy] is suited to his purpose of explaining as wide as possible a variety of social phenomena using the minimum number of explanatory principles. The unity of the *Moral Sentiments*, therefore, does not lie in an initial definition of morality but springs from the fundamental scientific generalizations on the basis of which Smith builds up his "moral" theory'. For Smith, the unifying principle was sympathy.

[154] At *TMS* vii. iv. 11 for a specific, single question; ibid. iv. 35 for his *De Officiis* in general (though a distinction is drawn between him and truly casuistic writers).

intricate network of petty rules and counter-rules, but on describing the sentiments that underlie every virtue and the way that these, as a matter of course, impel individuals to act. Even in their methodology, Smith found ancient systems of thought so much closer to his own.

2.13. THE DIVERSE ORIGIN OF THE CLASSICAL ASPECTS OF SMITH'S MORAL PHILOSOPHY

Stoicism, it will be abundantly clear by now, was the major classical influence operating on Smith. Although his interpretation of it was quite personal, he preserves some of its essential characteristics: the original motive for human actions is located in the natural care each individual takes to look after himself; due to the providentialist idea, the results of this self-interested behaviour are held to be good for society as a whole; and a certain detachment from one's emotions is considered necessary.

Against this background Smith focuses on the Epicurean virtue of prudence, and the Stoic one of self-control, as those most suitable for encouraging egoist behaviour of the right sort—behaviour, that is, designed to safeguard one's own interests without harming those of others. Recourse is also had to justice, a virtue with a somewhat Aristotelian character, not to mention an underlying element of resentment, ultimately Platonic in origin. The slight turn away from Stoicism already apparent in this is further emphasized by another aspect of Aristotelian, rather than Stoic, origin, namely attention to the circumstances. Smith rejects those parts of Stoic thought that distance themselves from the principles outlined above. Disinterested contemplation as an aim, whereby the Stoic becomes wholly independent of external affairs, and indeed of his own emotions, can hardly gain acceptance from a thinker who not only proclaims the supremacy of action, but above all bases his whole philosophy on the mutual correspondence of sentiment between individuals, and therefore requires that they be interdependent.

As regards the analogies that have been pointed out between some of Smith's fundamental philosophical ideas and certain classical concepts, one should emphasize that the latter were for him no more than starting-points: he developed these notions independently and incorporated them into his own philosophy. Even in these cases, therefore, his thought retains its originality. His manner of drawing diverse elements from various parts of ancient philosophy, weighing them up according to the extent that they fit with his own ideas—what might be called an 'alchemical' approach to the subject—can be gauged from the intricate relationship between, on the one hand, the Aristotelian/Peripatetic basis underlying his concept of sympathy and, on the other, the Stoic virtue of self-control. Aristotle and the Peripatetics allowed emotions up to the point represented by the golden mean, while Stoic self-control is what enables the individual to keep his passions down to the point of propriety—a point corresponding precisely with Aristotle's mean. Typical of Smith, furthermore, is his use of a virtue originally invoked to foster the wise man's *autarcheia* for quite contrary purposes, namely to make it possible for two individuals to achieve a sympathetic relationship. Stoic self-control is also what leads Smith on to approve the Epicurean virtue of prudence, which was valued in utilitarian terms rather than for its intrinsic worth: here too, then, we see the combination of elements of different provenance.

The fundamental problem in understanding Smith's relationship with the classics, perhaps, is that of aligning a general, universalist outlook, of Stoic origin, with his practical philosophy. The former—the so-called 'argument from design'—is optimistic in approach and, despite Smith's general opposition to dogmatism, essentially aprioristic.[155] His practical philosophy, on the other hand, starts out by recognizing that some of the individual's instincts are quite natural, and that the behaviour they lead to is therefore quite legitimate; it, however, requires him to moderate them, not in the hope of reaching moral perfection or spiritual independence, but rather (in the first place at least) for reasons that are thoroughly social, namely so that his behaviour, whether good or bad, will meet with a sympathetic response from others. This makes some degree of mismatch inevitable between the perfect order of providence and man's wickedness, which has therefore to be repressed.

It is truly regrettable that Smith's lectures on natural philosophy, the first part of the Glasgow moral philosophy course, are lost: these would probably have dealt with the problem of providence.[156] But for our purposes it is perhaps sufficient to make one point. Smith's use of the invisible-hand argument to apply a theory of providential type to economic reality in *TMS* and *WN* may not be completely assimilable to the Stoic approach to the topic: the latter, after all, was cosmological in essence, while Smith was examining precise economic situations from a very personal point of view. Nonetheless, there is a fundamental similarity in the way each theory regards reality. There is therefore greater reason to consider it a lucky circumstance that *TMS* furnishes us with Smith's critique of the Stoic theory in question, which he by and large accepts, adding only the important rider about individual responsibility in the face of wicked actions.

In this way too, then, the view that Smith would encourage self-interest but not selfishness seems confirmed. Above all, emphasis is again laid on the important role played in his thought by the necessity of moderating one's instincts. It is in any case clear that he tended to combine the frequent classical motifs in his works according to the varying extent to which they fitted with his own ideas: thus Stoic self-control merges on one side with the Aristotelian golden mean and on the other with Epicurean prudence, but has nothing to do

---

[155] Macfie (1967*e*), 110–22; cf. also above, Ch. 1 n. 102.
[156] Macfie (1967*e*), 106.

with Stoic apathy. Another example is provided by the impartial spectator, which can in all likelihood (and without detracting in any way from the originality of Smith's treatment of the idea) be derived from Aristotle's *phronimos*. This is certainly the main influence acting on the personification, but one can also perhaps discern combined elements of the Polybian 'witness' and the Epictetan 'neighbour' (to use Smith's translations), each understood as representing a viewer who sees an event and then relates it to himself, rather than a person producing a judgement. It would probably in fact be more correct to interpret these figures as examples of participation, rather than evaluation; but they also possess an element of reflection on what they observe. In other words, while the spectator's essential function is, as defined by Smith (and by Aristotle), the determination of the moral criterion, it is not impossible that the other two figures are in some way analogous to that of the spectator, taken as one who observes and mentally reacts to other people's behaviour. But the link with Aristotle is fundamental. The influence exerted by the other two authors is somewhat uncertain,[157] and would tend to have a character rather different from that of the spectator-judge—though no less appropriate in some ways to Smith's moral theory, if one recalls that the Polybian witness exemplifies the ideal of putting oneself in another's place, while the neighbour invoked by Epictetus hints at an attempt to keep one's passions at the correct level.

A suitable conclusion, then, is that the ancient moral philosophers provided Smith with elements of great importance, that cannot be considered merely items in the long list of distinguished exempla—though these are certainly not lacking. Their fundamental contribution is rather that of clarifying and deepening certain basic lines of thought which Smith reflected on, discussed, and argued about; he then made them his own or rejected them, according to the ideas he had formulated and matured in the course of this process, and with the help of the ancient doctrines themselves.

---

[157] Especially in the case of Polybius, whom I do not consider an overall influence on Smith's quite elaborate and wholly personal theory of sympathy. At most there is a partial coincidence, represented by the shared use of the figure of a spectator and his reaction. But this is in any case a conjectural relationship: this chapter is an attempt to indicate confirmed relationships between Smith's philosophy and that of his classical predecessors.

3

The Lectures on Jurisprudence and Roman Law[1]

3.1. INTRODUCTORY REMARKS

There was one academic project which can be said to have remained with Adam Smith throughout his life: that of writing a treatise on the general principles of the law and the way these had evolved over time. John Millar relates that Smith had planned a publication of this nature as early as the period of his Glasgow lectures, or at least had arranged the material in a manner appropriate to that end.[2] The idea reappears in Smith's letter to the Duc de la Rochefoucauld,[3] which reveals that he had to a large degree already got the necessary material together and in order, but that the fatigue of old age prevented him from drafting the work out and indeed cast uncertainty on it ever being brought to a conclusion. Despite this, in the sixth edition of *TMS*, which came out in the year of his death, he did not suppress the closing remark, reading though it does both as a justification for the lack of a historical treatment of jurisprudence in that essay, and a promise to undertake one in the future.

In many of the diverse intellectual fields that attracted Smith we are able to learn his views from works that were thought out, perfected, and revised. Occasionally we have recourse to pieces that are barely more than fragments; but even these were at least written by Smith himself. In the case of jurisprudence, unfortunately, we know only the great importance that he endowed the subject with; shortly before his death he had everything he had written on it destroyed. For this reason we must rely on a few authoritative pieces of evidence; the now well-known notes 'On Jurisprudence' published by Cannan in 1896; the second batch published by Meek, Raphael, and Stein in the Glasgow edition of Smith's correspondence; and, finally, the brief

---

[1] This Chapter revisits and develops in greater detail certain themes already dealt with in my essay 'La presenza della tradizione classica nell'opera di Adam smith', i.e. Vivenza *et al*. (1980). I was not able in that essay to take account of publications later than February 1977, and so could not make use of the group of lectures by Smith dated 1762–3, which were published for the first time in 1978.　　　　　　　　　　　　　　　　　　　　　　　[2] Stewart (1980), i. 19.

[3] *Corr*. 286–7 (no. 248) (1 Nov. 1785). The same letter refers to a project for a 'philosophical history' of literature, philosophy, poetry, and eloquence.

notes which Meek found in the commonplace book kept by Smith's colleague Professor John Anderson.[4]

The importance of these studies, relevant both to the history of jurisprudence and to the philosophy of law, arises from a variety of considerations. Smith lived in an era that was seeing the first fruits of the innovative thought of Montesquieu,[5] and an environment in which jurisprudence was a privileged subject. It is hard to grasp Montesquieu's 'tremendous originality' today, when the connection between laws and social circumstances is universally taken for granted,[6] but it marked a turning-point for juridical theory, taking it in a direction in which Smith carried it further still with his well-known theory of the four socio-economic stages. On the other hand, we should not lose sight of the contribution already made by jurisprudence to social and economic thought in an earlier period, a period which—if not exactly recent for Smith and his contemporaries—was still a living reality for them when they wrote. This contribution derived from the study of natural law, whose links with the growth of economic individualism in Britain from the sixteenth century onwards have received academic attention.[7] In addition there was also the great importance of arguments on natural law for the question of the political function of law in general.

Scotland's academic community, furthermore, was one with a heightened awareness of jurisprudential studies, and Smith's work in this area is associated with the names of certain famous jurists. It is also essentially defined by its intellectual associations, which look in two directions: towards moral philosophy, with which it was closely linked as a taught subject, and, as the clear source of its theoretical aspects, towards Roman law (and thereby towards the Continent, especially France and the Netherlands).

3.2. NATURAL LAW

On account of the extent to which this subject has already been discussed in the literature, what follows here will be no more than a commentary intended to establish its links with Smith's theory. Natural law is a classical concept in origin, and, despite the juridical implications of its name, it is a philosophical subject, with little practical relevance in antiquity at least, even though jurists were familiar with it. The theory's fundamental characteristic is the distinction it draws between objective natural law and the contingent norms of positive law. It is founded on a 'quest after some immutable standard or pattern,

---

[4] Meek (1976a), 466–7.

[5] As noted by Dugald Stewart in a memoir of W. Robertson presented to the Royal Society of Edinburgh in 1796, a great distance had been covered since Montesquieu's time, much of it through the efforts of Scottish writers, members of the Society in question; Stewart (1980), ii. 51 with n. 24 there.

[6] Stein (1979a), 625.   [7] Cf. Chalk (1951).

independent of their [i.e. men's] choice, and capable of carrying conviction'.[8] The contrast between what is by nature just and what is legally just dates back to pre-Socratic thought.[9] In tracing its history one needs to be aware of certain Platonic and Aristotelian views that are now slightly unattractive: Plato's recognition of the law's ethical and pedagogical function and rejection of any juridical one, and Aristotle's notorious justification of slavery on the grounds that certain breeds of men are naturally made to serve. Alongside these, however, one needs to set the important contribution made by Stoicism, whose strong connective tendencies gave natural-law theory a vital boost, drawing together its various versions and ascribing the superior status from which natural law derives its universal application to a set of principles which in Stoic thought, with its identification of divinity and nature, nature and reason, were in harmony. Stoic ethics and politics therefore retained the stamp of natural-law theory, seeing in natural law a necessary superiority that is divinely desired, physically inevitable, and the logical conclusion of right reason.[10]

Since not only philosophy but jurisprudence too is relevant to this matter, however, one should add that an obvious aspect of natural law's relationship with positive law is that the former ought to constitute the basis of the second, as is in fact affirmed, in the Stoic tradition, by Cicero, Seneca, and the jurisconsults.[11]

It is not easy to find agreement amongst academics on the extent to which this *ius naturale* is actually present in positive law. The majority place it in association with *ius gentium*, the system of rules governing dealings between Romans and *peregrini*, which developed as those dealings became more frequent, and was understood philosophically as dictated by *naturalis ratio* and therefore of equal validity among all civilized peoples. This, then, can be seen as the law of those nations not endowed with Roman citizenship; in concrete terms a body of largely commercial regulations. In contrast with this, established teaching placed *ius civile*, the body of laws of a specific city, namely Rome; though later on commercial relations between citizens were to be regulated by *ius gentium*. The association between *ius naturale* and *ius gentium*, which perhaps resulted from the latter's basis in *naturalis ratio*, and for which Cicero was partly responsible,[12] should not be regarded as a mere coincidence. In fact the two could occasionally conflict, the case of slavery being a well-known instance: it existed in positive law as an element of *ius gentium*, although jurists and philosophers such as Ulpian and Seneca, to

---

[8] Passerin D'Entrèves (1972), 16; cf. Cannata (1976), ii, 111.
[9] Fassò (1966), 29, 39, 43. For emphasis on Heraclitus' role see Struve (1921), 295–6.
[10] Fassò (1966), 108 f., and 77, 98–9 (on discrepant views of slavery in antiquity, for which see below).
[11] Kamphuisen (1932), 392–3; Levy (1949), 2. See also Pohlenz (1970), i. 133, 263–4.
[12] Costa (1927), i. 26–7; cf. Fassò (1966), 139; Kamphuisen (1932), 393, 397; Levy (1949), 3.

name but two, recognized the impossibility of justifying it in terms of law 'according to nature', which regarded all men as born free.[13]

The Stoic conception of natural law, received in particular by Cicero and the jurisconsults, was not without theoretical influence on Roman jurisprudence. In addition, it was transmitted into the theological enquiries of the Church Fathers and medieval Christian philosophy. In this way not just Stoicism, but Christianity too had a notable influence on philosophical and juridical thought, bringing to bear a concept that was to dominate medieval thought and lead to a vision of society divided into unequal parts; a state of affairs which, with Aristotle's help, might be considered to follow from the order of nature.[14]

In the meantime an event of great importance had taken place in the study of law, narrowly understood. As a result of the work of the glossators from the late eleventh century onwards and that of the commentators from the fourteenth, the *Corpus Iuris* (Code and Digest), having become a subject of study in European universities, not only infiltrated the canon law, but ended up being adopted as positive law by the whole of Catholic Europe, excepting England, but including Scotland. It now constituted a body of substantive law with validity throughout a large portion of western Europe, and was henceforth subject to a largely practical form of exegesis arising from the fact that for European courts and tribunals it was the working law. In these circumstances, natural law began to be conceived differently, as something distinct from the positive manifestation of Roman law.

The famous natural-law school of the seventeenth and eighteenth centuries, with the great names of Grotius, Puffendorf, and the lesser ones of Burlamaqui, Heineccius, Thomasius, Wolff, was a school of rationalist character: this is perhaps the link between the new teachings and classical *lex naturalis*, a form of law that is intended to be based entirely on pure reason. By now, however, this had come to mean independence of the Church and—in Grotius' notorious formulation—validity even if God should not exist.[15] The break in continuity which this represented was highly significant, inasmuch as it entailed a notion of 'mathematical' validity, outclassing all else in its unquestionable self-evidence. The extraordinary revolutionary potential which this piece of theory would later unleash is clear at once. The process was gradual, however, and one can still discern an analogy with classical teaching

---

[13] Rather than giving the whole bibliography on this subject I cite here only Arangio Ruiz (1945), 25–6; Burdese (1964), 14 f. and esp. 26–8; Fassò (1966), 143 f.; Passerin D'Entrèves (1972), 28–35 f.; Koschaker (1962), 424; Gierke (1934), pp. xxxiv–l. Burdese (1954), 419, states with reference to the age of classical jurisprudence (1st to 3rd centuries AD) that the subject then operated with a concrete 'concept of *ius naturale* as positive law in association with *natura* understood as a factual reality', and that only in the post-classical and Justinianic age was it elevated to an ideal law, superior to and distinct from positive law.

[14] Gierke (1934), 206; Chalk (1951), 332. On Christian theology's role as a bridge between Stoicism and modern natural-law theory cf. also Myrdal (1953), 28; Struve (1921), 298; Fassò (1966), 114, 245, 269.   [15] Cassirer (1951), 240; id. (1967c), 168.

in the fact that even now natural law was associated with the law of nations and found application in international relations, and use was still made of the *Corpus Iuris*. In practice, it is true, seventeenth-century natural-law theory faced situations of much greater complexity and diversity than those envisaged in Roman law; but the ancient world had a much wider experience of commerce than the Middle Ages, and ancient law, though requiring adaptation to the changed circumstances, could still furnish elements of value.[16]

Another distinction between natural and positive law was that the former was not enforceable. Observance of its rules was not something that could be imposed. But the modern era was to pursue as far as it would go the idea of a higher law than those that happened to be enacted in national codes, and arrive at the obvious conclusion that it was legitimate to withhold obedience to the latter when they came into conflict with the former.[17] The second half of the eighteenth century saw the explosive charge within this principle detonated in America and Europe, with results that continue to give the lie to the commonplace that there is no link between thinkers and reality. The conceptual basis, however, had already been expressed in the statement of an English judge in 1614 that 'even an Act of Parliament made against natural equity . . . is void in itself; for *iura naturae sunt immutabilia*, and they are *leges legum*',[18] referring to one of Bacon's aphorisms. As related by Dugald Stewart, Adam Smith's unfulfilled intention of producing a treatise on the general principles of jurisprudence can be formulated in Bacon's precise words; he planned to identify the *leges legum* from which 'one can seek an idea of that which, in specific laws, is well or badly disposed or established'.[19]

To recapitulate, the idea of a form of justice superior to that manifest in substantive law, an idea that can be traced back to earliest antiquity, by making an originally Stoic identification between natural law and the law of morality that ought to underlie positive law, influenced not only the jurists who compiled the *Corpus Iuris* but also a large section of modern thought.[20]

---

[16] Cannata (1976), ii. 115; see also Cavanna (1979), 326; Coing (1979), 29f.

[17] Passerin D'Entrèves (1972), 16: 'As far as natural law is concerned, it was Lord Bryce who remarked that, at a given moment, "that which had been for nearly two thousand years a harmless maxim, almost a commonplace of morality" was converted into "a mass of dynamite which shattered an ancient monarchy and shook the European continent" '.

[18] Barker, introduction to Gierke (1934), p. xlvi (italics as given there). The glossators drew a distinction between *leges legum* and *leges negociorum* (Vinogradoff (1929), 65), and tackled the important question of the relationship between law and equity. But in reality Bacon's *leges legum* resemble a view of social laws, perhaps even with historical existence, rather than 'natural law' in the strict sense. According to Taylor (1955), 88, Smith follows Bacon's and Montesquieu's notion of adaptability to local conditions; but his research into a set of universally applicable general principles is nonetheless a response to a requirement arising from natural-law theories.

[19] *Ex quibus informatio peti possit, quid in singulis legibus bene aut perperam positum aut constitutum sit*; Bacon, *De Fontibus Juris*, aphor. 6, quoted by Stewart (1980), iv. 7. See also Taylor (1955), 68, where Smith's project is said to reflect a natural law of a *moral* sort, typical of 18th-century social philosophy.

[20] Passerin D'Entrèves (1972), *passim*; Pohlenz (1970), i. 263, 470–1; Struve (1921), 298 f.; Coing (1979), 35.

Only rarely did Adam Smith make explicit reference to this debate. His *Lectures* contain the occasional suggestion of a link between a given law and 'natural reason', or the affirmation that no system of positive law, however good it might be, can coincide precisely with 'natural justice'.[21] Twice at the end of *TMS*, after an interesting 'historical' note on the (supposed) neglect of this question in the ancient world,[22] and the ritual act of homage to Grotius, founder of the discipline, he repeats a phrase about the '[general] principles which ought to run through and be the foundation of the laws of all nations', a phrase whose importance is evident from the privileged position within moral philosophy which the context gives to ethics and jurisprudence. The work then closes with the promise of a systematic treatment of the '*general principles* of law and government, and of the different revolutions they have undergone in the different ages and periods of society'.[23] It would seem, in other words, that for Smith these general principles should be read in evolutionary terms; this, at any rate, is implied by the second part of the sentence referring to 'different ages and periods'. Apparently contrasting with this, however, is a remark in the *Wealth of Nations*. There Smith draws an interesting distinction between the legislator, 'whose deliberations ought to be governed by general principles *which are always the same*', and the politician, 'whose councils are directed by the momentary fluctuations of affairs' (*WN* IV. ii. 39; my italics). This probably means that the principles of natural justice, the business of the legislator, are unchanging, while those underlying the various dispositions of 'police', inasmuch as they are contingent, can change over time or be adapted to circumstances. Rather than hypothesizing two sorts of general principle—the one referring to justice in the abstract, the other to situations in 'real life'— one should adopt Haakonssen's interpretation, according to which the legislator can be seen in terms of the 'man of public spirit', inclined to enact gradual political reform in accord with a moderate approach, as opposed to the well-known 'man of system', whose tendency is to impose an abstract model forcibly. The theoretical framework must come to terms with reality, and the ideal legislator[24] will be the one 'who will strike the perfect Smithian balance between the enlightenment of "some general, and even systematic, idea of the perfection of policy and law", and the piecemeal action to alleviate

---

[21] See e.g. *LJ* (A) i. 20, 24–5, 116; ii. 28, 145–6; iii. 35, 66; *TMS* VII. iv. 36.

[22] Smith doubtless sought some ancient analogy to modern natural-law theory; an impossibility. (It is not for me to repeat here all the differences between the two, for which see Passerin D'Entrèves (1972), 14–15, 53–62.) He sought it, furthermore, in the legal writings of Plato and Cicero, and complains of finding only positive law exemplified there, while in the moral works of Aristotle and Cicero the law is treated in the same way as the other virtues (*TMS* VII. iv. 37). He undervalues notably the Stoic contribution to the topic, and, despite naming Aristotle, does not give sufficient consideration to that author's references to the distinction between natural and positive law (*NE* $1134^{b}28$–$1135^{a}5$; *Rhet.* $1373^{b}4$ f.).

[23] *TMS* VII.iv. 37 (my italics); cf. the 'Advertisement' to the 6th edition, pt. 2.

[24] Exemplified by Solon, 'one of the leading figures in the republican "myth"': Winch (1979), 160.

concrete evils'.[25] For this reason we can conclude that at the basis of positive-law systems Smith saw general principles of 'natural reason' (a precise translation of *naturalis ratio*); principles which, however, cannot be considered universal and immutable, like elements of natural law, on account of their application to the changing realities of society.

Economic theory too was an area for which natural law had great importance. One brand of economic individualism was derived precisely from a statement of the principle of natural reason that certain specific modes of behaviour follow a law of nature that is common to all humanity, on account of its very humanity, and that it is thus not merely pointless, but actually harmful to try and prevent them. This way of thinking, so different from medieval notions of economic and social inequalities owing their origin to God's will, began to spread in the second half of the sixteenth century. While for medieval philosophers the law of nature, which was the same as divine law, required economic activity to be controlled, there was now a growing belief that it was better to allow natural human tendencies to express themselves. Within this can be discerned the outline of a very influential idea; the idea that economic activity is governed by laws that are universal and immutable, and for that reason similar to laws of nature.[26] Here we glimpse natural law's third aspect; in addition to its juridical and ethical sides, it had a scientific one, extremely important in the eighteenth century, when the mechanistic and teleological views of the universe went hand in hand, and influenced the psychological, social, and even economic strands of philosophy.[27] Like the other areas, economics saw the development of a concept of universal harmony. A society's economic system was conceived of as a mechanism in which 'labor, capital, business ability, goods and the money of consumers, have been pictured as "gravitating" to their best markets, with resultant interactions of supplies, demands, prices and incomes taking place according to "definite" laws',[28] and revealing thereby the creator's wise manner of promoting social welfare.

The changes that led up to the development of this concept took place in reaction not only to medieval doctrines, but also to the interventionist approach sanctioned by the complex apparatus of mercantile law constructed to direct the 'natural' flow of commerce. They can perhaps be seen as the conceptual result of the gradual change in economic circumstances. Certain important topics are relevant here: the justification for natural-law theory of private property; the coincidence of individual and collective interests; self-interest as the main motive factor in economic behaviour. The idea is, in short, one of the lynchpins of eighteenth-century liberalism. The extent to which Stoic philosophy can be regarded as a part of this

---

[25] Haakonssen (1981), 97.
[26] Chalk (1951), 336–7, 340–1; Taylor (1955), 54–5.
[27] Struve (1921), 300.   [28] Taylor (1955), 49–50.

conceptual framework is not something one can measure precisely; but that it was present in some degree is certain.

According to some commentators, Smith's position maintained contact with the scholastic one.[29] It is, at any rate, traditional to consider him the most distinguished exponent of the economic ideas recounted above: not, certainly, as promoting an indiscriminate *laissez-faire* approach, but rather a policy of allowing the natural order to develop and eliminating favouritism and restrictive practices, which, mostly made up of faulty provisions, impede the creation of an economy favourable to the harmonization of individual interests for the benefit of society.[30]

This approach, of course, presupposes that there is such an order of things in nature. In this respect, Smith's viewpoint is undoubtedly Stoic, at least to the extent that this can be said of the well-known idea that fundamentally selfish instincts are ultimately beneficial. For the Stoics, however, the presupposition of the perfect rationality of the real world admitted no human intervention; while for Smith the harmonious development of the natural order contains a residual element, the negative side of reality, doubtless constituted by those very elements that obstruct or impede the natural order itself.

Smith's position, though taking the theory of natural law as its starting-point, and paying homage to Grotius for his treatment of the primary elements of jurisprudence, is, in general terms, and despite the occasional statement of principle, too intimately bound up with concepts of evolution to be regarded as genuinely a natural-law approach. Although he admits the existence of fundamental principles, he does not describe them as immutable, mathematical, and eternal—an essential aspect of their character in natural law. There is, perhaps, reason to believe that Smith's evolutionary view of history and law influenced his moderate political stance; lacking belief in eternal and immutable schemes, he was unable to believe in movements for social regeneration they inspired.

For eighteenth-century social and economic thought, the manifold aspects of the theory of natural-law rights had a correspondingly wide range of implications, scientific, ethical, and juridical.[31] Though this is not the place for a full analysis, Smith's work reflects them all. Suffice it to say that his thought

---

[29] The reference is, of course, particularly to Schumpeter, and also to De Roover (1955), 188–9, both stating that scholasticism too contained certain hints of 'liberalism' (De Roover, op. cit., 184, with n. 6) and even the elements necessary for working out a theory of distribution: Schumpeter (1955), 272. Smith will have reached these ideas by way of the theory of natural law. On the latter, it needs to be emphasized how complex the classical influence was: Grotius was able to arm himself with Aristotelian weaponry to take on the schoolmen (De Roover, op. cit., 181); his originality, in comparison with the old Stoicism and Ciceronian texts, lay mainly in the way he treated them (Fassò (1968), 107–8). The historical origins of his fundamental creation, natural law, are to be found in the Stoic 'renaissance' of the sixteenth century: Coing (1979), 35.   [30] Rosenberg (1979), 24; Taylor (1955), 95 f.

[31] Taylor (1955), 71–3, 76–8, 87 f.

in the fields of law, history, and what would today be called sociology admits social inequality as a characteristic of the natural order (an admission found in scholasticism and deriving from the Stoics and from Aristotle). It is therefore, despite its basic evolutionary bias, opposed to hurried evolution, or—to be precise—to radical transformation. For Smith, the concept of natural law is thus dissociated from the idea of a superior justice in whose name it is legitimate to rebel against the established order of things, and is instead connected with the old Stoic idea of rational order in the cosmos.

3.3. LAW AND SOCIETY

Roman law had a crucial role in the birth of historical consciousness and political thought in modern Europe. The period between the eleventh and sixteenth centuries saw the so-called reception of Roman law in those countries of Europe that adopted the *Corpus Iuris* as their shared source of law up until the enactment of the modern codes. A large part in this process was played by the Church, which from the earliest advances of Christianity had breathed its own spirit into the last phases of Roman legislation, and had then, by means of canon law, which incorporated many elements deriving from the civilian code,[32] encouraged the adoption of the latter. This was particularly so in Scotland, where accepted academic opinion holds that it was precisely through the canon law that Roman law was adopted.[33]

The medieval interpretation of Roman law could be justly described as unhistorical and uncritical. It was assimilated to fit existing situations, and employed as a storehouse of arguments to resolve specific legal problems. The humanist approach which replaced this scholastic one submitted the ancient sources to philological enquiry, and constructed the basis for their historical interpretation.[34] The dawning appreciation of the historical background against which Code and Digest needed to be seen to be understood gave rise (in France at first, but under Italian influence) to the doubt that they were really of use in a modern society. This prompted a widespread re-evaluation of the ancient, unwritten, local customs that formed each country's framework of indigenous law. What resulted was the study of the antiquity of municipal institutions, and from it the impulse among the learned classes of Europe to study the remnants of their medieval and 'barbarian' past. This historical research was distinct from theorizing about natural law, which referred instead to an overarching unwritten law, possessing absolute validity and therefore in some sense immutable and

---

[32] Present in Gratian's *decretum*, compiled in the 12th century after the manner of the Digest, and later to form the basis of the canon law: Reulos (1975), ii. 672.

[33] See below, n. 42, and the relevant passage in the text. For doubts, see Campbell (1962), i. 78–9.

[34] What follows is principally drawn from Coing (1979); Reulos (1975); Pocock (1957); Bolgar (1958), 140–9, 291–5; Gierke (1934), pp. xxxix–xl; Stein (1969, 1979*a*, and 1980).

independent of time and place; almost an ideal paradigm of law, which particular systems of positive law ought to try and resemble as closely as possible.[35] Montesquieu's great insight (that though positive law should be based on the nature of things, this can itself be influenced by a wide diversity of factors such as climate, customs, administrative traditions) was foreshadowed by a long period of study arising from the humanistically inspired awareness that Roman law, though in operation throughout much of Europe, had belonged to a society that was radically different.

In consequence, the nature of the critical study of jurisprudence changed. The law, on principle, had to be adapted to fit the society it operated in. It was, furthermore, a historical circumstance that the Roman law 'received' from the medieval monarchies coexisted and to some extent conflicted with each nation's customary law. Accordingly, there grew up an atmosphere of enquiry in which all known legal systems (including the Roman one) were studied in the hope of finding the essential elements of jurisprudence shared by all systems.[36] Each was submitted to critical examination and placed in the context of the society that had given birth to it.

In contrast with this work of contextualization, the natural-law tradition, founded as it was on the universal value of pure reason, started from the presupposition that reason itself was the same for all peoples and in all times. It too was claimed to possess the general principles that are to be found, or should be found, at the base of all legislation; not, this time, as the result of a historical study but, rather, a priori. In spite of this, natural-law theorists recognized that the institutions deriving from these principles were not all the same; they did not exist in the state of nature, and were introduced only later. The principal focuses of attention were the apparatus of government and the question of property.[37]

This sort of historical-political enquiry did not give rise only to Montesquieu's great work; it was also the ultimate origin of Smith's much less well-known contribution. 'The great Montesquieu pointed out the road. He was the Lord Bacon of this branch of *philosophy*. Dr Smith is the Newton.' This remark of John Millar[38] referred to Smith's lectures 'On the History of Civil Society', which he considered it a privilege to have heard and to which he held himself in debt. Smith gave these lectures as Professor

[35] Smith too believed that natural law should be a model for positive law: *TMS* VI. ii. intro. 2; VII. iv. 36.

[36] See Pocock (1957), 23, and (for this whole topic) 8–29. The search for the principles common to all legal systems was, of course, precisely what Smith planned to undertake in his projected work on jurisprudence: *TMS* VII. iv. 37.

[37] Grotius, however, produced a 'comparative' study on various ancient authors to 'test' the principles of natural law. His comparison has thus been described as empiricist or a posteriori: Stein (1980), 3–5. In England the debate was carried forward in the 18th century by moral philosophers rather than jurists: ibid. 9f.

[38] In his *Historical View of English Government*, quoted in Stewart (1980), i. 19 n. 4; my italics.

of Moral Philosophy at Glasgow, a course which we have remarked was
divided into four sections: 'natural theology', 'ethics', 'that branch of
morality which relates to *justice*', and 'those political regulations which are
founded not upon the principle of *justice*, but on that of *expediency*'.[39] In
Millar's account the third section, on justice, appears to have followed the
very route marked out by Montesquieu, tracing the gradual evolution of
jurisprudence from the most uncultivated periods to civilized ages, and
emphasizing the role played by activities to do with sustenance and the
increase of wealth in the development of law and modes of government. But
it should again be observed that in the subdivision of the syllabus just given
this section is referred to as a 'branch of *morality*', being preceded by
theology and ethics, and followed by a fourth section, of a different character, in which not justice but utility is the basic criterion. It seems clear that
jurisprudence is the link between ethical behaviour, in the strict sense, and
political behaviour by means of 'changes in law and government'. Smith uses
the word 'jurisprudence' to mean the general principles on which laws and
governments are based,[40] and it covers the four well-known topics of 'justice,
police, revenue, arms' which made up the final section of his course in moral
philosophy as well as the essential nucleus of *The Wealth of Nations*. For this
reason, 'changes in law and government', connected on the one hand with
ethics and on the other with political economy, need a basis in justice while
also meeting the requirements of utility.

Smith is clearly well aware of the various directions in which the subject
pulls. He theorizes on its evolution, thereby opposing the notion of immutable (natural) law, and proposes the adaptation of institutions to meet the
relevant social situation. But at the same time he researches the general
principles that ought to underlie all legal systems, an intellectual task which
he derives not only from natural-law theory but also from the ultimately
humanist tradition of historico-legal research into the elements common to
all systems of law, referred to above. This doubtless explains why certain
principles are for Smith notably stable even if not strictly immutable.
Finally, he considers justice an essential part of ethical behaviour, while
appreciating that even if utility is not the basis of just activity,[41] regard must
still be had to 'expediency' in the administration of public matters.

3.4. THE SCOTTISH ENVIRONMENT

From the sixteenth century onwards English society evinces signs of a
natural-law approach in areas of economic activity. Free commerce was

---

[39] This is the definition given by J. Millar in Stewart (1980), i. 18–20 (author's italics).
[40] *LJ* (A) i. 1; (B) 5. Cf. the introductory remark by the editors of *LJ* on the great significance of
this term for Smith, wide enough to include the third and fourth parts of the moral-philosophy
course, i.e. justice in the true sense, but also 'police, revenue, arms' (*LJ*, 'Introduction', 4).
[41] Notoriously distinct from Hume on this point; Raphael (1973), 88.

man's natural right, and like its corollary, the right to property, one tending to promote the general good. Roman law, however, was not received into the system at all. In this, Scotland was very different. There Roman law made great inroads by way of the canon law, which had profound influence from the thirteenth and fourteenth centuries onwards. This influence was felt even in procedural matters, for the ecclesiastical courts offered a better guarantee of competence. The result was that civil procedure too came under Church law's shadow, and to this day bears the mark.[42] The Church, furthermore, had a wider jurisdiction, and therefore a wider and more systematic influence. The majority of texts held by Aberdeen and Glasgow cathedrals in the fourteenth century were texts on canon law, *Decretum* and *Decretalia*, as opposed to the more slender presence of the civilian tradition, represented by the Code and Digest.

From before the foundation of the Scottish universities in the fifteenth century, young men had been sent to study in Europe, particularly in France and Germany; after the protestant reformation the general preference was for the Netherlands. At the end of the fifteenth century a law required all substantial freeholders to educate their eldest sons in Latin and law, and during the sixteenth it was normal and regular practice for Scots lawyers to resort to Roman law. In 1567 canon law was abolished in Scotland, and with it, in theory, the civil law, or at any rate that part of it that was contrary to the protestant religion; but in practice it suffered no such fate, and its influence remained great.

In those countries which had received it, Roman law's great value was the subsidiary role it played in practical jurisdiction. When a given legal dispute was not resolved by any precedent or provision of local statute or customary law, recourse was had to Roman law.[43] In Scotland this was done in a wholesale fashion, local law being frequently inadequate, and the civilian code was accordingly often applied to local circumstances. The sparse system of indigenous law encouraged the historical approach that was impeded in England by the only organically evolved framework of national law in Europe. The habit of studying abroad, furthermore, allowed the absorption of Roman law to complement feudal, and gave Scottish students' historical outlook a European dimension.

There was clearly, therefore, a great deal of civilian influence on Scottish law, a subject that has been amply treated by Peter Stein, and which we need give only in outline here. Areas of particular influence include the wardship of minors, property, succession, and contract. In the case of wardship, Scots law retains the classical distinctions between pupils and minors and between tutors and curators, as well as the methods of appointment (by will or by

---

[42] The text is a brief résumé of Stein (1957*b* and 1968*b*) and Campbell (1962). See also Pocock (1957), 88 f. [43] Coing (1979), 30.

law) and the rules of administration of wards' goods. Property in land was governed by feudal law, but where this failed Roman law, as always, stepped in, especially where questions of praedial servitudes or usufruct were concerned. For moveable property Roman law was applied more widely, as well as for acquisition by means of *occupatio, accessio,* or *traditio.* The distinction between Roman and feudal law with regard to property was reflected in the rules of succession: real property was governed by the latter for inheritance purposes, personal chiefly by the former. Roman law's most profound influence was felt in the area of contract and quasi-contract (lease, sale, guarantee, etc.), both in general terms and in the detail of the provisions.[44] This degree of Roman presence in a national system was not, of course, unique to Scotland. Even after the great codifications of European national law, 'Roman law did live on in the codes themselves, since these took their systematic and conceptual framework from it and also many principles and rules, especially in the fields of contract, succession and testamentary disposition';[45] so even when its formal authority was a thing of the past, its influence remained.

The eighteenth century saw a decisive turn taken in the study of the law. The early part of the century was dominated by the work of James Dalrymple, Lord Stair, on the concept of natural law. Inspired by a fundamentally practical approach, Stair realized that Grotius' rationalist rigour, his 'mathematicization' of law, was excessive, and that the law, though founded on reason, cannot be constructed entirely by pure logic; authority must play a part too. He also held that, though respect was due to religion, jurisprudence needed to be independent of theological presuppositions. Onto this original and influential theory was grafted, in the middle of the century, the noteworthy impact made in Scotland by Montesquieu, whose work—as is well known—marks the watershed between the concepts of law as reason, and law as a creation of social circumstances.[46] In the decade following the publication of *L'Esprit des Lois*, academic attention centred on one of the factors conditioning man's social conduct, namely his means of subsistence.[47] The French thinker's influence was particularly strong on a group of Scottish students;[48] among them we will briefly consider Henry Home, Lord Kames, under whose patronage Smith was to start his teaching career. Kames was opposed to an excessively rigid adherence to authority, especially where supine acquiescence of this sort impeded the understanding of the principles behind earlier decisions. His defence of reason was, however, far from a return to natural

---

[44] Stein (1957*b*), 158 f.; cf. also Stein (1968*b*) and Campbell (1962) on the relationship between Roman and Scots law.
[45] Coing (1979), 36.   [46] The text here is a brief résumé of Stein (1957*a*), 3–8.
[47] Stein (1980), 18–19.
[48] In particular Dalrymple and Kames; but Hume, Smith, John Millar, and William Robertson should also be recalled: Stein (1980), 23 f.; (1957*a*), 8–9, 15.

law. For Kames, a rational study of the law could only be built on historical foundations, and history meant 'systematic analysis, comparison, and explanation', not merely antiquarianism. Apart from this vision of a truly comparative study, his approach was in part philosophical and psychological. The law should be studied historically from the earliest rudimentary systems used by savage peoples, and by way of its successive evolutions, up to the great advances of more civilized times. It is a theory that not only betrays the influence of Montesquieu in the emphasis it places on the connection between laws and economic and social circumstances, but also prefigures the stadial theory that was to have such importance in Smith's thought.[49]

Smith's contribution to jurisprudence 'was to combine the sociology of Montesquieu with the historicism of Kames'.[50] The law, for him, was an aspect of human history, and as such should be studied without aprioristic presuppositions. It should not be imagined, however, that he wholly rejected natural-law theory, as is shown by his well-known statement that that of Grotius was the best attempt made so far to find natural rules of justice independently of positive law. His two criticisms of natural-law theorists were that they made excessive use of Roman law (instead of using all legal systems as the sources for their general principles); and that they made no precise distinction between law and morality, and accordingly sought to impose precise, casuistic rules on what really came within the provinces of feeling or sentiment—the judgement of which requires close attention to the circumstances. Smith, in short, was more realistic about the law, taking a precise historical approach, with a marked emphasis on social and economic factors. He drew on Roman, English, and Scottish law for examples in his treatment of the topic, but he was able to put each of them into its correct historical context before comparing them. He is regarded as one of the main members of the Scottish school of juridical thinkers who, by way of an anti-rationalist, sociological, and flexible interpretation of law, had already challenged the rationalist European idea of natural law.[51]

3.5. ADAM SMITH'S PHILOSOPHY AND HISTORY OF LAW

For Adam Smith, 'the most important branch of political science is that which has for its object to ascertain the *philosophical principles of jurisprudence*'.[52] His view of justice was fundamentally anti-utilitarian. Despite his

[49] Stein (1957a), 10-11; (1980), 25-7. The first to publish a version of the stadial theory relating to subsistence were, however, Dalrymple and Kames: Meek (1971), 14–16 ld. (1976b), 99–107; Stein (1957), 8–15; ld. (1980), 23–9.

[50] Stein (1957a), 12. The 'Anderson Notes', roughly datable to the early 1750s, contain a notable quantity of references to Montesquieu, showing that Smith was already heavily under that influence; Meek (1976a), 465.

[51] Cf. Stein (1957a), 15–20; Bittermann (1940), 506.

[52] Stewart (1980), iv. 5; my italics.

recognition of the obvious fact that justice is 'useful' to society, he did not regard it as founded upon a consideration of this usefulness, but rather on the universal human instinct to detest criminals and wish to see them punished.[53] One consequence of this view is that justice assumes a negative character, at least in Smith's surviving work on the subject. The point of departure is the punishment of unjust acts or, in legal terms, the criminal law; and in psychological terms, the resentment that, in certain conditions and with regard to the circumstances, leads to approval of the reasonable punishment of the offender. Individual practice of justice, then, is limited to avoiding doing harm to one's neighbour: of Ulpian's three-part definition Smith seems most sensitive to the second element, *alterum non laedere*. The fundamental characteristic of justice in the social context, however, is that it can be applied with force. Smith's enquiry is therefore directed towards reconstructing the way in which a system of criminal law is initially imposed.[54] Further, as has been pointed out by a recent student of the topic, the link between Smith's moral and juridical thinking is to be sought in his concept of rights, but this too derives from his negative concept, injury: justice is violated when a person is deprived of that to which he has a right.[55]

Leaving aside this negative definition, however, what one might term the originating elements of the human desire for justice imply very little new that has not been encountered in Smith's moral thought. As has been pointed out, the principle of sympathy lies at the root of his theory of property, and an analogy can be drawn between the impartial spectator and the figure of the judge. The anti-rationalist nature of Smith's jurisprudential thought, furthermore, stands out from the fact that he regarded the law as a human phenomenon,[56] chiefly conventional in character and liable to evolve, by virtue of its fundamental links with the social circumstances. This set him apart from natural-law theorists on the foundations of such matters as contracts, acquisition of property by accession or succession, or wrongdoing.[57] Also essential to his approach is his anti-apriorism, his close attention to experience, which for him corresponds to 'nature': 'What is natural for a society is decided by the stage of development that that society has reached'.[58] This empiricism, however, does not mean that Smith neglects natural law. His starting-point, in fact, is that of Grotius; only later does he abandon that view.

---

[53] *TMS* II. ii. 3. 9. Of the several studies that have pointed out the anti-utilitarian nature of Smith's theory, I cite here only Raphael (1973), 95, and Haakonssen (1981), 87 f. On the extent to which Smith distanced himself from the natural-law theorists on this point see Stein (1979*a*), 635; (1979*b*), 268.

[54] Raphael (1973), 93–8; Giuliani (1954), 538. The negative character of Smith's jurisprudence has been noted by, among others, Bagolini (1967), 118–19, adding that Smith did not tackle the question of the genesis of the unjust act.

[55] Haakonssen (1981), 99–100.

[56] Giuliani (1954), 511, 522, 525; Haakonssen (1981), 137.

[57] Stein (1979*a*), 634–6.   [58] Stein (1980), 45.

A matter of fundamental importance for the theory of natural law, for which it was the basis of a model of legal development,[59] was the law of property. Natural-law theory, as is well known, allowed man a natural right to own property. Along with freedom, to which it was indissolubly linked, this right was considered fundamental.[60] Smith, on the other hand, regarded freedom as a fundamental right, but property as an acquired one. A brief outline of the significance of the concept of property in the culture of that time would not, perhaps, go amiss.

In Britain the tradition of 'civic humanism' had kept alive the Aristotelian view, coloured by other classical motifs (in particular Polybius' theory of the mixed constitution), that the autonomy of the individual's participation in public life was guaranteed by his ownership of property, especially in land. Accordingly, the most important part of politics was the relationship between the State and property: 'the claim to freedom of property was one of the claims to freedom that the individual made against the state'.[61] Recipro-cally, his ownership of property made him free of political dependence on others and on the government itself.[62]

Another classical motif also derived from Aristotle, originating in his defence of property against Plato's attack on it: the view that property is the only stimulus to care for and produce goods. This concept was taken up by the Church Fathers, and thus became, by way of the coming together of medieval theories of economics and politics with Roman law, on the latter's already described reception, the distant ancestor of *laissez-faire*.[63] The concept of property was thus inextricably linked with the principles of ethics and politics, as well as firm economic initiatives, and bound up with a whole range of considerations that were relevant not merely to the law, but more generally to man's place in society.

Smith's theory of justice preserves its essentially negative character even in regard to the law of property. The purpose of this, as he sees it, is to prevent the property to which the individual has a right from being taken away from him.[64] Civil government is instituted for the defence of property; to defend, in his effective (and only seemingly paradoxical) formulation, the rich from the poor. The poor, if not held in check by the law, would not

---

[59] Or rather, a means of getting closer to the creation of a model of legal development; Stein (1980), 25. [60] Bagolini (1967), 121.

[61] Fassò (1968), 219; cf. also Corsano (1948), 258.

[62] Pocock (1968), 179–83; cf. Winch (1979), 175.

[63] Viner (1960), 48–51. Viner sees in the Aristotelian concept of man as a political animal 'the keystone later of the case for laissez faire on the basis of a natural harmony of interests between individual and community' (48). See also Michels (1932), 99–100. This can be accepted on a very general level, but as regards Smith, in the light of his characteristic phrase by which egoist instincts are associated with beneficial results, I consider much more likely a Stoic derivation from the well-known principle of coincidence between individual and social interests.

[64] For Smith the concept of justice covers both natural and acquired rights: Haakonssen (1981), 102. The latter, as already stated, include property.

permit the rich to preserve their greater wealth intact, but would resort to violence to wrest it from them. He concludes that the aim of laws and government is to manage things so that the poor man either stays poor or, if he wishes to become rich, must do as the rich have done: work.[65] Smith thus belongs to the large group of thinkers for whom the right of each man to own property is founded upon his right over his own work.

The philosophical influences on Smith's theory are many and diverse, but there are also personal interpretations. He deploys his deep familiarity with the sources of, and historical background to, the law in support of the theory of evolutionary stages, in which is incorporated the history of institutions. It has been observed that with regard to property Smith begins to distance himself from the natural-law theorists, who sought to reduce this branch of the law to principles that would be applicable in every society; for him, the phenomenon of property was different at different socio-economic points, both in its fundamental characteristics and in terms of the methods of acquisition. These divergent outlooks have been shown up by the work of Peter Stein, which has also emphasized Smith's treatment of the history of Roman law, which he appreciated both for its fierce mode of argumentation and for the fine example it offered of an evolving system, stretching from the Twelve Tables to the legislation of the republic, principate, and late empire; a system that could be placed in historical context thanks to the rich volume of information about ancient society provided by the non-legal classical sources. The other body of law that was open to similar treatment, in other words to the design of measuring 'the changes in law and government', was the English common law. Accordingly, it was these two legal systems that Smith made particular use of when tracing in detail the development of specific institutions.[66]

In the course of his lectures Smith frequently offers a 'genetic' account of institutional evolution. Here too one can discern how everything turns on the concept of property. Laws and governments arise when society evolves in such a way as to make people feel the lack of them. As long as there are no occasions for dispute, the juridical machinery for resolving them is absent. For example, in the earliest economic state, when men were hunters, the lack of private property meant that there was no occasion for government, laws, judges, or tribunals to develop. In the pastoral state, property began to be defined, and with it developed not only political activity in the true sense but

---

[65] *WN* v. i. b. 12; *LJ* (A) iv. 22–3. At the latter place Smith does not specify how the rich acquire their wealth, but at *WN* v. i. b. 2 he tersely notes that great properties are obtained 'by the labour of many years, or perhaps of many successive generations'. His argument is in any case clear: it is wrong to acquire wealth by forcefully depriving other rightful owners of their property. This position explains his opposition to movements for agrarian reform and land redistribution in antiquity: see below, n. 99, and Ch. 2 above.

[66] Stein (1979*a*), 627–34, with n. 47; (1979*b*), 266–7; (1980), 33–43, where it is noted that the English system, which took less from Roman law than any other, was felt by Smith to be the closest to nature.

also laws to protect the property itself. One cannot speak at this point, of course, of a true legislative capacity, or of formal legislation worth the name: the range of circumstances in which disputes arose was somewhat simplified, given the far from diverse nature of 'business' carried on by such societies. There is only a form of conventional agreement in regard to property; but there is still relatively little space for private law, and the bulk of legal attention is directed towards criminal cases.

Smith did not, however, share Grotius' view that public utility is the motive for punishing crimes; the appropriate punishment for all crimes, whether committed against natural rights (homicide, calumny) or acquired ones (theft, extortion, robbery, etc.) is that approved by the sympathy felt by the impartial spectator for the resentment of the victim. But, since society is initially more conscious of itself as a collective unit than as a gathering of individuals, and since government, on the other hand, when newly established is too weak to take up firm positions on private matters, no provision is made for matters of private law, however serious.

It could be said that the character of justice at the outset is that of society's measures for its self-defence. With the passage of time, as peace, order, and tranquillity are achieved in social affairs, penalties are progressively softened, gradually arriving at the appropriate level or 'proper pitch', that is to say to propriety as reflected in the victim's reaction and the impartial spectator's resulting sympathy. This evolution is exemplified by the clear difference between the laws of the Twelve Tables, which date to a transitional period between pecuniary compensation and the very harsh penalties of the 'secondary state' of justice, characterized by the *lex talionis* and the death penalty even for minor offences, and those of the praetorian edict, which replaced the severest punishments with lighter and more equitable ones. A similar progression can be seen in the case of Athenian law, passing from the provisions of Draco to those of Solon.[67]

The pastoral stage of social development sees the formation of the 'leader' figure, usually the richest individual—a context in which Smith's use of Homer and Tacitus' *Germania* has received due attention.[68] But it is only in the third stage, with the development of property in land and the resulting distinction between those who possess means of sustenance and those who do not, that courts are created and a true concept of law grows up. In the fourth stage, when by accumulating produce and selling or exchanging it society has acquired a commercial character, the law broadens its scope, becoming more complex and more articulate. Smith's vision of this process likewise widens out at this stage. Embracing more than just the classical evolutionary model of government (monarchy–aristocracy–government) and the model of military development from the citizen army to the mercenary one (a less clearly

---

[67] What has been summarized here is principally drawn from *LJ* (A) ii. 89–95; 152–5; iv. 25–7; *LJ* (B) 182–4; 194–7. [68] Stein (1979*b*), 265.

identifiable model but still largely originating in the classics and Machiavelli and Harrington), Smith's vision also encompasses the fall of the Roman empire and the beginning of a new cycle marked by the invading barbarians, still themselves at the hunter or pastoral stages.[69] The necessity of making laws 'to maintain justice and prevent infringements of the right of property' is for Smith the lynchpin of his whole treatment of rights.[70]

An element of great importance in the first group of lectures is the more evident presence of Smith's moral philosophy, perhaps due to the greater length at which he treats the subject. There is often a clear link with *TMS*, which had been published only a few years earlier; and more than once explicit reference is made to it. The genetic account he gives of the progress of the legal *mentalité* is therefore given a philosophical tint, and it should be pointed out that Smith retraces each of the institutions that he mentions back to an origin in a specific human psychological characteristic. This brings him not infrequently into disagreement with the natural-law theorists, for all that he admires their work. For example, as has been pointed out, Smith opposes Grotius' thesis that criminal acts should be punished according to their degree of intentionality, objecting that no positive law treats with equal severity successful and attempted murder. This point supports instead his own theory that punishment is measured according to the resentment of the injured party.[71]

Again, in the matter of intestate succession, the natural-law theorists regarded this as regulated by law to give effect to the supposed wishes of the deceased. Smith objects that if that were so, succession at law should have developed after testamentary succession;[72] but the contrary is the case. Another explanation is needed; the one offered by Smith has shades of Locke, arguing that the law's design, far from paying homage to the presumed will of the deceased, is that his kin, having contributed their labour to the estate, should accordingly come into possession of it.[73] As for the

---

[69] A change in the property regime involves a political and, for that matter, a legal change: Stein (1980), 33–8. For these aspects of Smith's thought, and the classical influences that can be discerned in them, see Vivenza *et al.* (1980), 19, 37 f. On the changes in military matters see particularly Winch (1979), ch. 5.

[70] *LJ* (A) i. 35. Here Smith differs from ancient thinkers, who held that the more laws a republic had the more corrupt or degenerate it was: Viner (1960), 49.

[71] *LJ* (A) ii. 174–7; see above in the text, on Smith's different approach to crime from that of Grotius. Eckstein (1927), 381–3, rightly notes that the 'irregularity of sentiment' to which Smith ascribes man's tendency to judge actions not only by their intention but by their results (see above, Ch. 2.11) is also responsible for the juridical phenomenon referred to, namely that in all legal systems the penalties for attempted crimes are less harsh than those for crimes successfully perpetrated. Smith's way of phrasing his philosophy is thus of some importance, inasmuch as it marks how far removed he is in moral philosophy from the Stoic position, and in jurisprudence from the natural-law one.

[72] Because only thus would the need have been felt to secure by law what had not been successfully secured by the deceased's expression of his will; otherwise his supposed will would have been of no great weight. *LJ* (A) i. 90–2.

[73] Consistent with Smith's affirmation of man's right to the fruits of his own labour: Haakonssen (1981), 106, 110.

obligation to respect the later provision for succession by testament, this arises from man's sense of sympathy (albeit evanescent) for the deceased.[74]

Likewise, Smith does not derive the binding nature of contracts from the obligation of veracity, as was done by Grotius and Pufendorf, but from another moral duty; that of not disappointing the expectation created in the party that would be deceived by improper behaviour. This duty is ever present even if the resentment of the injured party will vary in intensity according to the gravity of the broken promise.[75] Finally, he locates the foundation of the law of property and ownership in sympathy; the impartial spectator will disapprove of anyone who seeks to take from someone else what is theirs.[76]

Certain aspects of Smith's jurisprudential thought thus derive directly from his moral philosophy. These aspects, furthermore, like his theory of institutions, also reflect his evolutionist concept not only of concrete political and juridical forms, but of the 'sentiments' that underlie these. For example, the sentiment of sympathy towards the deceased, referred to above, is 'a pitch of humanity, a refinement on it' (*LJ* (A) i. 151) that one cannot expect to find in the case of primitive peoples but only among those that have already made substantial progress. In conformity with this, testaments are quite a late introduction in the legal scheme of things, succession being regulated by other means previously.

As this section makes clear, the well-known elements of Smith's ethics are at the basis of his interpretation of justice and the laws that punish its transgression: solidarity with the victim's resentment, the impartial spectator, and the greater moral significance of the results of an act rather than the intention behind it. The canons by which judgment is made, however, vary according to the social situation. It is to this aspect of Smith's theory that we owe the various interesting discussions of long-forgotten ancient laws that he adduces as examples and 'explains' in terms of the criteria for, or better, the origins of or reasons for, their being formulated as they were. Social and juridical institutions, as much as political ones, are to be seen as the natural result of man's relationship with his environment, a changing relationship in which the crucial factor is that of economics.[77] Specific institutions that are overtaken by history end up as obstacles or restraints acting against natural liberty, a term which does not signify the absence of institutional restraints, but rather that the restraints should be of a sort to allow people to behave freely in a way fitting each specific stage of development.[78]

---

[74] *TMS* I. i. 1. 13; II. i. 2. 5; *LJ* (A) i. 154, 164; (B) 165; 'AN' 468.

[75] *LJ* (A) ii. 56–62; (B) 175–6. See Stein (1979*a*), 634; (1979*b*), 267; (1980), 39–40.

[76] *LJ* (A) i. 35–8; (B) 150–1.

[77] 'Adam Smith saw economic problems as problems of justice and therefore as problems of law': Cooke (1935), 332.

[78] The text here is a résumé of Stein (1980), 45–6; but see also Skinner (1974*b*), 79; Rosenberg (1979), 25.

In sum, Smith, like other members of the 'Scottish' group, goes beyond the humanist identification of property and civil personality by applying a historical scheme of modes of production through which humanity progresses by gradually increasing specialization and the division of labour. This approach results in the historicization not only of the concept of property but also of that of social personality: a view of the way man's political and social attitudes and needs, and indeed his intellectual capacities, change according to his surroundings. That this can on occasions have negative consequences (as, for instance, in the case of Smith's treatment of the division of labour) is due to the endurance of the humanist ideal, deriving ultimately from Aristotle, of the citizen as a participant in all positive social activities.[79]

3.6. BIRTH OF THE POWERS OF THE STATE IN ANCIENT SOCIETIES

As Smith saw it, then, institutions arise from the nature of property in society. This view exemplifies another characteristic aspect of his thought, not so far examined. As was pointed out by N. Rosenberg,[80] in the genetic account of judicial activity referred to above, this activity is itself the result of a certain form of division of labour. The progress of society, with its ever more complex ways of defining various forms of property and the agreements relating thereto, invariably brings with it an increase in disputes and conflicts. If these are not to remain unresolved, an individual or group must be appointed to sort them out. This also applies in the political arena (the two not always being clearly distinguished in Smith's account): when affairs of state become excessively onerous, the whole population is no longer convened in the earlier manner,[81] and executive and judicial functions are delegated to a body, which might coincide with the one selected to resolve disputes, or be distinct from it.[82] This act of delegation too substantially derives from a type of specialization: when there has arisen a mass of political business that would require more time than the citizen body as a

---

[79] Pocock (1968), 188–9: 'But it is of the highest significance that all the leaders of Scottish local science employed the humanist concept of personality's integrity as a normative control upon their scheme of historical development, and employed it on the whole pessimistically. In the three I have named—in Ferguson and Millar particularly, since few of Smith's teachings upon the point have survived—we find the idea that once a certain point in social specialisation has been passed, the personality begins to suffer, since its capacity to participate in social pursuits is now being impoverished'. The concept is probably also present in Smith, in his much-debated 'double interpretation' of the division of labour.

[80] Rosenberg (1976). It is interesting to note that Plato, advocate of a differently organized division of labour (see below, Ch. 4), asserts the appropriateness of specialization among high positions within the State; only thus will they be filled well.

[81] The whole people constituted the assembly by which executive power was exercised, under the leadership of the most valiant (*LJ* (A) iv. 14 (citing Tacitus as the source). (Cf. also, ib. 23–4).

[82] *LJ* (A) iv. 17–18. On Smith's view of the development of governmental forms and the powers of the state see Haakonssen (1981), 159 f., 219 n. 53.

whole, with the requirements of work, can allot to the task, it is more convenient to hand it over to a collection of individuals without other duties.

As was stated above, it was the pastoral stage that saw the rise of property, the beginnings of political activity, with the principal aim of conserving economic inequality in favour of the rich, and the appearance, if not of laws in the true sense, of property agreements. At first, government is fully democratic, and decisions of all sorts, especially on public matters, are made by the whole popular assembly. Later, however, when the authority of an individual has been established over the other members of the body, as well as over the 'councils' or judicial courts that have in the meantime grown up, and it has been made hereditary by man's natural desire to seek continuity through his sons, a form of government evolves in which executive and judicial power are exercised together by the monarch and the popular assembly. Judicial power itself transforms gradually from the simple friendly intervention of a third party, endowed with influence but no legal authority over the other two, into the power to decide issues submitted for the purpose, and to apply some mild form of punishment.[83] Legislation as such comes about later: 'Written and formall laws are a very great refinement of government, and such as we never meet with but in the latest periods of it' (*LJ* (A) iv. 35).

The pastoral age also gives Smith a chance to analyse political forms in relation to territory. Not yet sedentary in their habits, and lacking any *amor patriae*, the shepherds moved with ease from one area to the next in search of better pasture.[84] His main example is that of the Tatars, shepherds par excellence, with whom (on the basis of Herodotus and Justin) he compares various ancient peoples such as the Medes and Persians, the Thessalians, the Scyths, and the Parthians. These were peoples who readily banded together under a single leader, in response to the harsh country they lived in. The exceptions were the Scyths and Thessalians, and here Smith avers that it was precisely their lack of unity that prevented them from conquering all of Asia. Clearly what they missed was a leader; the Persians, who did not, were thus able to found an empire.[85]

The passage from nomadism to settlement takes place when a leader manages to assemble a range of tribes around himself. This may happen initially for warlike purposes,[86] but later on the aim is that of occupying a more comfortable territory. So it was with the Greeks, whose earliest captains of war (the Heraclids, Theseus, and—in a sense—the Homeric heroes) behaved no differently from the Tatars: their peoples were at the pastoral stage of development; the sources record their various migrations

---

[83] See, respectively, *LJ* (A) iv. 10–18, 31–5; (B) 23–4; *WN* v. i. b. 24.

[84] *LJ* (A) iv. 47–50. The examples furnished by the classical texts are the Elvezi, Cimbri, Teutons, and Germans; but invading barbarians are also found (*LJ* (A) iv. 114).

[85] *LJ* (A) iv. 53–4.

[86] Thus in the cases of Agamemnon (*LJ* (A) iv. 38) and Theseus (see the next note and the relevant passage in the text). The sequence clan–village–state is also outlined at 'AN' 47.

from one area to another; and even their disputes arose not over conquest but rather over booty, as evidenced by Homer. Attica turned out to be a suitable area from a defensive point of view; but the sea could still deliver a surprise, and Theseus, the founder of Athens, accordingly built a place where the various tribes and their flocks could find safety. This move diminished each tribal leader's authority in favour of that of Theseus, which assumed a monarchic form. At this early stage, however, there was not the financial support for lasting absolute power; the wealth held by the leader was not sufficiently greater than that of the other powerful lords, and after the dynastic vicissitudes of the monarchy Athens changed her form of government, and the series of archons began.[87]

It is interesting to note that Smith calls this new form of government 'democratic' because the whole legislative function and parts of the other two were vested in the 'general assembly'; but he points out that the participants, with great reason, called it 'aristocratic'; it was the *aristoi*, the men of power and authority, who had decisive influence over the populace.[88] Law-making, the choice of magistrates, and the declaration of war, however, remained the prerogative of the people.

The process described above (the two-hundred-year passage from Homeric kingship to this brand of aristocracy) was also undergone by other Greek city-states, and is characteristic of many other ancient peoples.[89] Among these pre-eminence naturally goes to the Romans, for all the significant distinctions necessary in discussing their case.[90] In discussing

---

[87] *LJ* (A) iv. 56–60; cf. 64–8; *LJ* (B) 32–3. Theseus' role in the beginning of Athenian history was already present in classical and Hellenistic rhetoric: Loraux and Vidal Naquet (1979), 182.

[88] *LJ* (A) iv. 60; cf. 67–8. More interesting still is the reference to 'republican monarchy', ibid. 149. In this connection it should be noted that the problem of getting to know Smith's use of terminology is a real brain-teaser, though not unique in this respect; Voltaire too used 'république' in a very elastic fashion, 'adaptable, it seems, to the widest range of possibilities' (Tortarolo (1983), 46–7). In *LJ* (A) iv. 60 and 67 the mode of government is termed aristocratic in name but democratic in fact, because power was with the people, though they entrusted it to the nobility (without any law compelling them to do so, according to *LJ* (A) iv. 67). The previous monarchic State was, in the case of the Greek world, 'a republican monarchy, that is, an aristocracy with a king at its head': *LJ* (A) iv. 149. This somewhat obscure phrase perhaps denotes a 'democracy', governed by a sovereign, and with the principal offices of state entrusted to aristocrats. In *LJ* (A) v. 44 Europe before the Roman conquest is described by Smith as 'republican' with the exception of Gaul and Spain, whose government was in part aristocratic; cf. ibid. iv. 71. The careless use of terms can perhaps be explained by Smith's observation that the ancients called democracies those governments in which the people had the same degree of access to the magistracies as the aristocracy did, something unknown in Smith's own day: *LJ* (A) iv. 68. He was accordingly inclined to consider democratic even those States where the popular assembly retained some power, such as legislative capacity or the right to decide questions of war and peace (ibid. 60, 67), inasmuch as, although the offices of state were filled by aristocrats, these were democratic forms not operating in his own time.

[89] The Germans and the greater part of the inhabitants of Europe (Gauls, Hispanic and Italic peoples) before the Roman conquest: *LJ* (A) v. 44.

[90] At *LJ* (A) iv. 72–95 Smith repeats and greatly amplifies his remarks at *LJ* (B) 35 f., examined in Vivenza *et al.* (1980). With reference to citizenship, Smith here adds that in Athens it conferred tax exemptions and was therefore sparingly granted: (A) iv. 92–3.

Roman legal history, Smith seems not to make any reference to the role of the *pontifices* in early legislation. He mentions instead the decemvirs as authors of the Twelve Tables, and indeed as tyrants; the praetor, both in regard to his edict and in more general terms in relation to fairer forms of law;[91] and, briefly and generically, the tribunals. Under the principate there were no important changes in the field of private law—'The private affairs of individualls continued to be decided in the same manner and in the same courts as before'—and although the emperor had gathered to himself all executive functions and most legislative ones 'right and wrong were as equitably determin'd as they ever had before' (*LJ* (A) iv. 97). Indeed one might say that there was an improvement: Smith maintains that new governments always make good law, it being their principal interest that the State is well run even in private matters.[92] The emperors, who needed to keep tight discipline, used the full weight of their authority to control elections and trials for offences against their own dignity, but in proceedings relating to private affairs justice was never better dispensed than under the cruellest sovereigns.[93]

The emperor thus combined within himself the various powers of the State: the executive; the legislative, which he had taken away from the comitia and given to the senate, a body which was in his control and always acted in accordance with his will (Smith finds it telling that in the reign of Augustus the prevalent mode of legislation was the *senatus consultum*);[94] and, finally, the judicial, likewise in the competence of the senate[95] and thus of the emperor himself. From the Antonine age, or perhaps later, laws were made by the emperors, under the name of *edicta* or *rescripta principum*; it is of these that the Code is chiefly made up. The provinces were better governed than they had been under the republic, on account of the closer control to which the activity of the governors was subject. The emperor, furthermore, had military power at his disposal to ensure that all his commands were carried out. As for the noblemen of the court, these might have led a precarious existence in Rome—to be precise, any opposition resulted in death—but if they lived at a distance they had peace and tranquillity. Rome thus presents a good example of the evolution of public law, from an initial experience of monarchy to a developed form of republican government by

[91] *LJ* (A) iv. 72; v. 57; (B) 36 (on the decemvirs). On the edict, *LJ* (A) i. 100; ii. 154; *LRBL* ii. 202. See also, on research into precedents in the practice of Roman law, *WN* v. i. f. 44, and Haakonssen (1981), 220 n. 61. The association between praetorian law and equity was already a matter of tradition: Arangio Ruiz (1937), 155, 159.

[92] *LJ* (A) iv. 98, with a reference to Caesar's intention of improving rather than altering the laws, which would seem an appreciation of his conduct had it been translated into reality.

[93] Domitian and Nero, named for the same reason at *LJ* (B) 45; cf. (A) iv. 98. See (A) iv. 107 for a reference to the improved provincial administration of the imperial period.

[94] Decrees of the senate with a significant role in the development of the law of succession: Arangio Ruiz (1937), 226.

[95] Whose power was not by original design judicial, but merely military recruitment, taxes, and the welfare of the State: thus *LJ* (A) iv. 106, cf. ibid. 17 and (B) 27.

means of senate and comitia, and thence to the wholly centralized power of a
system ruled by the imperial will.

This brings us to the question of crimes against the State, which Smith
illustrates in the Roman context with the offences of *perduellio*, *proditio*, and
laesa maiestas. These too evolved. The first two, originally consisting of an
attack upon the person of the ruler and the betrayal of the State into the
enemy's hands, were soon placed on the same level as each other and
considered more serious than that of *laesa maiestas*, which was constituted by
any affront to the State or the emperor.[96] Under the principate, however,
laesa maiestas too gradually acquired very serious connotations, even if the
act was a relatively trivial one such as defamation or an offensive gesture; as
in cases of high treason, the penalty was death, a fact which strikes Smith as
patently absurd.[97] But in monarchies the person of the sovereign is considered sacred, and nothing speaks more eloquently of the distinction in this
regard between the two basic political 'forms' than the different treatment
they accord to tyrannicide: in republics it is appreciated, as shown by the
great renown attained by Brutus, Timoleon, Harmodius, and Aristogiton;
while in monarchies there is no greater crime. In the former case, when a
tyrant or group of tyrants (such as the 'Thirty', or Pisistratus, or the
decemvirs) tramples on the republican liberties that embody popular
sovereignty, there is no other way to be rid of them than by suppressing
them; they are the traitors, in that they have violated the institutions of the
State. Monarchies, on the other hand, rely on the fact that whoever carries
out a function or bears arms for the sovereign (meaning in the absolutist case
the whole civil and military sides of the State apparatus) must be preserved
safe from all danger; this would not be the case if it were legitimate for
anyone to kill a person who represents the sovereign.[98] The different
evaluation made in republics and monarchies derives from the fact that
sovereignty resides in a different entity in each case. Smith is drawing a
comparison between the ancient world and the modern one, and the
different interpretation is a result of the different political structure, not the
fact that modern ways are 'better' than those of the ancients.[99] Tyrannicide
is today abhorred because it is the great monarchies that 'set the tone' for the
whole political mentality of Europe, including the small republics; while in
antiquity the opposite was the case, and in the ancient republics treason was
whatever offended the dignity of the people considered as a whole. Respect
for these republics was directed towards their institutions, not a specific

---

[96] *LJ* (A) v. 85. Mention is made of *perduellio* and *laesa maiestas* at 54–5.

[97] *LJ* (A) v. 85. *Crimen maiestatis* tended with time to absorb the other two, becoming a crime
against the State when the latter came to be represented by the emperor; Burdese (1966), 265,
270, 275; Arangio Ruiz (1937), 169, 243.

[98] *LJ* (A) v. 56–9; as long, however, as there are no excesses on the part of the sovereign. Cf.
ibid. 126–7, 133, and below, n. 104, with the relevant passage in the text.

[99] For an analogous suggestion relating to the fact that land distribution and remission of
debts are no longer requested see *LJ* (A) iii. 141.

person: Smith adduces the example of the Roman consuls, who were regarded more in terms of the office they held than as individuals. This, perhaps, helps to explain why treason is so much more easily discernible in a republic than in a monarchy.[100]

A specific aspect of Smith's 'historical' treatment is his account of the origin of laws. As soon as the concept of property was born, it will be recalled, it was necessary to create tribunals, or courts of justice; councils or assemblies whose whole function was to decide the questions arising from the disputes relating to property. They contained individuals on whom was bestowed the duty, and the authority, of passing judgment. But this type of authority, Smith states in commentary upon an ancient author,[101] is wholly intolerable to 'savage' peoples. On the other hand, once the notion of property is confirmed, a society cannot do without judges and tribunals. The problem was resolved by the devising of an instrument to control their activity and prevent abuses; this instrument was the law, which met the needs of the people; 'for when it is known in what manner he [sc. the judge] is to proceed the terror will be in a great measure removed'.[102]

This phrase contains two elements essential to Smith's thought on this topic: a 'psychologico-scientific' criterion of the sort already seen in his essays on natural philosophy (the idea that awareness and understanding of the action of a given force deprives it of its fearsomeness); and the somewhat 'defensive' nature of his juridical philosophy, taking the infraction of the law as its starting-point (in this case the presumed abuse by the judges of their authority and the consequent attempt to restrain the abuse by suitable means). In Smith's account, then, tribunals and courts came first, laws after; the power of the judges gave way to that of the legislators.

The view that 'savages' do not tolerate uncontrolled judicial authority does not prevent Smith from making his well-known statement that man is naturally disposed to respect authority. Of the two principles on which the State is founded, authority and utility,[103] the former is uppermost in monarchies, the latter in republics. But even in a monarchy, when the sovereign oversteps his position, behaving in an absurd and inappropriate fashion (Nero, Caligula, and Domitian being the customary examples), his subjects have the right to resist.[104]

---

[100] *LJ* (A) v. 54–60; cf. ibid. 122 and Haakonssen (1981), 127.

[101] Not Tacitus as Smith states, but Florus (cf. editorial note on *LJ* (A) v. 109). The tale of Varus is significant in Smith's eyes because it shows precisely the fact that the Germans could not tolerate the courts of justice. See also *LJ* (B) 92, and cf. Montesquieu (1964), xix. 2.

[102] *LJ* (A) v. 110. Smith relates that the peoples of Athens and Sparta requested legislation to govern the behaviour of their judges; an account that could perhaps be indirectly linked to the Aristotelian concept of the sovereignty of the law as a thing created to safeguard the liberty of the people and limit the power of their governors; *Pol.* 1292^{a}32–4. See on this Fassò (1966), i. 93, 131.

[103] *LJ* (A) v. 119–22; (B) 12–14. See Haakonssen (1981), 128–9. As is well known, Smith did not accept the contractual argument.

[104] *LJ* (A) v. 126, 133; (B) 94.

Smith's genetic account of the powers of the State, and the intimate association it draws between these and private property, might suggest that the earliest questions of law arose in the same connection; but in fact, as already stated, society's first punishments were directed against treason and cowardice, crimes with a public character. On the other hand, one should bear in mind the extremely close link between law and government (clearly apparent from the frequency with which Smith uses the two terms together), and the indissoluble bond joining both these with property: in eighteenth-century Great Britain only freeholders with a substantial property had the franchise; Adam Smith himself was unable to vote.[105] The power structure founded on the property–government–law nexus was therefore starkly visible to him, and, for all that property was in the humanist ideal a sign of the citizen's independence of government, he could not ignore the other side of the same coin: the citizens who were thus protected were precisely the ones who determined the course of public affairs. Property was not, therefore, an exclusively private matter; it had clear links with the State and therefore, in effect, with public law.

It is indeed true that, in a well-known passage opening with the elegant and terse quotation 'Wealth, as Mr. Hobbes says, is power' (*WN* I. v. 3), Smith distinguishes between power deriving from riches and political power in the true sense of the phrase, to the former of which he ascribes only the capacity of procuring the latter. This distinction, however, probably refers only to the attainment of specific positions, to which the rich man may or may not aspire. The other aspect of the question, familiar to modern historians, that is to say the fact that power (generally understood) resides with those groups that are characterized by a certain economic status, is not, I think, something that Smith fails to appreciate. On the contrary, it is a state of affairs he takes for granted and in substance approves of. Certainly with regard to ancient history his position is clear: in the classical 'republics' the right to vote was held by the whole citizen body, however mean and lowly their station. But, to dispel misunderstanding, Smith observes (probably with reference to the Roman system of *clientela*), that the mean and lowly were obliged to vote for the aristocrats who supported them. In other words, whatever the situation might have been in terms of rights, the effective result was not dissimilar, at least early on, from the reality of modern politics, where power is exclusively in the hands of the well-to-do. And as long as the system was maintained, everything went satisfactorily in the ancient world; it was only when the 'populace' acquired political weight that the disasters began.[106] It is but a short step from this account to the conclusion that the legal system which allowed this eventuality was a mistake; even though Smith does not make it explicitly, it is there to be understood in his treatment of the subject.

---

[105] Rosenberg (1979), 25.   [106] Vivenza *et al.* (1980), 22–31.

3.7. SMITH'S ANALYSIS OF ROMAN JURISPRUDENCE

Even a fleeting examination of Smith's *Lectures on Jurisprudence* reveals the great significance accorded to Roman law in his teaching. Not only was it a rich source of examples; it also gave him the chance, as we have already seen, to illustrate the evolution of a juridical system over time. Furthermore, its continuing presence in the Scots law of Smith's own day meant that his interest in it was not solely historical or antiquarian, but in the last resort had contemporary relevance.

In Smith's account, the evolution of the legal system and of the institutions within it is closely linked to and interdependent with the system of property holding, which constitutes an important and more or less direct relationship between the individual and economic good. Frequently it is in terms of this relationship, and not by recourse to 'natural reason', that Smith accounts for some specific aspect of the law as it stands or as it has evolved.

Smith's tendency to adduce economic factors as a structural mode of explaining the origin and spirit of specific parts of the law can be seen in his treatment of the law of succession. Here he invokes a bond between the heirs at law and the goods of the deceased rather than between the deceased himself and his close family circle. Similarly, in matrimonial law, the wife's relationship is plotted with regard to her husband's *patrimonium*, and to that of her own family. Even the development of *patria potestas* in Roman law is given the same treatment: the father's right to sell his son (already restricted by Numa to unmarried sons) and to take to himself anything earned by his son could not be extended to cover a son who had his own family, because that family would thereby be deprived of its means of support. The son owed his wife and his own issue (this too coming within the *potestas* of the grandfather) the benefit of his work. The right of sale, furthermore, is a corollary of the overarching right of life and death (*ius vitae et necis*), a very ancient right of the paterfamilias. Smith explains the origin of this right by an absence of obligation to bring up offspring, because no primitive people holds itself liable to support any persons who do not contribute to their own maintenance.

The origins of prescription, on the other hand, are discerned by Smith in the sympathetic participation of the impartial spectator in the plight of the person who has long made use of something that belongs to another, and has acquired an 'attachment' to it which the owner in title lacks;[107] here the emphasis is not only on the parts played by sentiment in the development of a legal concept, but also, once again, on the link between property and its possessor. This brings Smith to a further confutation of Grotius, who derives the right of prescription from the presumption of abandonment on

---

[107] *LJ* (A) i. 77. *Praescriptio* is treated ibid. 77–90; (B) 154–5. At (A) i. 26 he calls it 'Praescription or Usucapio'.

the part of the owner. Holding it improbable that anyone should consciously abandon their property, especially in land, Smith finds the only remaining explanation in the owner's ignorance of his rights. A lacuna in the manuscript at this point prevents a complete understanding of Smith's views of Cocceius' statement on this topic, but when the text recommences it does so with the realist observation, classical in origin, that 'The great benefit of prescription is that it cuts off numbers of disputes'.[108]

Smith's 'historical' reconstruction of the origins and development of testamentary practice is clearly debatable, in the light of what we now know, but this does not reduce its significance. He sees succession as founded not on an affectionate link—an aspect which came about later if at all—but rather on an economic one, namely the contribution that family members make to their own inheritance. From this arises the mode of succession that Smith considers the oldest: succession by descendants *ab intestato*. Later modes—succession by collaterals and ascendants—derive from the presumed wishes of the deceased.[109] In fact the compact structure of the Roman family found expression in a view of property that was based on the family rather than the individual. This was, in turn, reflected in the practice of succession which was characterized, at least at the outset, by the heirs living together. Only later did they move apart and thereby create separate family nuclei, the head of each one having the same powers as the deceased paterfamilias:[110] that is to say, in the current connection, absolute property rights over all family goods including those made or earned by family members under his control.[111] But as early as the Twelve Tables there developed a more individualist approach to property, becoming yet more individualist with the passage of time. As a result, many inroads were made into the powers of the paterfamilias over his family's property; these ranged from the *de facto* economic near independence of a son serving in the army (confirmed at the time of Caesar)[112] to the ever-increasing freedom of women, albeit only those in wardship, to possess and administer property on their own behalf (if necessary by means of a procurator)—a freedom that advanced most under the principate.[113]

Linked with the question of succession is that of 'domestic', or family, law. Smith's account of the position of women in the Roman world starts from an analysis of the rules of female-line succession there. These differed from the Scottish ones,[114] precisely because of the different position held by Roman wives, who had the status of a daughter and thus took a daughter's

---

[108] *LJ* (A) i. 86–7; cf. Dig. 41. 10. 5 *pr.*, though the term used there is *usucapio*.

[109] *LJ* (A) i. 103–4.   [110] Arangio Ruiz (1945), 426 f.

[111] Smith too speaks of it at *LJ* (A) i. 101; iii. 84; (B) 127.

[112] *LJ* (A) i. 101; (B) 129. In reality this measure dates to the time of Augustus, not Caesar (cf. editorial note ad loc.); but the matter is uncertain even for modern scholars, e.g. Bonfante (1925), i. 98.   [113] Bonfante (1925), 374.

[114] Similar in the matter of succession, apart from the wife's different position; *LJ* (A) i. 93–4; 110–11; (B) 158.

share of the inheritance.[115] The wife's subjection to the husband, exemplified by the fact that in ancient times he alone had the power to end the marriage by divorce, is explained by Smith as ultimately deriving from an economic factor: in the early days of Roman history dowries were small, and a wife had little opportunity to increase the patrimony of the family she had joined; this made her importance in the family correspondingly small and deprived her of any connection with its hereditable property. The later change in the position of women was due to the increase in the size of dowries, as well as to the fact that women generally enjoy better treatment in a rich and civilized nation such as Rome had by then become.[116]

Smith relates the evolution of Roman marriage from the ancient ceremonies of *confarreatio* and *coemptio*, the two sorts of marriage *in manu*, and the practices of marriage by *usus* and *deductio in domum*, up to the account given by Tacitus of the disuse of the ancient ceremony in the early principate.[117] The wife's kin, we are told, no longer accepted that her inheritance should irredeemably fall into her husband's hands, and it was found convenient for the husband merely to have administration of her property. In Smith's words, 'the husband, on consideration of such large summs of money as they might sometimes receive, gave up some parts of his authority'; in particular, an easier method of divorce was arranged, achieved by simple agreement of both parties.[118]

The resulting frequency of divorce led to a decline in morals which Smith illustrates by means of the four marriages of Cicero's daughter Tullia, thereby showing himself well read in the private lives of the great figures of the late republic.[119] But the ancient world had its own moralists, and from the time of the elder Cato onwards they were active in trying to limit the financial space that women had for movement; Smith cites the case of the tribune Oppius, who proposed a sumptuary law to suppress expenditure on luxury, and especially that by women. Later the *Lex Voconia* somehow prohibited rich men from naming women as their heirs.[120] This statute received some attention also from Montesquieu, who in a thoroughly classical and indeed almost Catonian manner treats moral corruption (in

---

[115] *LJ* (A) i. 94; iii. 6. The allusion is to the wife *in manu*, on which see Arangio Ruiz (1945), 434 f., 536.   [116] *LJ* (A) iii. 8; cf. also (B) 106–7.

[117] Tac. *Ann.* IV. 16. The *flamen dialis* had to be born *parentibus confarreatis*, but in Tacitus' day this type of marriage had fallen out of usage. See *LJ* (A) iii. 10, perhaps from Heineccius, i. 10. 9.

[118] *LJ* (A) i. 156–7; iii. 9–10. In reality it was necessary only that one party wanted it, as Smith himself states (iii. 9); see on this Arangio Ruiz (1945), 449–50.

[119] *LJ* (A) iii. 11.

[120] *LJ* (A) i. 157–9; cf. (B) 167. This law provided that those recorded in the census with an estate of more than 100,000 *asses* could not nominate a woman as their heir; Arangio Ruiz (1945), 533; Scialoja (1934), 209. The figure is given by Cassius Dio and was already known to Montesquieu; Smith, however, makes no mention of it and refers instead (unconvincingly) to a maximum bequest to a woman of one-quarter of the testator's wealth.

accordance with the motif of uncontrolled feminine luxury) as inseparable from wealth in the hands of women.[121] Smith's analysis, in contrast, is more accurate and quite modern in tone: by preventing women from having access to money, the *Lex Voconia* sought to put them back in their primitive state of subjection; since they were unable to acquire money other than by inheritance, its effect was to reduce the amount that they would be able to possess. The law must have applied also to intestate succession, Smith observes; otherwise it would have been the easiest thing in the world to evade it, namely by dying without making a will.[122]

Evasion was, however, made possible anyway by the *fidei commissum*,[123] by which the property was left to a friend who then made it over to the woman in question. As Smith points out, there were many instances of these 'trusts' not being respected, some recorded by Cicero;[124] but from the time of Augustus onwards they were held to be binding, with the result that the law was rendered entirely powerless.

The scandalous 'licence of divorce' that had arisen in the late republic continued unabated under the empire until a rescript of Valentinian and Theodosius allowed it only on certain conditions. Soon afterwards, however, Justinian restored the old approach.[125]

The economic and moral aspects of this historical episode are equally important. With regard to the former, Smith's reconstruction is broadly acceptable: the evolution of the institution of marriage and in particular the swift rise to pre-eminence of marriage *sine manu* and the development of measures to enable a woman to conjoin herself to a husband without falling under his *manus* (such as making sure that the period of continuous cohabitation necessary for *usus* to arise was not completed, a practice referred to by Smith more than once)[126] were brought about by the fact that the wife's agnates retained an interest in her patrimony.[127] Smith's account certainly emphasizes the importance of the dowry, although it does not deal with it in any detail; as

---

[121] Montesquieu (1964), xxvii (p. 721). It should be noted that, among the classical authors, at least Cicero was not favourably inclined to this regularly evaded piece of legislation, of which he wrote: *utilitatis virorum gratia rogata in mulieres plena est iniuriae* (*De Rep*. iii. 17; 'that law, passed for men's advantage, is full of injustice to women' (C. Walker Keyes's translation)).

[122] *LJ* (A) i. 158. On this point Smith is expressly opposed 'to the opinion of Perizonius and others'. This allows me to modify my doubts over whether Smith knew Perizonius or not; Vivenza *et al*. (1980), 58 n. 181. It needs to be added, however, that the latter's study of the *Lex Voconia* is mentioned several times by Heineccius, whom Smith certainly had recourse to.

[123] The obligation to preserve the object of a bequest and transmit it to a specified beneficiary; on testamentary *fidei commissa* in Roman law see Arangio Ruiz (1945), 573 f.

[124] *LJ* (A) i. 159–60. *Fidei commissa* of this sort were of course contrary to the *Lex Voconia*.

[125] *LJ* (A) iii. 10.

[126] *LJ* (A) i. 157; iii. 9; (B) 107. Like *confarreatio* and *coemptio*, *usus* was a form of matrimony *cum manu*, but prescribed a year of uninterrupted cohabitation. It became established that three consecutive nights spent away from home on the part of the wife were sufficient interruption, an expedient known as early as the Twelve Tables; Bonfante (1925), 53.

[127] Arangio Ruiz (1945), 435, 501.

he remarks (probably following Heineccius), it was precisely the presence of the dowry that distinguished between marriage and concubinage.[128]

Less typical is the account Smith gives of the immorality resulting from the frequency of divorce. It will be remembered that woman's complete subordination to her husband and her insignificant position within the family arose from the fact that her husband had every power over her, including the power to divorce her without justification.[129] Later, for economic reasons once more, the situation turned to the woman's advantage. The new form of marriage was worked out so that rich women, or rather the families into which they were born, could treat with their future husbands and negotiate the terms of the marriage settlement. This strengthened the woman's position, as indicated by the higher frequency of divorce. The moralist in Smith, however, perhaps harking back to Seneca and the other moralists of antiquity, could not accept this latter practice any more than he could appreciate the liberal fashions and modes of behaviour of the late republic and of the empire. On the other hand he could not accept the total subjection of the wife to her husband, arising from the fact that all the laws prejudicial to women—in regard not only to the legal nature of marriage but also, for instance, to the different treatment accorded male and female adultery—were, like all laws, made by men, by husbands with every interest in exercising as much legal domination over their wives as possible.[130] Analogously to this early Roman system, Smith notes, the barbarian populations that had invaded Europe at the time of the fall of the empire had also originally apportioned great legal power to the husband in respect of his wife;[131] but their approach had then been softened by the influence of the clergy who, themselves unable to marry, had regulated matrimonial matters with the impartiality of the uninvolved observer. It was also thanks to the clergy that marriage achieved its state of near indissolubility, and that equal rights were ensured in the extremely rare cases of divorce.[132] For Smith the

---

[128] *LJ* (A) i. 157; see Heineccius i. 10. 25; Arangio Ruiz (1945), 453.

[129] *LJ* (A) i. 110; 156; iii. 6; (B) 102; 'AN' 473 ('Of Divorce'). Smith's argument (which the loss of an entire page in the manuscript has rendered incomplete) seems based on the principle that the man alone had the power to divorce, on the grounds that he had all the other powers; it was simply not likely that a wife *in manu* (and thus in law *loco filiae*) could unshackle herself from her husband's burdensome guardianship by means of divorce (*LJ* (A) iii. 6–7; but cf. Heineccius' reference to Plutarch's *Life of Romulus*, which Smith too had perhaps seen). In reality a woman could, in the oldest Roman law, acquire a divorce only by the will of her husband or the paterfamilias in whose authority her husband was, or—if her marriage was *sine manu*—by that of the paterfamilias in whose authority she herself was; never, in short, on her own initiative as was later the case. See Bonfante (1925), 250–4.

[130] *LJ* (A) iii. 13, 16. An analogous point had been made about the slavery laws; ibid. iii. 102, 114; (B) 134.

[131] Similarly restricting the power of divorce to the husband; *LJ* (A) iii. 12–13. This exemplifies the 'cyclical' aspect of Smith's reconstruction; the invading barbarians were in a similar condition to that of the primitive Romans centuries before.

[132] *LJ* (A) iii. 16. In truth, the equal status of the sexes in respect of divorce is also of Roman origin, this principle being unknown to Judaic law on the matter: Basanoff (1936), iii. 180. This

best solution was clearly the one offered by Christian marriage, with its greater security and greater respectability for the wife, not to mention her more dignified position in economic terms.[133]

Smith's discussion of the regulation of contracts continually intermixes references to Roman law with other passages inspired by the Scottish and English systems and historical remarks on the development of each of these traditions. Thus *nuda pacta*, for instance, can be a basis for an action in Scottish law, but not in Roman; this difference, Smith explains, arises in part from the influence of religion, acting by way of canon law. Scottish courts, like those of many other European nations, were constituted at a time when both civil and canon law had strength enough to impose themselves; the latter of these, being based on principles of honour and virtue and therefore on the obligation resting on a good Christian to keep faith with his promises, did not take long (unlike the common law) to establish that every type of contract should be supported by a corresponding action at law.[134]

This form of historical evaluation of the influences of different types of legislation on a country's legal system leads Smith on to an observation regarding English law. England, where an indigenous system had grown up prior to the discovery of Justinian's *Pandects*, and where a framework of courts and the broad outline of legal procedure had been established before the institution of law courts in the rest of Europe, was beyond the reach of Roman law, and thus remained untouched by the influences of canon and civil law that operated on the legislation of other nations. Her system of law is therefore closer than any other to the 'naturall sentiments of mankind' and as such merits close academic attention. Central to this observation is not only its direct assimilation of natural law to English law (consequently necessitating a distinction between the former and Roman law) but its invitation to study English law as an example of the natural kind of jurisprudence.

The most interesting aspect of Smith's treatment of criminal law is his view that the evaluation of a crime is subject to changes throughout history. In relation to the obligations that arise from an offence, or 'delinquency', and specifically offences against private property, Smith notes that theft is punished in modern legislation much more severely than would be required

---

'new course' taken by marriage had, according to Smith, considerable effects on the sentiment of love, which acquired great significance in the modern world since it was bound up with the making of a choice for life. In the ancient world, where this choice was not irrevocable, it was considered a wholly negligible emotion. That is why classical literature, unlike its modern counterpart, has not provided any instances of tragedies based on love stories, other than that of Phaedra. Even verse works like the *Aeneid* or the *Iliad*, despite containing sentimental episodes, are not seriously influenced by the notion of romantic love. See *LJ* (A) iii. 20–2; cf. Stein (1979*b*), 269–70.

[133] *LJ* (A) i. 111; cf. 146. The wife now had a right to a third of her husband's personal estate; cf. ibid. 105. As to real estate, feudal law introduced the system of primogeniture which Smith regarded as contrary to nature, to reason, and to justice (ibid. 116). As at *WN* III. ii. 3, Smith's view was that a *natural* law of succession would divide land and other immoveable property between all the sons, as happened at Rome.

[134] *LJ* (A) ii. 72–4.

by resentment, because actions of this sort tend to arouse contempt rather than resentment in the true sense. One must conclude that in this connection Smith's personal preference was for Roman law, which condemned the thief to restore the value of the property stolen twice over or, if he was caught in the act, four times over,[135] rather than the modern law, of feudal origin, which often imposed the capital penalty.

The evaluation of resentment also comes into Smith's discussion of Montesquieu's interpretation of the *fur manifestus*. The harsher penalty imposed on flagrant acts of theft arises from the greater sense of resentment aroused by a thief caught in the act, and not from some supposed rule of Spartan origin designed to encourage (as Montesquieu had it) the development of skill in thieving, to which not being caught was obviously essential.[136]

One area where the difference between the modern evaluation of a crime and the ancient one is the opposite of that in the last case is the area of the 'minor' offences such as verbal insult, libel, and non-serious assault. The classical world did not treat these with great gravity, imposing only light penalties; Smith interprets the twenty-five *asses* which Gellius records as the established fine for *iniuria* under the Twelve Tables as two or three shillings.[137] As always he draws on ancient authors for passages that help his argument: the biting remarks made by Socrates to his interlocutors, for instance, are never presented by Plato as other than normal conversation; while Longinus, among his examples of the 'sublime', includes a passage of Demosthenes in which the orator details in full a beating suffered by his client[138]—proof positive that at that time it was not considered unseemly or disgraceful that a dishonour of that sort be recounted to all and sundry, when in Smith's own day it would have led to the client being heaped with ridicule and contempt. Here, however, Smith preferred the modern position. The inadequate penalizing of this sort of

---

[135] *LJ* (A) ii. 150, 158; (B) 195. Apart from theft, there was a form of damage to property which carried the death penalty among the Romans, the English, and the Scots alike, namely arson; *LJ* (A) ii. 145; (B) 194.

[136] *LJ* (A) ii. 150; see also (B) 195; 'AN' 472; and cf. Montesquieu (1964), xxix. 13. On Montesquieu's 'ingenious' interpretation, among the warlike skills the Spartans taught their youth was that of theft, which had to be performed with cunning and hence with stealth; and it was from this Spartan approach that Roman law derived its harsher punishment for those caught *in flagrante delicto*. Smith objects that the only evidence for this practice amongst the Spartans comes from Plutarch, not a convincing source in isolation, and that Roman customs neither tolerated nor encouraged theft, as shown by the fact that even when *nec manifestus* it was punished (if less severely).

[137] *LJ* (A) ii. 136. Smith states simply that: 'In the Roman law the penalty for such an injury was only about 2 or 3 shillings; and of the same little consequence was the recompense for all those injuries which would be reckoned the highest affronts', and goes on to say that if this did not lead to duelling in Rome, 'the different circumstances of the nations easily account for that'. Gellius (xx. 1. 12–13) tells of a deranged individual called Veratius who, always quick to lash out and slap those he met, took a slave with him ready to pay out 25 *asses* to injured parties. But Gellius' point (like Smith's) is that the penalty is clearly shown by the story to be too low, which fact led to the intervention of the praetor to give the offence a more suitable weight.

[138] *LJ* (A) ii. 138–9. The reference is wrong; in particular the violence was directed at Demosthenes himself (see editorial note ad loc.).

offence, evidently a relic of ancient indulgence, was to be held a *deficientia iuris*;
it was also responsible for the spread of the modern practice of duelling, a
response to the fact that the law does not provide satisfactory redress to the
injured party, who therefore seeks to obtain it himself.

A specific case of injury is that of criminal libel (defamation in writing),
for which the penalty is usually harsher where the wrong was committed
with malicious intention. Smith does not fail to point out that here too there
are notable differences according to the form of government, as shown once
again by Roman law: during the kingly and aristocratic regime of the
monarchy libellers were punished with death, as laid down by the Twelve
Tables; under the democracy the penalty was softened; but when monarchy
was brought back in by the principate the death penalty was re-established,
lasting from the age of Augustus and Tiberius to that of Valentinian.[139] It is
concluded that the liberty of a people can be judged by nothing so clearly as
by the penalty in place for that offence, tolerated by democracies but not by
despotic forms of government.

In regard to family relations, however, Smith notes a decline in the
strength of *patria potestas* allowed by Roman law to a man over his wife and
children, which he attributes to the concern of the relatives that those subject
to this power should not suffer excessively severe treatment.[140] However,
relations between husband and wife and between father and son, with their
gradual evolution from an initially harsh and rigorous approach to one of
ever-increasing fairness, did not constitute the entirety of Roman domestic
law. The third domestic relationship, that between master and slave,[141]
differs fundamentally from the others for the absence of any kind of check on
possible abuses of power by the paterfamilias, the slave thereby being left
completely at his mercy. Roman literary sources provide many cases of cruel
treatment of slaves, and there was no point in pretending that slaves had
affection for their masters; they were therefore constrained by discipline. To
compound the misery of their status, they were deprived of the right of
marriage and religious association.[142]

On the topic of slavery Smith makes two characteristic comments: first,
that slaves are accorded better conditions when the slave-owning society is
poor than when it is rich and cultivated; and, secondly, that the slaves'
well-being is in some way inversely proportionate to the degree of liberty

---

[139] *LJ* (A) ii. 143–4; cf. (B) 193.   [140] *LJ* (A) iii. 82–3.

[141] A tripartite division originating with Aristotle (*Pol.* 1253^{b}4–8) and transmitted to the
modern world by Aquinas: Camus (1979), 99. 'By considering slavery as an essentially domestic
relationship, Aristotle endowed it with the sanction of paternal authority, and helped to
establish a precedent that would govern discussions of political philosophers as late as the
eighteenth century': Davis (1966), 69.

[142] *LJ* (A) iii. 97–8, with the interesting observation (incorrect according to Bonfante (1925),
145–6) that ancient gods, in their tutelary role, did not look with equal favour on all, and that
the only slaves who could count on divine protection were those employed in temples. For the
legal status of slaves see *LJ* (A) iii. 89 f.; (B) 131 f.; 'AN' 475.

enjoyed by the citizens of the slave-owning society. The first of these observations clearly has its origins in the traditional motif of the poverty, frugality, and austerity of the earliest Romans,[143] who accordingly had very few slaves, whom they treated humanely; a motif that sits well with the fact that all the classical instances Smith provides of maltreatment of slaves come from the imperial age.[144] Furthermore, the great rise in the number of slaves under the principate brought about a reversal in the proportion of slaves to free, the former vastly outnumbering the latter. The result was that masters began to fear their slaves.[145]

This reconstruction appears to conflict with the second of the two comments referred to, according to which the condition of slaves under the absolute government of the principate was better than it had been during the 'free' republic. Here Smith makes use of an argument that he has already employed in relation to the condition of women: a democratic regime imparts legislative power to those who own slaves; therefore, given man's natural tendency to seek control over his fellow men, the greater the democratic liberty enjoyed by the citizenry, the less that of their slaves, and the worse their condition.[146] Now, bearing in mind that republican Rome is universally held to have been poorer than its imperial successor, there seems to exist here a contradiction between Smith's two approaches: the one just discussed, based on politics and ideology, and the economic one (the richer the slave owners, the worse the condition of the slaves). To pursue the schema *ad absurdum*, it would seem that slaves were badly off under the republic because of the freedom enjoyed by the citizenry, and that they were badly off under the principate because of the citizenry's wealth. To put the difficulty another way, Smith's examples from Roman history, drawn almost entirely from the imperial period, do not back up his claim that the loss of a people's liberty results in an improvement in the condition of their slaves. The only instance of intervention on behalf of the abused slaves (also cited in the *Lectures*) is that of Augustus' reaction to the cruelty of Vedius Pollio, a tale which evidently made some impression on Smith.[147]

As is well known, Smith ascribed two specific disadvantages to the institution of slavery: it was detrimental to the population as a whole; and the work it provided was not economically viable. As far as the first of these points

---

[143] *LJ* (A) iii. 109. The humanity of early slave owners is a motif also found in relation to other peoples such as the Germans: ibid. 106–7, 110. Cf. (B) 137 and 'AN' 475.

[144] With the sole exception of Cato's well-known advice that a slave who has become useless should be allowed to die; *LJ* (A) iii. 101; for the other instances see ibid. 92, 100, 103, 104; (B) 136. They are almost all taken from Hume, whose observations on slavery are of importance.

[145] *LJ* (A) iii. 106; (B) 136.

[146] *LJ* (A) iii. 103; 110–11; 114–15; 130; (B) 134–6. Smith's views of modern slavery are illustrated in Davis (1966), 433–5.

[147] *WN* iv. vii. b. 55; *LJ* (B) 135; (A) iii. 92–3. For the differences between *LJ* (A) and (B) see the 'Introduction' to *LJ*, p. 29 nn. 15 and 16. The episode of Vedius Pollio also appears in Bodin (1609), i. 5.

goes, Smith emphasizes that in the ancient world there was a general preference for sturdy male slaves, mainly imported from the East. Among the
evidence cited is the notorious story from Strabo of the 10,000 slaves sold at
Delos in one day. Few slaves indeed were born in the household, given the
great ease and cheapness with which new ones could be obtained from some
impoverished foreign country rather than brought up from infancy.[148] Few
female slaves were kept, furthermore; Demosthenes stated that his father left
fifty male slaves and two females,[149] as Smith records, without troubling to
wonder whether the orator's father, owner of a workshop producing weapons,
had need of women slaves.

In fact the major part of Smith's discussion of this topic is devoted to
modern slavery, and it can be held that the examples he draws from the
ancient world are there merely to confirm the general thrust of his argument.
He had, however, a general tendency to apply schematic interpretations to
different historical realities, and it is possible that he meant to include the
ancient world in his comments about how infants born to women in a state of
virtual prostitution, brought up in slavery, and maltreated from birth, were
highly liable to lose their health or die at a young age.[150]

Another aspect of slavery is its detrimental effects on free labour. In the
ancient world all labour was performed by slaves, the greater part of
agricultural produce being used for their upkeep,[151] and in the manufacturing sector they provided such damaging competition for free craftsmen that
the latter were reduced to economic ruin. The result was that all uprisings in
Greece or Rome were based upon a popular request for a new agrarian law
or the abolition of debts. Smith characteristically observes that there is in his
day no one so radical as to think of demanding such things. In explanation of
this fact he presents the evidence of the heavy debts that the lower classes
could fall into in antiquity,[152] constrained to sell what little they had and
watch as property and money all ended up in the hands of a few well-off

[148] Modern scholarship is not in agreement on this point; Finley (1959), 152; Treggiari
(1979), 188.
[149] *LJ* (A) iii. 131–2. The example from Demosthenes is wrong, as noted by the editors ad
loc.; all 52 slaves were male.
[150] For an argument of this sort, not referring necessarily to antiquity, see *LJ* (A) iii. 133. It
concludes with a generic discussion of the high rate of infant mortality, obviously highest
amongst the poor. There may perhaps be a link here with the pseudo-law of demography that
slave populations do not reproduce themselves; Finley (1959), 152.
[151] 'Five sixths of this was consumed by the slaves who cultivated it, so that here the greatest
part of the produce was bestow'd on the slaves'; *LJ* (A) iii. 140, cf. Vivenza (1990), 697 n. 33.
[152] *LJ* (A) iii. 140–4; cf. also 'AN' 476; *WN* IV. vii. a. 3; *LRBL* ii. 156–7. See Vivenza *et al.*
(1980), 22 f., for a brief discussion of this question. Here it is worth noting that Smith makes a
point of the manner of loans made: large sums were laid out at very high interest, making it
impossible for the debtor to free himself from the hold his creditor had over him; *LJ* (A) iii.
143. Smith could not make the observation made by Finley (1959), 155–6, that Greek history
provides many instances of calls to cancel debts and redistribute land, but no protests from the
poor free population against the competition they faced from slavery. The problem was
probably not posed in these terms.

citizens. This account is one of empathy rather than historical analysis in the true sense, but the underlying pattern described can be accepted. More typical of his general economic mode of analysis, and of his historical treatment of ancient economics, is the following remark:

We may see from this that slavery amongst its inconveniencies has this bad consequence, that it renders rich and wealthy men of large properties of great and real detriment, which otherwise are rather of service as they promote trade and commerce. (*LJ* (A) iii. 144)

Even here, however, even if indirectly, the reader recalls the perhaps too frequently cited words with which Pliny began the critique of the vast Roman estates of Italy: *latifundia perdidere Italiam.*

3.8. ROMAN LAW AS AN EXEMPLARY SYSTEM

One characteristic aspect of Smith's *Lectures on Jurisprudence* is the fact that they are not about jurisprudence alone. They deal with a wide range of topics interconnected with each other and with that subject by association of thought rather than in a systematic way. The fact that they contain elements of historical, juridical, socio-economic, and political import side by side makes it hard to follow the thread of Smith's argument, for all that it is an argument of some significance in the context of his thought in general. Furthermore, one cannot forget the initial purpose of the lectures: a 'general introduction to the law' for his students,[153] replete with illustrations and explanations, and not without digressions and some manifest failures to keep things in proportion.

The special character of the lectures can probably be derived from the fact that Smith is not only offering an evolutionary account of the law; he is also trying to identify its general principles; principles which one presumes must be endowed with a degree of stability and free from marked alteration either over time or in space. In this regard, Smith's comparison between the rules of justice and those of grammar has with reason been seen as significant, implying as it does a slow, long-drawn-out process of evolution, driven by social consensus and resulting in lasting (if not everlasting) social structures.[154] His philosophy of law thus retains something of the age-old contrast between positive and natural law, and the requirement that the former be constructed on the basis of the latter; the contrast, however, is no longer manifested by contingent rules on the one hand and abstract or ideal law on the other, but rather by specific legal systems born of particular historical events, and *leges legum*—laws of greater stability and wider application, almost universal but not quite because they too are subject to a form of change discernible only in the *longue durée.*

---

[153] Haakonssen (1981), 124.   [154] Stein (1980), 46.

The basis provided for positive law by a higher form of rule is thus relieved of the absolute, almost mathematic, quality that tends to characterize it in its usual Stoic, natural-law formulation. A better comparison would perhaps be with the passage of the *Nicomachean Ethics* ($1134^b28–1135^a5$) in which Aristotle states that he too saw natural law as subject to change.[155] The link between foundational natural-law theory and substantial historical material has already been made in the context of Smith's political thought;[156] it is clear from what has just been said that the same connection can be made in regard to his jurisprudence.

Smith's jurisprudence also recalls medieval thought in certain areas, most notably (in my opinion) the view of justice as an instrument devised to prevent men from doing wrong.[157] This conception accounts for justice's negative character in Smith, and indeed what one might term the defensive character of his jurisprudence: law's function is to protect property, in the sense of preventing poor people from taking it away from the rich; to prevent men's rights (even the natural ones) from growing strong enough to trample on the same rights held by others; to make it impossible for incompetent governments to harm the orderly run of affairs with their foolish policies; a series, in short, of prohibitions.

Roman jurisprudence was a subject of which Smith had a good grasp, as is quite natural when one considers its importance in the development of Scots law. Despite the fact that he ascribed Roman law no priority, and regarded it, in keeping with his research into the 'general principles' of law, as only one of many legal systems, it is quite likely that he was influenced directly by it. Indeed it could scarcely be otherwise, since it was the most conspicuous part of the law that he knew. His *Lectures* indeed are restricted to Roman, English, and Scots law, and the last of these is heavily based upon the first. For all that his theoretical approach submerged the significance of Roman law in a wider picture, the fact remains that the concepts, institutions, and procedural forms that came readily to him were Roman.

Smith's interpretation of Roman law is a composite one, stretching back within the tradition of English jurisprudence to Harrington and Moyle and the identification of landed property as the key to Roman history and, indeed, to history in general, as manifested in the pragmatic connection made between wealth and power that stands at the heart of the English treatment of Roman history in the eighteenth century.[158] The question of

---

[155] Of especial interest is the final reference to a piece of further research (which has not come down to us) into the nature and different types of law: 'But on each type of law, on the nature and the number of their forms and the nature of their objects, an investigation will be made later on' (*NE* $1135^a13–15$). It will be recalled that Smith too planned something of the sort.

[156] Winch (1979), 102.

[157] Originally expressed by St. Paul and St. Augustine in the terms that the law is made to restrain sinners, not for just men; Viner (1960), 49. Smith developed this, specifying its purpose of preventing men from harming their fellows, a function perhaps to be equated with the classical rule *alterum non laedere*.

[158] Momigliano (1980), i. 133–4. Harrington's writings were familiar to Smith.

property is a fundamental one in Smith's thought on the history of society, politics, and indeed of law. But the way he poses this question betrays an essentially modern conception of things: the idea that man has property rights over his person and over his labour. This notion, which acquired significance only in the modern era, has come to stand at the heart of economic liberalism and transform deeply the classical concept of property. (Labour would not have been considered a form of 'property' in ancient thought—at any rate, not a property belonging to the labourer.) The modern conception, however, was developed against a traditional theoretical background, of which the two main elements are the political and cultural relationship between citizen, property, and political participation (given prominence by the humanists but already identified in the ancient world), and the defence of private property, represented by Aristotle and the Stoics as the essential basis for legal order within the State. The role of labour in this schema was a problem which antiquity resolved in a wholly different way from Smith's. Smith's theory of property does not present it as one of man's natural rights, but he is familiar with the idea of man's right to the fruits of his own labour, and this influences his approach to law in general, and therefore to Roman law in particular. An example of the relatively modern viewpoint from which Smith looks at the latter can be seen in his account of certain changes undergone by venerable Roman-law rules; thus the prohibition on selling a married son arose not from juridical concerns, and still less from humanitarian ones, but rather from the son's family's right to his labour. The solidity and cohesion of the family entity itself, for that matter, is ascribed by Smith to the communality of economic assets obtained by the labour of all the family members, while its eventual fragmentation into a range of distinct family groups, which will in turn undergo the same process, is to be accounted for in terms of similar economic forces.

In other cases specific laws derive from measures to protect claims to estate. Though the most concrete and most frequent mode of explanation Smith offers for the creation or evolution of a wide range of diverse legislation, it does not merit description as a systematic account; but examination of his treatment of specific institutions of positive law shows it in recurrent use. Indeed it fits well with Smith's disenchanted approach to human activity, tending to view if not its ultimate causes then, at any rate, its immediate motivations in the light of realism. It is only right to add that this approach can sometimes leave the reader somewhat perplexed. Smith's 'economic' account of *patria potestas*, for instance, gives it a much less imposing character than the Roman one, even if one is obliged to admit that that institution's historical evolution was in part influenced by economic factors.

In addition, there is what might be termed the psychological aspect of Smith's treatment of the law, plainly connected with his moral philosophy and to that extent displaying a personal point of view. There is for that reason no point in discussing whether a contemporary scholar of the philosophy of law would be inclined to accept sympathy as the point of origin for the concept of property, the writing of wills, and so forth.

Smith's history of law, furthermore, is clearly couched in terms of the stadial theory. It has the relativist abstraction common to all historical reconstructions, and constitutes an example of what is customarily termed 'conjectural history'; and yet it is an important feature of his thought.

For this reason Smith's analysis of the law consists not only of a position founded in natural-law theory and interpreted in historical terms (whence the need to look for general principles), and an evolutionary account (incorporating the stadial theory) in which the part played by Roman law is not privileged in relation to those of other legal systems. Side by side with these elements, it contains a proportion of practical teaching whose lessons are heavily (if not solely) inspired by Roman law.

Smith's jurisprudential thought, therefore, is characterized by the criss-crossing influences of natural-law theory, the ideas of the philologically inspired humanists, and the work of Montesquieu received by way of the theoretical study of Scots law; all the above being melded and interwoven in Smith's own unfailingly original way. To the influences already mentioned can be added that of the particularly English line of thought which, starting from principles of natural reason, argued in favour of the free development of commercial activity on the part of the individual, interpreted as a consequence of his natural right to self-preservation. Locke, it will be recalled, had placed life, liberty, and property together on the same level as natural rights. A link can also be made between this and the seventeenth-century natural-law theory (especially characteristic of Pufendorf) which by comparing natural law and the law of nations had formulated a brand of international law for use not only in war but also in commerce; a response to the growing economic and political power of the bourgeoisie.

'Natural liberty' also inspired Smith's theories on international relations, where the regulations in place must be such as to ensure that affairs continue to follow the 'natural order' without favouritism and injustice, governed by general principles that represent the common denominator of the legal systems of all the participating nations, and thereby guarantee that there will always be a solid area of shared comprehension. Smith thus preserves, despite all the political and cultural differences between their situations, Cicero's analogy between natural law and the law of nations.

Another aspect of Adam Smith's jurisprudence, however, emerges clearly from one of his letters, in a passage which it is worth quoting at length:

In that year I would advise him to attend the Lectures of the Professor of Civil Law: for tho' the civil law has no authority in the English courts, the study of it is an admirable preparation for the Study of the English Law. The civil Law is digested into a more regular System than the English Law has yet been, and tho' the Principles of the former are in many respects different from those of the latter, yet there are many principles common to both, and one who has studied the civil law at least knows what a System of law is, what parts it consists of, and how these ought to be arranged: so that when he afterwards comes to study the law of any other country which is not so well digested, he carries at least the Idea of a System in his head and knows to what part of it he ought to refer everything that he reads.[159]

This clear and considered opinion is of some importance when one bears in mind how important the notion of system is to the whole of Smith's philosophy. A system of jurisprudence is evidently a very different creature from a system of natural philosophy, but both are characterized by connections made between certain fixed principles; in the latter case these connections take place in the imagination, while in the former they have a practical bearing, inaugurating relations that are first and foremost economic, and later on juridical.

The reference to Roman law, the study of which Smith recommends even to those who will not need to practice it, is enlightening because it reveals the exemplary status he attributed to its structure and organization, and the way in which he held that through it one could come to understand and resolve problems within quite different legal systems.

It is not an easy matter to estimate the extent to which Smith consciously valued the influence exerted by Roman law over his jurisprudential thought; but one can readily believe that, though he admired it as a system, it had more significance than he was disposed to credit it with. For, even if the notion of a superior form of justice was a Utopian idea (as amply demonstrated by the Romans themselves), contemporary legal systems could nonetheless be improved. To achieve this it was necessary to have a wide experience of the law; and the model for this was to be found at Rome.[160]

---

[159] Smith's letter to Lord Shelburne (*Corr.* 30 (no. 30)), suggesting a scheme of instruction for the addressee's son Thomas Petty-Fitzmaurice. It is worth adding another short passage from *WN* v. i. f. 44: 'This attention, to practice and precedents, necessarily formed the Roman law into that *regular and orderly system* in which it has been delivered down to us' (my italics), followed by the attribution of a superior character to the Romans over the Greeks for this reason.

[160] I do not mean to imply by this that Smith regarded the system of institutions at Rome as exemplary, merely that the Romans' capacities for systematizing legal matters should be taken as an example.

4

The Division of Labour and
the Theory of Value

4.1. PLATO AND ADAM SMITH ON THE
DIVISION OF LABOUR

Entrusted by Smith with a fundamental role in his theory of economic progress, the doctrine of the division of labour is a topic with many important implications and has, for that reason, been the object of much study.[1] In a widely read article of 1964 E. G. West homed in on an incoherence between books I and V of the *Wealth of Nations* regarding the ultimate effects of the division of labour on the intelligence, inventiveness, and character of the man who dedicates himself to one activity; in book I they are described as positive, but in book V as negative. This inconsistency, West thought, could be ascribed to the fact that Smith saw things both from an economic viewpoint and from a sociological one.

The following year a response from N. Rosenberg took a more fluid approach to the problem, looking not just at the development of the individual but also at that of society as a whole. In these terms, it can be seen that while the ever-increasing complexity of the social division of labour results in a diminution of the creativity of the individual, it gives rise to a reciprocal increase in social creativity. This comes about through a particular type of division of labour, one that can make the best application of technical and scientific advances to manual tasks. Indeed it is already a division of labour that attributes the most important and complex inventions not to the workers but to the philosophers, whose 'work' is precisely that of observing all things and (in Smith's well-known formulation) doing nothing.[2] The technological advances made by these ever more sophisticated discoveries means that the intellectual capacities of the individual worker are ever less adequate to master the whole field of knowledge relating to his occupation. In this way Rosenberg, invoking a

---

[1] Only specifically relevant references are given here: West (1964); Rosenberg (1965); Meek and Skinner (1973); Foley (1974); McNulty (1975); Foley (1975); id. (1976, ch. 8).

[2] *WN* I. 1. 9; cf. Rosenberg (1965), 132–3; Moscovici (1956), 6. Smith's remark would not have been received as pejorative in the way that it would be today; it does not represent the philosopher as a 'parasite' on society. Smith admired the philosopher's capacities for observation; cf. loc. cit., editorial note.

clear identification of two distinct stages in the specialization of labour, weakened Smith's apparent self-contradiction to the point of non-existence.[3]

In 1973 Meek and Skinner published an article attempting to show how Smith's theory of the division of labour developed; they did this by way of a close examination of all his relevant surviving work (including the then unedited first group of lectures on jurisprudence and the two fragments discovered and published by W. R. Scott). From the resulting chronology of Smith's ideas, it clearly emerges, for example, that he only gradually arrived, by way of his lectures and the 'Early Draft', at the theory that the division of labour depended on the extension of the market. More important for our enquiry was what was revealed about the meaning of the phrase 'division of labour'. Although there is a limited distribution of activity even in primitive communities, a division of labour in the true sense arises only when there is specialization both in the area of employment and in that of manufacture, which takes place in the fourth socio-economic stage.[4]

The next year saw the publication of an important article by V. Foley on the division of labour in Plato and Smith. The decidedly ambitious aim of this piece was to show the Platonic and indirectly pre-Socratic origins not only of the division-of-labour theory itself, but also of the stadial theory. Clearly being of considerable importance for this enquiry, these claims will be subjected to close examination here. Foley's most interesting statements are as follows: Smith's discussion of the division of labour in *WN* i has disconcertingly close similarities to that given by Plato in the *Republic*; both writers place the division of labour in the context of the fourth socio-economic stage; in book III of the *Laws*, Plato provides a model of the stadial theory.

Generally speaking this article is Foley's best contribution to the question, or at least the one with the most acceptable argument. The following year, indeed, saw a reply by McNulty concentrating on the clearest, and already well-known, distinction between the two authors: Plato bases his division of labour on the fact that different men are disposed towards different types of work, while Smith recognizes no natural variation in gifts of that sort, but only different conditioning brought about by environment and education.[5]

---

[3] Rosenberg (1976), 866–8, also deals with a very specific aspect of the division of labour, namely the separation of the duties of military commander and judge, enacted in some primitive societies and also in early Rome when (according to Smith's 'conjectural' history) it was realized that judicial activity risked being overlooked in favour of the military sort. He concludes that justice (a specific type of service exercised as a monopoly by the State and not obtainable by way of the free market), in order to be reliable, has to be entrusted to a restricted group of individuals. It thus constitutes an exception to the principle that the division of labour among many allows an increase in capacity. For the observation that Smith applied the concept of the division of labour, as a schematic account of development, much more widely than is usually thought see Lindgren (1973), 73 n. 9.

[4] Meek and Skinner (1973), 1109; cf. Skinner (1976), 117–18. In Smith's description, however, the fourth stage was never wholly achieved by ancient peoples: Skinner (1975), 159 n. 14.

[5] And also by the division of labour itself, as percipiently remarked by Bonar (1922), 155. Bonar indicated the differences between Plato and Smith; cf. also Morrow (1966), 168.

The conclusions to which these opposing viewpoints lead are themselves opposed: in the one, social and economic stratification and a lack of choice as to work; in the other, social mobility and a free labour market.

Foley replied by identifying classical origins even for this non-Platonist view of Smith's about the undifferentiated incidence of natural gifts. He pointed out that the well-known example of the philosopher and the porter, on which McNulty had based his argument, goes back to the note in Diogenes Laertius that Protagoras had worked as a porter before dedicating himself to philosophy; while the view that the philosopher 'does nothing but observes everything', thus nourishing his capacities for invention (especially the invention of machines), is also of classical origins, being found in Cicero and Seneca. This second article of Foley also enlarges the perspective somewhat, thereby anticipating the approach taken in his later work *The Social Physics of Adam Smith*, in which chapter 8 is entitled 'The Division of Labor'. Here Foley examined the division of labour in the context of a wholesale view of Smith's philosophy as dependent on certain formulations of pre-Socratic (and especially Empedoclean and atomist) physics—a mode of analysis which leads ultimately to the conclusion that the division of labour is a product of the cosmic separation of the elements.[6] A similar view had in fact been expressed at the beginning of the twentieth century: the principle of the division of labour (recovered rather than discovered by Smith) 'had been used by Plato in *The Republic* and, even before Plato, Anaxagoras and Diogenes of Apollonia had talked of progressive differentiation as the world-wide principle by which order is evolved from chaos'.[7] Without wishing to deny on principle that comparisons of this sort can be sustained, I must say that this analogy is too vague and remote to be of any use, and that it might have any significance or none at all. The relationship between the principle of the division of labour that lies at the heart of Smith's theoretical works and the separation of the elements in Empedoclean

---

[6] See Vivenza (1982a), 65–72, from which the present passage is necessarily synthesized. Foley adopts with insufficient caution Havelock's and Cole's hypothesis of a systematic set of ideas in pre-Socratic thought on the cultural origins and the nature of ethics, 'liberal' in political character and non-teleological in philosophical terms, overthrown and indeed covered up by Platonic and Aristotelian theology—though, of course, not so completely that twentieth-century scholars could not reconstruct the theories represented by the sparse fragments that survive. Notwithstanding the tremendous knowledge and meticulous work they showed in collecting and examining a huge mass of material, Havelock's and Cole's work was already highly conjectural and accordingly debatable. To attribute their findings to Smith who, working two centuries earlier, with the ancient sources in a very different state, was able to 'anticipate the findings of twentieth-century classicists' seems quite frankly absurd: Foley (1975), 380; (1976), *passim*. As for the frequent attribution of supposed allusions (enough to qualify for the designation of a method) to classical writers and Smith himself, together with the forced manner of employing scarce and often tendentiously interpreted documentary evidence, this removes all support from Foley's statement that the classical 'antecedents' of the division of labour are all connected with atomist physics. This theory will therefore not detain us long here, and the subject be tackled as far as is useful along traditional lines.

[7] Bryson (1945), 213, offering a synopsis of Benn (1906), 209–10.

physics and biology is in fact the single feature dominating Foley's larger study. It is a position leading to conclusions that lie beyond our purview, limited as it is to the demonstrably classical influences on Smith's work. The arguments of Foley's 1974 article, on the other hand, are acceptable with a degree of prudence, at least in part; that is, that all the illustrative elements in Smith's picture of the process of the division of labour (excepting of course examples such as the pin factory or the manufacture of nails) have classical antecedents, if by that one means not true and precise precursors of the doctrine, but merely descriptive and analytical elements relating to one or other technical aspect of the manufacture of goods. These elements can be found, it must be emphasized, in a range of contexts, without any link with the division of labour in the ancient writers and with only an indirect one in Smith, who carefully chooses modern examples (such as the pin factory referred to just now) to exemplify the theme most precisely.

Bonar had already demonstrated the connection between the division of labour and certain passages of Plato (*Rep.* ii. 369b–371b; *Politicus* 279–80) and Xenophon (*Cyr.* viii 2) which Foley later picked up and likened to the better-known sections of Smith's writings.[8]

Plato's argument (*Rep.* 369b–370c), in brief, is as follows. Men come together to live in the city because they are not self-sufficient and each needs the other's work. Thus it happens that, through their common need for food, housing, and clothing, the city comes to contain a mixture of farmers, builders, and weavers, each of whom then finds it convenient to practise his own trade both for himself and for others, exchanging products with them, rather than limit his own production to his personal needs and therefore be compelled to practise the other trades too for himself. Plato gives three reasons why this behaviour is more convenient: first, every individual is by nature different from the others, and thus better at one activity rather than another; secondly, by continually practising the same activity one gets better at it; and, thirdly, one will save time by carrying out an occupation professionally, inasmuch as one will not let the appropriate moment slip by, but will instead always seize it.

Smith's argument is likewise divided into three parts. First, the division of labour will bring about an improvement in the skill and dexterity of the worker. Secondly, time is saved by avoiding the changeover from one type of work to another. Thirdly, much labour can be facilitated or rendered unnecessary by the use of machines (*WN* i. i. 5–8; cf. also *LJ* (A) vi. 38 f.). Certainly, the coincidence of two out of the three arguments (Smith's first two and Plato's last two) is somewhat striking. One should not overlook the fact, however, that in at least one aspect the comparison is not between comparable entities. Smith is illustrating the division of labour within the

---

[8] Bonar (1922), 15 f.; already here it is remarked that Smith denied man's 'natural' predisposition for a specific activity, a point taken up by McNulty (1975), 376.

context of a single type of work; Plato is speaking of the professional distribution of labour throughout a whole city, and thus refers to particular trades
being apportioned to particular men, and wholly—or at least mainly—carried
out by those individuals. It is true that Smith makes fleeting reference to this
sort of division when, engaging in his customary mode of conjectural
reconstruction of the origins of human behaviour, he states that 'the separation of different trades and employments from one another seems to have
taken place, in consequence of this advantage'[9] (i.e. the increase in productivity). But the ensuing discussion, focusing as it does on the various phases of
manufacture, makes it clear that his real interest in this topic is in its 'modern'
aspect. Book III of *WN* does show some points of contact with Plato, though
even here Smith gives more attention to the relationship between city and
countryside than the Athenian philosopher, who limits himself to a mention
of agriculture as the producer of subsistence, without pointing out the fact
that it takes place in a different area from the other activities. In an unmistakable echo of Plato, Smith, at *WN* III. i. 1, indicates the convenience for
cultivators of exchanging their own agricultural surplus with the products of
urban manufacture, rather than having to make everything for themselves.
Further on, at III. i. 4, he points out the necessity of locating different forms
of manufacture close to each other so that the various aspects of social activity
can be co-ordinated, in relation again to the link between urban and rural
spaces. At *Rep.* 370c–d, another passage with distinct points of similarity to
Smith's theories, Plato states that neither the farmer nor the builder will be
able to make his own tools, and thus indicates the necessity for craftsmen and
other workers to stick together for their mutual benefit.

Finally, at *WN* I. iii. 2 mention is made of professional differentiation in
relation to the market, with the comment that, unlike the countryside, a large
city encourages specialization. The classical precedent for this remark is not
in Plato but rather in Xenophon who, describing the division of labour
within a single task such as the manufacture of shoes (where one worker cuts
the leather, another stitches it, and so on), states that this happens only in
large cities.[10] Leaving these points aside, however, 'division of labour' in

---

[9] *WN* I. i. 4; cf. also *LJ* (A) vi. 24–5; (B) 211–12.

[10] Xen. *Cyr.* viii. 2. 5. Diodorus Siculus iii. 12. 14 has an example of the distribution of tasks
in a mine, based in the main on differences of age and sex. See also Plato, *Politicus* 282a–283b,
where the various processes of weaving are described one by one, without any hint that each one
is carried out by different individuals; this is merely the account of a job in terms of its parts.
These examples show that a certain sort of division of labour was known in antiquity, and Smith
was doubtless aware of them; but I do not think he had them in mind, even at *WN* I. i. 11 where
he refers explicitly to weaving. Foley (1974), 238–9, links this passage with *Politicus* loc. cit., but
in fact Smith's approach, unlike Plato's, is to enumerate the various craftsmen involved at each
stage of the process; the Greek text presents a long series of verbs in the infinitive, or adjectives
to be taken with the noun *techne*, intended to show how the various operations can all be classed
under the two fundamental processes of 'separation' and 'composition'. In other words actions
are all that is mentioned, and no reference is made to the agent(s); nor can one be easily inferred,
as Plato, restricting his remarks to weaving pure and simple, distinguishes carding and the

Adam Smith's work is usually understood in the context of manufacture; the subdivision, that is, of a single manufacturing process into the various operations that make it up. This, certainly, is the sense in which Smith's work has made the concept famous, notwithstanding the fact that he uses the same phrase to describe the division of labour within society as a whole: the 'separation of different trades from one another', a phenomenon as old as society itself,[11] and one which to a certain extent constitutes the initial step on the road towards the other, more sophisticated, form of division of labour. This, at any rate, can be understood from *WN* I. i. 4, where Smith identifies the origin of 'separation' in an increase in productivity and goes on to state that: 'This separation too is generally carried furthest in those countries which enjoy the highest degree of industry and improvement; what is the work of one man, in a rude state of society, being generally that of several in an improved one.'

In any case we can exclude the idea that at *WN* I. i. 5, the passage under examination, Smith, although using Plato's scheme of reasoning, is referring to a kind of division of labour in the Platonic sense, whereby one man's job is that of a builder, another's that of a cobbler, and so forth. Along with the different sense in which they use the phrase, furthermore, they use different forms of argument. Thus, Smith's concept of 'dexterity' refers more or less to the ability to carry out a task at high speed. It is true that the text provides a single reference to the lower quality of work performed by a worker who is not used to the job, but with this sole exception the chain of his argument is unequivocal: the division of labour increases the workman's dexterity and with it the possibility of producing a greater number of objects (pins, in this case) in less time. It is easy to show that Plato did not intend to make any such point, though the relevant passage is a fleeting reference compared with Smith's long treatment of the subject. Plato's point is that the man who dedicates himself to one work only rather than to many will perform it better because he will do so with ever greater experience, an understanding of the way it works, and professional competence. The result, in short, is a better product, even if to put it like this is to misrepresent somewhat the thought of a philosopher whose principal concern is not so much for the product (a rather different concept for him from the one understood by an eighteenth-century economist) as for the man making it. The positive value of his recommendation is the chance it gives the worker to perform his task well. Plato admittedly concludes his three arguments in favour of the division of labour by saying that 'of each type of thing *more* is made to a higher quality and with greater facility when one man

passage of the shuttle between the strands of the warp among the movements that 'separate', and the twisting of fibres into strands and the weaving of the weft with the warp among those that 'compose'. The twisting of fibres into strands, furthermore, is itself divided into two parts, since it applies both to the warp and to the weft. Though I am not an expert in this area it does not seem likely to me that each of these actions was carried out by a different person.

[11] Meek (1956), 37–8.

performs one task according to his nature and at the right moment, and at leisure from other things' (370c; my italics). But it would be unwarranted to conclude from this that Plato was referring to an increase in production in the modern sense of the phrase, precisely because he did not refer to the different parts of a single branch of manufacture, but rather to a trade taken as a whole. His comment should therefore be understood in the obvious sense that by sticking to a single form of work one will get more of it done than if one were to carry out two or three together.

The increased 'professionalism' of Plato's worker accordingly brings with it a better use of time; and here we encounter the second argument common to the two thinkers, where they are somewhat closer to each other than in the first one. In this context, they both speak of the relationship between different trades: Smith, like Plato, deals with the case of a man who is simultaneously a peasant farmer and a weaver. He then states that by exercising a single trade one saves the time that is otherwise lost in the changeover between different jobs, whether they are carried out in the same place or not; the need to break off from one task before turning to the other encourages a certain indolence and weakens the powers of concentration and application. This will in turn result in a decrease in the amount of work done. Plato makes a more general reference to the fact that time will be wasted if the propitious moment for carrying on a task to its conclusion is not seized. Here the emphasis is rather on the lack of professionalism and the waste consequent upon carrying out different forms of work: the job, in Plato's words, does not wait at the workman's convenience; it needs to be carried out at the proper moment,[12] and not treated like a hobby that one can indulge in when one wishes or happens to.

It will be clear that the two arguments are not quite the same, but they do express comparable concepts. The two points that both Plato and Smith make (the gain in efficiency and the saving of time), furthermore, are similar in abstract, and work even in different contexts; thus greater dexterity and a saving in time will arise both when one trade is pursued instead of many, and when part of an activity is carried out rather than the whole activity.[13]

---

[12] The Greek word is *kairos*. Foley, following Shorey's English translation in the Loeb edition, refers to the need to seize 'the right *season*, the favourable moment in any task' (my italics), and swiftly constructs on that basis a parallel with agricultural labour, whose 'seasonality' according to Smith prevents it from being truly and fully divided, and to which Plato too referred, if only to make the opposite point. Thus 'both men do use the concept': Foley (1974), 233. The only thing demonstrated here is the riskiness of working on the basis of translations. In fact the concept is only employed by Smith; Plato makes no reference to seasonal work, Foley being deceived by Shorey's usage of 'season' in a somewhat archaic sense (even for 1930), for which cf. *TGL* and Liddell, Scott, and Jones, *Greek-English Lexicon*, s.v. 'kairos'. See also Shorey's own admission ('Introduction', p. liii) of having occasionally used redundant and apparently synonymous phrases to translate a single word. For a specific instance of *kairos* in this sense see Vernant (1983), 260 and n. 75.

[13] Foley (1974), 233 n. 72, notes the association between Plato's formulation of the point and Smith's version which Cannan showed to be derived from the *Encyclopédie*, and hypothesizes

Now we come to the third argument—or rather to the third pair of arguments, for as noted above they are different in each author. Here the classical background we need to examine extends beyond Plato. The statement in the *Republic* that men have different predispositions, so fundamentally different from Smith's views,[14] reveals a notion that we would today regard as far from progressive: men are by nature different; there are therefore better and worse; and, as Aristotle was later to argue,[15] some are born to command, others to follow. Smith was of a decidedly different opinion. Foley's brilliant discovery that the tale of the philosopher Protagoras beginning his working life as a porter prompted Smith's conclusion that philosopher and porter differ not in nature but in cultural and educational matters[16] in truth only reveals a *possible* origin; or rather, it shows why Smith chose a philosopher and a porter as his examples rather than, say, a lawyer and a sawyer; but that does not detract from Smith's intended meaning, namely that there is no difference in nature between the two. Foley, emphasizing that it was the atomist Democritus who 'discovered' Protagoras, and that Smith wrongly numbers the latter amongst the Atomists in his essay on astronomy,[17] draws support from these facts for his thesis that Smith looked back to the pre-Socratic Atomists and put together the scattered fragments of their thought in order to reconstruct its 'liberal' character that was supplanted by Plato. This he will have done without admitting it, for fear of reprisals. I have already indicated that I do not subscribe to this account, and here it will suffice for me to say that there is no need to search so far afield for the origins of Smith's 'liberalism' towards the dispositions and capacities of men. The idea that men were by nature equal and that they thereafter came to be different for a multitude of reasons ultimately due to their environment and to society was a widely and firmly held belief by Smith's day; it can be found, for example, in Montesquieu and Helvétius,[18] to say nothing of Rousseau, and it is highly likely that he shared it with these authors.

Whatever the case, it is certain that Smith's views on this matter are quite contrary to those of Plato. A full account of the matter, however, must include the fact that their respective concepts of the division of labour are divergent. It would clearly make no sense to see the type of division described by Smith in terms of individuals' different preferences or inclinations; it would be absurd to imagine that a person might better realize his innate capacities making the

---

that Smith's debt to the latter was in reality owed to Plato. For all that one might agree with Whitehead's felicitous comment that the whole of western philosophy is just a series of glosses on Plato, Foley's point here seems an over-simplification.

[14] See above, n. 5 and the relevant passage in the text. [15] Aristotle, *Pol.* 1252ª31–4.

[16] Foley (1975), 384–5; (1976), 44, 154.

[17] Foley (1976), 28–9. This interpretation, as a whole, is taken as showing that the birth of the modern economy can be regarded as a corollary to the scientific revolution in physics and astronomy seen in the previous century, id. (1975), 388.

[18] See Meek (1976b), 92; Imbruglia (1980), 318 f. According to Cropsey (1975), 144, Smith started from a Hobbesian position.

point of a pin rather than its head.[19] Plato's account, however, is based precisely on the consideration (re-emphasized in recent decades)[20] that people realize their potential better, both for themselves and in terms of their social function, when they undertake a job that they have an affinity for.

Finally, we come to Smith's third argument, for which there is no equivalent in Plato: the saving of time and effort by the use of machinery. The use of machines, of course, could not be a question that arose for Plato or the other ancient thinkers, not so much because they were ignorant of rudimentary instruments and mechanisms, or indeed the principles of mechanics by which it would have been possible to perfect them, but rather because they were not familiar with the need to save time.[21] Once this is accepted, one can ponder a question relative to the origins of machines that was raised both by Smith and by his classical predecessors: which is more likely, that the machine is invented by a workman whose daily practice of a trade sharpens his know-how, or by a thinker, a man of academic inclinations who has developed keener powers of observation than others? Smith's answer is the latter; in the classical age, however, the question (which perhaps ultimately derives from the mythical tales based on the concept of the *protos heuretes*, or initial discoverer) was answered differently by different authors; thus Seneca favoured the craftsman, but Posidonius (whose view Seneca reports critically in his ninetieth epistle) came down on the side of the thinker. It was perhaps precisely from Seneca that Smith took this debate,[22] but his immediate point of departure here too is different. Seneca illustrates his disagreement with Posidonius by recounting in full and varied detail his reluctance to accept that philosophy's role was the humble one of furnishing man with the little conveniences necessary for his life. Posidonius' position, on the other hand, according to which philosophy is the mistress of all the arts and sciences,[23] clearly seems reductive to Seneca, who states that any alert and competent individual will be capable of the invention of working tools and techniques; a process whose advance he inevitably identifies with an unnecessary and thus potentially damaging and corrupting increase in conveniences and facilities.

---

[19] The so-called 'alienation' felt by the worker who is constrained to repeat time after time the same actions has been studied by West (1964) and Lamb (1973); cf. also Winch (1979), 82. Some have seen in this a sort of prediction of the unpleasant results of large-scale manufacture, in Smith's own day not yet to be met with: Ginzberg (1979), 39. Smith considered that repetitive and oversimplified work would have deleterious effects on the finer human faculties not, perhaps, very different from those described by Xenophon (*Oecon.* iv. 2–3; vi. 5–7), which derive from a classical prejudice against manual labour. [20] Schumpeter (1955), 56.

[21] A need that became a high priority in the industrial era, along with the corresponding requirement to cut costs; Fiorito (1971), 47–8.

[22] As suggested by Foley (1974), 223–4, pointing to certain similarities between the examples used by the two authors. Less likely is any relationship between Smith's philosopher-inventor-observer and Cicero's (*Tusc.* v. 9): Foley (1975), 383–4. The latter is a model of Aristotelian 'disinterest' and the contemplative approach.

[23] A position that fits with a certain spiritual strain in ancient thought which esteemed and appreciated mechanical skills: Mondolfo (1982), esp. 57–8; 99–100.

In this way, the philosopher, whose tasks are of a loftier nature and appropriate to a discipline that should be concerned with the spirit, can remain untroubled.

Seneca's position, with its clearly discernible distinction between the material and spiritual worlds, contrasts with that of Smith, for whom the 'specialization' of philosophers in the field of invention is part and parcel of the division of labour; it is seen in the context of that principle and therefore incorporated into the new category; while intellectual speculation becomes an instrument of progress as conceived in Smith's day, a unitary phenomenon born of both mental and material labour. This fits perfectly easily with Smith's 'Posidonian' view of the figure of the philosopher-inventor, and—it may be added—with the eighteenth-century ambiguity over the frontiers between philosophy, science, and technology.

In brief recapitulation of what has been said so far, it can be observed that even in the form of the distribution of tasks within a single form of manufacture, the division of labour was known to the ancient world; but it should be sought in Xenophon, not in Plato. To quote the *Cyropaedia* (viii. 2. 5): 'Some make shoes for men, some for women; there are even those who live merely by stitching shoes, or only cutting the leather, or only cutting clothes, or without doing any of this, but simply putting the various pieces together.'[24]

Antiquity lacked, rather, the systematic application of this method, and thus failed to realize the scale of its potential. This is a topic that could divert us far from the one in hand. There were several areas of technology where the Greeks remained at a primitive level despite having all the scientific knowledge necessary to reach an almost modern stage of development. A few examples from physics will suffice. The Alexandrians, for instance, were able to construct a machine called an 'aeolipyle' which was, in effect, a true steam engine, a distant ancestor of the modern turbine. But the sole purpose of its conception, construction, and description was to provide an ingenious mechanical plaything to astound those who saw it. Many other such machines were built by Alexandrian scientists, especially by Heron, whose writings, it needs to be pointed out, have survived abundantly enough in the manuscript tradition for it to be quite clear that his inventions were far from unknown. In short, 'they were familiar with simple machines and gears, hydrostatics, the various applications of the siphon, the compressibility of air, and the motive power of steam. They possessed, in other words, both the technical elements and the scientific know-how to construct industrial machinery and anticipate the achievements of the eighteenth century.'[25] But from all this knowledge nothing more than wonderful toys and theatrical machinery came about; no one had the idea of applying it to the processes of

---

[24] By way of conclusion Xenophon adds that work carried out in this way will be done better; but that is not, for him, its most significant aspect.

[25] Gliozzi (1962), ii. 18; cf. also Gille (1956), ii. 630–6.

production; the only sector in which any advance was made was that of engines of war. The reasons for this strange phenomenon, which has puzzled no small number of scholars, are manifold, and it would be difficult, as well as out of place, to list them all here. Among them let us note only the well-known breach between pure and applied science; the fact that in some cases the design outstripped contemporary technical resources; the absence of the 'Baconian' spirit to inaugurate a constant interrelationship between specula-tion, empirical research, and its application; the aristocratic quality of science and philosophy in the Greek world, in comparison with which *techne* was a mean and humble activity. The fact that intellectuals dedicated them-selves principally to pure science took them away from practical issues, while, for their part, craftsmen and artisans could only offer modest innova-tions in the technology of manufacture, which thus shows few variations from the archaic period onwards.[26] Returning to the question in hand, I regard it as superfluous to ask why the Greeks though they had, and applied, the idea of the division of labour, did not apply it on a greater scale;[27] the reason, I believe will be the same as the reason they did not invent the steam turbine. In essence, they did not think of it.

Isolated intuition does not suffice when the social context lacks both the right mentality and the stimulus to put it to good use in a specific direction; the Greeks' machines were not made as labour-saving devices, because the Greek economy, and that of the ancient world in general, was not geared for the systematic increase of production, with the result that the profitability of the division of labour was not a concern to them. The principle in question was looked on not as an economic factor with its own testable characteristics, but as a curiosity of the organization of work within large cities—one of those occasional oddities of urban life.

This explains too why scholars who have studied this problem have more often discerned a connection between Smith and Plato than between Smith and Xenophon. The latter's reference to the division of labour is really *sui generis*: of great interest, inasmuch as it shows that the Greeks knew the practice and were able to think it out for themselves, but not to see its economic potential. The times were not ready for the division of labour within specific manufactures, even if, exceptionally, it was found. But the relationship between Smith and Plato is by its nature a conceptual one and

---

[26] Finley (1977), 120–8; cf. also M. Venturi Ferriolo's introduction to Mondolfo (1982), 29. Some have spoken in terms of a 'mental block', resulting from the Greek disdain for mechanical skill, and preventing the application of science to the manufacturing crafts; but this is a somewhat debatable concept (ibid. 28–30).

[27] In my opinion it was clear even to the Greeks that to do so would bring economic advantages. This does not emerge from the passage of Xenophon quoted above, but rather from one of Plato (*Laws* 846d), laying down a prohibition on two separate crafts being carried out by the same man: in practice he could only exercise one of them himself, and as regards the second would act only as a supervisor over others; he would inevitably end up dedicating more time and effort to the latter, because of the two operations it would bring him the greater profit.

therefore destined to last. Plato's division of labour, rather than offering concrete examples,[28] is an exercise of reason on a topic with economic implications; a thought-experiment, naturally limited both by the contemporary economic situation and, especially, by Plato's own outlook, with the phenomenon in question as its object of study.

At the risk of schematizing matters a little too much, it might be said that Xenophon offers a descriptive 'precedent', Plato a theoretical one; this, at any rate, clarifies the way in which the latter is closer in kind to what Smith provides. The radical economic changes that had taken place by Smith's day meant that the division of labour could no longer be treated as a curiosity. It was now a phenomenon of immense significance, and it is no surprise that Smith not only described it, but submitted it to investigation. But the fact that Plato too investigated this subject reveals once again the latter's calibre; he lived in an era when, as we have seen, the phenomenon in question was so limited that few became aware of it, while the mentality that he himself helped to produce was unfitted to take it into consideration. By one of those apparent incongruences that occasionally arise in cultural history, Greek intellectualism, possibly one of the obstacles to the development of the division of labour in the ancient world, is also the one that offers the greatest—in fact the only—possibility of analogy on this subject between the classics and Adam Smith.

Connected in some ways with our discussion of the division of labour is another theory of great renown: the theory of the four stages of history. According to Foley, Smith found this too in Plato; in book III of the *Laws*, to be precise. In fact it is a good idea to be cautious in ascribing classical precedents of this sort to Smith. The fundamental characteristics of Smith's stadial theory are its deliberate emphasis on mode of subsistence, and the relationship between the latter and institutions. These are not found in Plato who, like other ancient writers,[29] simply offers a mythological reconstruction of the origins of society based on what he regards as the likely course of development followed by primitive people. It has also been claimed that the successive stages described by the two authors neatly coincide, with a hunting phase followed by a pastoral one and then by the construction of towns. In reality, while Plato does refer simultaneously to hunting and pastoralism in the *Laws* (iii. 679a; cf. also 677b), he makes the latter predate the former. The stadial aspect of subsistence in Plato is thus, we would have to conclude, rather rough-and-ready—were it not better simply to avoid

[28] In the *Politicus* weaving is presented as a model for the subdivision of an activity into its component actions (cf. above, n. 10), to serve as an analogy with political activity. The *Republic*, on the other hand, deals with division of labour in society, not within manufacturing. It should be added that the abstraction of Plato's thought does not mean he did not closely observe and have genuine respect for craftsmanship; it is merely that, for him, 'it serves a lower-ranking good': Finley (1977), 127.

[29] On Aristotle, Lucretius, and Dicaearchus, see Meek (1976b), 7–12; Skinner (1974b), 30 n. 6.

treating him as setting a precedent for Smith in this area. A much more convincing reconstruction would focus on the obvious inherent likelihood of the notion that primitive man turned first to the simplest forms of activity, such as gathering uncultivated fruits and hunting animals with rudimentary weapons, before later learning more complex ones, such as raising livestock and cultivating the land; practices that require experience, powers of reasoning, and a range of understanding and knowledge, and are thus very improbable initial activities for people in a primitive state. This essential likelihood, in short, is doubtless what underlies the similarities between Smith's stadial theory and those found in classical authors, which are generally connected with schematic and theoretical accounts of social development, while including the occasional economic factor. These factors are, however, gathered in a rather different way and cannot be connected with the eighteenth-century stadial theory, as is shown by the mixture of forms of existence in Aristotle (shepherd, farmer, robber, fisherman, huntsman, trader, etc.) and the lack of distinction between pastoralism and agriculture in the otherwise percipient account given by Lucretius. The version of Dicaearchus, on the other hand, remains notably precise.

To call this sort of digression on mankind's legendary origins, present in many classical authors, a case of 'conjectural history' is perhaps going too far.[30] Conjectural history involves a rather different methodology and, though it does indeed have a classical principle at its root—the assumption that man's nature does not change—on which has been built a superstructure formed out of the mass of later documentary information deriving from geographical discovery, it is a matter of scientific analysis carried out largely on a comparative method; in the absence of documents relating to a given historical period it is assumed reasonable to suppose that men behaved then as we know they did in eras for which we have the documentary evidence. This approach is clearly a long way from that of the ancient world.

Furthermore, the division of labour is characteristic of the stage at which the process of manufacture undergoes specialization, that is to say the fourth stage. It will perhaps be recalled that among the similarities that Foley indicated between Plato and Smith was the claim that 'both men treat the origin of the division of labor in connection with the fourth stage'.[31] In fact it cannot be said that Plato's fourth stage is the one in which the manufacturing process is specialized. For classical writers the final phase in the development of human activity is the construction of cities and the related

---

[30] As does Foley (1976), 38, 45, 49, 62, 140, 151, 153, implying that the approach is similar to that of the 'Scottish school'; on which see esp. Skinner (1967), and id. (1974*b*), 29–30. It seems likely that Foley was making a loose, non-technical comparison on the basis that Plato too, at root, made 'conjectures' about the origins of humanity. On this see Raphael (1972), 335 n. 2: 'In my opinion the adjective "conjectural" is seriously misleading when applied to most of the historical interests of Adam Smith'. Raphael would prefer the phrase 'philosophical history'.

[31] Foley (1974), 225.

establishment of different trades and commercial exchanges between populations; but beyond this (apart from exceptional cases such as Xenophon's shoe 'factory') one cannot go, nor was it possible to go. Not only from Smith's viewpoint, but indeed from ours as well, 'both Greece and Rome had already passed through the stages of hunting and pasturage in reaching a stage of development which was more sophisticated than the agrarian, but without attaining all the characteristic features of the commercial stage'.[32] For that reason Plato and Smith refer to two 'stages' which are coextensive, but differently characterized.

A question that could not have been formulated by the ancients in general, furthermore, is that of the saving of time and the consequent saving of money; here, of course, I refer to the causal link between the two, not meaning to imply that they had no concept of saving money in itself. Smith, however, reflecting in full the economic realities of his day, concludes his tripartite argument by citing machines and their capacity to allow savings of time and, therefore, money. Plato too had noted the saving of time in his treatment of the division of labour, but he nowhere connects it with the saving of money, any more than he had been bothered to note the link between time-saving and increased production. Arguments of this sort held no value for him; what was valuable in his eyes was the possibility that the division of labour gave each man to work better, and thus realize his potential. Consequently his third argument (in the order followed by him, his first) is the one proceeding from the different capacities of different people, the correct application of which is an indispensable element in the creation of the perfect community of citizens. Spiegel's exegesis of Plato's position is, to my mind, entirely right: 'Division of labor, as every one knows, spells interdependence. The type of interdependence that Plato envisages does not stem from observation, not from a visit to Adam Smith's pin factory, but from a model of the ideal society, a construction of the human mind.'[33]

Adam Smith's position, though it has certain descriptive similarities to that of Plato and other classical writers, is first and foremost constructed on the basis of an empirical enquiry into an economic world that in terms both of the mode of production and of the market was quite remote from the one Plato had known. It is possibly the case that the third argument, which is different

---

[32] Skinner (1975), 158–9 n. See also the interesting remark by Scott (1940), 96, regarding *LJ*, where Smith states that the apprenticeship was unknown in ancient Greece: 'He [Smith] is careful to point out that Division of Labour had not proceeded very far.'

[33] Spiegel (1975), 611. Spiegel lays weight on the context in which Plato discusses the division of labour, namely the close relationship between the tripartite division of the soul and the corresponding division of society into three classes. It would not, however, be right to strip Plato's account of all economic value; it is simply that it needs to be seen in its historical context, which is what gives it its meaning. Thus Finley (1975), 71: 'The few ancient writers who mention the division of labour at all do so in a context and from a point of view which are essentially different from Adam Smith's. They were interested in the quality of manufacture, not in quantity or efficiency.' See also Vernant (1983), 259.

in the two authors, is more important than it seems at first sight, and that for each author it in fact expresses the fundamental reason behind, and the motivation for, the division of labour. This is more plainly evident in the case of Plato, who starts from an ideal schema and refers all human life back to it; but even for Smith the third argument is fundamental. Smith's formulation is framed so as to relate to the facts of the world of work as he observed it. The more frequent use of machines had allowed a greater specialization in human activity and a progressive increase in production. The example of the pin factory—for all that it was taken from the *Encyclopédie*[34]—is neither arbitrary nor trivial; it is the best example Smith could give of the form of labour whose division he was so firmly proposing.

In conclusion, then: Can it be said that Plato's argument is based on an idealist motif, and Smith's on the close observation of the world around him? In part, yes; though one must add, in fairness to the two authors, that Plato was also a sharp observer, and Smith for his part a sound theorist. The distinction made in the question just posed should be understood in relation to the initial connection in which each author raises the problem and the context in which he discusses it. It is, in any case, not perhaps inappropriate to emphasize once more that when two writers deal with a topic, regardless of their underlying theoretical motivations, there is always common ground between them, namely the shared object of their research. The fact that one author took an ideal city as his point of departure, and the other (writing twenty-one centuries later) a pin factory does not diminish the fact that, with all the differences here noted, they have ended up discussing a closely similar economic subject.[35]

Where Plato and Smith get out of kilter with each other, namely the question of efficiency and time-saving, it is ultimately due to historical factors. Plato was not in a position to treat efficiency in terms of increased production, while Smith could still deal with time-saving in relation to the man who performs one or more jobs alone, since that was a phenomenon still seen in his day. For that reason a more marked difference can be seen between the two authors in the first argument than in the second, but the simple analogy arising from their choice of similar economic topics remains. Furthermore, certain elements in Smith's brief treatment of the differentiation of trades and professions in society can be traced back to Plato. The arguments given above thus retain their validity, whatever perspective they are examined in, and they are, in effect, arguments common to Plato and Smith, without any implication that the latter 'copied' them from the former.[36]

---

[34] See the comment at *WN* I. i. 3 n. 3. It also seems that as a boy Smith had seen many factories of the sort in Scotland; Rae (1965), 103–9, and the editorial remark at *WN* I. i. 6 n. 11.

[35] Cf. the similar observation of Stewart (1980), 336 *ad fin.*

[36] 'There is no difficulty in finding references to division of labour through all ages from ancient Greece on, but I doubt whether any one anticipated Smith in tracing its relationship to

4.2. ARISTOTLE, ADAM SMITH, AND THE THEORY OF VALUE

The first of Pindar's *Olympian Odes* opens with the famous declaration: 'Water is the best of goods; gold, splendorous like fire burning in the night, outshines the treasures of proud wealth'.[37] The great poet could never have foreseen that these lines, apart from the triumphal way that was to be marked out for them in the literature of later ages, would have another, less obvious, road to follow that would take them into the heart of a most unexpected area, namely that of economic thought.

About a century after Pindar, Plato, in his dialogue *Euthydemus*, had recourse to the poet's imagery to illustrate Socrates' advice not to scatter the fruits of science to the four winds, but to hold them instead like precious things reserved for a few adepts: 'It is rarity, Euthydemus, that bestows value,' says Socrates; 'water is very cheap, for all that it is the first of goods, as Pindar wrote'.[38] Plato's most famous pupil also quoted Pindar, but he added something to the quotation; that is, he combined the two precedents available to him, putting together Plato's contrast between the utility and cheapness of water with the other commodity mentioned by Pindar but overlooked by Plato, namely gold. (Here it should be noted that Aristotle quotes only the first line of the ode in question, just as Plato does, and it is possible that the mention of gold that follows is purely coincidental, though I should be more inclined to consider it a reminiscence of Pindar.) Dedicating a book of his *Rhetoric* to the relativity of the good and the useful, Aristotle says:

The rarer thing has a greater value, like gold in comparison with iron, although it is less useful; and, indeed, to acquire it is more precious, because it is more difficult. But, in another sense, the abundant is more valuable than the rare, because its use is greater; indeed, 'often' exceeds 'rarely', wherefore it is said 'water is the best of goods'.[39]

The sceptic philosopher Sextus Empiricus takes up the question again more or less at the same point, though he gives it a slightly different tone:

Rare things are precious to us, while familiar and easily obtainable ones are not. Thus, if we imagine that water were rare, how much more precious it would seem to us than all the things that are so considered! Or, if we imagine that gold were spread

---

scale of industry, to scale of plant, and to the essential seasonal and raw-material characteristics of the various industries'; Viner (1965), 107. See also Gray (1931), 126–7.

[37] Pindar, *Olymp.* i. 1–2. The translation given follows roughly that of A. Puech in the Belles Lettres series (1922), 26; Pindar is notoriously resistant to translation. Note Puech's comment ad loc.: 'There is no need to bring in the influence of cosmological theories such as Thales' system to explain this opening. The mention of *gold* after that of *water* shows that Pindar judges *values* in relation to *man*' (italics as in original).

[38] *Euthyd.* 304b.   [39] *Rhet.* vii. 1364[a]24–8.

all over the earth like stones, who would think it precious and worthy of being treasured?[40]

The natural-law theorist Pufendorf knew these arguments, and used them to illustrate his argument about the providential diffusion of those objects that are of use to mankind, and the corresponding rarity of superfluous substances.[41] The die was now cast. Though formulated differently from time to time (with, for instance, different examples; Pufendorf contrasts pearls, gold, and silver with the abundant and 'useful' water), the notion became widespread. Locke stated that useful things, such as air and water, generally have no price, but that this would not be the case if they existed in smaller quantities, proportionate to their consumption; John Law added further precision to the concept with the comment that everything depends on the availability of the commodity in relation to the demand for it, and introduced a comparison between water and diamonds; and finally Adam Smith stated that water has great usefulness and little value, in complete contrast to diamonds;[42] a phrase which, like many others of his, has become famous and provoked yet more debate.

I have retraced the route taken by this characteristic image in the full knowledge that accounts of this sort do not always map direct and conscious links between the authors concerned. Dugald Stewart, countering the arguments of an early enquirer into the classical influences on Smith's thought, wrote that 'the marks of *Philosophical Plagiarism* . . . are easily separable from that occasional similarity of thought and of illustration, which we may expect to meet with in writers of the most remote ages and countries, when employed in examining the same questions, or in establishing the same truths'.[43]

Interesting discussions have arisen regarding the classical roots not only of the famous 'paradox' but also of the theory of value itself. Why Adam Smith, heir to a long philosophical tradition in which value was interpreted in terms of utility and scarcity of the commodities, should in the end have seen it as residing in labour, is a crucial question that has prompted a search for Aristotelian precedents for his views, to say nothing of other, more recent ones.

---

[40] *Pyrrh. Hypot.* i. 143.

[41] Pufendorf (1759) v. 1, 6; see also de Groot (1702) ii. 12, 14. On this topic cf. Viner (1972), 27–8; Bowley (1963), 133–4.

[42] *WN* i. iv. 13; *LJ* (A) vi. 8; 70; (B) 206. See also the comment on *WN* ad loc. for a list of 'precedents' for this motif, given also by Bowley (1963) and Pietranera (1963), 92–3, n. 33.

[43] Stewart (1980), 336 (author's italics). The remark was directed at John Gillies, who had asserted that the essential nucleus of Smith's moral theory was derived from Polybius: see above, Ch. 2, Sect. 2. In a footnote to this passage Stewart adds two of Gillies's comments on economic matters: that Smith had adopted Aristotelian principles on exchange value and national wealth; and that on the subject of money there was a clear link with the *Magna Moralia*. Stewart objects that one cannot conceive anything other than a chance similarity between Aristotle and modern writers on economics; the example he draws on is the *locus classicus* of usury, on which topic Aristotle is far removed from writers such as Smith, Hume, and Turgot.

In an article that aroused a degree of perplexity when it came out in 1953, E. Kauder stated that Aristotle can be considered the originator of the analysis of the subjective element in economic value, which he held to derive from the subjective aspect of the utility, scarcity, and costs of the commodity in question, and that he had a grasp of the concept of diminishing utility. According to these claims, which were made on the basis of passages in the *Politics* and *Topics*, Aristotle is the ancestor of the theory of marginal utility by way of a line of thought that proceeded from him and, after taking in the schoolmen, Davanzati, Montanari, Galiani, Condillac, and Bernouilli, who all elaborated upon his basic ideas, culminated in Adam Smith. To Smith is then ascribed the grave sin of having delayed the progress of economic thought by a century, inasmuch as his famous paradox effectively blocked any possibility of founding an economic theory on the calculation of marginal utility.[44]

Some years later, in 1957, Robertson and Taylor made the objection that, even if one can accept that Smith did not know or was not thinking of the works of the Italian and French authors mentioned above, he certainly knew well enough those of Grotius and, especially, Pufendorf, to which (by way of his teacher Hutcheson) he had been introduced by Gershom Carmichael, the translator of and commentator on the German natural-law theorist. He will therefore have been familiar with Aristotelian theories of value and the tradition deriving from them, which took as its basis the two elements of utility and scarcity. Hutcheson was a follower of this school, but Smith himself took a different approach, one that emphasized the importance of labour as an 'unvarying standard of value which would enable valid comparisons to be made through time'.[45]

Not even this new approach, however, was created from nothing,[46] and there was a theorist who sought to ascribe it to the same ultimate ancestry. In 1964 B. J. Gordon proposed, and attempted to prove, that Aristotle was the original begetter of *both* theories (i.e. value based on utility–scarcity and value based on labour); he was unable to work out a synthesis of the two because of the immature state of economic thought in his lifetime. Smith and Aristotle were thus joined by a double bond, with scholasticism in the middle; one associated with the traditional analysis of value in terms of utility and scarcity, and one with the newer analysis, more typical of Smith, which saw value in terms of labour and the costs of production. But as long ago as 1939

---

[44] Kauder (1953). Tozzi too maintains that the concept of value in Aristotle is 'understood . . . in terms we would use, as the decreasing subjective utility in the successive units of a particular commodity': (1961), 167; cf. also 164, where it is stated that 'something not much different' from the modern concept of the diminishing level of utility of successive units of the same commodity can be discerned in Aristotle. This view was championed first by Kraus (1905). Pietranera (1963), 98 f., challenged the appropriateness of this interpretation in relation to Smith, whose concepts of utility and demand he analysed percipiently.

[45] Robertson and Taylor (1957), 194.   [46] See on this Meek (1956), 12–14.

V. Johnson had carried out a primarily linguistic and literary analysis of the terms used by Aristotle, concluding that one can discern signs of a concept of value based on 'need' or 'demand' (*chreia*), but not two concepts; and that a theory of value in terms of 'labour' was certainly lacking.[47]

It is not my intention here to conduct a new analysis of Smith's theory of value, but rather to look for any links there might be between it and Aristotle's. It should first be stated that the works chiefly consulted in the course of the studies mentioned above were the *Nicomachean Ethics*, *Politics*, *Rhetoric*, and *Topics*. It is not appropriate, however, to quarry this diverse selection of texts indifferently for single passages, as if they were all written with the same end and did not each have their own underlying programme that ought to govern the way they are read. Thus the *Rhetoric* was written with the aim of establishing a rhetorical *techne* that would serve equally well in confirming or confuting a given proposition, and thus in bringing an argument equally easily to two opposed conclusions; thereby breaking rhetoric out of the servitude to morals in which Plato had left it.[48] To this end Aristotle recites long lists of controversial points, with many examples appended, designed to show how in each case conclusive arguments both for and against can be worked out. To return briefly to Smith's paradox of water and diamonds, this, as is well known, should be interpreted as showing that a widespread commodity, though useful, can be of low economic value, thus refuting the argument that value depends on utility. The same point is made by the case of the diamonds, a 'useless' commodity but one of great value because of its rarity. The argument is thus designed to locate the relationship between value-in-use and value-in-exchange; an account framed in entirely economic terms and directed towards a single end, namely the separation of the concept of value from that of utility. But the passage of Aristotle cited above, regarding water and gold, for all its apparent similarity to this section of Smith, is actually part of a series of arguments meant to show that there is not always agreement as to what is of greater or lesser use, by showing that on a single point there can be two opposite but equally well-founded opinions.

A similar point can be made in relation to another passage in the *Rhetoric*: 'Good, too, are things that are a man's very own, possessed by no one else, exceptional; for this increases the *value* put upon them' (Ross's translation, my

---

[47] For which see, respectively, Gordon (1964), 128, and Johnson (1939).

[48] A move which his erstwhile master would doubtless have disapproved of as being dangerously akin to a sophistic approach. In reality Aristotle's intention was to acquaint the rhetor with the opposing arguments and thereby enable him to overcome them; cf. Dufour's introduction to his Belles Lettres edition of *Rhetoric* i, pp. 7 f. The inappropriate nature of the *Rhetoric* and *Topics* for studying Aristotle's concept of value (they being 'works based on opinion rather than science, consisting merely of argumentative rules for use in debate') is emphatically stressed by Lotito (1980), 128–9, n. 5, with particular reference to the cited works of Kraus and Gordon.

italics).[49] With the right intention, one can discern in this passage a relationship between value and scarcity, though the Greek word rendered here as 'value' is *timé*, whose primary meaning is honour or prestige. This too, it is true, can be classed among 'goods' created by their rarity, and it is in this sense that Aristotle uses the word. I am not, however, certain of the extent to which he identified it with economic value, bearing in mind the primarily classificatory nature of the context, and its overt aim of producing a list of 'the things that are good' on the basis of syllogistic reasoning. The fact that there are things that are precious because they belong only to us and no one else does not necessarily lead to an account of economic value and scarcity. But, since it is above all important to understand what might be achieved by any potential 'economic' interpretation of this sort of terminology, I regard Polanyi's considered remarks on the topic as of vital significance:

> The *agatha* are the highest prizes of life, that which is most desirable and also rarest. This is indeed a surprising context in which to encounter that feature of goods which modern theory has come to regard as the criterion of the 'economic', namely, scarcity. For the discerning mind when considering those prizes of life must be struck by the utterly different source of their 'scarcity' from that which the economist would make us expect. With him scarcity reflects either the niggardliness of nature or the burden of the labor that production entails. But the highest honors and the rarest distinctions are few for neither of these two reasons. They are scarce for the obvious reason that there is no standing room at the top of the pyramid. The fewness of the *agatha* is inherent in rank, immunity and treasure: they would not be what they are if they were attainable to many. Hence the absence in early society of the 'economic connotation' of scarcity, whether or not utilitarian goods sometimes also happen to be scarce. For the rarest prizes are not of this order. Scarcity derives here from the noneconomic order of things.[50]

The *Topics* were part of Aristotle's logical works, and had the aim of using dialectic to enable statements endowed with verisimilitude and sustainable against contradiction to be made on any subject whatsoever. The fact that this work was an expression of ancient formal logic (which the Aristotelian school regarded as a tool of philosophical enquiry)[51] alerts us to the circumstance that here too Aristotle was not so much coming to grips with problems of ethics, politics, or, still less, economics, but was rather concerned with honing the rhetorical weaponry of debate and argument. This clearly

---

[49] *Rhet.* vi. 1363ª27–8, quoted by Gordon (1964), 119. As stated in the text, 'value' translates *timé*, which can also mean cost or price (*timios* is found in this sense in the passage from Plato's *Euthydemus* cited above, n. 38), but I am certain that here Aristotle is using it in the more usual and traditional sense of 'honour, esteem, prestige'; cf. the next note and relevant text.

[50] Polanyi (1957), 77–8. In my opinion this is the correct interpretation also of the passage cited in the last note (1363ª27–8); this emerges from the significant use of the term *agathà* (cf. 1362ᵇ29–31), 'good things' or also 'goods', but without specifically economic reference, for which Aristotle uses *chremata*. See on this Tozzi (1961), 152–3.

[51] One that had, however, 'only a place in the hallway of the building of philosophy': Lesky (1962), ii. 700.

diminishes the extent to which any apparent hints at economic language in the work can be interpreted as genuine signs of Aristotle's thought on questions relating to that subject. It seems preferable and safer, therefore, to stick to those passages in the *Nicomachean Ethics* and the *Politics* where one can be reasonably sure that Aristotle was intentionally speaking of economics.[52] These two dialogues are both dedicated to enquiring into what is good and what is bad for man, both as an individual and as a citizen, and in concrete terms rather than the abstract; programmatic works, so designed that they will inevitably include suggestions of an economic nature, just like most works in this vein in the classical and medieval traditions.[53]

The most important passages in the *Ethics* in this regard are almost all in book V, which deals with justice. This is a fact of some interest in itself, and one that was to influence scholastic philosophy, which located economics in the general context of ethical and juridical subjects. This was a scheme that not even Smith wholly abandoned, though he broke with tradition by dealing with economics not in those of his lectures that he devoted to justice, but rather in those on expediency.[54]

In *NE* v, then, Aristotle is concerned with the question of exchange value. The consideration that underlies his analysis is that for an exchange of two items to take place there must be some species of common denominator, so to speak. This is constituted by need or necessity, but it has also been translated as 'demand'.[55] It is need 'that unites everything', and that lays the basis on which the exchange can be made. The next step follows from the necessity to measure or quantify the two items in such a way that the exchange can be fair; that is, to find a means of translating the different needs represented by widely diverse objects into clearly commensurable data. The means in question is, of course, money: indeed money 'measures everything, and so measures excess and deficiency'.[56] This, though, is not the place to go in detail into Aristotle's treatment of the subject of money, the importance of which is indicated by Schumpeter's remark that it was the basis of relative economic theories 'to the end of the nineteenth century and even beyond', and that it had particular and direct influence on Adam Smith's own theory.[57]

Some modern scholars have claimed to discern in Aristotle's scanty remarks on exchange value the embryo, at least, of a labour theory of value.

---

[52] Cf. Finley (1970), 5; Spengler (1955), 381.   [53] Barbieri (1954), 824.

[54] De Roover (1955), 162–3, 188.

[55] The term is the Greek *chreia* at *NE* 1133ᵃ26–9 and 1133ᵇ6–8; cf. Johnson (1939), 449. Gordon (1964), 118, translates it directly with 'demand'. Tozzi (1961), 162–3, points out that it can mean 'utility' or 'common usage', and thus sees a reference to 'use' in the passage in question. I consider it better to translate it as 'necessity' or 'need'; when Aristotle wishes to speak of 'utility' or 'use' he employs *chresis* rather than *chreia*, as noted by Johnson (1939), 447–8 (see below, n. 82). Against this, see Lotito (1980), 129; against the loose and excessively 'modern' translation of *chreia* as 'demand', Spengler (1955), 385, who follows Soudek (1952); Finley (1970), 8 n. 22.   [56] *NE* 1133ᵃ19–21, Irwin's translation.

[57] Schumpeter (1955), 62–4, opposed by Gordon (1961), 608–11 (somewhat debatable). See also Bonar (1922), 156.

To justify these claims, it would be necessary to find in Aristotle secure references to the cost of production; and this a few of the scholars in question argue they have done, taking as their point of departure the passages in *NE* where Aristotle considers exchange between heterogeneous objects. In order for the exchange to be in accordance with justice, it is necessary to create an equation between the two objects, so that what is given can be gauged in proportion to what is received. Now in all these passages Aristotle compares not only the two objects in question, but also their respective makers: he thus conducts a comparison between *four* factors, the objects themselves and the men who made them; and states that the ratio that subsists between one pair must do so in the case of the other pair as well, or the exchange cannot take place.[58]

It is in my opinion largely this reference to the craftsmen whose artefacts are the object of exchange that has led certain scholars into thinking that Aristotle was referring to the *labour* of those craftsmen, and the different value placed on it according to the amount of work involved. This, at any rate, is my conclusion from reading the remarks of Schumpeter and Ross, as well as the admittedly cautious reference by Tozzi to the formulation of the relevant 'cost'.[59] Indeed in at least one place Aristotle makes a direct comparison between the two artisans' labour.[60] To move from these fleeting references, however, to a labour theory of value is, to say the least, a risky undertaking. It seems to me, first, that it is inappropriate to interpret the mention of the craftsmen who made the objects of exchange as a reference to their labour, or at any rate to base thereon a reconstruction in which their labour is the principal element. The essential condition for an exchange to take place, in Aristotle's analysis, is clearly need or necessity. There must be someone in need of shoes and someone in need of

---

[58] The passages in question are as follows: 'It is diagonal combination that produces proportionate exchange. Let A be a builder, B a shoemaker, C a house, D a shoe. The builder must receive the shoemaker's product from him, and give him the builder's own product in return' (*NE* v. 1133ª5–10); 'Hence, as builder is to shoemaker, so must the number of shoes be to a house; for if this does not happen, there will be no exchange and no association' (ibid. 22–4); 'Let A be a farmer, C food, B a shoemaker, and D his product that has been equalized; if this sort of reciprocity were not possible, there would be no association' (ibid. ᵇ4–6; Irwin's translation). The most accurate analysis of these and other Aristotelian passages is that of Lotito (1980).

[59] For the first two cf. Gordon (1964), 122, and Tozzi (1961), 166–7. I have doubts about Ross's interpretation, who though admitting that 'Aristotle does not expressly reduce the question to one of time', in fact explains the passage at 1133ª thus in his commentary. More prudently, Schumpeter (1955), 60–1 n. 1, observes that the reference to two craftsmen's work presupposes a reference to their produce, and that one might accordingly take Aristotle as aiming at a sort of 'labour-cost theory'; *contra* Finley (1970), 10.

[60] *NE* 1133ª8–10: 'the builder must receive the shoemaker's product, and give him the builder's own product in return' (see above, n. 58). See also, a few lines further on: 'since the product of one may well be superior to the product of the other. These products, then, must be equalized' (1133ª12–14). In both cases, however, Aristotle is referring not to the efforts of the craftsman, but rather to the work he completes, or—in modern terms—the end-product. See below, n. 70.

a house (to make use of Aristotle's own examples); otherwise there would
be no exchange, for the obvious reason that the two cobblers would only be
able to offer each other objects with which they are already equipped.
Aristotle makes this principle quite clear by stating that community of
exchange does not grow up between equals, for instance between two
doctors, or two farmers. It arises between people in different categories; a
doctor and a farmer, for example.[61]

What needs to be emphasized here is the reference to *community* of
exchange (*koinonia*): Aristotle repeats this frequently, and it is correctly
considered an essential point in his argument.[62] Within a community of this
sort, citizens follow different occupations according to the needs of the group
as a whole, and they exchange the produce of their work amongst themselves
so as to supply the wants of the whole rather than those of individuals.
Exchange takes place, in other words, between people with different
occupations and with reciprocal, interdependent needs. This fundamental
characteristic is Aristotle's reason for mentioning not just objects but people
also.[63] 'The first principle of market economy is, of course, indifference to
the *persons* of the buyer and seller; that is what troubles most commentators
on Aristotle';[64] indeed it often prompts them to conclude that the constant
presence of the craftsmen in Aristotle's analysis (the 'agents' of exchange, the
notion of the intermediary or professional merchant being overlooked at least
in the texts we have considered so far) entails a reference, albeit an implicit
one, to their capacity and therefore an evaluation of their competence for
labour, or even the time they spend on the task.

Now it is clear that in any economic evaluation of the artefacts exchanged
by the two craftsmen account will be taken of such matters as their costs and,
indeed, the time they spend on the work. Aristotle, however, makes no
mention of these factors, and it is sensible to be cautious in reading them
into his analysis, for the simple reason that an exclusively economic analysis
is a thing unknown in the ancient world.[65] It is also unlikely that Aristotle
had a concept of labour as a freestanding category, measurable in terms of
capacity and time and thereby affecting production costs, for such a concept
presupposes the existence of a market economy that in his day had not yet
developed, not to mention a form of abstraction that was similarly unknown

---

[61] *NE* 1133ª16–18.   [62] As by Polanyi (1957), 79; Finley (1970), 7–8; Lotito (1980), *passim*.

[63] That the exchanging parties are in different positions is a fundamental requirement of the
exchange, for which Aristotle has in mind specific products and real persons. Thus *koinonia* is a
relationship of specific difference and formal equality expressing the different exigencies of the
parties, 'unified' by need and made measurable by the latter's token, money: Lotito (1980), esp.
pt. ii. 32 f.; cf. also i. 162. The 'community' element in this, it can be argued, is found in Smith's
account too, in which society likewise depends on the reciprocal exchange of its members' work,
the difference arising precisely from the role this theory allots to work; Meek (1956), 62.

[64] Finley (1970), 10 (his italics).

[65] Economics did not exist as a free-standing science in antiquity; thus there could be no
truly economic speculation or analysis; Austin and Vidal-Naquet (1972), 19–22.

to the Greeks, by which the workman could be distinguished from his labour.[66] This does not mean that Greek thinkers had no conception of the role of labour in the economy. It is simply that it could not have developed the sense of independent workforce that it possesses in the modern economic context. I would add the perhaps banal observation that if Aristotle *could* have conceived something of the sort, it seems likely that he would have had the means to express it.

There are also other differences between the ancient and modern concepts of labour. When Smith speaks of labour as a measure of value, he defines it as 'toil and trouble'; his labourer 'in his ordinary state of health, strength and spirits; in the ordinary degree of skill and dexterity . . . must always lay down the same portion of his ease, his liberty and his happiness'.[67] There is no need to add that nothing similar is to be found in Aristotle. This is not the place to tackle the complex subject of the role of slavery in the ancient economy, still less so given that Aristotle refers to free labourers in the *Ethics*; but it is quite clear that the different structure and organization of work in the ancient world explains why there is in Aristotle's account of the goods of exchange no reference to the effort necessary for their production, whether in terms of the worker's 'disutility',[68] or—more reasonably—in terms that might, even vaguely, be compared with the typical formulation favoured by Smith, namely the labour 'embodied' in an object, and the labour 'commanded'.[69]

It therefore seems necessary to attribute the quadripartite structure of Aristotle's analysis of exchange to the indissoluble link between the fabric of society and its economic activity, because of which one could not imagine an

---

[66] Austin and Vidal-Naquet (1972), 27–8, 29–30. On the non-existence (or rather the embryonic existence) of the market economy in Aristotle's day see Polanyi (1957), 103, who argues against the tendency of economic historians to consider ancient civilizations of the East (and their supposed heir in Greece) to have been highly developed in commercial terms, and draws a distinction between commerce and market, whereby the former does not necessarily imply the presence of the latter. This fundamental distinction (the far-reaching implications of which were noted by M. Vegetti in the introduction to the volume in which Polanyi's essay appeared, p. 35) has received some attention, e.g. from Finley (1970), 13–14, on which see Lotito (1980), i. 171–2. This is not the place to deal with all the implications of this debate; we shall merely note that in Aristotle's day there was no market economy in the true, modern, sense, since it could not have the role in ancient society that it has in ours.

[67] *WN* I. v. 7. The phrase 'toil and trouble' occurs at I. v. 2.

[68] I agree with the suggestion by Johnson (1939), 447–8, 451, that the word Aristotle would have used for this is *ponos*—on the meaning of which see Mondolfo (1982), 13, 92. Though this is not identical with Smith's concept of 'disutility'—for which see Whitaker (1968), 18–19, 36— there is a likely degree of similarity between the two: cf. Plato's crude quantification of *ponos* and *chronos* at *Rep.* 369; Lotito (1980), iii. 62 n. 102. For the necessity and drudgery of *ponos* in Aristotle see Tranquilli (1979), 25 f.

[69] See Whitaker (1968), 21; Kaushil (1973), 63–4; Fiorito (1971), 82 f. Lotito (1980), iii. 63–4, states that for Aristotle 'value' is not entirely determined by need, 'but also by a value intrinsic to the object made up of technical know-how, ability of the workman, and labour examined in qualitative terms', and thus claims that Aristotle recognized the 'use-value of labour'. This, however, is somewhat different from the modern, abstract, and generalized concept, on which see Pietranera (1963), 111; Meek (1956), 60.

account that did not put the agents of exchange in the foreground of the picture. With regard to the product, one can approve the comments of Austin and Vidal-Naquet on the passage where Aristotle compares the labour of each craftsman: 'Non pas son travail en tant que catégorie abstraite, au sens marxiste de la valeur travail, mais le travail en tant qu'œuvre concrète'.[70] For these reasons I believe that the labour expended in the creation of a given economic commodity plays no part in Aristotle's conception of its value, and that that philosopher cannot therefore be considered in any way to have anticipated the labour theory of value.

As for the other important school of thought supposedly 'anticipated' by Aristotle, that of the marginalists, it seems equally hazardous to regard him as the standard-bearer of this group. For him, 'every product . . . is an indivisible organic unit, an *en tì* with its own *eidos*, its specific form, its unitary project, lying behind it. Therefore it is impossible to divide into parts the value-in-use of an object without destroying its essence.'[71] Accordingly, it is inherently difficult to associate Aristotle even remotely with marginalism, which presupposes the homogeneity and divisibility of all traded commodities. Furthermore, the association has been made, as usual, on the grounds of single phrases taken in the main from the *Topics*,[72] a process the inappropriate nature of which has already been commented upon.

Aristotle is justly considered the author of the distinction between value-in-use and value-in-exchange. In general it is noted that the former receives more attention in the *Politics*, while in the *Nicomachean Ethics* it is the latter. However, it is correct to say that even in the *Ethics*, while Aristotle certainly illustrates exchange, he subordinates value-in-exchange to value-in-use.[73] This priority is confirmed in the *Politics*, where he tackles the economic question from a more general position, but the keystone of exchange is still necessity or need; anything can be exchanged, because this action arises from the circumstance that men have less than they need of one sort of thing, and more than they need of another.[74] Here too, then, need is the fundamental element, though it is given a slightly more complex touch in that, instead of bringing all human requirements up or down to the same level, it is employed

[70] Austin and Vidal-Naquet (1972), 251 n. 10; cf. the rather reductive but still reliable comment by Johnson (1939), 450, that 'the equation of persons is to result, not from an evaluation of the labor contributed, but simply from an evaluation of the commodities offered'.

[71] Lotito (1980), i. 151.

[72] Such as: 'A thing is preferable if, added to the lesser thing, it makes the whole greater', *Top*. iii. 118^{b}16. (Later, Aristotle suggests a system of subtraction rather than addition. Note that the translation employed by Kauder renders the Greek neuter *to* with the word 'good'— which gives the sentence a more 'economic' flavour, for the reader inclined to see it in that light.) This, however, is not sufficient grounds for claiming, with Kauder (1953), 639, that 'the value of one good can be judged best if we lose or add it to a given group of commodities'; Aristotle merely meant to provide dialectic with a method of resolving the problem of making a choice between two or more things.   [73] Lotito (1980), i. 180; ii. 36.

[74] *Pol*. 1257^{a}14–17.

to indicate a possible use for an exchangeable object different from the one for which it was made, namely that of being exchanged. In both works,[75] however, one of Aristotle's main points is that for an exchange to take place there must first of all be someone who needs one thing and someone who needs the other; and if the exchange is made for money, then (except in cases of pure speculation, which he condemns)[76] this happens only because money is a means to an end, an intermediate element between two situations of necessity.[77] Money's essential function in the *Ethics*, as has already been noted, is that of 'interpreting' need and measuring value. In the *Politics*, on the other hand, certain other practical aspects are ascribed to it: intrinsic value; ease of handling; portability.[78] Money should, at any rate, be no more than a tool. It is possible that the fact that its chief job in the *Ethics* is that of turning need into quantifiable data accounts for the exchange of money for goods being less criticized than it is in the *Politics*;[79] the wider horizons of the latter and the stress it lays on the ease with which money can be acquired by means of 'unnatural' exchanges—those not driven by the primary require-ments of a self-sufficient community—doubtless resulted in weight being placed on the 'immorality' of chasing after wealth for its own sake in this way.

I shall not here go into the question of whether Aristotle's reasons for condemning commercial activity for profit were merely moralizing, or reflect a naturalist and materialist tendency; or even derive ultimately from the socio-economic situation of his own day.[80] What, I think, can be accepted is that value-in-use prevails in Aristotle's theory because he understood that

[75] The relevant passages are as follows: 'He who barters a pair of shoes *with one who has need thereof* in exchange for money or for food, uses the shoe in its role as a shoe, but not for its own use, since a shoe is not made for exchange' (*Pol.* 1257ᵃ10–13; my italics); 'It must therefore be that all things are measured in terms of one thing only . . . This thing is, in truth, need, which holds all things together; for if men had no need, or did not have the same need, exchange would not take place, or it would take place differently. And as a token of this need has emerged, by convention, money' (*NE* 1133ᵃ25–9). Each passage makes clear reference to need, but also to money. Thus Aristotle admits the notion of the exchange of goods for money in the *Politics*, even if not for gain.

[76] In other words 'chrematistics', i.e. 'speculation as known in the modern age': Barbieri (1958), 9.

[77] And also a pledge, when the exchange between goods cannot be completed at one time by both parties; Lotito (1980), iii. 32.

[78] 1257ᵃ31–41. Smith too, it should be said, includes an excursus on the origins of money at *WN* I. iv. 3–6, making mention of the primitive use of livestock as a measure of value, instanced by Homer's valuation of the armour of Glaucus and Diomedes 'in oxen'; a traditional example, repeated at *LJ* (A) vi. 98, and also used, for instance, by Montanari (1804), 23–4. The fact that the ox was a unit of measure does not mean that it was a means of exchange: Austin and Vidal-Naquet (1972), 221. Other comments by Smith on the origins of money are at *LJ* (A) vi. 105f.; (B) 235 f.

[79] Noted by Tozzi (1961), 159, and Johnson (1939), 449–50.

[80] For the first thesis see Finley (1970), 15–18; for the second Lowry (1974), 60; and for the third, deriving from Marx, see Lotito (1980), iii. 15–16. According to the last, Aristotle's theoretical outlook was limited by the restricted nature of commercial activity in his day, and his 'autonomous' interpretation of money reflects the autonomy of ancient commercial capital in regard to production.

unless firmly pegged to it, exchange value tends to be considered on its own account and leads to the fatal onset of the quest for gain for gain's sake. This, whatever his motive, he condemns. It is a point on which he is of course in fundamental disagreement with Adam Smith, whose famous paradox makes explicit reference to the fact that little or nothing can be had in exchange for water, but that a great deal can be had for diamonds. For Aristotle, then, it might be said that 'value' in its primary sense means use value, while for Smith it means value-in-exchange.

Attention must, however, be drawn to one point: from 'use' to 'utility', as translations of Aristotle's terminology, the step is short, but it has a disastrous effect here.[81] It is this that in some way seems to sanction, if not taking Aristotle as the ancestor of the marginalists, then at any rate attributing to him a certain subjective interpretation of value. In reality the key concept connected with value-in-use underlying his analysis is expressed by the term *chreia* in the *Ethics* and by *chresis* in the *Politics*. These words are almost, but not quite, synonymous; only the former has among its meanings (which range from 'use' to 'utility', 'advantage', etc.) that of 'lack, need'.[82] This is of vital significance to Aristotle's theory of the mechanism of exchange. It is therefore better to translate *chreia* as 'need' or 'necessity' than as 'use', as is sometimes done.

Certainly 'use' might well be the prevalent meaning of *chresis* as employed in the *Politics*, where emphasis is laid precisely on the usage that can be made of a given object: putting it to the use it was made for, or exchanging it for something of which one has *chreia*, need. Well-founded reservations about the translation of *chreia* as 'demand' have already been expressed;[83] but, though imprecise, this gets across the idea of an objective basis of value rather better than 'use' and 'utility' do. Aristotle only connects the concept of value with that expressed by the two latter words (that is, with *chresis*) in the sense that he rejects the potential for gain inherent in exchange, and focuses on it as the transfer of objects of equal value, destined for practical uses arising from life's necessities; this entails a certain privileging of 'use' and 'utility'. In today's language, however, reference to 'utility' in the context of value is something of a term of art, and even use value is influenced by subjective factors.

Smith's move was to dissociate the concept of value from utility and peg it to labour, thereby giving it what he felt was an objective basis. Aristotle too had constructed his theory on an objective and quantifiable factor, namely

---

[81] The effects have been seen, and criticized: cf. above, n. 55.

[82] Liddell, Scott, and Jones, *Lexicon*, and *TGL* s.v. On *chresis* see also the remarks of Tranquilli (1979), 43–7, though these relate to the relationship between production and consumption.

[83] See above, n. 55. Among others using this translation, Johnson (1939), 451 add., employs it to demonstrate a development within Aristotle's work from the concept of 'use' to one of 'demand'; for this it is necessary to argue that the first two books of the *Politics* predate *NE* book V. It is perhaps better to avoid chronological questions so far removed from our area, and adhere for the time being to the view of the *Ethics* and *Politics* as fundamentally unitary in concept; thus Polanyi (1957), 79.

that of need, which is the foundation of equality in exchange, and can be quantified by means of 'translating' it into money. But the fact that this concept of need is the constitutive ingredient in use value, which in turn is the essential factor in exchange, naturally leads on to the conclusion that the value of a thing derives from its practical, physical utility. Aristotle stands at the head of the tradition supporting the concept that value is objective utility for his assertion that exchange must take place solely on the basis of, and be contemplated purely in terms of, need; an assertion which emphatically depicts use and utility as the fruition of specific goods, and thus resolves value-in-exchange into nothing other than value-in-use. Expressed in figures, the two forms of value would therefore be precisely equal.[84]

Aristotle, it has been noted, speaks of exchange taking place directly between producers, without middlemen. It will be recalled that in his condemnation of ignoble occupations those of manual labour and commerce are associated with each other (*Pol.* 1328[b]37–41). How far this view (shared by Plato) of the different worth of different occupations goes back to ideas about their respective intrinsic dignity,[85] and how much it reflects the fact that the 'ignoble' ones were generally practised in the Greek world by non-citizens,[86] I cannot say. It remains the case that Aristotle's account of exchange is purely theoretical, and one cannot doubt that he was aware that things were rather different in reality.

Adam Smith, on the other hand, starts as always from experience. It is on this basis that he states that utility, in the long run, does not count for much. One can receive much in exchange for some things, and little in exchange for others, without there being any necessary relationship between this and the utility of the things in question (calculated as in Aristotle's schema according to a notional scale of essential requirements, classifiable as objective or given). Thus exchange value has to be sought elsewhere. Aristotle simply does not pose the question of why some things 'yield' more in exchange than others, even though he surely noticed the fact; his logical point of departure is an equal exchange. He does not, on principle, deal with the commercial exploitation of exchange because it is 'practised by some at the expense of others' (*Pol.* 1258[b]1–2), and confines legitimate exchange activities within the bounds set by use value. In other words, for Smith use value and exchange value do not coincide at all; for Aristotle they do; better still, exchange value only exists (or, perhaps, should only exist) as an expression of use value. Exchange, for

---

[84] The values, expressed in money, must 'equate' in the exchange: thus I can exchange an item worth five minas for another also worth five minas (*NE* 1133[b]23–6); the ratio is always 1:1. See on this Lotito (1980), ii. 42 n. 19; cf. also 49 n. 25: 'in Aristotle there is no concept of value independent of use-value, and thus of need'.

[85] For illustration and discussion of Aristotle's contempt for manual labour (directed not so much at the work itself as at the fact that the worker is dependent on another person) see Mondolfo (1982), 111, 118–24.

[86] Lotito (1980), iii. 43 n. 87—a lengthy note opposing Finley's thesis that the lack of the merchant as a social figure indicates that Aristotle was merely moralizing.

Aristotle, although indispensable for the community, cannot subsist outside it, and must depend totally on its needs; it is incapable of being distilled from solid, social necessities.

On the basis of what has been said so far, then, the closest link between Aristotle and Smith, from a purely formal and, in a sense, external point of view, is the famous paradox deriving from the ancient rhetorical tradition. Over the course of the centuries this has acquired an economic content which it did not have in Aristotle's day, the essential element not being expressed, namely that a thing's utility is not enough to give it value if it is also super-abundant; nor is it referred in any way to the question of exchange. Instead, we find the following statement (more clearly a passing reflection on an economic question) at *Pol.* 1323^b 7–10: 'a superabundance of these [i.e. external goods or tools] necessarily harms or brings no utility to whoever possesses them'. This isolated passage, however, is in my opinion chiefly to be under-stood in connection with Aristotle's concept of the narrow limits placed on needs and desires, and his corresponding condemnation of any attempt to satisfy them beyond these limits, which would transgress into chrematistics.[87]

In seeking to establish the degree of licence that exchange can be allowed, Aristotle has recourse to man's natural needs. His examples relate to a set of 'simplified' social circumstances, with conventional essential requirements: houses, shoes, beds, or oil, wheat, wine, etc.[88] Smith, in the famous paradox, is not referring to essential requirements; that is, his words relate to them to that small extent that the ease with which they are satisfied (thanks, for instance, to the great abundance of water) diminishes their exchange value. But if one looks not only at his most famous work, but also at his *Lectures on Jurisprudence*, one finds the subject dealt with at length. A highly significant passage of *LJ*, omitted in *WN*,[89] states that all occupations should serve man's 'natural needs'; among these he numbers not only what men need to live, but also the trivial refinements and niceties that meet specific inclina-tions or preferences in taste, which are felt by man alone among the animals, and which give rise (though Smith does not put it in these terms) to the pursuit of the 'superfluous'. All the evidence suggests that this is the explanation for the high value of precious stones, which owe their desirabil-ity in men's eyes chiefly to two characteristics, their colour and their rarity.[90]

This argument, by emphasizing the inherent links between human pleas-ures and human consumption, illustrates how the category of needs can be

---

[87] Austin and Vidal-Naquet (1972), 184–5; see also Barbieri (1958), 8.

[88] Lotito (1980), iii. 33. These are the so-called 'normal needs', today no longer the exclusive base for use value; Meek (1956), 72.

[89] Pietranera (1963), 88 f., analysed the difference between *LJ* and *WN* on this point; in his view, what remains of ethics in *LJ*, where the 'utility' described is of a feudal character, is easily outdone in *WN*, where it is of a decidedly bourgeois aspect. See also Meek (1956), 45 f.

[90] *LJ* (A) vi. 13, 15; cf. Hollander (1973), 135–6, stating that in regard to the determination of value Smith rejects utility or use value, understood as a matter of biological significance, not as what is desirable.

extended beyond vital necessities to include things that are desirable but superfluous. The difficulty in reconciling the concepts of utility, with its status as a social value, and desirability, and thus understanding subjective utility, 'is no doubt responsible for the comparative lateness of a satisfactory explanation of value on the basis of utility'.[91] The importance of the discovery of subjective utility, however, was not recognized only by authors such as Pufendorf; it had long been attributed to Aristotle himself, who would have considered 'needs' as including 'desires'.[92] According to Kauder, it was precisely this school of thought whose conclusions Smith was unaware of.

There is in fact a long tradition behind the phrase 'necessaries and conveniences'[93] going back to classical antiquity; but I believe that in drawing up an analysis of exchange on the basis of justice, Aristotle was thinking of an objective value.[94] That some of his phrases, plucked from contexts having nothing to do with economics, can be interpreted as somehow implying a subjective concept of utility does not suffice to cancel or outweigh the fact that his discussions of exchange are directed solely towards defining *the way in which exchanges should take place*. It is necessary to determine value so that the exchange can conform to justice and respects the requirements and the structure of the society in which it takes place, in accordance with a mechanism that is quite schematic, but also clear-cut enough to rule out subjective evaluations; these were surely attributed to the schema later on.[95] It is doubtless unwarranted to see in Aristotle the standard-bearer of those who would interpret value in terms of utility and scarcity; he certainly knew well enough that precious, useless objects could be very expensive, and it would be unfair to imagine that he had considered only how rare objects were, and not the additional factor of human vanity in pursuit of whatever is most costly.[96] But this played no part in his analysis of value, because these are attitudes that give rein to unnatural needs on the part of men, and make money serve ends that are not its proper function. They are, in short, attitudes

---

[91] Sewall (1971), 28.   [92] Sewall (1971), 120–1.   [93] Caruso (1973), pp. xlii–xliii.

[94] Sewall (1971), 119.

[95] Geminiano Montanari (1804), 42–5, following on from Davanzati, held that Aristotle had in mind not only needs arising from necessity, but 'voluptuary' needs as well. In propounding this thesis I believe he interpreted the text (which he read in the Latin translation conveniently giving *chreia* as *indigentia*) in a somewhat forced fashion. This can be seen from the key points in his argument: the difficulty of drawing a sharp line between what is necessary and what is not; and the somewhat 'modern' point that one man's luxury is another's opportunity for work. He generally renders *indigentia* with the hendiadys *bisogni e desideri* ('needs and desires'), which may well have given rise to a school of thought according to which Aristotle's theory took account of subjective value; but it remains based upon a forced reading of the text, and if anything it is to Smith's credit that he did not subscribe to this view.

[96] The fact that in *LJ* the determinant factors in an object's value are demand, scarcity, and the wealth of the person requiring it—see Pietranera (1963), 101 f., and Meek (1956), 49–50—associates Smith a little more closely with Aristotle's 'subjectivist' successors. This might in any case seem obvious, given that in his lectures he still adheres to general moral-philosophy schemes, without fully developing the concept of labour (as shown by Pietranera).

that come under the heading of the pursuit of wealth for its own sake, the contemptible chrematistics.

It will suffice by way of conclusion to emphasize once more that the presence of a subjective element in the determination of value began more or less with the later schoolmen and continued with the natural-law theorists;[97] the classic eighteenth-century theory of value, on the other hand, derived from the 'epoch-making discovery of the great productive potentialities of "free" wage labour organized on a capitalist basis'.[98] Little, I believe, need be added to this, other than to observe that Smith's rejection of subjective theories of value arises from the fact that these theories derive value-in-exchange from a subjective notion of utility.[99] Paradoxically, since (as argued here) it is wrong to take Aristotle as the ancestor of this strain of subjectivism, it may be that Smith was in fact closer to the 'true' Aristotle than to the way he was later interpreted.

Smith, in short, declined to participate in the debate over value-in-use, which had been fundamental to Aristotle, and concentrated instead on value-in-exchange; Aristotle had indeed dealt with this too, but in a completely different way, for all that both thinkers were at pains to strip it of subjective considerations. Smith's idea was to peg it to some 'objective' commodity, which he found in labour. Aristotle, not admitting exchange value as a thing in itself, but only as a function of use value, left standing only that thin sliver of the former concept that coincided with the latter, which thereby came to play the major role in his whole account of exchange. This, it must be stated, offers some justification to the interpretation of Aristotle as, in the subjective sense, a utilitarian, since the concept of utility in economic thought ends up meaning the evaluation of the subjective (and even the pleasurable) element in human needs.

Thus Aristotle's concept might, to modern eyes, seem a contradiction in terms. But in reality he saw value-in-use too as having a function within the *polis*. The Greek community was composed of different workers, who in order to survive had to exchange their produce with each other and thereby supply their respective wants; there had, furthermore, to be nothing left over, for Aristotelian justice allowed no gain arising from and in addition to the acquisition of necessities; any such gain would be both sordid and unjust, inasmuch as it would entail a loss on someone else's part. Value-in-use in Aristotle is not therefore to be understood in terms so much of subjective

---

[97] Meek (1956), 14 f.; Sewall (1971), 120–1; Pietranera (1963), 109.   [98] Meek (1956), 20.

[99] Pietranera (1963), 109 f., with reference to the strain of thought (mentioned above) stretching from the schoolmen, through the natural-law theorists, Davanzati and Montanari, to Barbon. If one accepts Hollander's thesis that Smith rejected not the economists' notion of utility and desirability, but only that of use value as a physical property of commodities (see n. 90 above), i.e., in essence, Aristotle's objective utility, it would be impossible to claim the similarities (referred to in the text) between the two arising from a shared objection to subjective valuations. The general critique, however, is that Smith broke away from this tradition in favour of objective valuation. For emphasis on the error of presuming utility and desirability synonymous in philosophical terms see Lindgren (1973), 103 n. 9.

utility, as of the requirements of the self-sufficient *polis* in all its constituent parts. Once again, Aristotle was considering not the individual, but rather the citizen, the well-known, typically Greek figure of the 'political animal'.

A question not raised here has been that of whether there really was any form of true economic analysis in antiquity;[100] nor have we attempted to ask whether later historical thought may itself have distorted the picture of the economic state of the ancient world.[101] To do so would have required a deep and precise examination into ancient doctrines and institutions, as well as the surviving contemporary evidence. We have also refrained from asking why Aristotle's account of exchange, composed in an age of quite sophisticated commercial relations, presents a model closely resembling simple barter and, in effect, amounting to an entirely theoretical analysis that may well have a given, specific objective, but is wholly divorced from the economic practice of the day. Here the question is one of deciding whether Aristotle's position was purely that of a moralist, or might somehow reflect certain aspects of contemporary economic systems;[102] this would have entailed a close exami- nation of the whole of his corpus, whereas here we are concerned only with his analysis of exchange. Some comment on the way in which Aristotle and ancient thinkers generally framed their theories, though this is a well-known question, is not out of place. Brunner puts it thus:

Economics as the study of matters concerning the *oikos* covers the entirety of human relations and the activities of the household, the relationship between husband and wife, parents and children, master and servant (or slave), and the fulfilment of duties arising in the context of domestic and agrarian economy. It also includes the creation of commerce, which is necessary and permissible to the extent that it assists the self- sufficiency of the household. It is however harmful when it becomes the end in itself, that is to say when its only aim is the earning of money. Economics is opposed to chrematistics, and *it is in the latter that the prehistory of today's economic science is to be found*. This was a subject so void of content that it gave rise to no theory—any such would have been regarded with disdain—and received occasional treatment only in ethical and political philosophy, then to be discussed only with regard to the limits that should be placed on it.[103]

In this picture Aristotle, whose aim is to present a structural analysis of exchange within the context of an 'economics' of the *polis* as a projection of

---

[100] On which (even in regard to Aristotle alone) there has been much disagreement amongst scholars of the first rank; suffice it to say that for Finley (1970), 18, there was no such thing, while for Polanyi (1957), 66, 'He [Aristotle] will be seen as attacking the problem of man's livelihood with a radicalism of which no later writer was capable—none has ever penetrated deeper into the material organization of man's life'. More recently, Lotito (1980), iii, 30, has ascribed certain theoretical advances to Aristotle.

[101] For the 'modernizing' way in which nineteenth-century ancient historians such as Edouard Meyer, Beloch, and Busolt interpreted the ancient Greek economy see Austin and Vidal-Naquet (1972), ch. 1. It is but a short step from such an approach to one ascribing to the Greeks a true, modern form of economic analysis.

[102] Respectively, the views of Finley and Lotito; see above, n. 80, with the relevant passage in the text.   [103] Brunner (1956), 35–6 (my italics).

the *oikos*, treats value from the point of view of use. Only two aspects of exchange itself concern him: that it should promote the self-sufficiency of the community, and that it should be conducted in accordance with justice. It is not inappropriate to recall that for Aristotle justice is 'une mediété proportionelle entre deux inegalités . . . le partage juste entre deux personnes inégales est un partage proportionnel, donc inégal, aux yeux des démocrates antiques, et c'est cette proportionalité qu'Aristote appelle "l'égal".'[104] After the making of the exchange (which must indeed reflect precisely 'reciprocity in proportion, not according to strict equality', *NE* 1132^{b}31–3), the preceding state of affairs has to be re-established. The two parties must have exactly what they had before, neither more nor less. Aristotle did not see exchange as a vehicle for either gaining advantages or suffering loss, but rather as the restoration of what was possessed by the parties at the moment of the exchange.[105] There is no need to emphasize the huge difference between this interpretation of exchange value and Smith's. The reason for the difference, however, resides in the fact that Smith's version of exchange derives from the area that Aristotle did not consider legitimate; chrematistics, the science of moneymaking, which could perhaps (and with great caution) be viewed as the ancient equivalent of market economics[106]. Aristotle's eyes were averted from the very type of value on which Adam Smith's were fixed.

[104] Austin and Vidal-Naquet (1972), 370 n. 3.   [105] Lotito (1980), ii. 33–4.

[106] 'the economy of ancient Europe has nothing to say to us on economic history as the history of the market, since the latter belonged not in the economic sphere, but rather in the chrematistic one; nor does this tell us much about its importance and the principles governing it': Brunner (1956), 59. *Pace* authors such as Polanyi (see n. 66 above), Brunner also argued that 'from the fact that the market economy was not capable of determining the fundamental characteristics of ancient Europe's social structure, and that it had only a limited significance in ancient European economic thought, one cannot conclude that it was devoid of importance, or primitive in character' (ibid. 56).

5

Adam Smith and Ancient Literature

5.1. SMITH'S LECTURES ON RHETORIC AND BELLES-LETTRES

Adam Smith in fact planned two publications, neither of which he succeeded in completing. In the letter in which he mentions a 'Theory and History of Law and Government' he also alludes to 'a sort of Philosophical History of all the different branches of Literature, of Philosophy, Poetry and Eloquence'.[1] Although he had already organized part of the material, the weariness of his advancing age prevented him from actually writing the planned work.

Shortly before his death, Smith ordered the manuscript of the lectures that he delivered in Edinburgh and Glasgow to be destroyed, the very manuscript which Hugh Blair in 1783 still hoped would be published.[2] We should remember that during his time in Edinburgh Smith was appointed to teach specifically these subjects, whereas in Glasgow he held the Chair of Logic for a year, before being appointed to the Chair of Moral Philosophy. The young professor's well-known aversion to logic and metaphysics, closely associated in his thought with scholastic philosophy, led Smith to digress into rhetoric and literature during his logic lectures. We read in the testimony of John Millar, who expressed considerable regret over the destruction of the original manuscript, that in Smith's opinion 'the best method of explaining and illustrating the various powers of the human mind, the most useful part of metaphysics, arises from an examination of the several ways of communicating our thoughts by speech, and from an attention to the principles of those literary compositions, which contribute to persuasion or entertainment'.[3] And so, as with the *Lectures on Jurisprudence*, all that remains is a set of notes taken during Smith's lectures by a diligent student. These notes, however, are less complete than the other notes available to us,[4] and do not seem to correspond so closely to any of Smith's published works. Certain passages of *LJ* closely resemble or coincide with *WN*, and in some

---

[1] Letter to the Duc de La Rochefoucauld, in *Corr*. 287 (no. 248).
[2] Howell (1975), 13.   [3] Stewart (1980), i. 16.
[4] The set of lectures on jurisprudence discovered in 1958, cited as *LJ* (A), provides much greater detail than those published by Cannan in 1896, cited as *LJ* (B). The so-called 'Anderson Notes' ('AN') should certainly not be overlooked, even though limited in scope.

instances through these we can trace and reconstruct the development of Smith's thought. In the case of the 'literary' lectures, there seems to be little connection with Smith's published work, though certainly we cannot say that there is no connection at all.

5.2. AN OUTLINE OF A 'CONJECTURAL' HISTORY OF LITERATURE

John Millar's testimony cited above is useful to us because it also explains, albeit briefly, Smith's aim in the teaching of literary subjects. In the first place Smith examined the structure of language, and then the principles underlying the rules of literary composition aimed at persuasion or pleasure. This may indeed be the theoretical part of Smith's unpublished literary work. However, from Smith's letter to the Duc de La Rochefoucauld mentioned above, we know that Smith intended to examine, from a philosophical angle, the *history* of the principal branches of literature. We can glean something more about this teaching from the *Lectures* too and from a few other sources. Smith's 'philosophical history' of literature has fairly well-defined characteristics, the first being that of its development in relation to progress in society.[5] Smith explains the fact that prose came after poetry in order of time as a result of the development of trade: 'no one ever made a bargain in verse' (*LRBL* ii. 116), in Smith's colourful phrase. Smith departs from the traditional distinction, of classical origin but reinterpreted during the Renaissance, between poetry as the expression of pleasure (or aesthetic emotion),[6] and prose, the language of civil life, used by the orator and the historian, and travels back in time to examine the condition of primitive men, and the dances performed for pleasure with music, which called for rhythmic language as an accompaniment: 'Poetry is a necessary attendant on musick, especially on vocal musick, the most naturall and simple of any. They [i.e. primitive peoples] naturally express some thoughts along with their musick, and these must of consequence be formed into verse to suit with the music'[7]. It is for this reason, Smith continues, that poetry is cultivated among savages, and even perfected: prose, on the other hand, is of no interest until some kind of commercial activity develops. This activity calls for appropriate language, namely prose, the 'natural' expression of commercial or other types of transactions, in the same way that poetry is the natural expression of enjoyment. (It is well known that Smith attributes the origin of trade to man's innate tendency to persuade. While persuasion has been, since

---

[5] I examined this issue, from a purely historical standpoint, in Vivenza *et al.* (1980), 51 ff.

[6] The well-known verses of Horace, who attributes to poetry the task of being useful or pleasant, or both (Hor. *Ars Poet.* 333–4), lead to a two-fold tradition, in which on the one hand poetry exists for moral ends, while on the other the sole purpose of poetry is enjoyment. It is evident that Smith refers exclusively to the latter, which goes back to Castelvetro (Cecchi and Sapegno (1966), 574–5).

[7] *LRBL* ii. 114. See also the essay 'Of the Imitative Arts', II. 1–4.

ancient times, the main purpose of some of the principal forms of prose, we shall see how Adam Smith came to link this classical purpose with his theory of economic growth, which ultimately influences some traditional literary principles, though in a rather personal way. The purpose of the classical authors, namely persuasion, has become in Smith's thought a cause which stimulates another of man's 'natural instincts', trade. The development of prose, an instrument appropriate to this activity, becomes a consequence of persuasion, or rather of the instinct to persuade.)

After these considerations of a practical kind, the next stage is of an aesthetic nature. In Smith's account, the two forms of expression are initially separate, since there is no need to make prose more pleasurable, given that poetry exists for this purpose. Prose offers no scope for amusement, and is therefore left without embellishment. However, the development of trade always creates wealth, and so there comes a time when pleasure above all else is sought in every activity—a condition generally brought about by prosperity, which, according to traditional moralizing, induces people to abandon the virtues by which they have become strong and rich in favour of comfort, luxury, and pleasures which will ultimately undermine their character. (Here, however, we could object that a refining of tastes will also result.) 'It is only when pleasure is the only thing sought after that Prose comes to be studied. People who are rich and at their ease cannot give themselves the trouble of anything where they do not expect some pleasure' (*LRBL* ii. 116). Thus prose also begins to take on qualities of aesthetic value.

In this lecture Smith speaks of eloquence and, in his customary fashion, 'reconstructs' its classical subdivision into demonstrative, deliberative, and judicial eloquence. Smith asserts that deliberative and judicial eloquence came first in time, because 'men would much sooner consider what was to be done, or consider the merit of those actions that have been done',[8] and would only later consider demonstrative eloquence, which consists mainly of panegyric.

Even from these fragments the consistency of Smith's approach, i.e. that in every branch of knowledge progress is encouraged by economic factors, is evident. We could perhaps note that in his *Lectures on Jurisprudence*, whilst Smith gives a fundamental role to trade in the foundation and development of legal systems, initially he focuses attention on the ownership of land (and before that, we may recall, the ownership of livestock). Ownership emerges as the economic factor which makes men feel the need for the power of the State and a legal regulation of interpersonal relationships. Subsequently, the

---

[8] *LRBL* ii. 111. I recall briefly Smith's concept of the origins of the power of the State: law courts and judicial and deliberative assemblies developed first (*LJ* (A) iv. 15–18 and *LJ* (B) 25–7; *LRBL* ii. 199). It is therefore consistent that the deliberative and judicial oratory came first, given that language was appropriate to these functions. In Smith's sentence, nevertheless, we can perhaps also detect a reference to Cic. *De Or.* ii. 43, which states that the demonstrative genre is 'less necessary' than the other two.

significant effect of trade is that it transforms institutions which are no longer suited to the new situation. In the *Lectures on Rhetoric*, on the other hand, it is trade that represents the starting-point, and ownership is not in itself sufficient to nurture literary aspirations, given that poetry was originally cultivated by savages in caves, who would appear to belong to the first socio-economic stage of society. Prose develops for practical purposes, and is perfected with 'the introduction of commerce' (*LRBL* ii. 114–15) and from the wealth which this brings.

In ancient Greece, the first impulse, in this and in other art forms, came from the colonies. Eloquence was brought to Athens by the Sicilian Gorgias, and economic progress following the Persian Wars did the rest. Nevertheless, this was already a rather advanced 'stage', and perhaps we can envisage a rougher and more primitive form of deliberative and judicial eloquence, with no artistic merit, which served merely to establish essential concepts and regulations, and which developed when men began to feel the need to consult each other for making decisions or giving judgements. On Smith's assumption, this coincides with the beginning of legislation and government. This primitive eloquence continues without further embellishment through the second and third socio-economic stages, until the changes caused by trade lead to the birth of literature, and prose begins to claim aesthetic value in the same way as poetry.

I hope I am not pushing Smith's intention too far when I suggest that in the fields of jurisprudence and politics, which were more 'concrete' and important for the material life of populations, the fundamental element was property, which was at the forefront of and propelled an activity (law and politics), which in turn served to protect and sustain it. In the case of poetry and other literature, the first (though not the sole) aim of which was to please, perhaps it is obvious that the most important element was trade, for two principal reasons: first, trade produced greater wealth, and therefore the development of a sense of beauty and refinement of taste; secondly, it brought populations into contact with each other, thus widening horizons which could and did have an influence on literature, particularly so in the case of the Greeks and Romans.

At any rate, the following sequence of events emerges from Smith's lectures: from the most primitive of times music and poetry are cultivated; from the beginning of the age of shepherds there is (probably) some sort of prose, used in making decisions or legal judgements. (In *LJ* Smith mentions the possible existence of agreements, even if they do not constitute proper laws, relating to the legal status of property which is in the process of being formed in that age.) As trade increases, or rather with the increase in prosperity which accompanies it, there is a need to add aesthetic value to prose as well, which probably developed in the meantime.

Poetry is still ahead from the artistic standpoint, and literary activity on public occasions is modelled on poetry. Smith reminds us of civilization in

Athens, with games, athletic contests, and poetry competitions, which were so dependent upon music, and the close links between poetry and the education of young people, based as we know on music and gymnastics. Thus in the games, which exalted the abilities of youth, the existence of competitions and prizes for music led to similar competitions for poetry, closely linked with music. But this was not all: in Athens, where the economy was already advanced in the fifth century, eloquence had also been perfected. The orators began to demand the same prizes and competitions as the poets, and so the histories of Herodotus and the orations of Isocrates were read in public.[9]

It is not for us to judge to what extent this 'reconstruction' of Smith's is convincing. It was widely accepted that poetry preceded prose, given that all great literature bears witness first to the poets and later to prose writers. Moreover, in seventeenth-century tracts considerable importance was attached to the distinction between poetry as a capacity different from rational thought and prior to craftmanship, and intellectual or logical reasoning. This distinction derives mainly from the idea that poetry was for enjoyment or play, and thus Smith's position is in keeping with his view of poetry as a source of delight.

5.3. **POETRY, OR DELIGHT**

So in Smith's teaching the purpose of poetry is enjoyment, and here he follows the classical and Renaissance tradition (originally deriving from Horace but also from Aristotle[10]). However, he avoids any mention of the other fundamental purpose attributed to poetry in classical tradition, namely moral teaching. It seems therefore that Smith's argument does not derive directly from classical ideas but rather from Renaissance commentators, such as Castelvetro, who assigns to poetry the sole purpose of providing enjoyment. I think that is a reasonable conclusion, despite at least one place in which Smith seems willing to ascribe a serious purpose to poetry and to primitive poetry in particular.

In Smith's most important work we find reference to moralistic origins of some of the first poetical compositions in Greece, where maxims of morality were expressed in verse, in the form of 'apologues' (didactic fables) and 'apophthegms' (wise maxims). Smith cites Aesop, Theognis, and Phocylides,

---

[9] *LRBL* ii. 119–20. At this time, in Smith's view, there was rivalry between orators and poets, and the orators imitated the poets both in content and in 'style': see Sect. 5.5. In my opinion Smith based this idea on a phrase from Cicero relating to rhythmic prose: it seems that Isocrates introduced an element of rhythm into prose, after realizing that people were serious as they listened to the orators, whilst the poets were listened to with pleasure (see Cic. *Or.* 174–5; *Brutus* 32–3). This phrase may well also have been behind Smith's argument on the need to make prose pleasurable.

[10] Howell (1976), 160. It is known that Horace in his treatise conforms to Aristotelian and Peripatetic doctrines: Marchesi (1971), i. 496.

part of Hesiod, as well as Solomon's proverbs. From the Greeks, with the exception of Aesop, Smith therefore quotes authors of epics and lyrics from the first period of Hellenic literature, more to underline the moralistic content than the poetic qualities of these early literary works.[11] I do not feel, however, that this in any way detracts importance from the fact that in *LRBL* Smith does not speak of a didactic or moralistic purpose of poetry.

We can also find indirect confirmation of this in a parallel, again of classical origin, that Smith makes between history and poetry[12] in which he affirms that the first historians were poets, and that they did their utmost to arouse 'wonder' in their audiences, by means of poetical language and the choice of exceptional and surprising subjects. (Note that *this* poetry, even though primitive, is already considerably different from the 'rhythmic language' of the savage, born in relation to music: here a precise intention exists, and is expressed with adequate techniques.) Poetry responds to the need to amaze[13] because it is a more expressive and sophisticated form of language than prose ('more difficult, but at the same time . . . much superior in beauty and strength', *LRBL* ii. 74). However, no edifying role is assigned to poetry at a first glance, and we are unable to detect any after special consideration either. For instance, in epic and tragic poetry attention is focused on the representation or description of the way in which characters behave in trying circumstances (*LRBL* ii. 83): but this is dictated above all by a technical necessity, in order to achieve the desired result of capturing the attention and participation of the spectator (or the reader). Nowhere, if I am not mistaken, does Smith refer to the catharsis of Aristotelian theory, nor does he adequately treat the problem of the enjoyment afforded by tragedy. 'The insistence in the lecture [ii. 82] on the tragic writer's heightening of the painful nature of his story in order to lead to a satisfying "catastrophe" is an oblique solution of the problem and one frequently given.'[14] It is, moreover, a technical solution, we might add. Smith is trying to show what means a writer must use to reach his desired result.

In his lectures on history Smith repeats that a historian must narrate events in such a way as to arouse the emotions of readers. There is no reason to suppose that this does not also apply to the composition of poetry, which, as we have already said, in Smith's opinion differs from history only in terms

---

[11] *WN* v. i. f. 25, with reference to the first non-systematic attempts to produce a moral theory. In *EPS* we also find reference to the poems of ancient Greece, which, like some more recent examples, 'may express merely some maxims of prudence and morality' ('Of the Imitative Arts', ii. 9, in *EPS*, p. 190).

[12] *LRBL* ii. 74; I have already mentioned this in Vivenza *et al.* (1980), 55 and n. 170, emphasizing the different stance taken by Smith in comparison with Aristotle.

[13] In literature the emotive aspect prevails over the feeling of wonder, which Adam Smith considers also to be present in 'scientific' literature, but in this case it produces a rational need for knowledge, while in a literary and artistic context it arouses sentimental involvement. See Ch. 1 n. 79.   [14] Bryce, 'Introduction' to *LRBL*, p. 20.

of the metre. If the aim of narrative, be it poetry or prose, is to inspire the reader, after having awakened a sensation of astonishment and interest, an active participation in the narrated events, we might conclude that in all this there is an ethical function, particularly if we recall what a phrase like 'We feel for them as it were for ourselves' meant to Smith (*LRBL* ii. 28). However, the doubt remains that even these efforts to find the best way to involve the emotions of the listener are in reality a technique; the more so, since, unlike history, poetry and narrative are fiction, and the reader is always aware of this.

When we consider the literary forms characteristic of poetry, it becomes clear that here Smith follows Aristotle's division between epic and tragedy, the former being principally narrative whilst the latter is dramatic, and this also explains why tragedy is generally much shorter.[15] In his treatment of the principle of the three famous 'unities', of action, of place, and of time, Smith echoes the approach of sixteenth-century critics, which should not surprise us if we recall that the unities do not appear in Aristotle (who, as is widely known, specified only one of them, unity of action, in *Poetics,* 1451^a28–34), but were elaborated amid the prolific writings of the Renaissance.[16]

The aspect of classical literary criticism which most interests Smith is, it appears, the characters, which once again give him an opportunity to adapt classical thinking to his own needs. 'The plot, then, is the first principle, and, as it were, the soul of tragedy; Character holds the second place', to quote Aristotle (*Poetics,* 1450^b2–3; S.H. Butcher's translation). Smith adapts this concept a little, affirming that in tragedy and in epic the plot is of greater importance than the characters, whilst in comedy it is the characters who are of greatest importance, principally because of the different purpose of the two 'forms'. The best characters for tragedy are kings and noblemen, grand figures. In *TMS*, the Scottish philosopher justifies the observed natural tendency of men to sympathize with illustrious (and rich) figures, explaining that men are generally more willing to share the joys than the sorrow of others. Thus those who are in a prosperous, fortunate, and enviable position are more likeable, and, conversely, when misfortune befalls them there is much greater participation than there would be for a common mortal.[17] Smith thus goes on to say that the best subjects for tragedies are the misfortunes that befall kings. In *LRBL* Smith adds that the misfortunes befalling important figures are less frequent than the misfortunes afflicting common people, to which we are accustomed. This rarity, together with the fact that

---

[15] Arist. *Poet.* 1459^b23–9; see also ibid. 1449^b10–15; and Smith's *LRBL* ii. 84–5.

[16] Cecchi and Sapegno (1966) 574–7; it may be of interest here that the enunciation of the three unities was by the very Castelvetro who dismissed the functions of poetry as solely for pleasure (see above, n. 6). Smith treats this issue in *LRBL* ii. 81 ff.

[17] *TMS* I. iii. 2. 1–2. See also ibid. VI. ii. 1. 21. Smith also notes with reference to prose, in particular to demonstrative oratory, that good fortune tends to attract consensus and admiration (*LRBL* ii. 100).

the well-being of important figures is linked to the fortunes of the masses, and with the natural human tendency to respect our superiors, explains this acknowledged circumstance.

Actually, Epictetus, the Stoic philosopher, writer of the well-known classical precedent to Smith's position, did not mean to say that man by his nature respects those who are in a superior position to him, but rather that it is impossible to fall from a great height if you are already in a humble position:[18] if you possess very little, you have very little to lose; the greatest misfortunes befall those who possess much, namely princes and kings.

In comedy, Smith ranks the characters first in order of importance, following on from the above reasoning: the inborn tendency which leads us to respect our superiors leads us also to ridicule only those who are below our station.[19] Here a faint similarity with the *Poetics* of Aristotle is apparent, where Aristotle states that the characters in tragedy are superior to those we encounter in life, whilst the characters we find in comedy are inferior or equal.[20] Thus Aristotle compares real life with the stage, and also tells us that the character of a tragedy must, taken as a whole, be 'noble'. However, any similarities between the two authors end here, because Aristotle is speaking of a form of temperament, rather than of a man's position in society. Smith on the other hand is referring specifically to the latter, with his realistic admission that human nature is inclined to be servile towards superiors and disparaging towards inferiors, and from his reasoning it follows that dukes and princes are misplaced characters in comedies, because the spectators have no natural inclination to ridicule them; while the humble are entirely suitable characters for comedy.

In the tradition of Plato and Aristotle poetry was dramatic or epic, and only later, in the Renaissance, was this division superseded with the addition of lyric poetry.[21] Smith examines lyric poetry in terms of *decorum*, the well-known principle of elegance and equilibrium of which the classical writers and their Renaissance followers were so fond.[22] This principle, which calls for the shunning of excess, was particularly congenial to Smith; indeed in *TMS*, commenting on the feeling of uneasiness which arises when sentiments are expressed too intensely, he voices his appreciation for pastoral poetry.[23] Smith thus follows the main stream of the seventeenth century inspired by 'pastoral' traditions, which evoked the country vision of Horace and Martial and rekindled the respect and affection for Virgil which had

---

[18] *LRBL* ii. 90. Cf. Epict. *Diss.* i. 24. 15–17.   [19] *LRBL* ii. 90–2.

[20] Arist. *Poet.* 1448ᵃ16–18; see also ibid. 1454ᵇ8–9 on the noble character of tragedy.

[21] Cecchi and Sapegno (1966), 582. As well as lyric poetry in the true sense, the similar forms of elegy, idyll, and epigram are also part of this category.

[22] Naturally not only lyric poetry was subject to the criterion of *decorum*; indeed it is likely that Smith echoes Scaliger's preference for Virgil over Homer among the epic poets, as a result of Virgil's closer adherence to the principle of *decorum*, which, although not present in nature, a poet should always respect in his work.   [23] *TMS* I. ii. 2. 2.

never died out.[24] In the *Lectures on Rhetoric* Smith comments that in short pieces such as odes, elegies, and pastorals, unlike tragic or epic works, there is little room for 'variety of incidents', and thus the tone will be that of a peaceful 'affection' or 'temper of mind'. Once again Smith expresses a preference for this literary genre, which is so close to the 'common tranquillity of mind' (*LRBL* ii. 95); the best of Horace also shows this quality.

On the other hand there is no 'connection' in the works of the lyric poets, especially in Pindar, because they are communicating passion, and passion calls for a fragmented style. In these few references we see an approach to poetry that is typical of Smith: great emotions, which belong to the more complex forms of composition, require a 'crescendo' of events and moods, but often it is not easy to arouse them in the reader. This is indeed so true that if the poet does not use extraordinary plots and the refined techniques of narrative, a 'desultatory [i.e. random] and inconnected' style is warranted, which expresses better than any other form the passions which are so characteristic of the lyric poets in general, and of one in particular: 'Pindar the most rapturous of all is the most unconnected or at least appears to be so' (*LRBL* ii. 121). No doubt, when he said this Smith was alluding to the so-called 'Pindaric flights' for which the poet is rightly renowned. However, the closing remark is of great significance, since it suggests that Pindar may not in fact be as unconnected as he appears, or rather that even in Pindar's poetry there is an inner logic, despite the thrusts which break up the syntactic structure of the discourse.

I do not wish to put words into Smith's mouth, but it is worth noting that in his 'History of Astronomy' he described 'wonder, surprise, admiration' as feelings which could rouse a man's sentiments up to the point where he loses control, as a result of the lack of connection between two subsequent events.[25] In *LRBL*, a few lines above this citation, Smith affirms that: 'All passions *especially admiration* express themselves in a very loose and broken manner' (*LRBL* ii. 121; my italics); here the context indirectly refers to primitive poetry, the precise aim of which was to arouse wonder. So it seems we can conclude that the amazement aroused by the unconventional language of Pindar is the result of a series of deliberately created 'want of connections', which have the precise aim of provoking man's sentiments; or, at least, this is the end result, whether deliberate or not. We might even think that Smith's methodical mind, which sought order and 'connection' in everything, struck by the vehement juxtapositions, the sudden transformations, the whimsically intersecting images of Pindar's magnificent style, perceived him as the best poetical representative of that uncontrolled passion which calls for unconnected, disjointed, and non-consequential phrases. The

---

[24] Ford (1975), 86, 255–6.
[25] See above, Ch. 1 Sect. 3. In particular, with regard to 'wonder', compare 'HA' II. 3: 'which occasion that staring, and sometimes that rolling of the eyes, that suspension of the breath, and that swelling of the heart', which describes the physical consequences of this agitation.

doubt remains whether in this case, once the reader has understood the logic underlying the boldest poetic licence, the 'wonder' is destroyed, in the same way as it is in the field of science. I cannot answer this (rather idle) doubt, except by observing that most of the beauty of Pindar's poetry would be lost if we were to replace in Pindar's poems the themes that are disjointed by his overwhelming poetic inspiration. At any rate, the appeasement of the imagination upset by 'scientific' wonder (so to say) responds to the cognitive need to reach a rational explanation; in this case, however, we are talking about emotions or sentiments.

'Great Passions as they are long of being raised in the Persons themselves so are they not to be raised in us but by a work of a considerable Length. A temper of mind that differs very little from the common tranquillity of mind is what we can best enter into, by the perusall of a piece of a small length', writes Smith (*LRBL* ii. 94–5), who seems to be far more at ease experiencing the quiet sentiments of the elegiac poets than the moving sentiments of the lyric poets.

I believe we can speak of 'sympathy' in poetry also. In *TMS* Smith tells us that man is not only sympathetic to real situations, but also to fictitious situations in tragedies and romances: we appreciate the good and detest the bad, we approve of consideration for the weak, and we participate in misfortunes, particularly if the victim is able to control his reaction.[26] In real life, sympathy is only aroused when individuals are able to moderate the violence of their passions. In a literary context, this is equivalent to a definite stance in favour of *decorum*.

Thus we understand why Smith appreciates the moderate sentiments of elegiac or pastoral poetry, and distances himself from the flights of lyric and the furious passions of dramatic poetry. In *TMS* Smith describes as 'breaches of *decorum*' attempts to arouse compassion through descriptions of physical pain in the great Greek tragedies, portraying the sufferings of Philoctetes, Hippolytus, and Hercules, and explains that man does not feel sympathy for excessive displays of pain.[27] Again in *TMS*, Smith states that love can only be given serious consideration by someone who loves, not by a spectator and even less so by a reader. Love must therefore be played down, in a certain sense, because only in this way will it not become ridiculous or tedious: 'We grow weary of the grave, pedantic, and long-sentenced love of Cowley and Petrarca, who never have done with exaggerating the violence of their attachments; but the gaiety of Ovid, and the gallantry of Horace, are always agreeable.'[28] Smith also states in *LJ* that love was not taken too

---

[26] *TMS* I. i. 1. 4; I. ii. 2. 3–4; I. ii. 5. 4; II. iii. 3. 5.   [27] *TMS* I. ii. 1. 11.

[28] *TMS* I. ii. 2. 1. Here there is an echo of sixteenth-century anti-Petrarch criticism, which accused the poet of excessive conceptualism and intellectualism (Cecchi and Sapegno (1966), 485–6). In the first five editions of *TMS*, I must say, Propertius rather than Petrarch was actually written. Propertius was an elegiac Latin poet who Smith mentions in *LRBL* ii. 170, including him among the epic poets (but this may be, as the editor notes, an oversight on the part of the

seriously by the classical poets.[29] On the whole, Smith seems to greatly appreciate their moderate approach in this sense. However, perhaps we should be a little wary of Smith's definition of Racine's Phèdre as 'the finest tragedy, perhaps, that is extant in any language' (*TMS* III. 2. 19), particularly in view of the fact that the French author explored the 'Latin' interpretation of the Greek heroine, the leading character in the one classical tragedy in which Smith is willing to acknowledge a sentimental content.[30]

Thus we can conclude that in Smith's appraisal of poetry also there are traces of a classical approach reflected through his great sensitivity. He follows the traditional classical canons (Aristotle and his Renaissance commentators; Horace; Longinus[31]) although not completely: for instance, he makes no mention of the concept that art should imitate nature, or that poetry should be instructive, as well as pleasurable.[32] He does allude, on the other hand, to the parallel between poetry and painting, derived from Horace and more widely used in the field of rhetoric.[33]

Smith offers an entirely personal interpretation of the classical 'rules', and this interpretation also reflects some of the fundamental characteristics of his philosophical reasoning. In Smith's view, the reader (or the spectator) is more greatly affected by certain events—or attitudes, or sentiments—than by others, and above all if these are portrayed in a certain way, with particular devices; the spectator will then share in the sentiment of the characters and the plot. A skilled writer will take full advantage of this and will write in such a way as to move the reader, using an accomplished technique in order to compel him to enter into the actual historical events or the fictional drama. However, it is not merely a question of technical ability on the part of the writer: the success of this technique hinges on the inborn tendency of man to become emotionally involved in the actions of those like him, and to share the passions that inspire them, provided that they are within certain limits. The choice of these limits is vital for the success of the poem and can explain why our sympathy is different with different approaches to situations,

---

student). Since Smith generally appreciates the elegiac poets, I feel this must have been an error, which slipped by unnoticed in the first five editions and was corrected in the sixth.

[29] Due to the fact that their matrimony was less 'permanent' than Christian matrimony: see *LJ* (A) iii. 20; *LJ* (B) 111, and above, Ch. 3 n. 132.

[30] *LJ* (A) iii. 20; in *TMS* I. II. 2. 4 Smith remarks that the 'extravagance and guilt' of Racine's Phèdre bestow upon her a certain charm because she is a woman, and the laws of society are lenient towards the weaker sex. But in reality Racine is evoking the drama of Seneca's Phèdre, torn between the refusal of guilt and the impossibility of not desiring it, cf. Grimal (1976), 366.

[31] See Ford (1975), 173–6. In reality Longinus is cited several times by Smith, but always in the context of prose writers. I am fully aware that a complete appraisal of Smith's literary background would require us to investigate how much Smith was influenced not only by classical literature but also by seventeenth-century French literary criticism, and certainly the Italian Renaissance as well; this is, however, beyond our scope.

[32] Howell (1975), 42, finds Smith's theory 'seriously weak' on this point.

[33] There was a precedent to the well-known verse by Horace, *Ut pictura poesis* (Hor. *Ars Poet.* 361), in Arist. *Poet.* 1454^{b}8–11; 1448^{a}4 ff. Smith speaks of an analogy between painting and poetry in *LRBL* ii. 95; but there is greater mention of this in oratory.

characters, and sentiments. Certainly 'sympathy' in real life is not the same thing, since here it refers to two or more persons who act and react to each other, whilst in poetry one of the two 'parties' concerned is a completed work which cannot be changed: however, if it is successful, each time it is read the reaction will be repeated.

The genius of the poet lies in his ability to arouse this reaction, a combination of all Smith's fundamental psychological elements: 'sympathy', 'wonder', 'admiration'. Here, while the rules that, in Smith's view, the true poet (in etymological terms, the creator) observes are of classical origin, the philosophical interpretation of the art of poetry has an essentially Smithian imprint. That is how I am inclined to conclude my analysis, despite a quotation from Horace which constantly springs to mind: *Si vis me flere, dolendum est primum ipsi tibi: tum tua me infortunia laedent.*[34] Thus there is also an element of emotional involvement in literary fiction. Indeed a Latin poet, not usually renowned for the strength of his sentiment and perhaps for this reason congenial to Smith, had acknowledged this fact long before.

5.4. PROSE, OR THE ART OF PERSUASION

Smith dedicated only one lecture to poetry, or rather to the language of poetry. The rest of the course comprises notes on the various forms of prose. It has been noted that Smith includes the theory of all the principal literary genres under the heading of 'rhetoric': history, poetry, didactic or scientific writing, and oratory.[35] Here we shall mainly deal with oratory, because something has already been said on the first two, and Smith refrains from commenting on scientific writing, since he considers its rules 'obvious'.[36]

In the twenty-fourth lecture, however, he tackles the subject from a methodological standpoint. Here he uses the terms 'Newtonian' and 'Aristotelian' method to refer to the two kinds of scientific explanation, which later came to be called synthetic and analytic. Both methods derived from concepts which were common knowledge in Plato's day, and continued to be of significance until Smith's day.[37] It would be superfluous here to underline the significance of Newton's method for Smith's doctrine. What is important to remember here is the fact that Smith explicitly acknowledges that this method applies to moral philosophy as well as to natural science.[38]

A preliminary issue, here expressed rather succinctly but I hope clearly enough, is this: the term 'rhetoric' has since classical times had two

---

[34] Hor. *Ars Poet.* 102–3: 'If you wish me to cry, you must first feel grief yourself, then your misfortunes . . . will injure me' (L. Golden's translation).

[35] Howell (1975), 20. See also 26: 'Thus it turned out that his nineteen final lectures dealt with four kinds of communication—instruction, entertainment, conviction and persuasion—and with four resulting forms of discourse—history, poetry, didactic writing and oratory.'

[36] See the brief reference in *LRBL* ii. 97.   [37] Howell (1975), 32–3.

[38] *LRBL* ii. 133.

fundamental meanings attached to it, depending on whether we give greater importance to argumentation or form. From the earliest origins in Magna Graecia[39] the principles of *inventio, dispositio,* and *elocutio* corresponded respectively to the content (the choice of arguments and their logical connection) and to the form.[40] These two approaches have been maintained with ups and downs to the modern age.

In the days of Cicero, supporters of argumentation were known as 'Atticists' while those in favour of form were the 'Asianists'. As we know, Cicero was somewhere between these two positions, since he aimed to reconcile the weight of argument with the splendour of form.

With the coming of the Renaissance, there was a revival of interest in the classical forms of rhetoric, although it was limited to *elocutio* as the doctrine of ornamentation. With the new teaching at the start of the seventeenth century came the idea that the orator should not merely persuade with reasoning, but should move his audience with marvellous, extraordinary, and sublime elements, and from here the natural progression was towards a psychological analysis of rhetorical figures. It was the task of the British theory of rhetoric to lay the foundations for a passionate or sentimental, rather than rational, interpretation of figurative speech.[41] This brief digression, certainly not adequate for this subject in its entirety, was warranted by the fact that Adam Smith plays an important role in studies of rhetoric in Scotland, and he takes a personal approach to the subject, rather than following accepted rules. What is special about Smith's approach is that he focuses more on the communicative[42] than on the persuasive aspect of rhetoric; furthermore, he examines not only the traditional genres of oratory, but also historical, poetical, and didactic composition; he also proposes simple, anti-Ciceronian language, the purpose of which was limited to posing a question and proving it. All this makes Smith 'the earliest and most independent of the new British rhetoricians of the eighteenth century',[43] and above all signifies that his rhetoric did not look to the glories of the past but rather to the live needs of the present.

[39] The first manual of rhetoric appeared in Sicily: see Cic. *Brutus* 46; *De Or.* I. 91.

[40] As well as the parts I have mentioned, classical rhetoric also included the elements of *memoria and actio*; however, the first three are fundamental to what is said in the text. Actually *dispositio* is in an intermediate position between the other two operations (retrieval of information and verbal expression).

[41] Here I would like to mention only the *Elements of Criticism* by Lord Kames, and the *Lectures on Rhetoric and Belles Lettres* by Hugh Blair, who acknowledges that he partly followed on from Smith. It is not true that in classical rhetoric there was no attention to the psychological aspect; indeed one of the aims of the orator was to move the audience, and this was considered of vital importance (see Cic. *Brutus*, 185; *De Or.* II. 185–9).

[42] In Howell's view, this fact distanced Smith from the classics (Howell (1975), 21); however, according to Sir George Campbell, author of a *Philosophy of Rhetoric* published in the same year as *WN* (cited in Bevilacqua (1976), 26) the rhetoric of Cicero was also a ' "grand art of communication" not of ideas only but of sentiment, passions and dispositions as well'. As we shall see, *this* type of communication is very close to what Smith considered the aim of every piece of literature, whether prose or poetry.   [43] Howell (1975), 43.

It is, however, an arduous task to break completely with the past, particularly in a field which is closely linked to jurisprudence. As we have already noted, Smith considered the principal task of the orator to be the proving of his case; but it is precisely through this notion of proof (the rhetorical-logical framework which developed significantly in judicial proceedings) that the tradition of rhetoric took hold in Scotland.[44]

5.5. ORATORY

In classical times, three divisions of eloquence existed: deliberative, judicial, and demonstrative or epideictic. This division was already criticized by Quintilian as well as by Smith;[45] but here we adopt this approach for greater convenience, as Smith himself adopted it. On the subject of demonstrative or epideictic eloquence,[46] which consisted principally in the panegyrics of illustrious Wgures, Smith has little to say other than that it offers the speaker an opportunity to show off his talents. What is surprising is that, although Smith considers demonstrative eloquence to be the last in chronological order, he draws more connections between this and poetry, at least in its origins, than between poetry and the other forms. Here perhaps Smith has been inXuenced unwittingly by Cicero (*Or.* 42), who detects the Wrst traces of oratory in epideictic eloquence, whereas in Smith's 'conjectural' reconstruction epideictic eloquence came last, following deliberative and judicial eloquence. Cicero had also acknowledged a *proxima cognatio* between poets and orators (*De Or.* III. 27). The Wrst panegyrists imitated the poets in their argument (hymns in honour of gods and heroes) and in their disconnected style. Isocrates maintained a taste for form and sound, which was admired by Cicero but not by Brutus (an Atticist, and thus in favour of plain eloquence relating to 'facts').[47] What is important in epideictic eloquence is the ability to accentuate, as appropriate, the character of the person or the events.[48] Typical of Smith's consideration of the results of human actions is

[44] Giuliani (1962), 249–51. Here we find an interesting question (caused by the observation that the person who developed the system of Scottish law was a philosopher, Lord Stair, who held the chair to which Adam Smith was later appointed): 'It would be interesting to inquire whether this tradition also penetrated Scottish philosophy in view of the dominance of lawyers in Scottish cultural life in the seventeenth and eighteenth centuries' (ibid. 251).

[45] As the editor of *LRBL* notes on p. 14 of the 'Introduction'. This three-way division dates back to Arist. *Rhet.* I 1358^{a}36–^{b}8.

[46] Aristotle and Quintilian are the classical sources, already identified by the editor Lothian: see comment on lecture 22, p. 124 nn. 1 and 2.

[47] Smith here alludes to Cicero's statement on this subject (with a degree of exaggeration, noted in particular by Lothian) see *LRBL* ii. 122 and n. 13 = Lothian, p. 134 n. 3. As well as Isocrates, Smith also mentions the following as occasional 'panegyrists': Lysias, Plato, and Thucydides, each of whom wrote such an oration in praise of the Athenians, at the time of the Persian expeditions (*LRBL* ii. 123–5).

[48] Smith mentions as examples from classical literature Xenophon's panegyric of Agesilaus and Cicero's *Pro lege Manilia* (*LRBL* ii. 108–10).

his observation that 'good fortune has a great tendencey to attract our admiration and applause' (*LRBL* ii. 100). But the subsequent observation, on the approval attracted by Wrm behaviour in the face of adversity, echoes Cicero (De Or. ii. 346).

Smith treats deliberative eloquence within the same framework as judicial eloquence. First he explains the general nature and principles of each type of eloquence, and then he proceeds to illustrate these further by examining the style of the orators in Greek, Latin, and English.

A splendid example of deliberative eloquence in classical literature can be found in the orations of Demosthenes and Cicero. Despite the greater 'simplicity' of this type of eloquence as against the judicial, and the fact that Smith intended to give it a more superficial treatment, his analysis is fairly lengthy, since he accounts for the technical differences arising from a detailed comparison of the two orators in sociological terms. The Athenian and the Roman, the two greatest orators of classical times (who had already been compared by Quintilian), provided the liveliest expression not just of differences in personal inclination, but also, and above all, of differences in social context.[49]

Thus the techniques adopted by the two orators are presented to us in a particular light, so that the comparison is not just a critique of their manners and their stylistic differences, but rather it is suggested that these differences stem from the state of mind and conditions in society, which influence the rhetorical style and to a certain extent even constitute this style, which in turn is appropriate only in that type of society.

The conciseness of Demosthenes, his familiar manner expressed in un-connected sentences, the frequency of simple examples (almost trivial, in Smith's opinion) mirrored a society which knew very little difference in wealth or station. Conversely, the more ornate, solemn, and excessive manner of the Latin orator, which avoided idiom and offered well-connected, precise, and accurate sequences, was indicative of the marked differences in status in the social structure of Rome, the enormous distance between the inestimable wealth of the 'great' and the misery of the populace, so that 'the Nobleman of Rome would . . . find himself greatly superior to the far greater part of mankind',[50] and this was reflected in his style. It is unnecessary to mention ancient criticism of Cicero's 'grand manner' (Smith mentions the criticism of Brutus and of another 'Atticist', whose name the student was unable to grasp, in *LRBL* ii. 169). None of the critics enjoyed the success of Cicero and of those who used a style similar to his, above all Hortensius Hortalus, a friend and rival of Cicero who represented the pompous 'Asianic' style.

---

[49] Demosthenes seems more suited to the modern world than Cicero, and thus Smith prefers him (Howell (1975), 40). Smith dedicated lectures 25–7 to deliberative eloquence.

[50] *LRBL* ii. 162. This argument is treated in lecture 26, particularly in *LRBL* ii. 164–70. I have dealt with this briefly in Vivenza *et al.* (1980), 48–9.

Smith's conclusion on the different nature of Greek and Roman style goes beyond the boundaries of oratory: 'This study of Ornament and Pomp was common not only to all the Roman orators but to the Historians and the poets themselves . . . When this Study is so generall we may be well assured that it proceeded not from any peculiarity or humour of the writers but from the nature and temper of the nation' (*LRBL* ii. 170). This idea that the oratory of one particular cultural 'establishment' is inappropriate to an-other[51] thus develops into a concept that can apply to all the literary work of a nation. Elsewhere, however, Smith explains the more elaborate nature of Cicero's style compared to Demosthenes by the fact that studies of rhetoric (and also of logic) were more 'fashionable' in Rome than in Athens, and hence Cicero did his utmost to show off his perfect grasp of all the 'rules'.[52]

Some other reflections on the two great classical orators are typical of Smith. In *TMS*, for example, Smith appreciates Cicero's orations against Catiline and Demosthenes' Philippics as examples of self-control: 'the command of anger', that is to say the attempt to restrain anger by cooling it down to a form of noble indignation with which the spectator can sympathize.[53] It is quite clear how much this evaluation reflects Smith's moral philosophy. In the *Lectures,* however, Cicero's fourth Catiline oration is offered as an example of uncertainty and havering, however well concealed in an ornate and perfect style. Here Smith considers that the orator must have been betrayed by his uncertain and cowardly character, in the stormy session in which Cato urged that the conspirators be sentenced to death and Caesar tried to defend them. Smith's invaluable conclusion is that if, despite this awkward situation, the oration was 'managed in a most artfull, ornate and elegant manner', one can imagine the elegance of Cicero's oration on other occasions when the orator was more certain of himself.[54]

On the subject of self-control, it is perhaps appropriate here to relate this virtue to the classical concept of *decorum*. Vincent M. Bevilacqua has effectively described the influence of certain elements of classical rhetoric on English aesthetics in the eighteenth century. At that time, the analogy drawn by Aristotle and Horace between poetry and painting was revived and applied to the relationship between rhetoric and painting.[55] Emphasis was placed upon similarities in the method of the painter and the orator, who

---

[51] This implies a relativistic approach to rhetoric: see Howell (1975), 37–8.
[52] *LRBL* ii. 214–16. Smith rejects the theory that the difference is attributable to the diverse nature of the two languages (*LRBL* ii. 151–2).   [53] *TMS* vi. iii. 9.
[54] *LRBL* ii. 170–2. It is interesting that here Smith translates Cicero not because he doubts that his disciples can understand him, but because it would be 'unfair' to compare an original from Cicero and a translation from Demosthenes. This leads us to think that Greek was not used in these lectures, despite the occasional use of phrases in Greek which seems to vouch for a knowledge of Greek on the part of at least the student who took these notes.
[55] Bevilacqua (1976), 11 ff. This author speaks of the 'pervasive historical influence of traditional rhetorical theory on the intellectual development of the study of literary aesthetics' (ibid. 27).

share elements such as the choice of subject, what to bring to the forefront, or leave in the shadows, and the propriety of expression. An example of *decorum* (on the lines of Cicero and Quintilian) is the well-known representation by Timanthes in the painting inspired by the sacrifice of Iphigenia (the Greek painter represented Agamemnon with a cloak over his head, so as to hide his face, finding it impossible to depict Agamemnon's grief as a father). This theme was present in literary criticism at Smith's time, and Smith himself uses the example of Timanthes in the context of historical narration. That context is related to the effectiveness of the indirect narration of a dramatic event. Smith feels that the best results are to be achieved by describing the emotional reactions which the events inflict on the sensibility of the main characters, provided that these emotional reactions are within reasonable limits. Here Smith makes no direct mention of either *decorum* or self-control, but it is natural to think that, in art as in everyday life, it is impossible to sympathize with an excessive display of sentiment and thus it should be avoided. The reason for this, however, far from being for classical purposes of equilibrium, is emotional involvement, and thus more Smithian than Aristotelian.

Smith tackles a lesser methodological issue concerning deliberative eloquence when he describes *insinuatio* and *principium* as respectively the Socratic and the Aristotelian method; these are classical procedures which he applies to the entire oration and not just to the *exordium*.[56]

Finally, Smith makes clear to his students the secrets of judicial oratory. This genre is more complex than the other two, as a result of the extensive reasoning required by forensic practice, and thus there has been since classical times a virtually unlimited array of distinctions, divisions, and subdivisions. These exasperate the Scottish philosopher, and he invites keen students wishing to discover more to examine Quintilian's works.[57]

Judicial, or civil, eloquence, which had the aim of defending a person or upholding certain rights, came into being as a consequence of the 'division of labour', since the various tasks, of judge, military leader, and legislator, once entrusted to the same person, were separated because it was inevitable that one would otherwise be neglected in favour of another.[58] In describing this type of eloquence, Smith gives some information about the different organization of law courts in Athens and in Rome. Greek judicial orations concerned both public and private affairs, but for private affairs there was no such figure as what today we call the counsel for the defence, and the party directly concerned pleaded on his own behalf, even if his speech was written by a professional. In ancient Greece there was no institution similar to the

[56] Howell (1975), 35–6. These are the possible 'openings' in oration, depending on whether the orator introduces his argument gradually, slowly capturing the audience, or directly.

[57] *LRBL* ii. 197. The following phrase is cited several times: 'They are generally a very silly set of Books and not at all instructive' (*LRBL* i.v. 59), referring to ancient and modern treatises on rhetoric.   [58] *LRBL* ii. 199 ff. See also Rosenberg (1976), 865–6.

Roman patron–client relationship.[59] The Roman courts were rather better organized and less disorderly than those in Athens, and this, according to Smith, explains the greater political stability in ancient Rome.[60]

There are many surviving examples of speeches from judicial oratory, and Smith analyses the distinguishing features of the best known of these. I do not need to comment here on the classical subdivision of a speech into *exordium*, *narratio*, *confirmatio*, *refutatio*, and *peroratio*, which Smith considers in lecture 29. What is perhaps of greater interest is the observation that in the *narratio* the task of the orator is to provide a complete account, including details of which he has no proof together with elements which can be proved to be true, thereby making his argument more forceful. In this context Smith examines the famous *pro Milone* speech and the *pro Cluentio*, his favourite Ciceronian orations.[61] Here, in oratory too, one can glimpse a development of the same 'connective' methodology to which Smith attends explicitly in several other disciplines. Although here it is not part of a coherent 'historical' reconstruction (in the well-known sense of 'conjectural' history), we can see that Smith's argument tends towards the idea of a gradual improvement of this technique. We recall how he attributed to the early Greek orators an 'unconnected' and almost poetic style, whilst the supreme Roman orator, representing the height of the art of oratory, shows clear progress towards clarity, coherence, and proper sequence of argumentation. It is no coincidence that here Smith uses words such as 'connected' or 'connections' to describe this process: it is a case of 'filling in the gaps', so that the whole account seems probable.[62]

Perhaps with the aid of this principle we can explain the apparent contradiction between *LRBL* ii. 139 and ibid. ii. 197, discussed by Howell (1975), 36–7. Smith asserts in the first of the two passages that Cicero and Quintilian considered the choice and arrangement of arguments of little consequence, since they paid greater attention to embellishment; yet in the subsequent passage he states that the art of the orator consists principally in the appropriate arrangement of arguments. The first statement is probably inspired, as pointed out by the editor, by Cic. *Or.* 44, where the Latin author maintains that *inventio* and *dispositio* are more a question of common sense than of oratory (*in Brutus*, however, all the five parts of rhetoric are qualified as exacting sciences without distinction: see Cic. *Brutus* 25). The reference to Quintilian originates with all probability from Quintil. VIII. iii. 2, more in favour of embellishment than the other two parts (the editor also notes Quintil. III. iii. 1—in reality III. iii. 11—in which, however, Quintilian takes

---

[59] *LRBL* ii. 217–18.   [60] *LRBL* ii. 208–9.

[61] *LRBL* ii. 209–10. Smith's examination of the *Pro Milone* is criticized by Howell (1975), 41. On the subject of Smith's interpretation, we should remember that the proof true and proper was given in the *confirmatio*; but, since not all arguments are open to proof, the adept orator provided a probable reconstruction also in the *narratio*.

[62] *LRBL* ii. 206 ff. Compare also ibid. ii. 247. Cf. 'Introduction' to *LRBL*, p. 13.

a critical stance). In the second passage, in relation to *dispositio*, Smith makes a significant statement: 'These [sc. arguments] when placed separately have often no great impression, but if they be placed in a naturall order one leading to the other their effect is greatly increased. The best method to answer this is to throw them into a sort of *narration*, filling up in the manner most suitable to the design of the Speaker what intervalls they may otherwise be. By this means tho he can bring proof but of very few particulars, *yet the connection there is makes them easily comprehended and consequently agreeable*, so that when the adversary tries to contradict any of these particulars it is pulling down *a fabric with which we are greatly pleased and are very unwilling to give up*' (*LRBL* ii. 197; my italics). It seems in the first case that Smith is referring to rhetoric in general (*inventio*, *dispositio*, etc. are parts of this discipline, and not subdivisions of the speech): shortly before this he speaks of deliberative eloquence, in which arguments are generally rather simple and do not require elaborate proof. The second passage, however, falls within the context of judicial oratory, and originates from a discussion of the argumentation of proof: as a result, *dispositio* takes on considerable importance, because it means *how* arguments are presented (in the second part of the speech, i.e. the *narratio* which Smith almost certainly has in mind, and indeed he uses the English term). The way in which elements which have been proved and elements that are yet to be proved intertwine to form a kind of 'connection' which is in itself convincing and pleasing ('with which we are greatly pleased') is obviously essential in a judicial speech. It is unnecessary here to comment on the similarity of this concept with that of scientific theory, and of astronomy in particular, in which phenomena are explained by hypotheses (see above, Ch. 1). Here we can detect a parallel with unproven parts (that cannot be proven) of the procedure, which become more believable in reconstruction by means of the 'connections' between one argument and another. Howell's observation remains valid, that Smith is incoherent with himself (or rather with his first assertion) when he shows a thorough knowledge of the classical doctrines of *inventio* and *dispositio*, thereby revealing that he must have been aware that these doctrines were not of little consequence to Cicero and Quintilian.

As regards the feelings which oratory must arouse, we read that 'those passions which are chiefly to be excited by oratory' are 'compassion and indignation' (*LRBL* ii. 223–4). Consequently orators whose character is not suited to these feelings, or who introduce an element of humour, fail in their principal undertaking (Smith is referring to Aeschines). Smith perceives a fundamental difference between deliberative and judicial oratory: the former deals with questions of a political nature, and concerns society as a whole. However important these issues are, they 'will never affect the passions so highly as the distress of a single person or Indignation against the Crimes of an individuall' (*LRBL* ii. 227), which are the subject of judicial eloquence. This attention to the individual reminds us of Smith's theory of sympathetic participation, and means that orators who find the right touch to arouse compassion and indignation, or who have the temperament for this, will excel in the third type of oratory. Smith gives the example of Demosthenes with his severe and passionate character, which stands out even more in judicial than in deliberative orations, despite a certain similarity between the two.[63] This trait is the reason why Smith has a preference for Demosthenes despite all his defects:[64] thus we may conclude that Smith's preference is due not only to the fact that Demosthenes fits in better with modern needs, but also to his exceptional ability to touch the chord of feelings which arouse greatest sympathy, an essential requisite for persuasion in Smith's opinion, we may think, since it enables us to understand all human behaviour.

5.6. **THE CHARACTERS**

Differences in style between the orators is thus explained by differences in their temperament as well as by differences in their environment. Smith's final lecture is given up to an analysis of the characters of Aeschines, Demosthenes, and Cicero.

As we have already seen, in Smith's opinion Demosthenes more than any other possesses all the necessary qualities which are essential to a good orator. Aeschines lacks gravity, while Cicero has a singular character, described by Smith with the aid of Cicero's letters and other writings: he rightly believes that a careful reading of Cicero's works yields a far better knowledge of Cicero than any critical interpretation. From his reading of Cicero Smith concludes that the Latin orator possessed great sensitivity, but also that he was vain and ostentatious. Here Smith digresses in order to explain how sensitivity is an admirable virtue, but one that is often accompanied by a certain frivolity; what is more, those with this trait are able to sympathize deeply with the feelings of others, but are excessively sensitive towards their own, and so are too prone to enthusiasm or depression. Cicero possessed precisely these qualities, and thus was liable to become elated or disheartened at the success of his plans or a reverse of fortune for himself or his friends. This, as Smith observes, made him unsuitable for public affairs, but was an advantage in oratory because he was more communicative than he would have been had his character been calm and balanced.

Smith touches briefly on Cicero's education as a young man, without supplying any great detail, and stressing that when he returned after concluding his studies in Athens Cicero discovered that the eloquence used

---

[63] *LRBL* ii. 226. Later on (ii. 232) Smith mentions Demosthenes' solid philosophical background, noting the influence that Plato had on him; this is already mentioned by Cicero (Cic. *Or.* 15–16; *Brutus* 121).

[64] This is the opinion of Howell, who interprets Smith's preference for Demosthenes not as a stance in favour of Greek rather than Roman rhetoric, but as the expression of Smith's conviction that Demosthenes was more suited to the modern world. This explains the fact that he prefers Demosthenes to Cicero (Howell (1975), 40; cf. Vivenza *et al.* (1980), 50).

in Rome was more elaborate by far than that used in Greece, and so he adapted to this, aiming to achieve the splendour and formal dignity contrasting so much with the 'familiarity' of the Greeks (expressed in Rome, I repeat, by the 'Atticists' whom Smith mentions on another occasion). Logic and rhetoric were much more common in Rome than in Greece, where Aristotelian dialectic was still widely used; thus Demosthenes' orations (the comparison between the two orators continues despite the fact that Demosthenes preceded Cicero by a considerable period of time) were not divided into five parts. Moreover, Demosthenes possessed a stern character, and was more prone to violent indignation than to compassion. Thus: 'Upon the whole Cicero is more apt to draw our Pity and Love, and Demosthenes to raise our Indignation. The one is strong and commanding, the other persuasive and moving', Smith asserts (*LRBL* ii. 242–3), concluding that Quintilian's description of Cicero corresponds perfectly to his own.

Character is important not only for orators. In the seventeenth century the French moralist La Bruyère produced a work that he declared was inspired by the *Characters* of Theophrastus, a short treatise the purpose of which is not known and which contains thirty or more sketches of human behaviour, focusing on deviations from normality. This was not the only treatise of this kind in the ancient world: Theophrastus' teacher Aristotle also showed an interest in this field of study.

The fame of Theophrastus in Smith's day was pretty well bound up with that of his French popularizer, who based his work on the Latin edition of Theophrastus' *Characters* by Casaubon, but he also knew Greek and was therefore able to read the original. His work was rather different from the original, but at the same time he spread abroad the knowledge of Theophrastus' writings and the 'fashion' of the study of characters, even though a tendency to do this already existed.[65] The main difference between Theophrastus and La Bruyère, already recognized in the seventeenth century, was that Theophrastus' characters are abstract and universal, while La Bruyère portrays characters belonging to seventeenth-century French society.[66]

Smith analyses the work of the two writers in terms of style. As in other disciplines (historiography in particular), description can be direct or indirect; the indirect form is always more effective. However, it is necessary to distinguish a further subdivision: indirect description may be general (La Bruyère) or specific (Theophrastus), depending on whether behaviour as a whole is described, or only certain circumstances. In conclusion, the approach adopted by Theophrastus is, according to Smith, more pleasing than that of his French imitator.[67]

---

[65] Navarre (1914), 431 n. 1.

[66] Navarre (1914), 439. In 1693 a French academician told La Bruyère that while his 'characters' resembled individuals, those of Theophrastus represented 'the man' (ibid. 403).

[67] *LRBL* i. 194–5. A little further on we find the careful observation that the characters of Theophrastus, although agreeable, are all described using a particular method: they are all very

In lecture 15, digressing from the distinction, of distant Aristotelian origin, between characters and actions, Smith explains how the characters should be described in literary composition. Of interest here is an example from classical literature, the comparison between the descriptions of Catiline by Sallust and Cicero. Sallust uses the 'direct' method, while Cicero opts for the 'indirect' method, and Smith finds the latter more complete and more interesting: 'We will see likewise by this comparison that the latter is considerably more interesting and gives us a fuller view of the character' (*LRBL* i. 194).

Without doubt the students will have had in mind, as we have today, Sallust's splendid Catiline, portrayed 'directly' with all his merits and defects, or rather his strengths and weaknesses pushed to the limit, making him a truly exceptional character, summed up in the unforgettable beginning:

L. Catilina, nobili genere natus, fuit magna vi et animi et corporis, sed ingenio malo pravoque (Sallust, *De Coniuratione Catilinae*, 5; 'Lucius Catilina, scion of a noble family, had great vigour both of mind and of body, but an evil and depraved nature' (J. C. Rolfe's translation)).

The wicked character that emerges from Cicero's second Catiline oration is the epitome of all possible vice. The indirect description to which Smith refers is probably explained by the fact that Cicero represents Catiline through a repetitive and detailed account of all the jailbirds of whom he is a friend, all the crimes that he has commited, and all the wicked deeds that he has at heart. Basically, Catiline is depicted as a negative character because no crime exists that he has not committed or does not intend to commit.

We have no way of knowing whether Smith's students were overwhelmed to a greater or lesser extent than we are today by Sallust's 'direct' Catiline. Smith himself makes no mention of the artistic qualities of Cicero's portrait, but touches only on the greater completeness and interest. On this point we cannot but agree, since Cicero, in the ardour of his oration, certainly did not overlook even the slightest detail. Here, however, Smith would have been wise to remind his students that Cicero subsequently spoke of Catiline again, in the oration defending Caelius Rufus. Despite the fact that in this oration Cicero's task is to minimize and excuse the youthful intemperance of his client, who for a certain time was a follower of Catiline, this second portrait is not entirely insincere, and perhaps in certain parts reminds us of Sallust: a man of vice, but not without virtue, contradictory and passionate, endowed with great charm.[68]

---

similar, and so they tire us (*LRBL* i. 197). Modern criticism also acknowledges this ('caractères, tous coulés dans une moule identique': Navarre (1914), 419), in comparison to the luxurious variety of forms in La Bruyère.

[68] Cic. *Pro Cael.* 12–14. Smith does not say which of Cicero's descriptions he is referring to, but it seems fairly evident that he intends the Catilinarian. However, in *TMS* vi. iii. 30 he asserts: 'Had Caesar, instead of gaining, lost the battle of Pharsalia, his character would, at this

Smith does not limit his study of characters to this lecture alone. In part VI of *TMS* we find a series of descriptions that 'follow the model of Aristotle and Theophrastus but also declare Smith's own scale of values',[69] as is often the case with Smith and the classics. In the same work Smith frequently uses the characterization of actions or attitudes as a yardstick: consider the comparison (originally from Plutarch) between the king of Macedon and the Roman Paulus Aemilius as an example of Roman 'magnanimity' against Macedonian feebleness; the affirmed supremacy of the Roman citizen over the father, the basis of the capital punishment inflicted by Brutus on his own son; the frequent reference to the cruel Roman emperors as totally negative characters.[70]

Cato as described by Seneca is a perfect example of these moral characters, and indeed it is striking that Seneca's appreciation contains all the elements of Smith's psychology, as if Smith were able to find no better example of strength of mind;[71] however, elsewhere Cato is presented as a product of 'literature'.[72] In short, Smith uses the study of characters for two purposes: in a truly literary sense, in order to understand the temperament of a character or of an author by reading and carefully analysing the work; and in an interpretative sense, when he cites well-known historical events as examples of typical human traits. Certainly it is difficult to leave literature aside, because our knowledge of historical events comes also from literary sources, and we may sometimes have reasonable doubts as to their impartiality, apart from the fact that the technical skills of the author may be to the advantage of the character. Generally speaking, in *LRBL* 'characters' are predominantly literary, whereas in *TMS* their moralizing nature is evident, as we would expect.

Smith's interest in this field of study is readily explained: character shows the individual, and 'sympathy' is an individual trait *par excellence*.

5.7. PSYCHOLOGICAL AND RATIONAL FOUNDATIONS OF RHETORIC

It would have been possible to examine the *Lectures on Rhetoric* at greater length, and we would have found many other classical references, useful both to illustrate aesthetic theories (not all of classical origin) and to offer

hour, have ranked a little above that of Catiline', in whom later on he acknowledges 'many great qualities', but who did not achieve success in enterprise, whereas Caesar did.

[69] Raphael and Macfie, 'Introduction' to *TMS*, p. 18.

[70] Compare also *TMS* I. iii. 2. 6; IV. 2. 11; and, on the cruelty of the emperors, ibid. v. 2. 1; compare also *LJ* (A) v. 126.

[71] 'The sentiment of complete *sympathy* and *approbation*, mixed and animated with *wonder* and *surprise* constitutes what is properly called *admiration* . . . Cato, surrounded on all sides by his enemies', etc. (*TMS* I. iii. 1. 13; my italics).

[72] Particularly in *TMS* VII. ii. 1. 32, on the subject of suicide, see above, Ch. 2.10.

what we might call a structural approach, in which elements taken from classical literature lay the foundations of the complex discipline of rhetoric.

It would have been inappropriate to examine the various *figurae verborum* and *figurae sententiarum*, the metaphors, hyperboles, compound words, and metonymies. What is interesting is Smith's opinion that these figures of speech have no intrinsic value but are only of value inasmuch as they communicate precisely the sentiment of the speaker.[73]

These figures of speech should thus only be used when they constitute the most precise and 'appropriate' natural form of expression. Two elements which are typical of Smith's moral theory in this way form the basic requisites of communication through language: sympathy, and propriety of expression, or the ability to express sentiment in a perfectly appropriate manner. The grammatical and stylistic elements of speech should be judged according to these criteria. In his lectures Smith wished to achieve two main aims (according to the testimony of John Millar mentioned at the beginning of this Chapter): here we have emphasized above all the second of these. Smith's first aim is certainly also worthy of attention, but falls within the category of linguistics. (A part of these early lectures forms the core of *Considerations Concerning the First Formation of Languages*, which I have not treated here since it is a modern discipline, despite the frequent examples Smith gives from Latin and Greek. Perhaps the only element with classical origins is analogy.[74]) It is more useful here to discover something more about how Smith's conception of literary production fits into his general thinking on philosophy.

It has already been observed, and I repeat it here to conclude this point, that Smith's rhetoric is not simply a return to classical rhetoric, but rather a study of the psychological foundations of rhetoric, which allows a use of this discipline suited to a modern context.[75] Rejection of the traditional subdivision of oratory into five or six parts, and a certain 'pragmatic' tendency to limit didactic and oratorical eloquence to the laying down and proof of a proposition[76] show us that Smith's approach to this discipline is very rational, leaving no room for classical expedients used to persuade and move the audience. Smith is doubtful not only of Cicero's tearful perorations and his booming clauses, already criticized in antiquity, but also of his digressions, which in some cases serve only to divert the attention of the judges, and are quite out of place.[77]

---

[73] 'When the sentiment of the speaker is expressed in a neat, clear, plain and clever manner, and the passion or affection he is possessed of and intends, by *sympathy*, to communicate to his hearer, is plainly and cleverly hit off, then and then only the expression has all the force and beauty that language can give it' (*LRBL* i. v. 56; Smith's italics).

[74] Not as linguistic doctrine in general (here the absence of any allusion to the doctrine of anomaly is significant) but as a 'conjectural' reference to similarity (analogy) of terminations (see 'Considerations', 10, in *LRBL*, p. 208).   [75] Bevilacqua (1968), 560–1; Howell (1975), 40.

[76] *LRBL* ii. 14 and ii. 206; cf. Howell (1975), 39–40.

[77] Cf. *TMS* v. 2. 10; *LRBL* i. 50; ibid ii. 243–4.

Nevertheless, Smith's rhetoric has sound psychological foundations. It is important to be aware of the different aims of the various parts of this discipline; but in any case it appeals quite often to pathos.[78] The fact that sad and dramatic events are more moving is fundamental for historians, poets, and to some extent for orators too. The choice of subjects will thus be influenced by this.

In *LRBL* questions of a technical nature often prevail, while in *TMS* we frequently find elements of literary origin which serve to illustrate or back up moral theory. A significant remark, even if it is a chance reference, is the statement that 'poets and romance writers . . . are . . . better instructors than Zeno, Chrysippus, or Epictetus' (*TMS* III. 3. 14); that is, the Stoic philosophers. Why so much honour for the romance writers? Because they work on the sentiments, while the Stoic philosophers, even though greatly respected by Smith, with their doctrine of apathy were unable to recognize that sentiment is the basic driving force of all human behaviour.

The supremacy of sentiment, however, does not mean that Smith is in favour of abandoning oneself to passion: on the contrary, self-control is essential both in real life and in fiction. This 'mean' (or propriety), in its aspect of an equilibrium between excesses, as I have already said, is of classical origin: what is characteristic of Smith is the assertion that it is essential in order to obtain sympathy, both in morals and in literature.

The fact that poets, or narrative writers in general, work on the imagination, while in philosophy (or in science) it is reason that is stimulated, is not enough to create a clear-cut distinction between the two. As we may remember, the first faculty to be involved in scientific activity is the imagination, and this continues to be true: not even a truly scientific discipline such as astronomy is an exception to this.

Science thus uses reason to explain the various phenomena, but with the aim of restoring the 'tranquillity' which the imagination demands, faced with the insecurity of conflicting evidence. Here we might emphasize the classical origin of *tranquillitas animi*, well documented in modern times.[79] Perhaps this comparison is imprecise, given that *tranquillitas* (mainly Stoic) has more ethical connotations, meaning the absence of passions, while Smith is referring to scientific doubt: some relationship exists, however. It is no coincidence that in literature the starting point is a 'wonder', which may be a way of attracting attention, but all the same it is a sensation that requires satisfaction. The fact is that the various human faculties are closely interrelated, and it is logical that this is reflected in the productions of the spirit. Plato had already asserted the link between all the human 'arts' (meaning by this the various branches of culture) and Cicero echoed this.[80] Today this

---

[78] It is an appeal of classical origin (Vivenza *et al.* (1980), 53), whose importance was recognized also by the moderns.   [79] For example in Muratori: see Badaloni (1973), 788.

[80] Plato, *Epinomis*, 991^e5–992^a1; cf. Cic., *Pro Archia* I. 2; *De Or.* III. 21.

concept is hard to grasp completely, but in Smith's day intellectuals could truly embrace the essential relationships between the various disciplines.

In his literary lectures Smith appraises poetry and prose by the same fundamental criteria which guide his philosophical thinking ('wonder', 'admiration', 'sympathy', 'propriety', and an idea of *decorum* which is rather close to 'self-command'). He assigns to at least one part of rhetoric the task of persuading through 'connections' which offer a complete and logically constructed explanation; and he offers a history of literature using the same analytical tools as for legal and political history (though he does not examine these in depth here): the development of trade, the division of labour, and the theory of socio-economic stages, even though only in broad outline.

At this point we can explain why Smith's thinking, taken as a whole, is so coherent. Rational generalizations of observed facts exist in science, in ethics, and in the arts. But tranquillity of mind is demanded in all disciplines: in philosophy as in literature, where, as we have seen, Smith prefers elegiac poetry to lyric poetry precisely for this reason. We could say at this point that Smith seeks a satisfactory rational explanation for the imagination, in order to achieve tranquillity of mind; and art which is expressive but without violent contrasts, in order to maintain it.

Conclusion

Smith's ties with the classics are not easily defined, and perhaps it would be best to say that the relationship is more complex than it appears at a first glance. At times when we examine a classical theme in one of Smith's works, and the thought connected with this theme, we discover that the final result takes a curious turn. An example of this is when the philosopher in Smith's account begins to speculate in consequence of 'wonder', the very wonder of Aristotle, but his ability to reflect leads him to invent such things as machines to save human labour, thus introducing a practical element which could not be further from Aristotle. A further example might be the supposed derivation from Polybius of the sympathy which an individual experiences with the offended party's feelings of resentment; even if we accept this, we must acknowledge that the spectator who shares the indignation of the offended party does so initially as a result of rational calculation in Polybius, and from a stir of emotion in Smith. In terms of moral philosophy, the strong Stoic influence clashes with Smith's basic assumption that sentiments formed the ground of ethical behaviour and so men were constrained by the reciprocal nature of their reactions, as a result of which they became dependent on one another. The true Stoic had no need to depend upon his kind, and even less upon his own passions.

This is why the classical influence in Smith's thought appears as a composite set of elements, among which we could perhaps identify a Stoic theoretical principle (sometimes called universal harmony, which upholds the principle that the interests of the individual are not opposed to those of the community), with which Aristotelian, Epicurean, or again Stoic elements intertwined to regulate individual behaviour so that harmony could be reached. The fact is that Smith was a realist as well as an optimist, and he never believed that things could fall into place of their own accord, even in economics, where he envisaged the consequences of individual self-interest purely in terms of its bringing benefit to society as a whole, and in this respect he was critical of the laws in force in his day.[1] Similarly, he wished that man's aggressive tendencies would be restrained by the law, as he could not accept that the order of nature, perfect as it was, could be reconciled with any kind of iniquity. Smith's greater sensitivity towards individual

---

[1] Rosenberg (1960), 560 and *passim*.

responsibility had a precedent in the classical Aristotelian maxim which defined man in relation to others. So whereas on the one hand in Smith's philosophy, as in Stoicism, the natural instincts which drove man to pursue his own interest led to results which were beneficial to society as a whole, on the other hand men were required to regulate their own behaviour in order to cooperate for the achievement of this beneficial result. This was to happen spontaneously (remember that in Smith's view men 'naturally' possessed a certain degree of self-control), but if this were not the case, then justice was to intervene.

Smith never considered 'natural liberty' to mean that man should be free to do whatever he pleased; but his 'optimism' was due perhaps more to his conviction that man, by controlling his passions and his behaviour, could contribute, albeit unwittingly, to positive social results than to a belief that self-centred behaviour could in some way automatically lead to beneficial results.

The objective of Stoic self-control, however, was to reach self-sufficiency, whereas Smith's self-control focused more on the essence of man's social behaviour and his relationship with other individuals than on the fact that self-control was also necessary to impose reasonable limits on the intensity of passion. It is in this respect that Smith was closest to Aristotle. (Note that such comparisons are rather schematic: both Stoic and Aristotelian philosophy underwent considerable development over time; this is particularly true of Roman Stoicism, to which Smith has been considered closest, and which differed significantly from the original Greek doctrine. Indeed in this field it is difficult to trace clear boundaries and recognize influences with certainty: this is above all because the ideas attributed to the various philosophical schools of thought developed over time, so that even their basic concepts were no longer uniform. What is more, Smith himself had a strong philosophical personality and he gave a personal interpretation to what he could find in classical literature.)

Thus we can detect (partial) echoes of Aristotle and Stoicism in the spectator who judged from a distance and found the 'point of propriety'; in the formidable Stoic virtue of self-control, which in an appropriately modified version taught man to moderate his passions so that sympathy was aroused and a proper social relationship resulted; in Epicurean prudence, which encouraged the calculation of future benefits and taught man to be virtuous in his own interest, and to avoid (again in his own interest) excess and abuse. Prudence, together with self-control, ensured that legitimate individual aspirations were harmonized for the well-being of society.

Roman jurisprudence deserves separate treatment, as it offers the best example of a legal system (in terms of its structure, rather than its content) and so we can infer that it also offered the best guide for reasoning on 'laws and governments', which were essential for human life. The value of Roman

jurisprudence was pre-eminently methodological, and it was of great importance not only from a theoretical but also from a practical point of view.

Smith has at times been considered more a systematizer than an original
thinker, and it has been suggested that some of his positions had nothing
new to offer with respect to scholasticism, whose fundamental principles
were still those of Aristotle;[2] in other words, the economy was subordinate to
ethics, or rather to an ethical concept of justice. I too believe it is significant
that in his study of economics Smith started out from traditional principles,
and perceived economics within an ethical, theological, and juridical
framework. Up to this point we must acknowledge his connection with the
scholastic tradition and with Aristotle also. I apologize for quoting once
again John Millar's words: 'In the last part of his lectures, he examined those
political regulations which are founded, not upon the principle of *justice*, but
that of *expediency*, and which are calculated to increase the riches, the power,
and the prosperity of a State.'[3] It probably did not constitute a manifesto for
the study of economics as a science in its own right, but it was still a significant step. Even if it were true, as authoritative commentators have
suggested, that Smith did not offer anything significantly 'new' with respect
to his predecessors, at times even a change of outlook can be revolutionary.

Economic measures were thus not based on the principle of justice but of
expediency: here clearly Smith distanced himself from Aristotle, and was
closer to the rational–sociological approach which was widespread in the
Enlightenment. This approach originated from the consideration of landed
property as the first material element regulating social life, and from the
need to modify laws, not because they were intrinsically just or unjust, but
rather because they favoured or hindered the production of wealth.[4] The fact
that the new instruments of legislation were necessarily to be founded on a
knowledge of economics derived in part from the conviction (which Smith
shared with Voltaire and the Encyclopaedists, as well as with some Italian
followers of the Enlightenment) that intellectual and civil progress was
linked to economic progress.[5] The emergence of commercial society and the
ensuing changes in social and political life were studied within the general
reflections in the field of ethics and social institutions; not only scholars of
history, economics, and law considered this kind of question: even men of
letters—known as 'Augustans' in eighteenth-century England on account
of their classical perfection—turned their attention to this and to the study of

---

[2] In addition to the authors cited above, p. 91 n. 29, here I will mention De Roover (1951)
and Lindgren (1973), 129, who considers Smith close to Aristotle in the way that he perceives
commercial activity within a framework of justice, and on the other hand close to modern
anthropologists in the way he judges it a function of the customs of a community.
[3] In Stewart (1980), I. 20, in *EPS*, p. 275 (author's italics).
[4] Badaloni (1973), 813.   [5] Woolf (1973), 76.

how the new economic goals were compatible with the classical conceptions of public and private virtue.[6]

It is generally recognized that Adam Smith did not propound as perfect economic behaviour that went against justice; on the contrary, he supported the introduction of legislation to remove abuse and breach of trust, and he considered this sufficient to guarantee a regime in which justice and expediency coincided.[7] But the fact remains that economic advantage was now at the forefront, although it was perceived as the due consideration which every man should have for himself and for his basic needs, and not as an impulse to outdo others, or as a vile desire for money. I think that, just as Aristotle considered these feelings despicable (and on this ground he justified his condemnation), Smith did the same. However, Smith started from a European, or even a world, perspective, far more widespread than the 'domestic' economy of Aristotle, and his analysis, although theoretical in principles moreover developments, always took reality into account. Finally, in Smith's time the classical distinction between science and technique had faded; moreover, it was no longer possible to subscribe to Cicero's disparaging definition of the merchants: *nihil enim proficiant, nisi admodum mentiantur* (*De Officiis*, I. 150; 'they would get no profits without a great deal of downright lying' (W. Miller's translation)).

Without wishing to embark upon a vast issue, which would perhaps be out of place here, namely an analysis of the differences in the state of mind, albeit of a purely economic nature, between the two different periods of history, we can say briefly that changes both in the contingent reality of economic 'facts' and in the theories examining and evaluating them were so great that we cannot draw any valid parallel between the two. We have already seen that the classical authors were by no means uninterested in the economic world, but, since it occupied a lower place in their scale of values,[8] they treated it in a peculiar way. To take just one example from the previous pages, we recall that Aristotle did not avoid economics, and realized its importance in the formulation of his ethics and his politics, which had to take account of it in their organization. Aristotle nevertheless took what we would consider a strange approach, namely a theoretical scheme that was oversimplified in relation to the economic reality of his time. This was probably an attempt by Aristotle to *restore it to order*, to guarantee the survival of the city according to justice, and nothing more. In Smith's day speculation on economic issues was already considered of scientific value, and, having originated from a treatment within the context of ethics and jurisprudence, had gradually led to the definition of economics as an independent reflection on issues which, at this point, even political theory

---

[6] Winch (1979), 72–3.   [7] Rosenberg (1979), 24 ff.

[8] The economic world has been defined, in the context of Greek thought, as 'the world of necessity, *against* which and *upon* which . . . the Greeks constructed their scale of values' (Musti (1984), 10–11; see above, Ch. 1.4).

recognized as of prime importance. The 'world of necessity', to which the ancient freeman did not dedicate any sort of theoretical treatment except to define its limits, was by now seen as a stage upon which the shrewd and flexible tactics of intellectuals and governors could regulate human actions in the most appropriate way, achieving what were judged the most opportune results. Thus we cannot detect analogies between classical thought and eighteenth-century thought in the field of economic doctrine, and I realized early on that this study of the classical culture of Adam Smith would have not produced any important changes in the evaluation of his economic theories. However, I think I have contributed to the confirmation of certain interpretations which link Smith to the classical authors, without overlooking that the direct influence of classical culture on Smith's general philosophy may have had indirect repercussions on his economic theory, if it is true, as many maintain, that the origins of the *Wealth of Nations* are to be found in the *Moral Sentiments*. In the various chapters of this book I have drawn conclusions on each topic, and it would be superfluous to repeat these here. On a general note, we can say that this attempt to discover how the classical authors influenced the thought of Adam Smith, and how he reacted to their teaching, leads us to the conclusion that their presence in his work and in his life was more than just the 'flirtation' of a man of great culture and many interests; it influenced not only his tastes but also his mind and his ideas.

Traditional intellectual history has sarcastically been defined as 'a kind of foxhunt for ideas through the centuries (which usually ended with Aristotle and Plato)',[9] but clearly this type of search would be idle if the sole aim were to demonstrate that nothing new exists under the sun. I feel, however, it would be rather hazardous to maintain that it is pointless to learn as much as possible about the cultural background of a man of ideas, since his thought, new and important for the development of future knowledge, does not spring from nothing, but consists, at least in part, of personal reflection on and critical elaboration of what he has received, and of the use of logical tools from the distant and recent past. Smith's classical perspective was influenced (and today we would say partially distorted) not only by humanistic, Renaissance, and Baconian interpretations, but also by his own philosophical concepts (above all his concept of sympathy). But it constituted a constant reference point for his ethical, political, and even scientific thought. His spirit was exercised and nourished by the classics, in complete freedom, and he maintained a stance with respect to these influences which is summed up in the phrase attributed by Politian to Cosimo de' Medici: 'Rare talents are celestial forms, not carrier donkeys.'[10]

I hope I have demonstrated that Smith was greatly indebted to the classical authors of whom he was so fond. Perhaps he would not have acknowledged all the influences that I have identified, and would have admitted

---

[9] Stone (1981), 14.   [10] Garin (1967), 51.

others: the pleasure of reading; the opportunity to appreciate great poets and prose writers, to evoke memorable events and to examine the history of thought from its origins; the ability to converse in the pleasing manner of an 'initiate' with friends of similar background as well as with well-read chance acquaintances, or even prestigious thinkers (all men of learning were at home with classical texts); the opportunity to show off a precise and punctual knowledge of grammar and etymology;[11] his return, at an advanced age, to the beloved texts of his youth.[12] A personality as exceptional as that of Adam Smith clearly has drawn upon numerous and varied cultural sources, and perhaps it may be useful to further our understanding by highlighting those that may seem of little importance to his audience of economists (and in this context, we must not forget the report that Smith always considered the *Theory of Moral Sentiments* to be his most authoritative work).

Today it is generally accepted that a man must know his past to under- stand the present and project himself responsibly into the future. The same is true for the history of a man's thought, in the sense that we cannot leave aside his past and the cultural experiences of his formative years. Classical studies form only a part of these experiences, and so the picture that emerges is incomplete. It is, however, an important part for its contribution to thought, scholarly worth, and nobility of expression; and perhaps it deserved to be studied also on account of the special affection that the father of modern economic science had for it.

---

[11] We know that this weakness was anything but rare in the learned scholars, and Smith was not an exception (Stewart (1980) I. 10 n., in *EPS*, p. 272). Smith offers frequent observations and explanations of a linguistic nature in *Lectures on Jurisprudence*, in which he is often called to explain the precise meaning of Latin and even Greek terms (see for example *LJ* (A) i. 48, 97; iv. 70; v. 92; vi. 1; *WN* IV. vii. a. 3; *Of the Imitative Arts* III. 7 in *EPS*, p. 209. The lengthy historical digression on the grammatical term *idea*, in the note on Plato's theory of ideas in 'HALM' 3 (see above Ch. 1, pp. 34–5) is also interesting.   [12] Rae (1965), 333.

Postscript

I

The original version of this book was published in the same year as the article by N. Waszek, which I did not see prior to the publication of my book. Waszek's article significantly influenced a number of English-language authors, and indeed several works on Adam Smith followed which emphasized the Stoic aspect of his writings, in certain cases inspired by ideas expressed by Waszek himself.

Waszek's analysis centres on two fundamental points: the identification of Smith's propriety with Cicero's *kathekon*, or *decorum*;[1] and a parallel between the virtues described in *TMS* and the four cardinal virtues. I have reconsidered the issue, and I still feel that *decorum* is best confined to literature, and that Smith's propriety is, rather, related to the *medietas* of Aristotelian origin. This seems an appropriate opportunity to examine this more closely.

Waszek bases his reasoning on a passage (*TMS* I. i. 5. 7) in which Smith defines 'mere propriety' as behaviour which is morally acceptable but not perfectly virtuous. This leads him to suggest that propriety is an intermediate level of virtue, which can be attained by the majority of men, while virtue is a prerogative of the 'wise few'. Waszek adds that these two levels of virtue are of Stoic origin, and that Smith in his tract gave priority to the 'intermediate' rather than the perfect virtue, since 'the standard of propriety is generally traceable'.[2]

Let us take the passage analysed by Waszek as our starting-point: a few lines below, Smith attributes a different meaning to propriety. In *TMS* I. i. 5. 9 (and likewise in *TMS* VI. iii. 23) Smith refers to two 'different standards' of judgement in evaluating moral action: 'complete ['exact' in VI. iii. 23] propriety and perfection', the highest standard, and a lower standard represented by 'that degree of proximity or distance from this complete perfection, which the actions of the greater part of men commonly arrive at'.[3] It is evident that in

---

[1] He was not the first author to express this idea: compare Scott (1940), 84, on whom see above, Ch. 2 n. 24. [2] Waszek (1984), 594.

[3] Waszek cites this phrase on p. 602, but without noting that Smith used 'propriety' to qualify the higher standard; thus his conclusion 'virtue of the wise, propriety of the multitude' seems rather strange, when a few lines above it is clear that Smith refers propriety to the wise few. In

this case propriety represents perfection, and not vice versa. The same is true of certain forms of self-control dictated not by 'the sense of propriety' but by 'prudential considerations' (*TMS* VI. concl. 5).[4] Smith also alludes to propriety in several passages as if it were a precise degree of intensity, using expressions such as 'point of propriety'(*TMS* I. ii. intro. 2; VI. iii. 14), or 'pitch of moderation' (I. i. 5. 8). This gives the idea of a yardstick, and an exact yardstick I would say; however, one that is not easily established. It is well known that no system, only the impartial spectator, can establish this 'precise and distinct measure' (*TMS* VII. ii. 1. 49).

It is interesting to note that Smith himself traced the classical antecedents to his propriety. In *TMS* VII. ii. he classifies the moral theories according to whether they are founded upon 'propriety', 'prudence', or 'benevolence'. Smith emphasizes that prudence and benevolence (*TMS* VII. ii. intro. 2–3) are the virtues which inspire, respectively, actions to one's own advantage, or to that of others. Propriety is quite different, and in a certain sense it is more neutral: it is, in short, a yardstick and a relationship (*TMS* VII. ii. intro. 1). Above all it is not a virtue (*TMS* VII. ii. 50). In keeping with this definition, Smith—who illustrates 'those Systems which make Virtue consist in Propriety' with the theories of Plato, Aristotle, and the Stoics—declares that his propriety bears affinity to both Aristotle's 'habit of mediocrity' (*TMS* VII. ii. 1.12) and Plato's 'state of mind in which every faculty confines itself within its proper sphere' (*TMS* VII. ii. 1. 11). But there is a significant difference between the two aforementioned systems and the third, the Stoic system; and Smith never parallels his propriety to the Stoic concept.

Stoic propriety consists of living according to nature, and of totally conforming to the rational order of the universe. Thus the will of the individual is expressed simply as the acceptance of his role in this order, without any sort of opposition (see in particular *TMS* VII. ii. 1. 21–3). This behaviour which is taken to extreme consequences in Stoic philosophy is not in reality consistent with Smith's moral teaching, and indeed Smith rejects it (*TMS* VII. ii. 1. 43 ff.). The Stoic's acceptance of one's own fate derives from a knowledge of the cosmic order and it is exclusively rational and wholly detached from passion, which the Stoic philosophers generally thought should be suppressed. Stoic virtue is founded upon reason, or rather 'on principle', and not on sentiments.[5] Smith knew this well and, in a passage which was removed from the sixth edition of *TMS* but can be found in the first five, we read that the Stoic philosophers 'appear to have regarded every

---

TMS VI. iii. 23 the expression relating to the lowest standard is slightly modified, but not in substance: 'that degree of approximation to this idea which is commonly attained in the world'.

[4] In this case, there is even 'some degree of propriety and, if you will, even of virtue; but it is a propriety and virtue of a much inferior order' (ibid.) in conformist behaviour. It is all judged by the impartial spectator, the subject of the phrase. This demonstrates that this character enters into the judgement both of 'perfect' actions and of actions inspired only by convention (*contra* Brown (1994), 114).   [5] Edelstein (1966), 2.

passion as improper, which made any demand upon the sympathy of the spectator' (*TMS* VII. ii. 1. 17, p. 273). Smith then rightly observes that the true Stoic does not admit any dependence upon the sentiments of others. Naturally things are not as simple as they seem. However, we must remember that Smith refused to do away with passion, and he also refused to be content with contemplating the perfect order of nature. Man is born for a purpose and all told he cannot 'better his condition' if he accepts it willingly whatever it may be.

Waszek is nonetheless correct when he considers the two levels of virtue which, as Smith says, the Stoic accepted (*TMS* VII. ii. 1. 42). Undoubtedly Smith's philosophy also accepted this, as we can see from numerous passages in *TMS*.[6] We might also add that in the passage quoted above Smith once again uses the term 'propriety' to describe that 'imperfect but attainable virtue' upon which Waszek founds his argument. Smith writes: 'they called the imperfect virtues . . . not rectitudes, but *proprieties*, fitnesses, decent and becoming actions' (my italics). It seems evident to me, however, that the use of the plural and the string of quasi-synonyms makes it clear that here the term takes on a slightly different meaning: we are no longer dealing with the 'exact propriety and perfection' nor the Stoic 'virtue and the propriety of conduct' of *TMS* VII. ii. 1. 16 (note that virtue and propriety are on the same level). In this case we are dealing with 'proper' and 'decent' behaviour and this leads Waszek to liken Smith's 'propriety' to the *decorum* with which the Stoics defined aspects of conventional moral behaviour.[7]

This identification has also been taken up by other authors, and so perhaps some clarification is called for. Cicero's *decorum* is an aesthetic as well as a moral value. In *De Officiis* I. 93, and *De Oratore* 70 Cicero translates *decorum* with the Greek *prepon*: this is again an aesthetic concept, which principally means 'appear' and which maintains—even when applied to ethics—the meaning of a visible manifestation of qualities. This word is used predominantly in art, literary criticism, and rhetoric.[8] *Decorum* means a perfect proportion, a correspondence between the exterior expression and the impulses of the soul. It is always connected with appearance, and it is something that is projected to the exterior.

Since it is connected with a sense of equilibrium and moderation, *decorum* could be related in some way to the golden mean; but, to the best of my knowledge, this has happened rarely.[9] At any rate, I believe this relationship is a coincidence, and one that is more apparent than real. The golden mean is something of a precise measure, almost a kind of mathematical intuition

---

[6] This has already been observed by Bonar (1926), 345.

[7] Waszek (1984), 600–1.

[8] On this see Pohlenz (1933), Philippson (1930), 386–413, North (1996b), 221–2, and Dyck (1996), 238–59.

[9] There is a brief mention in North (1996b), 223, and one in Griswold (1999), 183 n. 5. Philippson (1930), 394, also alludes to this relationship, but only within the context of rhetoric.

(Arist. *NE* 1142ª27–9), although it cannot be measured in a concrete sense but only by the sensibility of the wise man. *Decorum* is rather a form of 'bon ton', of conformity to people and to situations, of behaviour which is appropriate to a given role or status.

Decorum is not absent in Smith, but in my opinion it does not correspond to propriety. It is true that *decorum* leads to moderate and appropriate behaviour; however, I think that this is the result more than the cause.

In sum, I remain of the view that Smith's propriety is closer to Aristotle's concept of *medietas*; and, as I suggested in 1984, Smith's personal interpretation is that the point of propriety has the purpose of producing a sympathetic reaction in others. In the (rare) cases in which Smith uses propriety to allude to mediocre behaviour in the sense of 'not perfect', we cannot exclude some sort of overlap with the concept of *kathekon*. Indeed in one case this is certain and Smith himself acknowledges the fact by referring to the Stoics (*TMS* VII. ii. 1. 42). It is useful to remember, however, that the two levels of virtue do not belong exclusively to Stoicism.[10] Ethics is a discipline in which there has been so much overlap that it is not always easy to attribute ideas with certainty. Waszek maintains that the two levels of virtue in Smith's moral thought derive from Stoic philosophy; but in my opinion this is not the case. The '(certain) mediocrity' of which Smith speaks in *TMS* I. ii. intro. 1–2 is more evidently related, as I have tried to demonstrate,[11] to Aristotle's ethics than to Stoicism.

II

Another recent trend in Smith studies is the analysis of virtues. My brief outline of 1984 may seem of little substance today; but at that time the topic was far less treated.

As I have already said, Waszek was the first to link the cardinal virtues to Smith's moral philosophy. Since then other authors have taken for granted the 'canon' of the four virtues, namely prudence, justice, benevolence, and self-command.[12] Here I wish merely to express reservations over the fact that the above-mentioned virtues of Smith, considered 'cardinal' and even of Stoic origin,[13] make Smith more indebted towards Stoic philosophy.

---

[10] A distinction between the perfect virtue of the wise and conventional virtue based on habit or conventions can be found both in Plato and in Aristotle: see Sorabji (1980), 211–14.

[11] Vivenza (1984), 56–7 and nn. 30–1; according to Waszek, this was a case of mediocre behaviour typical of conventional morality. Cf. Waszek (1984), 596.

[12] Cf. Fitzgibbons (1995), 104–14; Griswold (1999), 202–10. In reality Griswold simply affirms that 'the cardinal virtues for Smith are self-command, prudence, benevolence and justice' (p. 202), which may signify a relevance for Smith, but not an identification with the theological cardinal virtues. Brown (1994) takes into consideration the four virtues, but subdivides them using different criteria (cf. Vivenza (1999*a*), 104–7).

[13] Waszek concedes Stoic origins for three only; he attributes to justice an Aristotelian origin (Waszek (1984), 604).

It has long been thought[14] that the four virtues indicated by Plato in book IV of the *Republic* as essential to the perfection of the city and individuals were the precursors of the cardinal virtues of Christian ethics. I do not know to what extent this depends upon the fact that they are four, or upon the similarity between some of these and the virtues which were subsequently elaborated by the thought of the Church and scholasticism. Essentially the argument is that the canon of the four virtues was founded by Plato,[15] ignored by Aristotle, but taken up by the Stoics, and thus made its way into the Christian religion. Reputable research has been done on this aspect, and I would prefer not to take the issue any further, as it would lead us well away from our theme. However, we should be very wary of considering Adam Smith's virtues to be cardinal virtues.[16]

The fact that Christianity used (and naturally adapted) classical motives is well known; but one should not attribute to ancient literature a meaning which it could not have had.[17] I believe that I can spare myself the task of establishing if and to what extent Smith's virtues are akin to the cardinal virtues.[18] Here I will try to expand on what I said in my original book about their classical origins.

---

[14] In modern times, I would say with the first publication (1902) of J. Adams's commentary on Plato's *Republic*. It is true that in the commentaries on Cicero's *De Officiis* of the 16th, 17th, and 18th centuries there are certain parallels between the three virtues of prudence, justice, and strength and the cardinal virtues, and for the fourth (temperance) *decorum* tends to be used. It was St. Ambrose who originally made these identifications (North (1966*b*), 360–2).

[15] But Plato's virtues, as they belong to different classes of persons, are profoundly different from the Christian virtues; indeed in this case the four virtues have a mark of inferiority, given the class to which they belong (Sorabji (1980), 214).

[16] It is indeed true that Smith mentions the cardinal virtues as illustrated by Cicero (*TMS* VII. iv. 5), and there is also a reference to this group of virtues in Plato's *Republic* (*TMS* VII. ii. 1. 6–9). But precisely these two references demonstrate that Smith is describing traditional doctrine, and no reference is made to any possible relation between these and *his* four virtues mentioned above, which—at the very most—I think are in some way effectively related to justice, and a certain type of prudence.

[17] Just one example, from a scholar who generally takes the utmost care, and thus cannot be (excessively) criticized. On p. 270 of her book (1966*b*), Helen North affirms that Cicero 'put the social virtue of *communitas* (Cicero's rendering of *dikaiosyne* in his list of the four virtues in *De Officiis* 1. 153) at the top of the hierarchy' and remarks in the notes that in *De Officiis* 1. 43. 153 'the four cardinal virtues' are here 'called *cognitio, communitas, magnanimitas, moderatio*'. Now neither in the passage cited from *De Officiis* nor in any other work by *Cicero* can *communitas* signify *dikaiosyne*; it means *socialitas*: social bond. It is clear that the scholar had in mind the *communitas vitae* which is the basis of the second part of *honestum*, namely justice/benevolence (*De Officiis* 1. 20); but *communitas* cannot be directly identified with justice. If we wish to take this further, it is not true that in *De Officiis* 1. 153 Cicero lists the four above-mentioned virtues, signalling the conflict which may rise from all four. On the contrary, he alludes to the possible conflict between *two* types of wisdom, theoretical and practical (*sophia* and *phronesis*, which he translates as *sapientia* and *prudentia*), from a clear Greek–Roman viewpoint. Basically H. North *wanted* to find a link between Cicero's treatment and the four cardinal virtues, and so forced the text to the point of attributing an entirely improbable meaning to a word whose meaning is well known. In this way, it is easy to find 'cardinal' virtues everywhere, starting from Plato, or even before, as North has shown us.

[18] It is obvious that in the case of Smith we must take into account the fact that he, unlike the classical authors, knew Christian ethics and could not help being influenced in some way. As I mentioned in n. 16, he speaks of the cardinal virtues in *TMS* VII.

Let us take prudence for example. Prudence is particularly interesting because on the one hand it has an obvious economic application and perfectly describes the modest saver who is excessively cautious and perhaps even downright mean. On the other hand, for those arguing the case of the four cardinal virtues, this is the only virtue which might correspond to wisdom. This obstacle is wisely avoided by resorting to the 'superior prudence' of *TMS* vi. i. 15.[19] However, it is quite clear that this is different from the 'inferior prudence' to which Adam Smith dedicates far greater attention.

In reality, the origin of this 'dual' prudence belongs to classical antiquity. Cicero, in *De Off.* 1, 153, emphasized a contrast which had already been put forward by the Greeks, and paved the way for a concept which was later to become one of the principal elements both of divine providence and of another, more earthly, type of prudence.

At the time of Aquinas, prudence was a virtue which enabled individuals to choose the right means with which to achieve a moral purpose.[20] Two types of prudence existed: individual prudence, by which individuals governed their own behaviour, and public prudence, which served to rule the community. The latter prudence was divided into four parts which Aquinas derived from Aristotle:[21] legislative, political, domestic, and military.

The relationship between Smith's well-known superior prudence, which the legislator, the statesman, and the military commander have to prove, and the above form of prudence is singular. (What I have defined as 'domestic' prudence corresponds, of course, to the Greek *oikonomikè*; I have avoided the term 'economic' because I do not wish to attach an excessively modern meaning. Interestingly, in *TMS* vi. i. 15 Smith mentions the other three varieties, and omits precisely this variety of prudence. I believe this may depend, at least in this context, on the fact that he perceived *oikonomikè* at a private level and thus as connected with inferior prudence. Public prudence is part of political prudence, and so it is formed by the three varieties of superior prudence.[22])

---

[19] This expedient had already been employed by Waszek (1984), 602–3; cf. also Fitzgibbons (1995), 105, and Griswold (1999), 204, who assimilates it to the 'Platonic *sophia* (vii. ii. 1. 6)', probably on the basis of the comment on *TMS* ad loc. He goes on to say that the aforementioned *sophia* is 'self-command over all emotions to the appropriate degree and in the right manner', which is not correct. Heise takes a different view, and identifies prudence with self-interest (Heise (1995), 23).

[20] I do not wish to go into highly specialist issues, such as establishing whether Aristotelian *phronesis* and Thomistic *prudentia* were related to the means but not to the end: cf. Westberg (1994), 16 and n. 6.

[21] Aquinas cites in this context numerous passages from Aristotle and Isidore's *Etymologiae* (*Summa*, ii. iiae, Q50). The direct comparison of the four parts of *phronesis* was passed down from Stobaeus, from the epitome of Arrius Didymus: cf. Stobaeus, *Eclogae*, Meinecke, ed. ii, 328, p. 93.

[22] The view expressed by Young (1997), 184, is incomprehensible: 'Smith's "superior prudence" is the same as Platonic justice, the perfect balancing of the different parts of the soul in a virtuous and just whole'. Further evidence that Smith's virtues have been identified with just about everything.

From Italian humanism onwards the nature of prudence became more political than moral. Its 'secularization'[23] led to a definition which was more material and closer to the economy: individual behaviour which regulated itself according to the (changing) circumstances and therefore differently in each case, but was always focused toward the achievement of personal advantage.

In sum, I think I can confirm what I wrote in 1984. On the subject of prudence, I would only add that Smith gives much more space to the domestic variety,[24] making only fleeting reference to superior prudence, a prerogative of politics. It is also interesting that he attributes the 'paternity' of superior prudence to Plato and Aristotle, and that of inferior prudence to Epicurus.[25] In reality, as I have already said, Aristotle was the father of all four varieties, but Smith's affirmation is nonetheless founded. Let us turn to Diogenes Laertius, an author to whom Smith himself makes reference and an important source on Epicurean thought: 'while therefore all pleasure because it is naturally akin to us is good, not all pleasure is choiceworthy, just as all pain is an evil and yet not all pain is to be shunned. It is, however, *by measuring one against another, and by looking at the conveniences and inconveniences*, that all these matters must be judged' (x. 130; R. D. Hicks' transl., my italics). This passage offers reasons both for Smith's adversity expressed in *TMS* VII. ii. 2. 13 (Epicurus is interested only in the 'utility', the finality of the choice) and for its hidden similarity. In the careful calculation of the present or future advantage, there is something more than the cold Stoic rational choice. The Epicurean chooses a future advantage which is within his reach, and performs a calculation of practicality which leads neither to indifference towards the final outcome, nor to intellectual abstraction. This calculation may only inspire 'a certain cold esteem' (*TMS* VI. i. 14), but it is wise and justified behaviour. In 1984 I wrote that the two schools have much in common in this respect, and indeed this is so. However, the Epicurean, unlike the Stoic, pursues a practical outcome. For Smith this represents a valid argument, despite a certain anti-utilitarian element in his thought.[26]

I will not dwell upon virtues such as temperance and courage which in my opinion do not correspond to Smith's self-command and benevolence in any

---

[23] I have borrowed this term from a well-known review by Hans Baron (1960).

[24] In Aquinas' *Summa* we can find the elements of prudence which constitute a set of 'minor' virtues: memory, understanding, docility, shrewdness, reason, foresight, circumspection, caution (II IIae, Q49; cf. *TMS* VII. ii. 3. 15).

[25] Waszek (1984), 603, defines 'inferior prudence' as 'strongly reminiscent of Roman Stoicism'. My opinion is that Smith was perfectly capable of judging, and he defines it as Epicurean.

[26] Vivenza (1984), 65 and nn. 61–2; 86–7; 128 and n. 88. Smith does not approve of utility as an *end*, because the virtue has value in itself (note the classical, and 'pagan', position). He is, however, ready to admit that virtuous behaviour usually produces advantageous results (*TMS* III. 5. 8).

way,[27] except for the obvious, purely exterior, resemblance between temperance and self-control.[28]

Another virtue which has attracted great attention is justice, and above all 'distributive' justice. A little clarification of this concept is warranted, at least in terms of its well-known classical derivation from Aristotle. Some recent authors start from a contraposition of commutative and distributive justice, thus automatically adopting an Aristotelian-scholastic stance, and then proceed to investigate Smith's concept of 'fair' distribution (in an economic sense).[29] I believe it is wrong to associate the latter with distributive justice.

Smith expresses opinions on justice on numerous occasions: he reminds us of the Aristotelian distinction and its modern equivalent; he criticizes the classical philosophers, because they treated justice in the same way as the other virtues,[30] and, above all, he likens justice and beneficence (or benevolence) in a way that is often underlined, as it is puzzling for the modern reader. How many times have we seen the phrase quoted from *TMS* II. ii. 3. 4, that only justice is the pillar of society, while beneficence is an entirely optional embellishment? Well, this comparison is less singular than it seems. Once again Cicero is partially responsible, because while on the one hand Aristotle made a clear distinction between the two virtues, on the other Cicero treated them as one virtue divided into two parts (*De Officiis* I. 20). In this way, Cicero connected justice in its true sense with *liberalitas/beneficentia*, which had come to be identified with that form of justice which supposes that the parts are unequal—namely distributive justice. I do not intend to repeat here what I have already said elsewhere, nevertheless it is true that Cicero's version fitted the many queries over the 'just' behaviour in a society with a strong hierarchy. The purpose of distributive justice is to maintain differences in merit (a kind of proportionality, according to Aristotle (*NE* 1131 ^{a}23–7)), and it is suited to a society in which marked inequality exists. Indeed the classics had no difficulty in stating that men are *not* equal, and Aristotle merely enunciates the diverse nature of the two types of justice.

Christianity, however, considered all men equal and thus should have taken a different stance. But it was all too convenient to have an argument which made the given fact accepted that all men were not equal, and justified the authority which certain men had over others without the possibility of rebellion. In distributive justice it was considered just that certain individuals (the sovereign of a State, the aristocracy, the father of a family[31]) had authority over others.

---

[27] Fitzgibbons (1995), 104–5, finds a connection.

[28] In reality the virtue which constitutes temperance is prudence in the sense of 'practical wisdom': Plutarch defined temperance as *phronesis* in the Moralia (Plutarch, *De Vir. Mor.* 441A; *De Fort.* 97E). Smith naturally was well acquainted with this argument: cf. *TMS* VII. ii. 2. 9.

[29] Endres (1995), 92; Noell (1995), 239–43; Young (1997), pt. II, 5 and 6; Griswold (1999), ch. 6.

[30] Cf. *TMS* VII. ii. 1. 10; VII. iv. 37, and the fragment published in app. II to *TMS*.

[31] On the model of God for the universe cf. Lambertini (1985), 67.

The latter's task was to recognize as just their own subordinate role and allow themselves to be governed. This argument was naturally not only political, and applied to all family and social relationships. It was an excellent means of preserving situations of subordination and dependence. The initial configuration of benevolence/beneficence excluded equal relationships: this virtue was the prerogative of those in 'high' positions, with the power to command and responsibility for administrative duties. In theory, it was taken for granted that they acted for the good of all.

Thus we see that benevolence was an important element in this argument. It suits the powerful to do good, it is just that they do so, but no man can order this, or punish them if they fail. Conversely, it is clear that those in positions of weakness have no rights: they can ask, but they cannot demand. The discretion of the donor cannot be questioned, and it is in a certain sense inversely proportionate to the rights bestowed upon the receiver. The poor man has no claim to the property of the rich man even in extreme cases,[32] otherwise benevolence would cease to be voluntary. It is clear that this type of argument cannot in any circumstances be treated with the tools of commutative justice, in which parties are assumed to be on an equal footing: it has to be treated as a distributive justice.

By the eighteenth century it perhaps began to seem slightly incongruous that both forms were called 'justice', when in fact they represented opposing concepts. In Smith's terminology, a certain degree of dissatisfaction seems to emerge:[33] *true* justice is commutative justice, which provides precise rules, and can be imposed with force upon those who do not wish to abide by it spontaneously. If it is to be a spontaneous and voluntary act, which men are free to perform or otherwise, it is better to call it something else: benevolence.[34] Now, as far as I can see, this aspect of justice has not been sufficiently grasped by authors writing on Adam Smith today, as if it were directly linked with distribution in the economic sense of the word.[35]

---

[32] Hont and Ignatieff (1983), 24–6. Cf. also ch. 6, 'Distributive Justice', in Pieper (1966), 81–103.

[33] I refer principally to the fragment on justice in which Smith clearly affirms: 'the former, *which can alone properly be called Justice*, has been denominated commutat [. . .] Justice' (*TMS*, 390; my italics); and to *LJ* (A) i. 15.

[34] Smith followed centuries in which the existence of two varieties of justice had given rise to excess; for example, in *De Legibus Naturae* by R. Cumberland, ch. VIII. 5, at a certain point everything seems to boil down to one or other form of justice: '*Liberality is Justice conspicuous in Actions . . . Providence* and *Frugality* may be defin'd *Justice in acquiring and in preserving*', etc. (cf. Cumberland (1727), 332, author's italics).

[35] I have not examined this issue in depth, but there may have been a parallel between distributive justice (or at least so-called) and social justice at the time of the utilitarian theories in the 19th century, when the relationship between justice and utility was analysed, by John Stuart Mill in particular, and distributive justice took on a more 'egalitarian' meaning, with distribution of 'rights' subject to various criteria. The connection with economic distribution was not immediate, but transpired in some cases. My impression, however, is that Stuart Mill used the adjective 'distributive' almost as a synonym of 'social' (in *Utilitarianism* at least: cf. Plamenatz (1949), 225), without intending any sort of reference to Aristotle.

The most authoritative author on this issue, J. Young, in practice identifies distributive justice with benevolence,[36] which may be accepted. Subsequently, on the basis of a number of remarks made by Smith to the effect that the State can impose certain forms of benevolence or 'good offices', Young first criticizes feudalism and mercantilism as erroneous or rather unjust forms of distribution, and then concludes by remarking that distributive justice is 'an important normative concern in his [Smith's] political economy'.[37]

It is not for me to interpret what Smith intended by 'just' economic distribution; however, I feel I can reasonably discount, when he speaks of 'distributive Justice' or even of benevolence, the idea that this is what he was referring to. In the case of distributive justice, the subject is exclusively philosophical and I think Smith has adequately placed it in historical context. In *TMS* VII. ii. 1. 10 he is also keen to underline that Aristotle's distributive justice is not the same as the distributive justice of certain other authors[38] nor the *iustitia attributrix* of Grotius, which means the bestowal of additional benefits left to discretion.[39] It is enough to read a few lines above ('we are said to do injustice to a man of merit . . . though we abstain from hurting him in every respect, if we do not exert ourselves to serve him and to place him in that situation in which the impartial spectator would be pleased to see him') and a few lines below ('which [i.e. distributive justice] consists in proper beneficence, in the becoming use of what is our own, and in the applying it to those purposes either of charity or generosity, to which it is most suitable, in our situation, that it should be applied') to realize that *this* justice has nothing to do with the other variety. It represents the two faces of justice considered as a virtue in the classical and medieval world. If we are in a position to serve or honour a person, then we must do so;[40] if, conversely, we find ourselves in a higher position, it is for us to decide how, how much, and to whom we give.

I have observed elsewhere that while Smith considers the rules of benevolence to be 'loose and inaccurate' (*TMS* III. 6. 9), Cicero and to an even greater extent Seneca had no difficulty in offering a number of practical

---

[36] Young (1997), 130, 132, 198. Griswold does the same (1999), 250, 252. In reality the concept of benevolence had been considerably broadened by Hutcheson: cf. Vivenza (1996), 35.

[37] Young (1997), 155. I have rather brusquely summarized ch. 6 of Young (and B. Gordon) taken from a previous article, which posed itself the impossible task (in my opinion) of unifying commutative and distributive justice.

[38] 'Some' in the text; I do not know whether they are the 'schoolmen' mentioned slightly above. Raphael has appropriately noted that the observation concerning Aristotle was probably the result of checking information prior to publication (*TMS*, app. II. 396–7).

[39] And which was of course of no use in legal practice: 'The confusion in Grotius had led to distinctions that were wholly unnecessary and useless for legal practice, for example between *justitia attributrix*, which is really benevolence and is voluntary, and *justitia expletrix*, which is justice proper' (Forbes (1982), 188).

[40] Smith's observation that it is not sufficient merely to abstain 'from hurting him' is significant; it is our duty to serve him and treat him as a superior.

examples. Smith takes Cicero as a starting-point, though he makes no direct mention of him, to question whether it really is so easy to return a favour appropriately.[41] We must remember that in the classical world, from Seneca onwards, a distinction came to be made between the personal relationship between benefactor and beneficiary, and the impersonal nature which was characteristic of a mercenary relationship.[42] All the more in the eighteenth century, the difference between the establishment of any kind of relationship on precise (and redeeming) rules and being forced to leave these to the discretion of one or other party had become quite clear.

The classical authors from Cicero onwards (who is principally responsible for the likening of the two virtues), and in the same way medieval and modern thinkers, were able to keep justice and benevolence united particularly in terms of political thought, since both were among the gifts deemed essential to anyone in a position of power and authority, in roughly equal proportions. Benevolence was discretionary, and merely a moral obligation, whilst justice rendered to each his own. The fact that certain differences were explained in terms of 'to each his own', thus resolving them in terms of justice, merely reveals one of the expedients adopted by men in order to justify privilege.

Smith came after centuries in which distributive justice had been used to identify actions which depended entirely on the will of those who performed them. Naturally certain rules, instructions, and suggestions had been formulated in order to avoid the actions being simply the whim of the person who performed them. However, if the individual wished to act entirely of his own accord, then no one could prevent this. At times Smith speaks of 'proper' and 'improper' benevolence[43] and so reflects precisely this issue, well known in classical times, of granting benefits to deserving people, in the correct manner and so forth. All was in the name of a principle which Cicero had already identified,[44] that a misplaced benefit does more harm than good. Nevertheless, if an improper benefit were granted it would be impossible to punish the person who bestowed it (as would occur when an unjust action is committed), because the benefactor is not answerable to anyone on how he allocates his benefits.

When Smith asserts that distributive justice consists in 'proper beneficence', he echoes this philosophical distinction. His is what we might call a technical definition by a moral philosopher, used to explain how the duty to make 'becoming use of what is our own' is not a legal obligation. Those

---

[41] Vivenza (1995), 528 n. 91.

[42] When payment is involved, the debt can be calculated with precision. This is not possible when the debt depends on a 'benefit': cf. Seneca, *De Beneficiis*.II. 18. 5, and Vivenza (1996), 26, on the same subject.

[43] For example, cf. *TMS* II. ii. 1.6; VII. ii. 3.4 and the fragment in app. II. p. 390.

[44] In his treatment of the topic in *De Officiis* II. 62 Cicero repeats a verse by Ennius: *Bene facta male locata male facta arbitror*.

authors who have transferred a long-established philosophical argument to the economic field of distribution have given to Smith's words a meaning which suggests the opposite of what he had in mind. Classical distributive justice aimed to *maintain* inequality,[45] while, in the field of economics, distributive justice aims to correct it. Here naturally I am not disputing that certain questions raised by these authors[46] may refer to some true concern of Smith for 'distribution'; however, when he refers to 'distributive justice' this is not what he alludes to.

To conclude, I believe we can say that the most important virtues for Smith are those mentioned above, but they do not correspond to the cardinal virtues of Christianity, or even those of the classical world. Strength and temperance, for example, mentioned by Smith (*TMS* VII. ii. I. 7–8), are not among his four fundamental virtues. Benevolence, rather than being acknowledged as part of 'civic commitment'[47] or distributive justice, may have some relationship with 'charity',[48] which, if anything, is a theological virtue. Parallels drawn between Smith's virtues and the cardinal virtues go a little too far, and it can easily be demonstrated that the same virtue is identified in different ways by different authors.

III

Generally speaking, Paul Heise is perhaps the author who more than any other has offered a 'pan-Stoic' interpretation of Smith.[49] He suggests that Smith starts from Stoic principles in *EPS* and continues with Stoic morals in *TMS*, and ultimately 'applies' them in *WN*.[50] This interpretation, however, is based on unproven affirmations.

The methodological significance of the essay on astronomy has long been acknowledged. Once its value from a historical and epistemological stand-point has been recognized, Heise presents it as offering a model for human behaviour. From a historical point of view, perhaps it might have been interpreted as a missed opportunity. Stoic cosmology might have been of special interest in the seventeenth and eighteenth centuries, since, unlike Aristotelianism, it did not separate physics from astronomy. In this sense, it might have been considered more 'modern'.[51] However, from Roman

---

[45] Spiegel (1983), 30–1.

[46] Young and Gordon (1996); Young (1997). Neither Witztum (1997) nor Griswold (1999), 250–4, emphasizes the derivation from Aristotle, so my criticism is mainly of Young's approach.

[47] Fitzgibbons (1995), 95, cf. also 105–6.

[48] It is well known that Smith uses this word in *LJ* (A) vi. 46 as a synonym of benevolence (that of the famous passage in *WN* I. ii. 2). I do not deny that benevolence may have certain political aspects, of which Smith speaks in *TMS*, and which I have already briefly considered in Vivenza (1996).

[49] Heise (1995), 17–30. This author has written another article on this issue, which I have been unable to read; my analysis is therefore based on the 1995 article.

[50] Heise (1995), 18.   [51] Todd (1989), 1368–9.

Stoicism onwards Stoic cosmology slipped into second place in relation to moral philosophy, and was avowedly neglected.[52]

Heise, however, presents 'HA' as if it were more a question of moral philosophy than scientific theory (or at best a combination of the two). He suggests that its purpose is to enable men to 'know the data well enough to make rational choices about what is or is not in conformity to nature'.[53] The purpose of astronomy is certainly not to make rational choices, nor to behave in conformity to nature, but rather to offer an abstract explanation of observed phenomena. No models of action are proposed because this is the task of ethics or politics, or even of economics: in short, of practical philosophy but not of astronomy, which is first and foremost a theoretical science.[54]

It is perplexing to read that 'Smith rejected that part of Stoicism which made God the impartial spectator',[55] an incomprehensible statement which concludes with an equally incomprehensible reference to *TMS* VII. ii. 1. 40. At this point in *TMS* Smith only refers to paradoxes which serve to illustrate the well-known Stoic principle that no intermediate level between absolute good and absolute evil exists. Later Heise repeats this argument, by stating that the Stoic 'in attempting to make God his impartial spectator, removed himself from the level of human understanding. From the perspective of a transcendent God, nothing man does has much relevance'.[56] Much can be said of Stoicism but not that it had a transcendent God. The idea is totally alien to this philosophy and while we can accept the idea that Smith's impartial spectator is human, we cannot consider this 'a proper remedy' to the Stoic divine spectator, because the latter simply did not exist.

At this stage it is clear that the implications which Heise draws from these assumptions are, to say the least, debatable, although one conclusion is acceptable: Smith holds man responsible for his actions, in contrast to Stoic determinism.

Moreover, Heise's idea that human propensities deriving from 'reason and speech' are 'the cause of all troubles of mankind'[57] is quite incredible, and I do not know where Smith said or even hinted at such an idea. Heise connects this affirmation with another metaphor, that of the partial spectator, the very character who in *TMS* III. 3. 42 is in contrast to the impartial spectator and is aroused by a feeling of partisan spirit. In Heise's view, the former represents

---

[52] Lapidge (1989), 1380.   [53] Heise (1995), 22.

[54] Heise states—after having said that *EPS* 'provided a model of animal behaviour and propensities to survival'—that 'Smith is proposing a model for scientific or philosophical action' (Heise (1995), 22). I wonder whether he means, in a modern sense, that 'words are deeds' and theories are facts, but this was certainly not the thought of Adam Smith.

[55] Heise (1995), 19.

[56] Heise (1995), 22. Griswold is also struck by the 'cosmic perspective' that the Stoic philosopher endeavours to adopt, but his definition is rather less bold: a 'synopticism' which is the 'standpoint of nature, or the whole' (Griswold (1999), 318–19).

[57] Heise (1995), 23.

the negative and self-destroying elements in the system, which need to be compensated for by the Stoic instinct of regard for the self, family, friends, and the State. The fact that Heise and others consider this principle (*oikeiosis*, of which I shall speak shortly) Stoic is comprehensible, given that these authors are better acquainted with recent literature on Stoicism than with the texts themselves, and the majority of recent literature attributes the principle to Stoic doctrine.[58] At this point, given that the source of the sequence in question (family, friends, the State) is precisely the same as for 'reason and speech', namely Cicero, I see no reason to attribute Stoic origins to one but not the other. Both the instinct of self-preservation and *ratio et oratio*, as typical characteristics of mankind, go back to the accounts of the origins of society. The version offered by Cicero was naturally the most appropriate to the minds of the eighteenth-century thinkers, not only because of the extensive studies conducted on this author, but also because of the Latin orator's 'special affinity' with that century.[59] It is beyond me why one of the two characteristics should be deemed beneficial and the other harmful, and why this conviction should be attributed to Smith.

It is true that from classical antiquity onwards Stoicism embraced many positions which were less rigorous than the original doctrine. It is possible to draw on these, at times with reasonable foundation, and find connections with certain elements of Smith's thought. However, we must remember that the revival of Stoicism in modern times, resulting from the reinterpretation of many classical authors in a modern key, has led to the adoption of a number of different contrasting positions. This fact should invite us to proceed with caution, because an array of elements have been grouped together under the label of Stoicism. Thus we find that on the basis of Stoic doctrine it was possible to be in favour of both the republic and absolute monarchy;[60] of both aggressive and retiring behaviour;[61] of the famous self-regarding instinct as well as of universal benevolence.

The interpretation and development of Stoic thought certainly did not cease with the coming of the modern age. To take an example not mentioned by Waszek but by others, the well-known *oikeiosis* came to be attributed to Stoicism mainly as a result of Max Pohlenz's great authority in the twentieth century. It is therefore unlikely that Smith could have interpreted it as such as early as the seventeenth century.[62] This is not to say that the classical texts

---

[58] Both Brown (1947), 97 and 137, and Heise (1995), 19, tend to identify the above version of *oikeiosis* as the basis of Smith's social theory, which actually leads them to opposing conclusions: a clear rejection of Stoic doctrine (Brown); and its acceptance and further development (Heise).

[59] Stewart-Robertson (1983), 4.

[60] Oestreich (1982), 33–6 and *passim*; Peltonen (1995), 124–30; Barbour (1998), 16, 247. D'Angers (1964), 136.

[61] Shifflett (1998), 29–30; 45; 108–10; Barbour (1998), 107; 176–7.

[62] In reality Grotius linked *oikeiosis* to justice; but its Stoic origin (M. Aurelius) is incorrect, and his commentator Barbeyrac (n. 4 to Prolegomena VI of the comment to *De Jure*) emphasized the Aristotelian origin (Palladini (1990), 187 n.17).

on this subject (with which he was certainly extremely familiar), did not influence Smith; however, the type of theory that emerged has connotations that are clearly Peripatetic rather than Stoic. As I have already observed,[63] although Smith starts from the Stoic self-regarding instinct, he assumes a gradual evolution of family and social relationships derived from Aristotle and even Cicero, but which in my view is not essentially Stoic. Scholars cannot agree either on the origin of *oikeiosis* (Peripatetic or Stoic) or on its character. To attribute to Stoicism the 'differential' *oikeiosis* (if I can call it that) does not seem to fit with the assumptions of the doctrine, even if some representatives (Greek and Roman) of the middle Stoa may have subscribed to this view (namely Hierocles and Cicero). Great effort has been dedicated by modern critics in ascertaining how to progress from the self-regarding instinct to regard for others, not in the sense of similarity or relationship with *all* other human beings (which corresponds to the Stoic version of *oikeiosis*) but as a specific interest for the members of one's own family, friends, compatriots, and so forth. It is easy to see that the first form involves an attitude (in terms of both relations of affection and duties to be performed) which is undifferentiated; in the second version certain behaviour is imposed towards relations of affection and the performance of duties which cannot be easily evaded, but the obligation gradually becomes less binding as the relationship becomes more distant. The latter approach is clearly of Aristotelian origin, and to attribute it the Stoics would be to distort their doctrine.

We are certain of three points in the Stoic doctrine: the self-preserving instinct, the special instinct of parents towards their offspring (but *not* vice versa), and a bond with all mankind.[64]

We could also object that Hierocles the Stoic presented the famous image of the concentric circles, which represented a well-developed hierarchy; if we turn to Cicero, undoubtedly the famous gradation 'sons, relations, friends, *res publica*' echoed in all the modern studies on Stoic *oikeiosis* could not be closer to the spirit of the Roman orator. It is, however, in reality Peripatetic.[65] Cicero himself in *De Finibus* demonstrates that for the individual with public duties the practicable philosophy is the Peripatetic, and not the Stoic or Epicurean.[66] On the other hand the original spirit of Stoicism had been 'softened' by Panaetius, the source of Cicero, as well as by Carneades, Diogenes of Babylonia, and Antipater of Tarsus, in order to reconcile it with the needs of everyday life. The result was that essential Aristotelian moral values had been integrated into the Stoic system, and thus elements such as fame, social standing, glory, and wealth were included. It was in this way that in the golden age of the Roman republic the 'model' of the wise ruler

---

[63] Cf. Ch. 2, pp. 58–9 and (1999*a*), 119–20.
[64] Isnardi Parente (1989), 2214; Inwood (1983), 193–8.
[65] Magnaldi (1991), 33–41.   [66] Gigon (1988), 260–1.

would have been able to coordinate Stoic principles within political activity and government. But these are 'impure' elements with respect to the original doctrine, and have given rise to what has been defined as 'syncretism' between the Stoic doctrine, the academic-Peripatetic doctrine, and the 'mixed' moral teaching expounded by Cicero in *De Officiis*.[67]

Certainly Stoic doctrine of the middle Stoa is still Stoicism, and indeed its influence was far greater, precisely because it was more practicable. This, however, is not a valid motive for failing to recognize the Peripatetic nature of *oikeiosis* 'in concentric circles'. The original Stoic doctrine related *oikeiosis* first to the self and then to humanity; the preferential relationship with one's offspring was instrumental, in so far as it is essential to their survival. It is no coincidence that supporters of the 'differentiated' *oikeiosis* developed this relationship, on condition that offspring reciprocated the affection of their parents in some way.[68] By derivation it was suggested that, after the parent–child relationship, other altruistic ties developed towards a series of relations—not so close but nevertheless significant—which intervene between blood relatives and the rest of mankind. This, however, I repeat once again, does not correspond to the original spirit of Stoicism, which moreover lacked that characteristic (and Aristotelian) figure of the man at the head of the *oikos*:[69] husband, father, master, and administrator, the emblem of a hierarchical society.

IV

The majority of critics thus tend to label Smith as 'Stoic', or at least a partial Stoic—since the fact that he explicitly distanced himself from this doctrine is generally taken into account. One recent exception is Griswold,[70] who considers Smith a follower of scepticism, which became a driving force behind modern scientific thought following the discovery of ancient sceptic writings during the Renaissance. Griswold's interpretation is suggestive, well argued, and highly coherent.[71] It is even, in my opinion, a little too well construed. By this I mean that it contains many ideas attributed to Smith that he certainly never himself expressed: Griswold seems to rely rather heavily on the fact that he never actually denied these ideas either.

I suppose that the metaphor of the spectator has been an important element in directing recent criticism towards an interpretation of Smith's works based on the concept of 'seeing', and of reality as a performance.[72] Naturally, similar

---

[67] Grimal (1989), 1970–3; 1978–9.

[68] This did not exist in Stoic philosophy, as Inwood has commented (1983), 193–4 and 197.

[69] Zeno affirms that the sage must be *oikonomos*, but simply because he must have all the capabilities (Isnardi Parente (1989), 2222–3 and n. 56).

[70] Clearly it is impossible to enter into any great detail here. Cf. Vivenza (1999*b*).

[71] I wish to distinguish between the 'scepticism' in Griswold's reconstruction, and the 'relativism' which the evolution of society creates, in Smith's view, in moral teaching. No principle can be so absolute as not to undergo change in the long run: cf. Ch. 3, pp. 121–2.

[72] Marshall (1984), Griswold (1999), 65–70; Fleischacker (1999), 43.

metaphors which liken the world or our existence to a theatrical scene abound in literature, including classical literature. Some authors have attempted to unify Smith's thought under this principle, but I am not sure whether this unity belongs more to these authors themselves than to Smith. In Griswold's work Smith's methodology presented in 'HA' is extended to cover all Smithian philosophy, including his moral teaching. According to Griswold, in Smith's view we can draw only from external appearances in all fields of knowledge; consequently there is no objective reality (or we cannot reach it). So Smith is associated with the current of scepticism which in the sixteenth and seventeenth centuries had begun to separate science from metaphysics, denying that it was possible to discover the 'final causes', but claiming that knowledge could be built on the basis of what appears to our senses. In this way, by underlining our author's well-known aversion to metaphysics, the final result is the extension of the principles contained in 'HA' to all Smith's theoretical works. In all of them, it is a case of 'saving the appearances': with the aid of the imagination, psychological and sensible data are arranged into a system.[73]

Smith limited the presentation of his methodology to 'HA' (with the exception of a reference in *LRBL* ii. 133). His analogy with Hume's position of 'scepticism with regard to the senses' (Treatise, i. iv. 2) is limited to the working of the imagination and psychological association. However, it has already been observed that 'Smith is adapting Hume's account of the imagination from the one subject [i.e. our belief in the existence of material things] to the other [i.e. scientific theory]'.[74] We also should remember that although Smith is speaking in general about 'philosophical enquiries', he is expounding theories on astronomy in this essay, which, unlike other theories, were traditionally declared to be hypothetical. He states that he will not consider 'their absurdity or probability, their agreement or inconsistency with truth and reality' ('HA' ii. 12). This was an entirely orthodox position in astronomy, and was not sceptical. It is true that Smith reaches as far as Newton's theory, which was of a different nature altogether. At any rate, the general methodology of scientific thought in Smith's day was empirical and experimental, which does not mean sceptical. In other words the methodology which emerged from the scientific revolution refuted hypotheses in favour of demonstrated facts, but it was thought unnecessary to reach the ultimate cause, which up to that time had clearly been metaphysical, and as such unverifiable.[75]

It is quite another matter to place systems of moral philosophy on a par with other systems. Griswold deduces from Smith's anti-rationalism that he is exclusively a subjectivist (157–8), and that he rejects any form of 'moral

---

[73] David Levy (1995) has a more limited objective, and concentrates on the absence of an (impartial) spectator in *WN* to gather a series of elements to suggest that Smith uses the concept of vision and perspective to explain how the majority of economic problems derive from an incorrect way of 'seeing' things, and how the solution lies in the correction of this vision.

[74] Raphael in 'General Introduction' to *EPS*, 18.

[75] I have treated these points more thoroughly in Vivenza (1999*b*), 195–9.

realism' in the sense of objectivity of moral values. Morals are exclusively as our imagination construes it, and are 'construed' in the same way as any other system. But the fact that the initial perception of good and evil is the result of 'sense and feeling', and that with experience reason is relegated to the formulation of ethical rules (*TMS* vii. iii. 2. 6–9), is not necessarily equivalent to saying that rational and objective elements are so totally irrelevant as to allow room for such subjectivism that the imagination is totally free, and can build any image or appearance. Griswold himself is aware of this trap, and repeatedly declares that in Adam Smith's view man should behave 'as if' moral teaching existed, 'as if' virtue had intrinsic value, and 'as if' there were a rational correspondence between moral judgement and reality.[76] It would be superfluous to say that this intricate issue does not belong to Smith, who actually states, in a passage from *TMS* already mentioned, that a system of 'natural philosophy' may seem totally plausible even though unfounded, while this cannot be allowed in systems of 'moral philosophy', which are based on our own experience.[77]

Smith poses questions of epistemology and method almost exclusively in his early works as a young scholar. He does not subsequently return to these themes, although he maintains his original position: anti-metaphysical, anti-dogmatic, empirical, perhaps even with an element of scepticism related to empiricism itself. I do not believe, however, that this element was a principle with which he defined himself as a man and as a philosopher, or an indirect means by which to embrace a doctrine without acknowledging it. And certainly one theory, scepticism alone, would not be sufficient: modern science owes much to all three of the principal Hellenistic philosophies. Stoicism and Epicureanism are both materialistic;[78] scepticism was important in so far as it freed science from metaphysics.[79] If we were to identify a methodology which is close to Smith's, we might recall that Epicurus' Atomism provided a model for Gassendi which allowed experiences to be considered and related to each other without this necessarily becoming an account of 'reality'.[80] As far as ethics is concerned, the Epicureans unlike the Stoics founded ethics on sensation and not on reason—and this too may represent a fundamental analogy with Smith. By saying this I do not wish to suggest that Smith was an Epicurean,[81] as it has been suggested that he was a

---

[76] Griswold (1999), 165–7.

[77] *TMS* vii. ii. 4. 14; cf. Raphael (1979), 92. On the use of this passage by Griswold (1999), 56 and 161, cf. Vivenza (1999*b*), 194 n. 14.

[78] It is well known that Epicureanism had a greater influence on modern philosophers; cf. Barker (1991) and Moreau (1964), 301–2.   [79] Popkin (1969).

[80] According to the greatest authority on ancient and modern scepticism, Gassendi's method combined sceptic and Epicurean elements: Atomism in particular became a scientific hypothesis with which to 'relier les phénomènes entre eux' (Popkin (1969), 700). Modern science developed from an amalgam of Epicurism and scepticism.

[81] In theory, this is the thesis put forward by Foley (1976), who considered Smith a follower of Democritus rather than Epicurus.

Stoic and a sceptic. As I have already said, Smith brings together many different elements of classical philosophy and culture.

V

Turning now to the historical survey in *TMS* VII. ii. 1.1–47; in my opinion what clearly emerges is the bias towards Stoicism. Smith rapidly dismisses Plato and Aristotle, and he makes no mention of sceptics and the pre-Socratic schools.[81a] There is, however, a torrent of words on the Stoics. Why should this be so, if their system bears no resemblance whatsoever to what 'Nature has sketched out for our conduct' (*TMS* VII. ii. 1.43)?

This, along with the fact that many recent authors have commented on the Stoic influence on Smith, has led me to ask myself once again what influence (certainly undeniable, even if it does not always correspond to their identification of it) this current actually had on the Scottish philosopher.

Naturally I do not deny the 'mixed' influences which I have attempted to emphasize in this book, and the unconventional use which Smith makes of them. It is precisely this aspect of classical heritage, functional to Smith's own theories, which is attractive and valid, given Smith's ability to accept and arrange elements from various sources into his own system. But was it predominantly Stoic, as it is generally thought, and as I myself have suggested in certain passages?

In terms of content, there are indeed many Stoic elements and perhaps more than from other philosophies, even if these are also well represented. Some of the principles connected with fundamental aspects of Smith's thought, including his economic thought, are derived from Stoicism. However, as I noted in 1984, other elements which are of great importance are not Stoic. I also remain convinced that when Smith declares that the Stoic system is incompatible with his own, we ought to take heed of his words.

One issue leaves us perplexed, and once again we regret the loss of the notes on natural religion, which seems to be the only subject upon which Smith had *no* intention of writing a tract.

Stoic philosophy survived alongside Christianity because it proclaimed what appeared to be total submission to providence. This point, so deceptively similar to Christian doctrine, is derived from Plato and in a certain sense is opposed to the very assumptions of Stoic philosophy.[82] The result was that a fact which is totally incompatible with Christianity was ignored (or concealed): the Stoic God is not made from a different substance to the rest of the material world, and did not create anything different from

---

[81a] Only a short hint to the 'ancient Pythagoreans' in VII. ii. 1.9. Epicurus is treated with some length at *TMS* VII. ii. 2.1–17.

[82] Jagu (1989), 2177–80.

himself.[83] Transcendence is alien to Stoicism, and the autarchy of Stoicism contrasts with Christianity's dependence on the grace of God. Christians must put their trust in God, and cannot act on their own. The Stoics do not recognize any external authority which imposes, in the name of a divine will, a hierarchy of relationships and duties. It is true that where these relationships already existed the Stoics never proposed to overturn them; on the contrary, they proclaimed the greatest respect, obedience, and submission. The reason for this, however, was that these were in fact relationships of no consequence: the Stoic obeyed nothing other than his nature. Internally he was free, and immune from relationships of authority. This was clear to the modern authors who speak of the arrogance of Stoicism, its disregard for magistrates, and so on.[84]

The paradox which so struck Adam Smith (*TMS* VII. ii. 1. 40—indignation, of classical origin, mentioned by Cicero) is open to ridicule or to exaggeration, because it is an extreme example, namely the well-known principle that the unmotivated killing of a cockerel is as grave as slaying one's own father. Original Stoicism knew no half measures, and was endowed with what has been defined as 'intellectual totalitarianism'.[85] When the Stoic affirms that *philanthropia* must be nurtured towards all humanity, despite the apparent resemblance with Christian doctrine this means that the individual feels no particular duty towards any particular person: there is no difference between one's own father and a total stranger. It is difficult to control a man who thinks in such a way. It is no coincidence that modern advocates of 'universal benevolence' were considered supporters of the French revolution.[86]

Smith did not make this type of contrast clear, other than by a couple of references in which he is not writing on the subject of Christianity, but of nature.[87] It is true that Smith avoided dealing with certain issues in depth, so that his position is not entirely clear, but this does not justify excessive inference. For example, Smith's position on problems of a religious nature is not readily defined: all that he says is orthodox, but he says as little as possible. His aversion to metaphysics, and his empirical approach even in the field of moral philosophy, at times have led critics to consider him an atheist, or at least detached from questions of faith. I do not believe that *firm* elements to support this exist, and I do not wish to hazard deductions which may be unfounded. Neither do I believe that Smith was a man to employ

---

[83] Edelstein (1966), 8–9; Jagu (1989), 2174; Hershbell (1989), 2161; Barbour (1998), 196–8; D'Angers (1964), 142 ff.; Bouwsma (1975), 9–12.

[84] Lipsio, *Manuductio* I, xiv–xv, cf. Sams (1944), 74–7.

[85] Moreover, this had already been recognized and criticized by Seneca, cf. Grimal (1989), 1983.

[86] Radcliffe (1993), and Forbes (1982), 199 (referring to Lord Kames).

[87] In the well-known case of suicide, *TMS* VII. ii. 1. 34; and on an active life, VII. ii. 1. 43–7. Even the fact that Smith is for Peripatetic *oikeosis*, in other words a hierarchical structure to relationships in the manner of Cicero, shows a well-known stance in favour of maintaining the 'distinction of ranks'.

indirect means, as has twice been suggested, to subscribe to theories (of classical origin) which have been accused of atheism, without, however, admitting to this. The only reasonable explanation is that questions of a strictly religious nature interested Smith less than others. After all, Smith made it clear from his boyhood, and before he had any other plans, that he was not cut out for the clergy.

Certainly, given the times, religious issues were not only that, but embraced other arguments which were more closely connected to religion then than they are today, and so the lack of this kind of element in Smith's thought prevents us from furthering our understanding of it. We can give a few examples of this. Whether he believed in God or not, and in the Christian God, Smith was convinced of a hidden plan, of an order in nature and of things, and in this sense he was closer to Stoicism than to the Epicurean casualism. However, he wrote a treatise on moral teaching, and tried to offer arguments taken not from authority but from human nature; and we may think that he was in line with the Epicureans rather than with the Stoics when he stated that it is feeling and not reason which prompts human actions and judgements. In any case the Hellenistic philosophies, which intended to offer mankind a concrete hand in the problems of everyday life, attracted Smith more than the doctrines of the two great Greek philosophers.[88] The practical aspect of moral teaching (which was also perfectly in line with classical philosophy) and the value attributed to the 'minor' virtues which encircle prudence confirm Smith's anti-metaphysical disposition.

I have asked myself why, shortly before his death, Smith rewrote Part 6 of *TMS* with so much Stoicism. I am unable to provide an answer, and I generally tend to abstain from expressing opinions other than those based on texts. Thus I will do no more than to suggest the possibility, perhaps a remote one, that something in this philosophy disturbed Smith, and at the same time something attracted him.

He certainly did not want to do away with hierarchy and achieve revolutionary egalitarianism. In the passages where he broaches this subject, he is always contrary to it. But, as we have said a little earlier, Stoicism in practical terms was in favour of exterior respect for authority, and did not propose to rebuild the world: the existing order could remain as it was.[89]

It is well known that Smith considered the philosopher and the porter to be born equal, and, as I have already said, I believe that he takes this element from modern philosophy rather than from Stoicism. However, Smith, like the Stoics, readily accepts social inequality, and even considers it to be

---

[88] This was a tendency that Smith shared with the Scholarship of his time: many of the treatises on the history of philosophy (e.g. the *History of Philosophy* of T. Stanley and the *Historia Critica Philosopiae* of J. Brucker, both present in Smith's Library) gave more room to Stoicism and Epicureanism than to Plato and Aristotle.

[89] I agree with Brunt (1975), 17, that all forms of government were the same for the Stoics. They perceive a fundamental equality, but do not support subversive action to achieve it.

useful, thus refuting any sort of revolutionary tendency, despite the fact that at a human level he comprehends the motives which lead the lower levels of society to rebel (*WN* I. viii. 12–13; I. xi. p. 9). When life ill-treats the porter, the worker, or the helpless poor man, Smith, while in no way justifying rebellion, expresses himself in such a way as to inspire J. Viner's renowned comment that the flaws in the natural order that Smith points out 'would suffice to provide ammunitions for several socialist orations'.[90]

The society in which Smith lived practised the 'division of ranks', and it had been accepted for centuries that the supposed moral equality of men would lead to a strongly hierarchical structure which was respectful of authority for reasons of public order and social peace. The interior freedom of the Stoic in its essence was a challenge to all consolidated relationships, and represented a challenge founded upon reason. This philosophy always held a special charm, and indeed many of the changes to the original doctrine from times of classical antiquity were due, as it is generally acknowledged, to the desire to apply the doctrine to social life. This would have been practically impossible if it had remained in its original form.

Once the sharpest edges had been smoothed, it was possible to adapt the theory, or at least to appear to adapt it, to the many duties of life in society. Stoicism, however, maintained something ambiguous in its independence.

Smith in turn felt that certain requirements were just,[91] but not when taken to extremes: he believed that it was sufficient to do away with errors and bad faith and everything would fall into place without the need for violence. Indeed this was the challenge of *his* reason. Perhaps he meditated on Stoicism so deeply in order to discover why this philosophy, which left no room for sentiment, which did not recognize authority, and could not serve as a guide for human behaviour, attracted him so much.

---

[90] Viner (1966), 136.

[91] Proof of this is his will to guarantee a minimum of well-being, education, and consideration even to the less fortunate classes: something that the Stoics would not have been concerned with.

References

ABBAGNANO, N. (1961). *Storia della filosofia*, Turin, UTET.

ANSPACH, R. (1972). 'The Implication of the Theory of Moral Sentiments for Adam Smith's Economic Thought', *History of Political Economy*, 4.

ARANGIO RUIZ, V. (1937). *Storia del diritto romano*, Naples, Jovene.

—— (1945). *Istituzioni di diritto romano*, Naples, Jovene.

ARRIGHETTI, G. (1969). 'La Structure de la lettre d'Epicure à Pythoclès', *Actes du VIII Congrès de l'Association G. Budé*, Paris, Les Belles Lettres.

AUBENQUE, P. (1963). *La Prudence chez Aristote*, Paris, PUF.

—— (1964). 'La "Phronésis" chez les stoiciens', *Actes du VII Congrès de l'Association G. Budé*, Paris, Les Belles Lettres.

AUSTIN, M., and VIDAL NAQUET, P. (1972). *Economies et sociétés en Grèce ancienne*, Paris, Librairie Armand Colin.

BADALONI, N. (1973). 'La cultura', in *Storia d'Italia, iii. Dal primo Settecento all'Unità*, Turin, Einaudi.

BAGOLINI, L. (1966). *La simpatia nella morale e nel diritto*, Turin, Giappichelli.

—— (1967). *Esperienza giuridica e politica nel pensiero di David Hume*, Turin, Giappichelli.

—— (1975). 'The Topicality of Adam Smith's Notion of Sympathy', in A. S. Skinner and T. Wilson (eds.), *Essays on Adam Smith*, Oxford, Clarendon Press.

—— (1976). *David Hume e Adam Smith. Elementi per una ricerca di filosofia giuridica e politica*, Bologna, Pàtron.

BALDWIN, T. W. (1944). *William Shakespere's Small Latine and Lesse Greeke*, Urbana, University of Illinois Press.

BARBIERI, G. (1954). 'Le dottrine economiche dell'antichità classica', in U. Padovani (ed.), *Grande antologia filosofica*, ii, Milan, Marzorati.

—— (1958). *Fonti per la storia delle dottrine economiche*, Milan, Marzorati.

BARBOUR, R. (1998). *English Epicures and Stoics: Ancient Legacies in Early Stuart Culture*, Amherst, University of Massachusetts Press.

BARKER, P. (1991). 'Stoic Contributions to Early Modern Science', in M. J. Osler (ed.), *Atoms, Pneuma, and Tranquillity*, Cambridge, Cambridge University Press.

BARON, H. (1960). 'Secularization of Wisdom and Political Humanism in the Renaissance', *Journal of the History of Ideas*, 21.

BASANOFF, V. (1936). 'Les Sources chrétiennes de la loi de Constantin sur le repudium', *Studi in onore di S. Riccobono*, iii, Palermo, Arti grafiche G. Castiglia.

BENN, A. W. (1906). *The History of English Rationalism in the Nineteenth Century*, ii, New York and Bombay, Longmans, Green and Co.

BEVILACQUA, V. (1968). 'Adam Smith and Some Philosophical Origins of Eighteenth-Century Rhetorical Theory', *Modern Language Review*, 63.

—— (1976). 'Classical Rhetorical Influences in the Development of Eighteenth-Century British Aesthetic Criticism', *Transactions of the American Philological Association*, 107.

BIONDI, B. (1933). *Corso di diritto romano. Le servitù prediali*, Milan, Giuffrè.

BITTERMANN, H. J. (1940). 'Adam Smith's Empiricism and the Law of Nature', *Journal of Political Economy*, 48.

BODIN (1609). *De republica libri sex*, Frankfurt, ex typ. Nicolai Hoffmanni.

BOLGAR, R. R. (1958). *The Classical Heritage and its Beneficiaries*, Cambridge, Cambridge University Press.

—— (ed.) (1979). *Classical Influences on Western Thought, 1650–1870*, Cambridge, Cambridge University Press.

BONAR, J. (1922). *Philosophy and Political Economy*, 3rd edn., London, Allen & Unwin.

—— (1926). ' "The Theory of Moral Sentiments", by Adam Smith, 1759', *Journal of Philosophical Studies*, 1.

—— (1966). *A Catalogue of the Library of Adam Smith*, New York, Macmillan.

BONFANTE, P. (1925–33). *Corso di diritto romano*, Rome, Sampaolesi.

BOUWSMA, W. J. (1975). 'The Two Faces of Humanism: Stoicism and Augustinianism in Renaissance Thought', in H. A. Oberman with T. A. Brady (eds.), *Itinerarium Italicum: The Profile of the Italian Renaissance in the Mirror of Its European Transformations*, Leiden, E. J. Brill.

BOWLEY, M. (1963). 'Some Seventeenth-Century Contributions to the Theory of Value', *Economica*, 30.

BROWN, V. (1994). *Adam Smith's Discourse: Canonicity, Commerce, and Conscience*, London/New York, Routledge.

BRUNNER, O. (1956). 'Das "ganze Haus" und die alteuropäische "Ökonomik" ', in *Neue Wege der Sozialgeschichte*, Goettingen, Vanderhoeck & Ruprecht.

BRUNT, P. A. (1975). 'Stoicism and the Principate', *Papers of the British School at Rome*, 43.

BRYSON, G. (1945). *Man and Society: The Scottish Enquiry of the Eighteenth Century*, Princeton, NJ, Princeton University Press.

BURDESE, A. (1954). 'Il concetto di "ius naturale" nel pensiero della giurisprudenza classica', *Rivista italiana per le scienze giuridiche*, s. III, 8.

—— (1964). *Manuale di diritto privato romano*, Turin, UTET.

—— (1966). *Manuale di diritto pubblico romano*, Turin, UTET.

CAMPBELL, A. H. (1962). 'Diritto scozzese e diritto romano', in *Bartolo da Sassoferrato. Studi e documenti per il VI centenario*, Milan, Giuffrè.

CAMPBELL, T. D. (1971). *Adam Smith's Science of Morals*, London, Allen & Unwin.

—— (1975). 'Scientific Explanation and Moral Justification in the *Moral Sentiments*', in A. S. Skinner and T. Wilson (eds.), *Essays on Adam Smith*, Oxford, Clarendon Press.

CAMPBELL, W. F. (1967). 'Adam Smith's Theory of Justice, Prudence, and Beneficence', *American Economic Review, Papers and Proceedings*, 57.

CAMUS, P. (1979). 'L'esclave en tant qu'*organon* chez Aristote', in *Schiavitù, manomissione e classi dipendenti nel mondo antico*, Rome, 'L'Erma' di Bretschneider.

CANNATA, C. A. (1976). *Lineamenti di storia della giurisprudenza europea*, Turin, Giappichelli.

CARUSO, S. (1973). 'Nota alla traduzione', in Adam Smith, *Indagine sulla natura e le cause della ricchezza delle nazioni*, Milan, ISEDI.

CASSIRER, E. (1951). *The Philosophy of the Enlightenment*, trans. F. C. A. Koell and J. P. Pettegrove, Princeton, NJ, Princeton University Press.

—— (1953). *The Platonic Renaissance in England*, trans. J. P. Pettegrove, London, Nelson.

—— (1967a). 'Il platonismo di Galileo', in *Dall'Umanesimo all'Illuminismo*, collected essays, ed. P. O. Kristeller, Florence, La Nuova Italia.

—— (1967b). 'Keplero nella storia del pensiero europeo', in *Dall'Umanesimo all'Illuminismo*, collected essays, ed. P. O. Kristeller, Florence, La Nuova Italia.

—— (1967c). 'Il problema della verità in Galileo', in *Dall'Umanesimo all'Illuminismo*, collected essays, ed. P. O. Kristeller, Florence, La Nuova Italia.

CAVANNA, A. (1979). *Storia del diritto moderno in Europa, i. Le fonti e il pensiero giuridico*, Milan, Giuffrè.

CECCHI, E., and SAPEGNO, N. (1966). *Storia della letteratura italiana, ii. Il Cinquecento*, Milan, Garzanti.

CHALK, A. F. (1951). 'Natural Law and the Rise of Economic Individualism in England', *Journal of Political Economy*, 59.

CLARKE, M. L. (1945). *Greek Studies in England, 1700–1830*, Cambridge, Cambridge University Press.

COING, H. (1979). 'Roman Law and the National Legal Systems', in R. R. Bolgar (ed.), *Classical Influences on Western Thought*, Cambridge, Cambridge University Press.

COLLETTI, L. (1979). 'Nel bicentenario della *Ricchezza delle nazioni*', in L. Colletti, *Tra marxismo e no*, Bari, Laterza.

COOKE, C. A. (1935). 'Adam Smith and Jurisprudence', *Law Quarterly Review*, 51.

CORSANO, D. (1948). *U. Grozio. L'umanista, il teologo, il giurista*, Bari, Laterza.

COSTA, E. (1927). *Cicerone giureconsulto*, Bologna, Zanichelli.

CROPSEY, J. (1977). *Polity and Economy: An Interpretation of the Principles of Adam Smith*, The Hague, M. Nijhoff.

—— (1975). 'Adam Smith and Political Philosophy', in A. S. Skinner and T. Wilson (eds.), *Essays on Adam Smith*, Oxford, Clarendon Press.

CUMBERLAND, R. (1727). *A Treatise of the Laws of Nature . . . made English by John Maxwell*, London, R. Phillips.

D'ANGERS, J. E. (1964). 'Le Renouveau du stoicisme au XVI et au XVII siècle', *Actes du VII Congrès de l'Association G. Budé*, Paris, Les Belles Lettres.

DAVIS, D. B. (1966). *The Problem of Slavery in Western Culture*, Ithaca, NY, Cornell University Press.

DE ROOVER, R. (1951). 'Monopoly Theory Prior to Adam Smith: A Revision', *Quarterly Journal of Economics*, 65.

—— (1955). 'Scholastic Economics: Survival and Lasting Influence', *Quarterly Journal of Economics*, 69.

DIJKSTERHUIS, E. J. (1961). *The Mechanization of the World Picture*, trans. C. Dikshoorn, Oxford, Clarendon Press.

DREYER, J. L. E. (1953). *A History of Astronomy from Thales to Kepler*, 2nd edn., New York, Dover.

DUHEM, P. (1908). 'Sozein tà phainomena', *Annales de philosophie chrétienne*.

—— (1913). *Système du monde*, Paris, A. Hertmann and Son.

DYCK, A. R. (1996). *A Commentary on Cicero, De Officiis*, Ann Arbor, Mich., University of Michigan Press.

ECKSTEIN, W. (1927). 'Adam Smith als Rechtsphilosoph', *Archiv fur Rechts und Wirtschaftsphilosophie*, 20.

EDELSTEIN, L. (1966). *The Meaning of Stoicism*, Cambridge, Mass., Harvard University Press.

EINARSON, B. (1936). 'Aristotle's Protrepticus and the Structure of the Epinomis', *Transactions of the American Philological Association*, 67.

ENDRES, A. M. (1995). 'Adam Smith's Advisory Style as Illustrated by his Trade Policy Prescriptions', *Journal of the History of Economic Thought*, 17.

ENGBERG-PEDERSEN, T. (1990). *The Stoic Theory of* oikeiosis: *Moral Development and Social Interaction in Early Stoic Philosophy*, Aarhus, Aarhus University Press.

FASSÒ, G. (1966). *Storia della filosofia del diritto*, i. *Antichità e Medioevo*, Bologna, Il Mulino.

—— (1968). *Storia della filosofia del diritto*, ii. *L'età moderna*, Bologna, Il Mulino.

FINLEY, M. I. (1959). 'Was Greek Civilization Based on Slave Labour?', *Historia*, 8.

—— (1970). 'Aristotle and Economic Analysis', *Past and Present*, 47.

—— (1975). *The Use and Abuse of History*, London, Penguin.

—— (1977). *The Ancient Greeks*, London, Penguin.

FIORITO, R. (1971). *Divisione del lavoro e teoria del valore. L'economia sociologica di Adam Smith*, Bari, De Donato.

FITZGIBBONS, A. (1995). *Adam Smith's System of Liberty, Wealth, and Virtue*, Oxford, Clarendon Press.

FLEISCHACKER, S. (1999). *A Third Concept of Liberty: Judgement and Freedom in Kant and Adam Smith*, Princeton, Princeton University Press.

FOLEY, V. (1974). 'The Division of Labor in Plato and Smith', *History of Political Economy*, 6.

—— (1975). 'Smith and the Greeks. A Reply to Professor McNulty's Comments', *History of Political Economy*, 7.

—— (1976). *The Social Physics of Adam Smith*, West Lafayette, Ind., Purdue University Press.

FORBES, D. (1982). 'Natural Law and Scottish Enlightenment', in R. H. Campbell and A. S. Skinner (eds.), *The Origins and Nature of the Scottish Enlightenment*, Edinburgh, John Donald.

FORD, B. (ed.) (1975). *The Pelican Guide to English Literature—From Dryden to Johnson*, Harmondsworth.

GARIN, E. (1941). *L'illuminismo inglese. I moralisti*, Milan, Bocca.

—— (1967). *La cultura del Rinascimento*, Bari, Laterza.

GEE, J. M. A. (1968). 'Adam Smith's Social Welfare Function', *Scottish Journal of Political Economy*, 15.

GEYMONAT, L. (1970). *Storia del pensiero filosofico e scientifico*, Milan, Garzanti.

GIERKE, O. (1934). *Natural Law and the Theory of Society 1500 to 1800: With a Lecture on the Ideas of Natural Law and Humanity by E. Troeltsch*, Cambridge, Cambridge University Press.

GIGON, O. (1988). 'The Peripatos in Cicero's *De finibus*', in W. W. Fortenbaugh and R. W. Sharples (eds.), *Theophrastean Studies: On Natural Science, Physics and Metaphysics, Ethics, Religion, and Rhetoric*, New Brunswick, NJ/Oxford, Transaction Books.

GILLE, B. (1956). 'Machines', in C. Singer, E. J. Holmyard, and A. R. Hall (eds.), *A History of Technology*, Oxford, Clarendon Press, ii.

GINZBERG, E. (1979). 'An Economy Formed by Men', in G. P. O'Driscoll (ed.), *Adam Smith and Modern Political Economy*, Ames, Iowa State University Press.

GIULIANI, A. (1954). 'Adamo Smith filosofo del diritto', *Rivista internazionale di filosofia del diritto*, 31.

—— (1962). 'The Influence of Rhetoric on the Law of Evidence and Pleading', *Juridical Review*, 3.

GLIOZZI, M. (1962). 'Storia della fisica', in *Storia delle scienze*, ii. Turin, UTET.

GORDON, B. J. (1961). 'Aristotle, Schumpeter and the Metallist Tradition', *Quarterly Journal of Economics*, 75.

—— (1964). 'Aristotle and the Development of Value Theory', *Quarterly Journal of Economics*, 68.

GRAMPP, W. D. (1948). 'Adam Smith and the Economic Man', *Journal of Political Economy*, 56.

GRAY, A. (1931). *The Development of Economic Doctrine*, London, Longmans, Green and Co.

GRILLI, A. (1953). *Il problema della vita contemplativa nel mondo greco-romano*, Milan/Rome, Bocca.

—— (1992). *Stoicismo, Epicureismo e letteratura*, Brescia, Paideia.

GRIMAL, P. (1976). 'Permanence de la littérature latine', *Bulletin de l'Association G. Budé*, 35.

—— (1989). 'Sénèque et le Stoicisme romain', in *Aufstieg und Niedergang der römischen Welt*, II. 36. 3.

GRISWOLD, C. L. (1999). *Adam Smith and the Virtues of Enlightenment*, Cambridge, Cambridge University Press.

GROOT, H. DE (1702). *De iure belli ac pacis*, Amstelodami, *apud* H. Wetstenius.

HAAKONSSEN, K. (1981). *The Science of a Legislator: The Natural Jurisprudence of Hume and Adam Smith*, Cambridge, Cambridge University Press.

HEILBRONER, R. L. (1982). 'The Socialization of the Individual in Adam Smith', *History of Political Economy*, 14.

HEISE, P. (1995). 'Stoicism in the *EPS*: The Foundation of Adam Smith's Moral Philosophy', in I. H. Rima (ed.), *The Classical Tradition in Economic Thought*, Perspectives on the History of Economic Thought, xi, Aldershot, Edward Elgar.

HERSHBELL, J. P. (1989). 'The Stoicism of Epictetus: Twentieth-Century Perspectives, *Aufstieg und Niedergang der römischen Welt* II. 36. 3.

HIGHET, G. (1949). *The Classical Tradition*, Oxford, Clarendon Press.

HOLLANDER, S. (1973). *The Economics of Adam Smith*, London, Heinemann.

HONT, I., and IGNATIEFF, M. (1983). 'Needs and Justice in the *Wealth of Nations*: An Introductory Essay', in I. Hont and M. Ignatieff (eds.), *Wealth and Virtue: The Shaping of Political Economy in the Scottish Enlightenment*, Cambridge, Cambridge University Press.

HOWELL, W. S. (1975). 'Adam Smith's Lectures on Rhetoric: An Historical Assessment', in A. S. Skinner and T. Wilson (eds.), *Essays on Adam Smith*, Oxford, Clarendon Press.

—— (1976). 'Poetics, Rhetoric and Logic in Renaissance Criticism', in R. R. Bolger (ed.), *Classical Influences on European Culture*, *A.D. 1500–1700*, Cambridge, Cambridge University Press.

IMBRUGLIA, G. (1980). 'L'utopia "philosophique" di Helvétius', *Rivista storica italiana*, 92/2.

INWOOD, B. (1983). 'Comments on Professor Goergemann's paper', in W. W. Fortenbaugh (ed.), *On Stoic and Peripatetic Ethics: The Work of Arrius Didymus*, New Brunswick, NJ/London, Transaction Press.

ISNARDI PARENTE, M. (1989). 'Ierocle stoico. Oikeiosis e doveri sociali', *Aufstieg und Niedergang der römischen Welt*, II. 36. 3.

JAGU, A. (1989). 'La Morale d'Epictète et le Christianisme', *Aufstieg und Niedergang der römischen Welt*, II. 36. 3.

JOHNSON, V. (1939). 'Aristotle's Theory of Value', *American Journal of Philology*, 60/3.

KAMPHUISEN, P. W. (1932). 'L'Influence de la philosophie sur la conception du droit naturel chez les jurisconsultes romains', *Revue historique du droit français et étranger*, 10.

KAUDER, E. (1953). 'Genesis of the Marginal Utility Theory: From Aristotle to the End of the Eighteenth Century', *Economic Journal*, 63.

KAUSHIL, S. (1973). 'The Case of Adam Smith's Value Analysis', *Oxford Economic Papers*, 25.

KOSCHAKER, P. (1962). *L'Europa e il diritto romano*, Florence, Sansoni.

KRAUS, O. (1905). 'Die aristotelische Werttheorie in ihren Beziehungen zu den Lehren der modernen Psychologenschule', *Zeitschrift für die gesamte Staatswissenschaften*, 61.

LAMB, R. (1973). 'Adam Smith's Concept of Alienation', *Oxford Economic Papers*, 25.

—— (1974). 'Adam Smith's System: Sympathy not Self-interest', *Journal of the History of Ideas*, 35.

LAMBERTINI, R. (1985). 'Per una storia dell'*oeconomica* tra alto e basso Medioevo', *Cheiron*, 2.

LANDUCCI, S. (1972). *I filosofi e i selvaggi*, Bari, Laterza.

LAPIDGE, M. (1989). 'Stoic Cosmology and Roman Literature', *Aufstieg und Niedergang der römischen Welt*, II. 36. 3.

LE HIR, J. (1954). 'Les fondements psychologiques et religieux de la morale d'Epictète', *Bulletin de l'Association G. Budé*, 13.

LESKY, A. (1962). *Storia della letteratura greca*, trans. F. Codino, Milan, Il Saggiatore.

LEVY, E. (1949). 'Natural Law in Roman Thought', *Studia et documenta historiae et juris*, 15.

LEVY, D. M. (1995). 'The Partial Spectator in the *Wealth of Nations*: A Robust Utilitarianism', *European Journal of the History of Economic Thought*, 2/2.

LIMENTANI, L. (1914). *La morale della simpatia*, Genoa, Formiggini.

LINDGREN, J. R. (1969). 'Adam Smith's Theory of Inquiry', *Journal of Political Economy*, 77.

—— (1973). *The Social Philosophy of Adam Smith*, The Hague, M. Nijhoff.

LIPSIUS, I. (1637). *Manuductio ad Stoicam philosophiam*, Antwerp, B. Horetus.

LORAUX, N., and VIDAL NAQUET, P. (1979). 'La Formation de l'Athènes bourgeoise', in R. R. Bolgar (ed.), *Classical Influences on Western Thought*, Cambridge, Cambridge University Press.

LOTITO, G. (1980). 'Aristotele su moneta scambio bisogni', *Materiali e discussioni per l'analisi dei testi classici*, 4/5/6 (1981).

LOVEJOY, A. O. (1970). *The Great Chain of Being*, 9th edn., Cambridge, Mass., Harvard University Press.

LOWRY, S. T. (1974). 'Aristotle's "Natural Limit" and the Economics of Price Regulations', *Greek, Roman and Byzantine Studies*, 15.

MACFIE, A. L. (1967a). 'The Scottish Tradition in Economic Thought' (1954), repr. in Macfie (1967).

—— (1967*b*). 'Adam Smith's *Theory of Moral Sentiments*' (1961), repr. in Macfie (1967).

—— (1967*c*). 'Adam Smith's *Moral Sentiments* as Foundation for his *Wealth of Nations*' (1959), repr. in Macfie (1967).

—— (1967*d*). 'The Impartial Spectator', in Macfie (1967).

—— (1967*e*). ' "The Invisible Hand" in the *Theory of Moral Sentiments*', in Macfie (1967).

—— (1967). *The Individual in Society: Papers on Adam Smith*, London, George Allen & Unwin.

—— (1971). 'The Invisible Hand of Jupiter', *Journal of the History of Ideas*, 32.

McNULTY, P. J. (1975). A Note on the Division of Labor in Plato and Smith, *History of Political Economy*, 7.

MAGNALDI, G. (1991). *L'oikeiosis peripatetica in Ario Didimo e nel 'De finibus' di Cicerone*, Florence/Turin, Casa Editrice Le Lettere.

MAGUIRE, P. G. (1947). 'Plato's Theory of Natural Law', *Yale Classical Studies*, 10.

MALUSA, L. (1981*a*). 'Le prime storie generali della filosofia nell'Inghilterra e nei Paesi Bassi', in G. Santinello (ed.), *Storia delle storie generali della filosofia*, Brescia, La Scuola.

—— (1981*b*). 'Le premesse rinascimentali all'attività storiografica in filosofia', in G. Santinello (ed.), *Storia delle storie generali della filosofia*, Brescia, La Scuola.

MANCINI, G. (1940). *L'etica stoica da Zenone a Crisippo*, Padua, Cedam.

MARCHESI, C. (1971). *Storia della letteratura latina*, 8th edn., Milano/Messina, Principato.

MARSHALL, D. (1984). 'Adam Smith and the Theatricality of Moral Sentiments', *Critical Inquiry*, 10.

MEEK, R. L. (1956). *Studies in the Labour Theory of Value*, London, Lawrence & Wishart.

—— (1971). 'Smith, Turgot and the "Four Stages" Theory', *History of Political Economy*, 3/1.

—— (1976*a*). 'New Light on Adam Smith's Glasgow Lectures on Jurisprudence', *History of Political Economy*, 8.

—— (1976*b*). *Social Science and the Ignoble Savage*, Cambridge, Cambridge University Press.

—— and Skinner, A. S. (1973). 'The Development of Adam Smith's Ideas on the Division of Labour', *The Economic Journal*, 83.

MICHELS, R. (1932). *Introduzione alla storia delle dottrine economiche e politiche*, Bologna, Zanichelli.

MITTELSTRASS, J. (1979). '*Phaenomena bene fundata*: From 'saving the appearances' to the mechanisation of the world-picture', in R. R. Bolgar (ed.), *Classical Influences on Western Thought, 1650–1870*, Cambridge, Cambridge University Press.

MIZUTA, H. (1975). 'Moral Philosophy and Civil Society', in A. S. Skinner and T. Wilson (eds.), *Essays on Adam Smith*, Oxford, Clarendon Press.

MOMIGLIANO, A. (1980). 'Polybius between the English and the Turks', *Sesto contributo alla storia degli studi classici e del mondo antico*, i, Rome, Edizioni di Storia e Letteratura.

MONDOLFO, R. (1903–4). *Saggi per la storia della morale utilitaria*, Padua/Verona, n.p.

MONDOLFO, R. (1982). 'La valutazione del lavoro nella cultura classica', in *Polis, lavoro e tecnica*, Milano, Feltrinelli.

MONTANARI, G. (1804). 'Della moneta', in P. Custodi (ed.), *Scrittori classici italiani di economia politica*, iii, Milan, G. G. Destefanis.

MONTESQUIEU, C. (1964). C. L. de Montesquieu, 'De l'esprit des Lois', in *Oeuvres Complètes*, Paris, Éditions du Seuil.

MOREAU, J. (1964). 'Le Stoicisme et la philosophie classique', *Actes du VII Congrès de l'Association G. Budé*, Paris, Les Belles Lettres.

MORROW, G. (1969). *The Ethical and Economic Theories of Adam Smith*, New York, Augustus M. Kelley, reprint (first printed 1923).

—— (1966). 'Adam Smith, Moralist and Philosopher', in J. M. Clarke *et al.*, *Adam Smith, 1776–1926*, New York, Augustus M. Kelley, reprint (first printed 1928).

MORROW, G. R. (1923). 'The Significance of the Doctrine of Sympathy in Hume and Adam Smith', *Philosophical Review*, 32.

MOSCOVICI, S. (1956). 'A propos de quelques travaux d'Adam Smith sur l'histoire et la philosophie des sciences', *Revue d'histoire des sciences et de leur applications*, 9.

MUSTI, D. (1984). 'Economia, politica, mentalità', *Studi storici*, 25/1.

MYRDAL, G. (1953). *The Political Element in the Development of Economic Theory*, London, Routledge & Kegan Paul.

NAPOLEONI, C. (1970). *Smith, Ricardo, Marx. Considerazioni sulla storia del pensiero economico*, Turin, Boringhieri.

NAVARRE, O. (1914). 'Théophraste et La Bruyère', *Revue des études grecques*, 27.

NEUGEBAUER, O. (1957). *The Exact Sciences in Antiquity*, 2nd edn., Providence, RI, Brown University Press.

NOELL, E. D. (1995). 'Adam Smith on Economic Justice in the Labor Market', *Journal of the History of Economic Thought*, 17.

NORTH, H. (1966a). Canons and Hierarchies of the Cardinal Virtues in Greek and Latin Literature', in L. Wallach (ed.), *The Classical Tradition: Literary and Historical Studies in Honor of Harry Caplan*, Ithaca, NY, Cornell University Press.

—— (1966b). *Sophrosyne: Self-Knowledge and Self-Restraint in Greek Literature*, Ithaca, NY, Cornell University Press.

OESTREICH, G. (1982). *Neostoicism and the Early Modern State*, Cambridge, Cambridge University Press.

PACCHI, A. (1978). 'Hobbes e l'epicureismo', *Rivista critica di storia della filosofia*, 33.

PALLADINI, F. (1990). *Samuel Pufendorf discepolo di Hobbes*, Bologna, Il Mulino.

PAOLUCCI, M. (1955). 'Studi sull'epicureismo romano', *Rendiconti dell'Istituto Lombardo di Scienze e Lettere*, 88.

PAPPÉ, H. O. (1979). 'The English Utilitarians and Athenian Democracy', in R. R. Bolgar (ed.), *Classical Influences on Western Thought, 1650–1870*, Cambridge, Cambridge University Press.

PASSERIN D'ENTRÈVES, A. (1972). *Natural Law: An Introduction to Legal Philosophy*, London, Hutchinson University Library.

PELTONEN, M. (1995). *Classical Humanism and Republicanism in English Political Thought, 1570–1640*, Cambridge, Cambridge University Press.

PHILIPPSON, R. (1930). 'Das Sittilichschöne bei Panaitios', *Philologus*, 85.

PIEPER, J. (1966). *The Four Cardinal Virtues*, Notre Dame, Ind., University of Notre Dame Press.

PIETRANERA, G. (1963). *La teoria del valore e dello sviluppo capitalistico in Adamo Smith*, Milan, Feltrinelli.

PLAMENATZ, J. (ed.) (1949). *The English Utilitarians*, Oxford, Blackwell.

POCOCK, J. G. A. (1957). *The Ancient Constitution and the Feudal Law*, Cambridge, Cambridge University Press.

—— (1968). 'Civic Humanism and its Role in Anglo-American Thought', *Il pensiero politico*, 1.

POHLENZ, M. (1933). '*To prepon*. Ein Beitrag zur Geschichte des griechischen Geistes', *Nachrichten von der Gesellschaft der Wissenschaften zu Goettingen*, Philologisch—Historische Klasse. Fachgruppe I (Altertumswissenschaft), no. 16.

—— (1970). *Die Stoa. Geschichte einer geistigen Bewegung*, Goettingen, Vandenhoeck & Ruprecht.

POLANYI, K. (1957). 'Aristotle Discovers the Economy', in K. Polanyi, C. M. Arensberg, and H. W. Pearson (eds.), *Trade and Market in the Early Empires, Economies in History and Theory*, New York, The Free Press.

POPKIN, R. H. (1969). 'Epicurisme et scepticisme au début du XVIIe siècle', *Actes du VIII Congrès de l'Association G. Budé*, Paris, Les Belles Lettres.

—— (1979). *The History of Scepticism from Erasmus to Spinoza*, Berkeley, Calif., University of California Press.

PUFENDORF, S. (1759). *De iure naturae et gentium*, Frankfurt/Lipsiae, ex Officina Knochiana.

RADCLIFFE, E. (1993). 'Revolutionary Writing, Moral Philosophy, and Universal Benevolence in the Eighteenth Century', *Journal of the History of Ideas*, 54/2.

RAE, J. (1965). *Life of Adam Smith: With an Introduction 'Guide to John Rae's Life of Adam Smith' by Jacob Viner*, New York, Augustus M. Kelley.

RAPHAEL, D. D. (1969). 'Adam Smith and "the Infection of David Hume's Society" ', *Journal of the History of Ideas*, 30.

—— (1972). 'The Impartial Spectator', *Proceedings of the British Academy*, 58.

—— (1973). 'Hume and Adam Smith on Justice and Utility', *Aristotelian Society*, 73.

—— (1979). 'Adam Smith: Philosophy, Science and Social Science', in S. C. Brown (ed.), *Philosophers of the Enlightenment* (Royal Institute of Philosophy Lectures XII)', Brighton, Harvester.

REULOS, M. M. (1975). 'Le Droit romain au XVIe siècle', *Actes du IX Congrès de l'Association G. Budé*, 2.

ROBERTSON, H. M., and Taylor, W. L. (1957). 'Adam Smith's Approach to the Theory of Value', *Economic Journal*, 67.

ROSENBERG, N. (1960). 'Some Institutional Aspects of the "Wealth of Nations" ', *Journal of Political Economy*, 48.

—— (1965). 'Adam Smith on the Division of Labour: Two Views or One?', *Economica*, 32.

—— (1976). 'Another Advantage of the Division of Labour', *Journal of Political Economy*, 84.

—— (1979). 'Adam Smith and Laissez-Faire Revisited', in G. P. O'Driscoll (ed.), *Adam Smith and Modern Political Economy*, Ames, Ia., Iowa State University Press.

SALVUCCI, P. (1966). *La filosofia politica di Adam Smith*, Urbino, Argalia.

SAMS, H. W. (1944). 'Anti-Stoicism in Seventeenth- and Early Eighteenth-Century England', *Studies in Philology*, 41.

SANDYS, J. (1908). *A History of Classical Scholarship*, Cambridge, Cambridge University Press.

SCHALK, F. (1971). 'Aspetti della vita contemplativa nel Rinascimento italiano', in R. R. Bolgar (ed.), *Classical Influences on European Culture, 500–1500*, Cambridge, Cambridge University Press.

SCHIAPARELLI, V. (1873). 'I precursori di Copernico nell'antichità', *Memorie del R. Istituto Lombardo di Scienze e Lettere*, 12.

—— (1875). *Le sfere omocentriche di Eudosso, di Callippo e di Aristotele*, Milan, Pubblicazioni del R. Osservatorio di Brera.

SCHUMPETER, J. A. (1955). *History of Economic Analysis*, London, George Allen & Unwin.

SCIALOJA, V. (1934). *Diritto ereditario romano*, Rome, Anonima Romana Editrice.

SCOTT, W. R. (1937). *Adam Smith as Student and Professor*, Glasgow, Jackson.

—— (1940). 'Greek Influence on Adam Smith', in *Etudes dédiées à la mémoire d'André M. Andréadès*, Athènes, Pyrsos.

SEWALL, H. R. (1971). *The Theory of Value before Adam Smith*, New York, Augustus M. Kelley.

SHIFFLETT, A. (1998). *Stoicism, Politics and Literature in the Age of Milton*, Cambridge, Cambridge University Press.

SKINNER, A. S. (1967). 'Natural History in the Age of Adam Smith', *Political Studies*, 15.

—— (1972). 'Adam Smith: Philosophy and Science', *Scottish Journal of Political Economy*, 19.

—— (1974*a*). 'Adam Smith: Science and the Role of Imagination', in W. B. Todd (ed.), *Hume and the Enlightenment (Essays Presented to Ernest Campbell Mossner)*, Edinburgh/Texas, Universities of Edinburgh and Texas.

—— (1974*b*). *Introduction* to '*The Wealth of Nations*' (i–iii), London, Pelican Classics.

—— (1975). 'Adam Smith: An Economic Interpretation of History', in A. S. Skinner and T. Wilson (eds.), *Essays on Adam Smith*, Oxford, Clarendon Press.

—— (1976). 'Adam Smith: The Development of a System', *Scottish Journal of Political Economy*, 23.

—— (1998). *Adam Smith: The Philosopher (and the Porter)*, Discussion Papers in Economics, 9807, University of Glasgow.

SORABJI, R. (1980). 'Aristotle on the Role of Intellect in Virtue', in A. Oksenberg Rorty (ed.), *Essays on Aristotle's Ethics*, Berkeley, University of California Press.

SOUDEK, J. (1952). 'Aristotle's Theory of Exchange', *Proceedings of the American Philosophical Society*, 96.

SPENGLER, J. J. (1955). 'Aristotle on Economic Imputation and Related Matters', *Southern Economic Journal*, 21.

SPIEGEL, H. W. (1975). 'A Note on the Equilibrium Concept in the History of Economics', *Economie appliquée*, 28.

—— (1976). 'Adam Smith's Heavenly City', *History of Political Economy*, 8.

—— (1983). *The Growth of Economic Thought*, Durham, NC, Duke University Press.

STEIN, P. (1955). 'Osservazioni intorno ad Adamo Smith filosofo del diritto', *Rivista internazionale di filosofia del diritto*, 32.

—— (1957*a*). 'Legal Thought in Eighteenth-Century Scotland', *Juridical Review*.

—— (1957*b*). 'The Influence of Roman Law on the Law of Scotland', *Studia et documenta historiae et iuris*, 23.

—— (1968a). 'Lo svolgimento storico della nozione di "regula iuris" in diritto romano', in *Antologia giuridica romanistica ed antiquaria*, Milan, Giuffrè.

—— (1968b). 'Roman Law in Scotland', *Ius Romanum medii Aevi*, v, 13b.

—— (1969). *Roman Law and English Jurisprudence Yesterday and Today*, Cambridge, Cambridge University Press.

—— (1979a). 'Adam Smith's Jurisprudence—Between Morality and Economics', *Cornell Law Review*, 64.

—— (1979b). 'Adam Smith's Theory of Law and Society', in R. R. Bolgar (ed.), *Classical Influences on Western Thought, 1650–1870*, Cambridge, Cambridge University Press.

—— (1980). *Legal Evolution: The Story of an Idea*, Cambridge, Cambridge University Press.

STEWART, D. (1828). *The Philosophy of the Active and Moral Powers of Man*, Edinburgh, Adam Black; and London, Longman, Rees, Orme, Brown, and Green.

—— (1980). 'Account of the Life and Writings of Adam Smith', in *EPS*.

STEWART-ROBERTSON, J. C. (1983). 'Cicero Among the Shadows: Scottish Prelections of Virtue and Duty', *Rivista critica di storia della filosofia*, 38.

STONE, L. (1981). 'Il ritorno della narrazione', *Comunità*, 35.

STRUVE, P. (1921). 'L'Idée de loi naturelle dans la science économique', *Revue d'économie politique*, 35.

TAYLOR, O. H. (1955). *Economics and Liberalism*, Cambridge, Mass., Harvard University Press.

TAYLOR, W. L. (1965). *Francis Hutcheson and David Hume as Predecessors of Adam Smith*, Durham, NC, Duke University Press.

THOMSON, H. F. (1965). 'Adam Smith's Philosophy of Science', *Quarterly Journal of Economics*, 79.

TODD, R. B. (1989). 'The Stoics and their Cosmology in the First and Second Centuries A.D.', *Aufstieg und Niedergang der römischen Welt*, II. 36. 3.

TOLOMIO, I. (1981). 'Il genere "historia philosophica" tra 500 e 600', in G. Santinello (ed.), *Storia delle storie generali della filosofia*, Brescia, La Scuola.

TORTAROLO, E. (1983). 'Sul linguaggio della storiografia illuministica', *Studi storici*, 24/1–2.

TOZZI, G. (1961). *Economisti greci e romani*, Milan, Feltrinelli.

TRANQUILLI, V. (1979). *Il concetto di lavoro da Aristotele a Calvino*, Milan/Naples, Riccardo Ricciardi.

TREGGIARI, S. (1979). 'Questions on Women Domestics in the Roman West', in *Schiavitù, manomissione e classi dipendenti nel mondo antico*, Rome, 'L'Erma' di Bretschneider.

USSHER, R. G. (1966). 'Some Characters of Athens, Rome and England', *Greece and Rome*, 13.

VEGETTI, M. (1977). Introduction by M. Vegetti (ed.), *Marxismo e società antiche*, Milan, Feltrinelli.

VERNANT, J. P. (1983). *Myth and Thought Among the Greeks*, London, Routledge & Kegan Paul.

VINER, J. (1966). 'Adam Smith and Laissez-Faire', in M. L. Clark *et al.*, *Adam Smith, 1776–1926*, New York, Augustus M. Kelley (reprint).

—— (1960). 'The Intellectual History of Laissez-Faire', *Journal of Law and Economics*, 3.

VINER, J. (1965). Introduction to Rae, *Life of Adam Smith* [1895], New York, Augustus M. Kelley.

—— (1972). *The Role of Providence in the Social Order*, Phila. American Philosophical Society.

VINOGRADOFF, P. (1929). *Roman Law in Medieval Europe*, Oxford, Clarendon Press.

VIVENZA, G. (1982*a*). 'Adam Smith e la fisica antica,' *Economia e Storia*, 3/1.

—— (1982*b*). 'Elementi classici nel pensiero di Adam Smith: giurisprudenza romana e morale stoica,' in R. Faucci (ed.), *Gli italiani e Bentham. Dalla "felicità pubblica" all'economia del benessere*, i, Milan, Franco Angeli.

—— (1984). *Adam Smith e la cultura classica*, Pisa, IPEM.

—— (1989–90). 'Studi classici e pensiero moderno: la sintesi di Adam Smith', *Atti e memorie della Accademia di Agricoltura Scienze e Lettere di Verona*, 166.

—— (1990). 'Lavoro e attività politica: Motivi classici e moderni nel pensiero di Adam Smith', in G. Gaburro, R. Molesti, and G. Zalin (eds.), *Economia Stato Società. Studi in memoria di Guido Menegazzi*, Pisa, IPEM.

—— (1995). 'Origini classiche della benevolenza nel linguaggio economico (dall'evergesia del mondo antico alla "benevolence" della società commerciale),' in R. Molesti (ed.), *Tra economia e storia. Studi in memoria di Gino Barbieri*, Pisa, IPEM.

—— (1996). 'Benevolenza pubblica, benevolenza privata e benevolenza reciproca: la virtù del dono e dello scambio dall'antichità al Settecento', *Studi storici Luigi Simeoni*, 46.

—— (1999*a*). 'Ancora sullo stoicismo di Adam Smith', *Studi storici Luigi Simeoni*, 49.

—— (1999*b*). Adam Smith e la filosofia scettica', *Nuova economia e storia*, 5/3.

—— *et al.* (1980). 'La presenza della tradizione classica nell'opera di Adam Smith', in *Aspetti della formazione culturale di Adam Smith*, Verona, Istituto di Storia economica e sociale, vi.

WASZEK, N. (1984). 'Two Concepts of Morality: A Distinction of Adam Smith's Ethics and its Stoic Origin', *Journal of the History of Ideas*, 45.

WEST, E. G. (1964). 'Adam Smith's Two Views on the Division of Labour', *Economica*, 31.

—— (1969). 'Adam Smith's Philosophy of Riches, *Philosophy*, 44.

WESTBERG, D. (1994). *Right Practical Reason: Aristotle, Action, and Prudence in Aquinas*, Oxford, Clarendon Press.

WHITAKER, A. C. (1968). *History and Criticism of the Labor Theory of Value in English Political Economy*, New York, Columbia University Press.

WIGHTMAN, W. P. D. (1975). 'Adam Smith and the History of Ideas', in A. S. Skinner and T. Wilson (eds.), *Essays on Adam Smith*, Oxford, Clarendon Press.

WILLEY, B. (1940). *The Eighteenth-Century Background: Studies in the Idea of Nature in the Thought of the Period*, London, Chatto & Unwin.

WILSON, T. (1976). 'Sympathy and Self-Interest', in A. S. Skinner and T. Wilson (eds.), *The Market and the State: Essays in Honour of Adam Smith*, Oxford, Clarendon Press.

WINCH, D. (1979). *Adam Smith's Politics*, Cambridge, Cambridge University Press.

WITZTUM, A. (1997). 'Distributive Considerations in Smith's Conception of Economic Justice', *Economics and Philosophy*, 13.

WOOLF, S. J. (1973). 'La storia politica e sociale', in *Storia d'Italia, iii. Dal primo Settecento all'Unità*, Turin, Einaudi.

YOUNG, J. T. (1997). *Economics as a Moral Science*, Cheltenham/Lyme, Edward Elgar.

—— and Gordon, B. (1996). 'Distributive Justice as a Normative Criterion in Adam Smith's Political Economy', *History of Political Economy*, 28/1.

ZELLER, E. (1881). *A History of Greek Philosophy*, i, trans. S. F. Alleyne, London, Longmans, Green and Co.

—— (1932). *La filosofia dei Greci nel suo sviluppo storico*, ed. R. Mondolfo, Florence, La Nuova Italia.

Index of Personal Names

Index of Subjects